The Montanans'
FISHING GUIDE

DICK KONIZESKI

Revised and updated by
JAMES A. DERLETH

Volume II

MONTANA WATERS EAST OF CONTINENTAL DIVIDE

1982

MOUNTAIN PRESS PUBLISHING COMPANY
Missoula, Montana 59801

Copyright © 1982
Mountain Press Publishing Company

4th Edition

Library of Congress Cataloging in Publication Data (Revised)

Konizeski, Richard L., 1917-
    The Montanans' fishing guide.

    Vol. 2 rev. and updated by James A. Derleth.
    Contents: v. 1. Montana Waters west of the Continental
Divide.— v. 2 Montana waters east of the Continental Divide.
    1. Fishing — Montana. I. Burk, Dale A.
II. Derleth, James A.   III. Title.
SN517.K64   1982   799.1'1'09786   81-1530
ISBN 0-87842-139-4 (v. 1)
ISBN 0-87842-144-0 (v. 2)

MOUNTAIN PRESS PUBLISHING COMPANY

Box 2399 • Missoula, MT 59806 • (406) 728-1900

Dedication

to the fishermen
        to the spirit
        of the seekers;
        the perpetuators
        of Montana's
        great wild places

to fishermen
        this is your book.

                        Jim Derleth

Acknowledgments

It is almost two decades since Dick Konizeski wrote the first Montanans' Fishing Guide. His diligent research, fishing and hiking experience, and reporter's thoroughness is evident in the excellence of previous editions of the guide. And he is owed special tribute for compiling this useful and informative book with his appealing "on target" phrasing. It is within this tradition and framework that this new edition is revised and updated.

Little worthwhile remains static. Trails and roads constantly undergo access change and new trails and sites are acquired. The productive capacity of Montana fisheries is changed by many factors: management plans; lakes newly stocked; new species tried; and ponds and reservoirs built. Dams wash out, creeks and rivers flood(or go dry), lakes freeze out (or silt in), and various forms of pollution take their toll. But the great Montana fishery endures, even prospering here and there.

This revised edition is essentially an inventory of the state's fishery resource. Extensive research reflects over 850 new or revised entries in the guide to update fishing and access information. Such updating is possible only with the cooperation of personnel of the Montana Department of Fish, Wildlife and Parks, the U.S. Forest Service, and the Soil Conservation Service, and by a myriad of ardent fishermen and backpackers. Introductory articles to most of the 24 major drainages are by knowledgeable fisheries biologists or by local fishermen with years of "on the stream" experience. Many new photographs come from various government agencies, studios and skilled amateurs.

Perhaps no goal is worth obtaining unless the getting there is painful. This applies to "sweating it up to" a mountain lake or re-working a fishing guide. Yet hours spent putting it all together pale next to the gratification I feel at being given the opportunity to help fellow anglers enjoy our sport. Whether I'm floating a wild river, or wading waist deep in a quiet stretch, or simply browsing this book, researching fishing in Montana is fun. Now it's your turn.

Jim Derleth

Introduction

Montana's size requires two volumes to The Montanans' Fishing Guide: East and West. *This volume, East of the Continental Divide, covers three-quarters of the state and five of seven official fishing districts. It describes some of the most incredibly varied and superb fishing in the U.S., including most of the "blue-ribbon"*[1] *trout water of the state. From alpine lakes and wilderness brooks to accessible valley reservoirs, farm ponds, creeks and prime rivers, this volume details an enticing collage of angling for you to explore.*

The lifeblood of Montana's fishing flows from the smowmelt of its mountain ranges, forming world-renowned rivers like the Big Hole; the Madison, Jefferson and Gallatin; the Yellowstone; the Big Horn; and the mighty Missouri. These drainages are the heart of trout fishing U.S.A. But this guide will also describe other famous fisheries like Big Spring Creek; the Beaverhead and Smith Rivers; Fort Peck Reservoir; and the Beartooth high lakes country as well as all the productive waters known both statewide and locally. The book lists access routes, the kind and size of fish you can expect to catch, and other helpful fishing information.

Catches here include brown and rainbow trout from frying pan to state record size, cutthroat trout, prolific eastern brook trout, deep-dwelling lake (Mackinaw) trout, exquisite golden trout, grayling and silvery kokanee. Underutilized is the abundant, good eating mountain whitefish. And of growing importance, the state's warmer waters yield sauger, walleye, perch, ling (burbot), tackle-busting northern pike, largemouth and smallmouth bass, channel catfish, unique paddlefish, and pre-historic sturgeon.

---

[1]Designated by the state as a nationally significant fishery resource. Six such rivers exist east of the Continental Divide in Montana.

Wildlife, too, is a part of the Montana scene. Mule and whitetail deer, elk, moose, bighorn sheep, mountain goat and plentiful small game are frequently seen. A keener eye and a touch of luck is what you'll need to see the wolverine, the grizzly and black bear, the bobcat and mountain lion.

In these pages you'll find the key to your own special fishing trip. The information you need is here, and the world's best fishing is waiting for you.

Jim Derleth

Contents

Montana Game Fish

The following seven pages reproduce Montana fish paintings by wildlife artist Ron Jenkins. Many of the individual paintings are available as prints suitable for framing. For information write Mountain Press Publishing Company, Box 2399, Missoula, Montana 59806.

BROOK TROUT. Range up to 9 pounds; are distinguished by variable dark brown-to-olive-to-scarlet red (in some alpine lakes) color, round red spots with blue margins on the sides, wavy lines across the back, and white margins along the ventral fins. This species is especially common in the Big Hole drainage and the lakes of the Beartooth Plateau (Clarks Fork of the Yellowstone drainage).

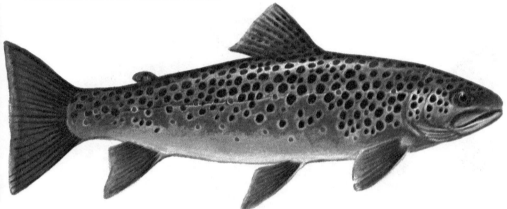

BROWN or GERMAN BROWN or LOCH LEVEN TROUT. Range up to about 20 pounds and are common to 5 pounds; are distinguished by their yellowish-brown color, relatively large dark spots on the back and a few red spots (sometimes with a narrow bluish band) on the sides; see especially the Yellowstone, Madison, Judith, Mussellshell and upper Clark Fork drainages.

RAINBOW TROUT. Range up to 20 pounds and are common to 5 pounds; are distinguished by usually light sides and somewhat darker back with numerous irregularly-shaped spots and a broad red band along the midline of each side. They are abundant in all of the drainages and frequently cross with Cutthroat with hard-to-identify results.

CUTTHROAT TROUT. Range up to 15 pounds but are generally under 12 inches in the small headwaters of most Montana drainages, and up to 5 pounds in many lakes; are distinguished by a dark red or orange slash along the bottom of each jaw, and numerous dark spots on the posterior parts of the body.

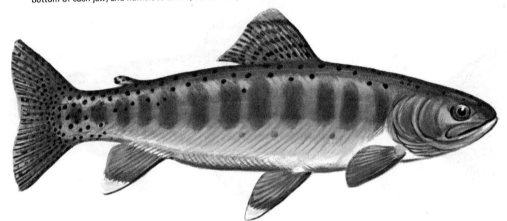

GOLDEN TROUT. Generally average less than 1½ pounds; are distinguished by their beautiful coloration, generally yellowish color with bright carmine strips along the belly from the throat to the anal fin, small scales; have been introduced in suitable (alpine) lakes in most of the major drainages.

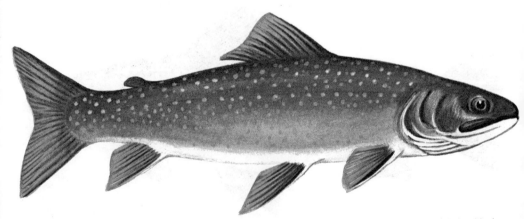

DOLLY VARDEN or BULL TROUT. Range up to 30 pounds and are common to 15 pounds; are distinguished by their large mouth, olive color, with round orange to yellowish spots on the sides, and a white border on the ventral fins, are generally slenderer than the Brook trout; see especially the South Fork of the Flathead drainage.

ARCTIC GRAYLING. Mostly average between 6 and 12 inches but range up to 2 pounds or 20 inches; are distinguished by their large beautifully colored dorsal fin, large eyes, small mouth, grayish-silver color and irregularly-shaped black dots; are found in several lakes in most of the major drainages, and in many lakes in the Big Hole and Clarks Fork of the Yellowstone drainages.

LAKE or MACKINAW TROUT. Range up to 40 pounds are common to 15 pounds; are distinguished by their light or greenish-gray color, many irregular light spots on the sides and back, large mouth and deeply forked caudal fin; see especially Whitefish and Flathead Lakes in the Flathead drainage, Spar Lake in the Kootenai drainage, and Twin Lakes in the Big Hole drainage.

WHITEFISH. Range up to 5 pounds or 24 inches; are distinguished by their small mouth, silvery sides and belly, and olive drab back; see especially Rock Creek in the upper Clark Fork drainage, and the Kootenai and Yellowstone Rivers.

COHO or SILVER SALMON. The sea-going variety ranges up to maybe 30 pounds or so, but they've only recently (1969) been introduced to Montana waters so it's still too early to say how big they'll grow here. Otherwise they need no description except perhaps to say that they're not only large, they're fighters from the moment they feel the hook, and are truly an Epicurean's delight.

KOKANEE or SOCKEYE SALMON. Range up to 5 pounds but average between 12 and 14 inches; are distinguished by their dark-greenish color on the back, silver on the sides and belly, height of the anal fin is shorter than the base line, small teeth, and the mature males are a bloody red with no spots and a hooked nose; see Flathead Lake and the Clearwater on the Blackfoot drainage.

STURGEON. Several species are found in Montana. Some range up to several hundred pounds. They are distinguished by their flat belly, ventrally located mouth, cartilagenous nobby plates along the sides and back, and 4 barbels or wiskers directly in front of the mouth, see Kootenai and Yellowstone Rivers.

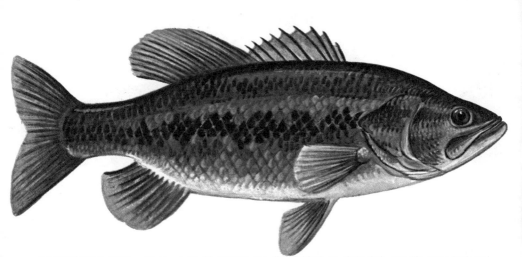

LARGEMOUTH BASS. Range up to 14 pounds; are distinguished by their dark metallic green back and greenish-yellow sides, a broken dark greenish band from the eye to the caudal fin, a large mouth that extends to well behind the eye in adults, and large scales; see Blanchard and many of the pothole lakes in the Flathead drainage, and sloughs along the upper Clark Fork drainage and many reservoirs in the eastern part of the state.

SMALLMOUTH BASS., Range up to 4 pounds but average around 1½ to 2½ pounds; are usually distinguished from Largemouth Bass by a shorter jaw that ends below the reddish colored eye, and a dorsal fin that is hardly emarginate; see Horseshoe Lake in the Swan River drainage.

YELLOW PERCH. Are reported up to 21 inches but mostly range between 5 and 15 inches; are distinguished by their deep greenish back with indentations extending down across their yellowish sides, and a dirty white belly, coarse scales, and an arched back leading to the head which has a more or less concave adult profile; they are common in many lakes in all drainages.

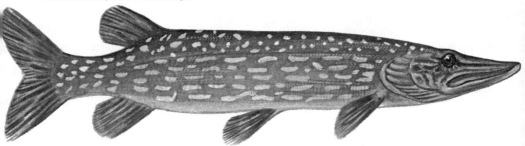

NORTHERN PIKE. Range up to 27 pounds but average between 3 and 8 pounds; are distinguished by their long narrow body and equally elongate head with its deep mouth and large vicious teeth, forked tail, and dirty greenish-yellow mottled body; see especially Pike Lake in the St. Mary drainage, and Dry Fork Reservoir in the Flathead drainage.

5

WALLEYE. The average angler cannot tell these from Sauger. Both are large members of the perch family. The average size creeled is 12 to 14 inches. Walleye and sauger are common in the reservoirs and large rivers in the eastern part of the state.

SUNFISH or PUMPKINSEEDS. Green sunfish and Bluegills have all been introduced into Montana. Mostly about the size of your hand (4 to 6 inches long), flat-bodied with coarse, iridescent scales. Bluegills have been widely planted in ranch ponds in eastern Montana. Pumpkinseeds alone are found west of the Continental Divide.

PADDLEFISH or SPOON-BILLED CATFISH. Are usually from 2 to 4 feet long (two in the 120 pound class have been taken in Montana). Smooth and very large gill slits; are caught (snagged) in the Lower Yellowstone and Missouri river drainages.

6

CHANNEL CAT. This hard looking but good eating fellow has a slender, smooth skinned body with a small head, whiskers on his chin, spines on his dorsal and pectoral fins, a long anal fin and a forked tail. He's bluish to greenish-gray on top and white below and you'll find him in sizes ranging up to 30 pounds or so in the lower Missouri, Yellowstone and Musselshell rivers.

BULLHEAD. Black bodied, smooth skinned, up to maybe 5 pounds in weight, big headed, wide mouthed with whiskers, more or less square tailed and plenty attractive in a frying pan. You'll find them here and there in the Lower Missouri, Yellowstone and Musselshell drainages and a few over the Divide in the lower Clarks Fork of the Columbia River and the Flathead drainage.

LING. If your wife took one horrified look, screamed and threw rod and all in the drink — that, brother, was a ling — a gruesome-looking half brother to the sea-going cod but resembling more closely the slippery eel. Many are those who claim its flesh is a toothsome as its looks are revolting — especially in the Kootenai River area although it's not bothered much elsewhere in the state.

UPPER BEAVERHEAD
Courtesy Bridenstine Studio

Beaverhead River

The Beaverhead River originally began at the confluence of the Red Rock River and Horse Prairie Creek. The Lewis and Clark expedition reached this juncture in 1805 after having maneuvered their heavy boats up the Beaverhead in late summer. They noted that the Beaverhead was heavily brushed and meandered so circuitously that eleven river miles had to be travelled to make four miles by land. The brushy banks and frequent meanders remain today and are extremely important to the tremendous wild trout fishery that exists.

The river begins today in the roaring tailrace below Clark Canyon Dam. The dam was built in 1964 and provides irrigation water to a large diversion project nearly fifteen miles downstream. High flows in the upper river are the rule from May through September when up to 100 cfs runs through the narrow, twisting river bed. The banks are extremely brushy and fishermen should step carefully since the river is very swift and deep. The only way to effectively fish the river during the high water period is to float fish. Float fishing is extremely popular on the upper Beaverhead today and there are several old timers who have been floating the river since the 1940's. The trout population is composed of rainbows and browns and there are tremendous numbers of them. Trout grow extremely fast in the upper Beaverhead. The heavy bank cover provides ample undercuts and overhanging cover for trout to rest in and the combination of security cover and rapid growth has produced a remarkable fishery. Flow releases from Clark Canyon Dam have been very favorable for trout reproduction since 1975 due to excellent cooperation from the East Bench Irrigation District and numbers of trout have increased dramatically.

Fly fishing is the favored technique on the upper Beaverhead and as you float down the river you will see the various favorite patterns hanging from the willows, the result of errant attempts to hit the little pockets that harbor the big trout. Rubber-legged patterns, the Beaverhead Special and large streamers are the favored patterns. Big flies and heavy tippets are the rule here for float fishing. Walk-in fishing is at the discretion of the landowners, so please ask permission.

9

Downstream from Pipe Organ Rock, the river changes somewhat. The river has been channelized in places due to highway construction and rock riprap has taken the place of brushy banks. Anglers can still catch trout but the brushy banks harbor far more trout.

Flows below the large diversion at Barretts are much less during the irrigation season. The river can still be floated but is more easily fished from the banks. Rainbow and brown trout continue to provide the fishery as the river continues north. There is a large fishing access just south of Dillon that includes Poindexter Spring Creek and lots of river frontage. Below Dillon, the river leaves the highway and meanders for miles before it joins the highway again at Beaverhead Rock. This rock formation was mentioned in the journals of Lewis and Clark. Access in this reach is more difficult although a polite request to fish will usually be granted.

Downstream from Beaverhead Rock, the effects of irrigation season dewatering, high summer water temperatures and sediment combine to depress trout populations. There are still trout though, including some lunker size browns. As the river continues downstream from Silver Bow Lane Bridge, it begins to pick up spring creek flows and eventually the Ruby River. Below the mouth of the Ruby, trout numbers increase again due to the summer cooling effect of the Ruby River and several spring creeks. This is brown trout water and is a pleasure to fish. Access is somewhat difficult although a polite request to fish should prove productive.

The river from Dillon to the mouth is floatable, although there are a few low bridges and occasional wires to negotiate. Access points are at bridges and floats from Dillon downstream are quite long. The Beaverhead River is also a waterfowl paradise and the river bottom abounds in whitetail deer.

The brushy Beaverhead is a difficult river to fish and can prove frustrating to the first time angler. However, the jolt of a big Beaverhead rainbow or brownie on the end of your line will make you a believer.

Jerry Wells

Beaverhead River Drainage

Blacktail Deer Creek. A really beautiful fishing stream flowing to the northwest down a broad open valley between the south end of the Ruby Range and the Red Rock Mountains. It heads at the junction of the East and West Forks (27 miles by good county roads southeast from Dillon), and joins the Beaverhead River at Dillon. The creek is relatively slow and deep with one nice hole after another — loaded with 8 to 10 inch brook, rainbow and some good brown trout in the lower reaches, and some cutthroat in the upper (canyon) reaches. Unfortunately much of it is posted but those stretches that are accessible to the public are heavily fished indeed.

Bloody Dick Creek. This was once a good cutthroat creek, until planted with brook trout by a local rancher. It heads away up above Reservoir Lake below Selway Mountain and flows for 14 miles down a partly timbered, partly open valley and then for 5 miles across open hay meadows to Horse Prairie Creek near Red Butte. The entire stream is paralleled along its northeast side by county and USFS roads. Almost all of the private land is posted but the public reaches are heavily fished (mainly by Butte-ites). It's excellent fishing for eastern brookies 6 to 11 inches long, some rainbow to 15 inches, and whitefish to 18 inches. The stream drains some really nice elk and mule deer country.

Blue Creek. A small southeastward flowing creek in a narrow, rocky, timbered canyon at the headwaters of Grasshopper Creek, reached by the Grasshopper road a mile south of Elkhorn Springs. There's a horse trail along it; about 1½ miles of fast fishing water with lots of boulders and good holes that harbor a few small brook and cutthroat trout. A good wild raspberry spot in season.

Clark Canyon Reservoir (or Hap Hawkins Lake). A 4995 acre Bureau of Reclamation irrigation project at the head of the Beaverhead River 21 miles south of Dillon on I-15, right above the original site of Armstead. It's a triangular reservoir, fed by the Red Rock River and Horse Prairie Creek at the south and west corners and drained by the Beaverhead River to the north. There are a couple of 50 acre rock islands in it, and open grazing land all around. This is one reclamation project that has recreational water, tables, fireplaces, toilets and boat launching ramps. The reservoir is stocked regularly with rainbow trout and provides good fishing for 1 to 7 pounders plus temperamental browns in the 2 to 10 pound class. It's heavily fished in the summer, and more-than-somewhat in the winter for the above, plus 16 to 26 inch ling, and whitefish to 20 inches. Not only is it good fishing but the added suspense of the probability of netting a real lunker keeps the crowds coming. Also, a new "wild spring spawning" strain of rainbow is now being stocked, and doing well.

Clark Creek. The outlet of Sawtooth Lake, drains 4 miles west down a steep, timbered valley above, through many beaver ponds in the middle reaches, and out across open grass-sagebrush-aspen-and-willow grazing land below to Grasshopper Creek. It's reached by the Grasshopper road 3 miles north from Polaris where you turn right on a jeep road a couple of miles and then take a good USFS trail. There is some fair (although limited) fishing here for small brook and cutthroat trout, plus a rare golden or cutthroat-golden hybrid from the lake. The lower reaches are on mostly private land.

Dad Creek. Heads in Deadman Pass and drains Dad Creek Lake 5 miles southeast through open sagebrush hills to Medicine Lodge Creek 19 miles by road south of Clark Canyon Reservoir. The lower reaches are mostly dewatered for irrigation, but a jeep trail takes you up above where there are lots of small beaver ponds that are good fishing for 5 to 12 inch brook and cutthroat trout. It's too small to stand much pressure and doesn't get much.

Dad Creek Lakes. Two, 100 yards apart, reached by a 3 mile hike up the drainage from the end of the Dad Creek jeep trail which goes through some private land, so stay on the road. The upper lake is barren. The lower one lies at 8800 feet above sea level in the head of a rock walled basin below steep, timbered talus slopes to the south. It's 3½ acres, rather pear-shaped from the air, has an average depth of around 8 feet with a 15 foot maximum and pretty steep dropoffs except along the north side. There are many submerged logs and snags here, pushed in by old snow slides. The fishing is perhaps a little better than fair (for 12 to 16 inch cutthroat). You can see every fish in it but not many people look.

A GHOST OF BANNACK
Courtesy Bridenstine Studio

A BEAUTY?
Courtesy Bill Browning

East Fork Blacktail Creek.
Heads below Olson and Sunset Peaks and is followed by trail for 5 miles and then a private dirt road for 11 miles westward to the head of the main stem. The roaded reaches are mostly in sagebrush flats between open hills with some willow and brush along the margins. There are occassional beaver ponds and lots of nice deep holes that are excellent fishing for mostly 8 to 15 inch brook, and some rainbow trout to 16 inches, mountain whitefish to 18 inches, plus a few cutthroat trout. The whole bit is moderately popular with Dillonites and others from over the hill. A few years back, the MDFWP purchased 20,000 acres in the area for elk winter range, helping the hunter and fisherman with much more public access.

Estler Lake.
Take the Rattlesnake Creek road northwest from Dillon for 10 easy miles, then 5 truck miles and finally a ½ mile trail to this one. Once there, you'll find it's 57.8 acres in timber at 7859 feet elevation behind an earth dam that gives rise to 15 foot water-level fluctuations that in turn raises havoc with the fish. It's shallow to the north, steep to the south and only poor-to-fair fishing for 8 to 10 inch rainbow, and rainbow-cutthroat hybrids. There are better places to go and most people do.

Eunice Creek.
A real small tributary of Bloody Dick Creek, flowing east through heavy timber to the main stem a mile below Reservoir Lake. There's a USFS trail and the first mile is fished a little for eat'n trout.

French Creek.
Take the Rattlesnake Creek road 3 miles above the old silver mining town of Argenta to the mouth of French Creek, then gravel and dirt roads upstream for perhaps a mile of fair cutthroat and brook trout fishing (good for small fish). The stream is quite small, partly in timber but with its share of willow and aspen. The water is fast and clear and the trout just fit a skillet. You can pitch your wigwam anywhere.

Gheny (or Geinnie) Pond.
A 3 acre by 3 foot deep borrow put just east of State Highway 41, one and a half miles south of Twin Bridges on the Big Hole-Beaverhead floodplain. It's in open pastureland, has his'ns/n/her'ns, is stocked annually to the living limit with catchable rainbow trout (some biggies) and gets fished to a frazzle after each planting. Mosses up a bit come late season.

Grasshopper Creek.
Flows southward for a couple of steep miles down a timbered mountain canyon below Elkhorn Hot Springs, then meanders slowly for 20 miles through open hay fields to Bannack (the first capital of Montana Territory and now a ghost town) where it enters a narrow rocky canyon and stays there for 12 more miles until it joins the Beaverhead River 10 miles south of Dillon on U.S. 91. You can drive all along the upper reaches for 4 or 5 miles. It doesn't get fished much but is easy to negotiate above Bannack — and pretty fair too, for 8 to 10 inch brook and rainbow trout. There are also some beautiful holes down in the canyon below that are hard to reach but fair when you do for some fair-sized brownies (8-18 inches), some rainbow to 15 inches, and whitefish. Better take your snakebite kit along; you might need it.

Hap Hawkin's Reservoir. See Clark Canyon Reservoir

Horse Prairie Creek. Heads on Bannack Pass and flows northward across high open
prairie land for 14 miles to Red Butte where it turns east for 15 miles to Clark Canyon Reservoir. It's all in (posted) open hay and pastureland — permission is needed. The upper reaches are perhaps the most "willowed-up" in Montana. Much water is taken at times for irrigation; but the fishing is still good where you can get to it, for 8 to 14 inch brook and rainbow trout and 12 to 14 inch whitefish. The lower end of this stream (when it carries water) contains some nice brown and rainbow trout up to 4 or 5 pounds. P.S.: There are one H--- of a lot of suckers in the lower reaches, migrating out of Clark Canyon Reservoir.

Kelly Reservoir. At 7005 feet elevation above sea level, 92 acres, fairly deep behind a dam. It is up Rattlesnake Creek (through Argenta) about 15 miles west and a little north from Dillon, reportedly on a "four wheel" type road that gets real steep, rocky, and narrow in the last ½ mile or so; so much so a lot of folks walk in. Good (and popular) for 8 to 10 inch brookies and rainbow.

Lake Canyon Lake. A 2½ acre by 6-to-10 foot deep pothole in rocky, open timber and sagebrush mountains reached 5 miles up (barren) Lake Canyon Creek from Medicine Lodge Creek 11 miles up from Clark Canyon Reservoir. You can get 2 miles from the lake (on a dry day) with a pickup, then hoof it, or as some do, use a scooter. It's seldom visited but fair fishing for 12 to 15 inch cutthroat — if you hit it right.

Lotts Slough. Is really a natural 2 mile long brushy drain ditch in open grazing Jefferson River bottomland just east of Twin Bridges. It used to be stocked annually and is still fished occasionally by Twin Bridges' kids.

Medicine Lodge Creek. Heads in a high, wide, open hayland valley between the Tendoy and Beaverhead Mountains and is followed by gravel road for 25 miles north to junction with Horse Prairie Creek a mile above Clark Canyon Reservoir. It's dewatered here and there for irrigation but is real good fishing for 8 to 13 inch brook and rainbow trout at a ratio of about 3 to 1. The fishing pressure is about the same, i.e. light to moderate as in accordance to ease of access, as most angling requires permission. This is also good bird and big game country.

Minneopa Lake. Is really a marshy 12 acre reservoir at 8160 feet elevation behind an earth dam in a timbered mountain valley at the head of Rattlesnake Creek, reached a circuitous 1½ miles north from Estler Lake by a logging road to within 2 miles of the lake. The dam may have "blown"; the extent of damage to the fishery is yet unknown. It doubles in size when full but is mostly drawn down in summer. If you can get out to the deep water, it's good fishing for 10 to 11 inch cutthroat (and reportedly a few rainbow) trout.

North Frying Pan Creek. Take the Lemhi Pass road a mile west of the Selway Ranch and then a jeep road 2 miles southwest to the mouth of North Frying Pan. It's in willow and grassbottoms with no trail and has a few 5 to 6 inch cutthroat trout and not many fishermen except a stray prospector now and then with a craving for fish and nothing better to do.

Peppercoff Pond. See Gheny Pond, translate the locale about a mile south and to the other (west) side of State Highway 41 — and there you have it — litter and all.

Poindexter Slough. Two and a half miles long as the wild goose goes, but 4 brushy miles by water. U.S. 91 crosses it in the middle reaches, in open hay-meadowland 3½ miles south from Dillon. It's heavily fished and very good too — for 10 to 20 inch browns, 10 to 12 inch rainbow and a very few 8 to 9 inch brook trout and 16-18 inch whitefish. A really nice bit of water to have so close to town. Thank your lucky stars (actually the MDFWP) — ½ mile or so of it is public.

Polaris Lake. You gotta climb to this alpine (Pioneer Range) lake, 1790 feet in 4 miles from Grasshopper Creek just north of Polaris, up the Lake Creek drainage to Polaris at 8190 feet elevation above sea level. Once you're there, you'll find it to be about 11 acres, fairly deep with steep dropoffs all around, timbered on the north with talus slopes to the south and very temperamental fishing indeed for 12 to 24 inch rainbow trout. Not many people figure the fish are worth the hike — but — they forget the scenery and solitude. Access to the lake (through some private land) is with permission.

Rattlesnake Creek.
Drains Estler, Minneopa, Tent and several barren lakes in the southern Pioneer Mountains southeastward for 6 miles down a mile-wide timbered valley above and 11 miles across private hay and pastureland on the "Rattlesnake Flats" below before it sinks a few miles southwest of Dillon. It's the Dillon water supply and some water is also taken for irrigation. You can drive it all on county and USFS roads but it's really brushy and difficult to fish. There is a fair population of 6 to 8 inch brookies though, plus a scattering of rainbow and cutthroat trout. Quite a few Dillonites picnic along it and give it a whirl now and then on their way to and from the lakes.

Reservoir Lake.
Take the Horse Prairie Creek, then Bloody Dick road (State 181) west from Clark Canyon Reservoir, 19 miles beyond Red Butte and you're there. Its 40 acres lie just to the right (east) of the road behind an abandoned dam at 7200 feet above sea level with alpine timber and lodgepole pine all around and a good public campground you can pull into and spend a night or a week. There are shallow dropoffs with lilies at the upper end but it's deep (60 feet) and cold out away from shore, and provides plenty of good fishing for 9 to 10 inch brookies. It's closed to all motorboats, gets moderate usage, and is not as crowded as you'd think.

Sawtooth Lake.
Lies at the head of Clark Creek in a truly beautiful wilderness setting at 8511 feet above sea level, 500 feet below nearly vertical slide rock and talus slopes on the north side of Goat Mountain in the Pioneer Range. It's 16 acres, bordered by alpine timber, has shallow dropoffs to the north but is steep-to-the-shore to the south, and used to be barren. The fair population of colorful golden trout (up to 16 inches) that now fight for survival in its ice cold waters offer anglers a rare treat although they're harder than H--- to catch. A USFS spray plane crashed into the lake in the late '50s. Might be you can still see the wreckage.

Scott Lake.
No trail (a 2 mile scramble west up the inlet to Estler Lake) and it is seldom visited. It's 9 acres, in a partly wooded, alpine cirque at 8700 feet above sea level but almost 2000 feet beneath the great rocky talus slopes of Baldy Mountain. The view is truly stupendous from the top and you can get there by an old USFS trail up the north side. The lake? — well, it used to have real nice 12 to 24 inch rainbow, cutthroat, and rainbow-cutthroat hybrids and still did as of 1981. A good one to hit if it hasn't frozen out, and the scenery is terrific, except for an old (breeched) dam scar. The Black Mountain logging road and a 3 to 4 mile hike is another way in here (cross-country).

Selway Creek.
A small stream with limited recreation potential. Take the Bloody Dick road 1½ miles east from Reservoir Lake, and then turn left (north) up Selway Creek for 2 or 3 miles of fair fishing. It's all in private mountain meadow pastureland, is easily fished and fair too for small brook trout, eating size.

Shoestring Creek.
Here is a pretty little meandering mountain meadow creek that flows southward down the slopes of Seymore Mountain for 4½ miles to Grasshopper Creek, ½ mile south of Elkhorn Hot Springs. There's about 3 miles of easily fished water (for 6 to 8 inch cutthroat trout) accessible by trail — and a USFS campground ½ mile above its mouth. A nice place to take "Molly and the baby don't-cha know!"

Silver Bow Pond.
Lies a fast mile south on State Highway 41 from Gheny Pond, is about 3 acres but otherwise similar to Gheny in all ways, i.e. it's an old borrow pit in open grazing land on the east side of the road, is crammed full of catchable rainbow trout each year and fished like mad in spurts as soon as the good word gets around. It's littered like mad, too.

Smith Pond.
Is an even 2 miles south of Gheny Pond by State Highway 41 on the same side of the highway and in all other things a duplicate. Fine fishing at times for the tourist but not very exciting. After all, you can buy your fish at the market with less effort and expense. The kids like it and a few lunkers are caught.

Taylor Creek.
Is an open foothill, grass, sagebrush, hay and pastureland, willow bordered stream that heads just west of Argenta and flows 9 miles south to Grasshopper Creek a couple of miles upstream from Bannack. It's crossed by State Highway 278 a couple of miles above its mouth, and is mostly accessible by private roads for about 4 miles of fair (6 to 8 inch brook and a few cutthroat trout) fishing — but gets very little attention.

CLARK CANYON RESERVOIR
Courtesy USBR

SAWTOOTH LAKE
Courtesy Bridenstine Studio

Tent Lake. Isn't shaped like a tent but more like a 6 acre hot water bottle with the stopper (outlet) at the east end. There's a big marshy area above it (to the west) and open banks along the north side but with alpine timber all around. The lake itself is 8340 feet above sea level, has fairly good dropoffs along the south side, but it's hard to get out to fishable water elsewhere. It's fair though, at times, for camp-fare cutthroat trout. You get there by trail a mile above Minneopa — if you're not looking for company.

Trail Creek. Take the Horse Prairie road 3 miles south from Red Butte and then the Trail Creek road 10 miles west to the top of the drainage divide where you will find a USFS campground (also available from Idaho up the Agency Creek road). Trail Creek is all on private (mostly hay meadow) land, loses a lot of water for irrigation, but is still large enough to support good populations of 8 or 9 inch brook and rainbow-cutthroat hybrids. You'd better ask permission because the owner is tired of closing gates, repairing fences and picking up beer bottles.

Twin Lakes (Upper, Lower). On the Rattlesnake Creek drainage. Two lakes, Upper and Lower, 8.2 and 3.9 acres at 8745 and 8720 feet above sea level, lie below a great rock ridge to the south in sparsely timbered country a mile up the western inlet to Tent Lake. They both had fish years ago but those in Lower Twin have long since suffocated. Upper Twin is deeper and used to have small brooks and large rainbow, but may be kapoot now too. Almost nobody goes there — why don't you try it and let me know?

West Fork Blacktail Creek. A small stream, heavily fished by "locals" (as far away as Butte) who drive to the head of main stem and then take a dirt road on up the West Fork for about 16 miles of easy going. It's mostly in open sagebrush and grassland hills with scattered patches of conifers and aspen. There is an occasional beaver pond and only fair fishing all around for 5 to 7 inch — sometimes up to maybe a foot long brook, rainbow and or cutthroat trout in descending order of plentitude. You can jump it above and wade it at the mouth. It's one of the heaviest used elk areas in the state.

Respect Private Property — Ask Permission **First**

BIG HOLE RIVER BELOW WISDOM
Courtesy Ernst Peterson

Big Hole River

The Big Hole country is a land of beauty, legends and wild trout. Arising in extreme southwestern Montana, the Big Hole River flows for 113 miles before it is joined by the Beaverhead River to form the Jefferson River near Twin Bridges. Throughout its length, the river is undammed, a wild river in the truest sense and one of the most scenic rivers in Montana. The first non-Indians to see the Big Hole were probably members of the Lewis and Clark expedition who reached the confluence of the Big Hole and Beaverhead Rivers in August of 1805. Captain Meriwether Lewis named the river "Wisdom" in honor of President Jefferson. However, the river soon took on its own name – the Big Hole – mountain man parlance for the broad, deep valley of the upper basin.

The river has changed a great deal since 1805, mostly due to man's influence, and so has its fish population. When Lewis and Clark came into the country, game fish in the river were cutthroat trout, artic grayling and mountain whitefish. Cutthroat trout are nearly gone now, victims of competition from rainbow, brown and brook trout which were introduced to the drainage in the 1920's. Grayling remain in the upper river only where they represent the last major stream-dwelling population in the United States south of Alaska.

The fishery of the river is perhaps best described in three separate reaches. The upper reach, beginning at the headwaters in the Skinner Meadows country near Jackson, extends down to the mouth of Pintlar Creek below Wisdom. It is a small stream here, and meanders its way across the Big Hole Basin, a high sparsely populated valley surrounded by the scenic Pioneer, Beaverhead and Pintlar mountain ranges. Wild hay is still put up with beaverslides in this valley, sometimes called the valley of the thousand haystacks. The fishery of the upper river is essentially comprised of brook trout, grayling and mountain whitefish. There are scrappy brookies up to 15 inches here as well as fair numbers of the beautiful artic grayling. There are also occasional rainbow trout and plenty of mountain whitefish. The upper river is a joy to fish, particularly during long summer evenings when large hatches of caddis flies provide a bonanza of surface activity for the fly fisherman. Public access is limited and fishing is at the discretion of the landowners. The respectful fishermen who asks permission to fish will generally receive it. Please respect this privilege. The river can be floated downstream from Wisdom although low flows after early July make it an uncomfortable float.

The character of the river changes as it heads east from the mouth of Pintlar Creek. It enters a narrower valley and the banks are lined with conifers and grasses. The river begins to pick up velocity as it continues down toward Wise River and the fish population begins to change. Brook trout diminish in

17

numbers, their place taken by rainbow trout. Grayling remain in small numbers, and as the river nears Wise River we first encounter the king of the river, the brown trout. The river is floatable in this reach, although after mid-July it is generally too low to float comfortably. There is public access on the south side of the river above Dickey Bridge and a BLM campground near the mouth of Bryant Creek. Fishing for rainbow trout can be very productive in this reach, particularly during the salmon fly hatch of mid-June. Rainbow up to 15 inches are fairly common and there are fish much larger. Mountain whitefish are numerous and can provide fast action for the fly fisherman when the trout aren't biting.

Downstream from Divide, the Big Hole River is designated Blue Ribbon in recognition of its national importance as a trout fishery. It is a stretch of river that anglers dream about. The most popular and most productive stretch is from Divide to Glen. Brown and rainbow trout make up the fishery here with brown trout the dominant species on downstream. Float fishing is extremely popular and there are boat access points at Divide, Maiden Rock, Melrose and Glen. The salmon fly hatch of mid-June marks the peak of angling pressure each year.

After leaving the scenic Maiden Rock Canyon, the river enters a broad valley of irrigated hay and cattle ranches. There are walk-in access points between Melrose and Glen courtesy of the landowners. Please respect their generosity and treat this privilege with respect. Fishing can be very productive in this reach of the river. Trout up to 16 inches are common and there are brown trout much larger. There is a special regulation area between Divide and Melrose that is designed to increase numbers of large trout. Anglers should read the regulations before fishing this stretch of river. While artificial flies and lures are the rule in the special regulation area, bait fishing is allowed on the remaining 98 miles of the Big Hole. Angling techniques vary but bait fishermen who can effectively fish sculpins are generally successful. Spin fishermen have success with rapalas, mepps and the hammered brass. For the fly fishermen, the wooly worm, rubber legs, muddler minnow and marabou muddler are the favorites. They are fished in sizes from #6 to #2. Dry flies are also effective, particularly during the salmon fly hatch.

Downstream from Glen, the river offers some fine brown trout angling but as we continue downstream, irrigation dewatering results in very low flows and high water temperatures during late summer.

The Big Hole offers a variety of angling opportunities in its 113 mile length. From the rare and beautiful grayling of the headwaters to trophy brown trout below Divide, the Big Hole is a joy for the angler to experience.

Jerry Wells

Big Hole River Drainage

Ajax Lake. Is reached by 4 miles of poor jeep trail from the end of the Big Swamp Creek road. At 8522 feet elevation, Ajax is about 20 acres, 93 foot maximum depth with mostly shallow dropoffs, in scattered timber and parkland, but with lots of down timber around the margins. The long abandoned Ajax Gold Mine is about a half mile above the lake, and from it the old timers used to ship gold by mule train to Bannack. The lake is reported to be good fishing for 10 to 15 inch rainbow as well as rainbow cutthroat hybrids. Usually the road is closed during hunting season and the lake is closed to all motorboats.

Albino Lakes. Are reached by following the outlet (there's no trail) for ¾ of a mile from the (barren) Ajax Creek trail. Lower Albino is about 3½ acres, in scattered trees just at timberline. It is good fishing for 10 to 12 inch cutthroat. Upper Albino (at 8817 feet above sea level) is about 8 acres, in a cirque above timberline. Both lakes are out of the way, seldom visited and at last report — barren.

Alder Creek. Flows from Foolhen Mountain for 9 miles to the Big Hole River 4 miles above Wise River. This is a small, seldom fished stream that is fair for 6 to 8 inch brooks, a few rainbow and grayling. There is a trail all the way to headwaters.

Anchor Lake. See Pear Lake.

Andrus Creek. Flows through meadowland with considerable willow bank cover for about 8 miles to Governors Creek, 10 miles south of Jackson, and is followed to headwaters by jeep road and trail. The lower reaches are excellent fshing for 10 to 12 inch brookies and a few small cutthroat and grayling. It is seldom visited since these lower reaches are on private property; an alternate route would be the Bloody Dick and Selway roads from the south.

Baldy Lake. An 85 foot deep, 32.5 acre alpine lake in timbered country right at the top (above 8000 feet elevation) of the Wise River-Big Hole River divide and reached by a trail 2 miles from the Ibex Mine which is easily accessible by the Lacy Creek jeep road. However, this road is reported closed about 5 miles downstream (below Schwinegar Lake a few miles). Baldy is moderately popular and fair-to-good fishing for 11 to 13 inch rainbow trout.

Bear Creek. A small stream flowing south to the Big Hole River 2 miles east of Ralston and followed by a road for 5 miles through open timber to headwaters. It is fished occasionally for fair catches of pan-size brookies.

Bear Lake. Elongated 19.8 acres, in dense lodgepole at the lower end and about ⅔ of the way up the sides, but in open meadow above, and reached by horse trail 3½ miles up Bear Lake Creek from the Warm Springs Creek trail. It has a fair population of 8-10 inch brook trout but is marshy all around and very hard to fish which is no doubt why most folks never try.

Bear Wallow Creek. A short, meadowland, willow-bottomed tributary of Old Tim Creek. It contains 6 to 8 inch cutthroat in the lower reaches but they are hard to catch and seldom fished for. The road was closed recently — try the Bull Creek road.

Bender Creek. A small tributary of Johnson Creek paralleled by a trail to headwaters. The lower (meadowland and scattered timber) reaches are fished occasionally by local residents for good catches of 6 to 8 inch brook trout. Here is an easily fished stream — if you can get permission.

Berry Creek. Flows from Berry Lake (mostly through meadowland with willow bank cover) for 12 miles to Pioneer Creek. The lower 2 miles are braided, not too much water here, but the next 4 or 5 miles are fair fishing for brook trout that average about 10 inches and range up to 16 inches. This stream is easily accessible by road and trail for its entire length. The lower to middle reaches are heavily fished, the upper reaches contain a few cutthroat trout but are seldom fished.

Berry Lake. A real hard one to find but worth it. Take the Pioneer Creek trail to Pioneer Lake, then ¼ mile to Highup Lake, then another ¼ mile to Skytop Lake, and thence 1½ miles along the Continental Divide by way of mountain goat trails, such as they are, to Berry Lake just west of the Divide. An 11 acre, real deep, cirque lake in barren rocky country that is (you'd better believe it) seldom fished for cutthroat to 15 inches and reported to better than 6 pounds (rarely). It was stocked in 1972, '76, and '79 with 2 inchers — and is excellent fishing.

Big American Creek. An open meadowland and scattered-timber stream that is crossed at the mouth by the Big Hole-Anaconda highway 4½ miles south of the Continental Divide. This one is small but easily accessible and moderately popular for good catches of 6 to 8 inch brook trout and some small rainbow-cutthroat hybrids.

Big California Creek. A small, open meadowland stream that is crossed at the mouth by the Big Hole-Anaconda highway 6 miles south of the pass and followed by the highway for 4 miles to headwaters. It is seldom fished and poor at best for 6 to 9 inch brook and rainbow trout.

Big Lake Creek. Flows for 17 miles from Twin Lakes north to Rock Creek about 2½ miles south of Wisdom and is easily accessible by road all the way. The lower reaches are mostly dewatered for irrigation but the first 6 miles below the lakes are good fishing for 10 to 12 inch brook and a scattering of rainbow and cutthroat trout. A point of interest about 2 miles below the USFS boundary is the first campsite of Chief Joseph and his little band, survivors of the massacre by white soldiers only a few hours earlier at the Battle of the Big Hole.

Big Moosehorn Creek. This creek flows through timbered country to junction with Ruby Creek 1 mile west of Wisdom and is followed by a poor road upstream for 2 miles above Little Moosehorn and crossed at the mouth by the Swamp Creek road 19 miles above the mouth. This is a fairly good fishing stream for 6 to 8 inch brookies.

Big Swamp Creek. Heads in timbered mountains above but the lower reaches flow for 10 miles through meadow, swamp and willow land to the Big Hole River 12 miles south of Wisdom. The lower 6 miles are mostly dewatered for irrigation but the next 4 or 5 miles are easily fished and fair to good for 8 to 10 inch brook and cutthroat trout. There are private roads all the way.

Birch Creek. A clear, rapid stream in timbered country above and almost all used for irrigation below (in foothill country). Birch Creek is easily accessible along most of its length by a good gravel road and is crossed near the mouth by the highway 15 miles north of Dillon. It is poor fishing for 8 to 10 inch brook, a few cutthroat averaging a foot long, and is good mule deer and rattlesnake hunting here. You can two wheel to Dinner Station campgrount but you'll need four wheels and a good rig beyond that.

BIG HOLE RIVER NEAR JACKSON
Courtesy Ernst Peterson

Blacktail Creek. A small, steep little tributary to Camp Creek, accessible at the mouth by the Camp Creek truck road and followed by a jeep road for 3 miles to headwaters. It reportedly contains small brook and cutthroat trout.

Bobcat Creek. Drains Schwinegar Lake for 9 miles eastward through steep, timbered mountains to the Wise River, and is followed by a jeep road to within a few miles of the lake where the road has been closed by the USFS to vehicles over 40 inches wide. It is only lightly fished but good for 6 to 8 inch rainbow and some cutthroat trout.

Bobcat Lakes. Three (about ¼ mile apart) in a timber-bottomed, rock-walled cirque just below Bobcat Mountain between 8300 and 8400 feet above sea level and reached by the Bobcat Creek trail 4 miles from the end of the Lacy Creek road in the Wise River drainage. North and South Bobcat are about 5 acres each, by 20 or so feet deep and excellent fishing for 6 to 12 inch grayling and some rainbow. West Bobcat is only a couple of acres and has only grayling. They host horsemen and hikers but are not overcrowded.

Bond Creek. A small stream that drains Deerhead Lake for 2 miles to Bond Lake, and thence for 2 miles to Willow Creek. It is accessible at Deerhead Lake by the Birch Creek road but is seldom fished for the few 8 to 9 inch cutthroat that enter it from the lakes. The road is reported in bad shape after it leaves Birch Creek and may be closed.

Bond Lake. In a lodgepole forest, 20 acres (5 in aquatic vegetation), dammed with a maximum depth of 12 feet, drained by Bond Creek and reached by a mile hike up from the Willow Creek (via Birch Creek) road 7 miles past the guard station. It is spotty fishing but good at times for 9 to 11 inch rainbow, cutthroat, and some grayling. Note well: This is an irrigation reservoir and is drawn way down each summer exposing acres and acres of mud flats. Let's go somewhere else and maybe not tear up our rig getting there.

Boot Lake. In rocky, lodgepole country, 28 acres, dammed, with a gradual dropoff; the outlet flows to Birch Creek. This lake is reached by the Birch Creek road 7 miles past the guard station. The last few miles you need a four-wheeler. It gets its share of visitors and is spotty fishing but good at times for 9 to 11 inch rainbow, cutthroat, and some grayling.

Brownes Lake. A 60 acre lake on public land in timbered mountains with slide rock on the north side and lots of old wrecked cars scattered hither and yon. It is reached by the Rock Creek road 6 miles above the mouth of that stream, and is heavily fished for poor to fair catches of 8 to 10 inch brook and a few rainbow trout. There is a nice public campground here. The access in (the road) was a lot of trouble acquiring so stay on the road through all the private land.

Bryant Creek. Flows from Trident Meadows for 10 miles through timbered country to the Big Hole River 11 miles west of Wise River and is followed by a jeep road to headwaters. A heavily and easily fished stream that is good for 6 to 8 inch brook trout.

Buckhorn Creek. A small stream flowing through a flat bottomed, timbered canyon for about 3 miles above the Joy Cow Camp. This is a real brushy and rough one to fish and is not recommended, although it does contain pan-size brookies and cutthroat trout.

Bull Creek. This small stream flows for 10 miles south around Butch Hill by the Big Horn Pass to Governor Creek and is followed most of the way by road. The lower 3 miles are mostly dried up for irrigation, but the next 4 or 5 are good fishing (although seldom) for 7 to 9 inch cutthroat, brook and a few rainbow trout with here and there a grayling.

Camp Creek. Crossed at the mouth by the Butte-Dillon highway at Melrose and followed by a poor road for 16 miles to headwaters. This is mostly an open rangeland stream that is poor to fair fishing for 7 to 12 inch brookies and some rainbow trout.

Canyon Creek. A real pretty little stream that flows for 20 miles through timbered canyons and willow-bordered reaches to the Big Hole River about 3½ miles south of Divide. The middle reaches are accessible by a road from about 1 mile above the Kambich Ranch on Trapper Creek, then 2 miles north to Canyon Creek and thence 9 miles along the stream to an improved USFS campground and guard station — the jumping-off point to the Canyon Creek Lakes in high "mountain goat" country. The upper reaches of Canyon Creek contain few if any fish but the lower reaches are good fishing for 8 to 12 inch rainbow, cutthroat, some hybrids, and brookies, too.

Canyon Lake. A shallow 19 acre, 9 foot deep, swampy lake in alpine timber at 8392 feet above sea level, it's reached by a good USFS trail 4 miles from the Canyon Creek Campground. Canyon Lake is good fishing for cutthroat trout from 8 to 12 inches, boasting not only an occasional fair sized fish (up to 4 lbs. or so) but an old cabin to keep the weather out in a pinch.

Cherry Lake. A high, alpine basin lake at about 8830 feet above sea level, is perhaps 8 or so acres with talus slopes on the west side and timber on around. It's barely accessible up the (barren) Cherry Creek road about 16 miles from Melrose, is spotty fishing, but generally fair-to-good for 10 to 12 inch cutthroat trout. You can jeep to about 2 miles below — then a trail bike (or foot power) is allowed over the last stretch. It's closed to vehicles over 40 inches wide.

Corral Creek. A very small tributary to Tenmile Creek in mostly open, private rangeland that is poor fishing for small brookies.

Cow Bone Lake. At 8600 feet elevation, it's a deep, 9 acre, cirque lake timbered on the east side with talus on around. It can be reached by a poor jeep (if you feel like trading it in) road 5 miles from Skinner Meadows some 20 miles from Jackson. Cow Bone is moderately popular and spotty but sometimes excellent fishing for ½ to 2 pound cutthroat trout. Planted last in '79 and '76 with cutts, it's planted every third year. There are some hold-over rainbow and rainbow-cutthroat hybrids. The name — well, there's a lotta cow bones lying around.

Cow Creek. A very small, upland meadow tributary of Ruby Creek, crossed at the mouth by a gravel road. It contains a few small brookies that seldom see a hook.

Cox Creek. This small stream flows for a few miles through meadow and willow land to Warm Springs Creek near the Clemow Cow Camp and is paralleled by a jeep road all the way. It is seldom fished (mostly during hunting season) but is pretty good for mostly 8 to 10 inch brook trout, plus a few rainbow and cutthroat too.

Crescent Lake. Twenty-four acres, 22 feet deep in slide rock and scattered timber "goat" country at 8600 feet above sea level, reached by a trail ½ mile above Canyon Lake and 4¼ miles from the Canyon Creek campground. Crescent is better than fair fishing for 8 to 15 inch cutthroat and rainbow-cutthroat hybrids. It was stocked with tiny cutts in '76 and '79, the catching of which pleases more than a few people.

Crystal Lake. At 7810 feet above sea level, an alpine lake in gently sloping parkland set in heavily timbered country reached by 12 miles of rough gravel road north from Wisdom, then 9 miles by a USFS trail up Thompson Creek. Crystal is about 4 acres, 30 feet deep with mostly steep dropoffs and some vegetation around the margins. It is seldom fished but fair for 8 to 14 inch rainbow that are in poor condition.

Dark Horse Creek. A heavily fished stream followed by a dirt road from just below headwaters at Dark Horse Lake for 8 miles to Pioneer Creek. It is good from Skinner Meadows to the mouth for 6 to 8 inch brook and a very few cutthroat trout.

BOOT LAKE
Courtesy Bridenstine Studio

BROWNIES LAKE
Courtesy Bridenstine Studio

CANYON CREEK
Courtesy USFS

Dark Horse Lake. At 8700 feet above sea level Dark Horse is a 10 acre, blue water, cirque lake in a beautiful hanging valley. The lower, south end is shallow and timbered around the margins, the upper end drops straight off from talus slopes. Dark Horse is reached by a very poor jeep road 5 miles from Skinner Meadows and ¼ mile above an old abandoned copper mine. It is excellent fishing for 6 to 14 inch cutthroat and rainbow-cutthroat hybrids planted in '68, '71, '76, and '79 as wee 2 inch cutts.   It is attracting anglers fairly consistently all summer long.

David Creek. A small stream (the outlet of Schultz and Tahepia Lakes) flowing for 9 miles through steep, timbered canyons, meadow and willow-bottomed valleys past the Mono Campground to join with Wyman Creek. There are a lot of falls just above the campground and very few fish. It's fair fishing below though for 10 to 14 inch cutthroat, plus a few rainbow and hybrids. It's followed all along by a road.

Deep Creek. A slow, open meadow and willow-bottomed stream followed for 5 miles above the mouth by an oiled (Mill Creek Pass) highway. The upper reaches are on Mount Haggin wildlife management area land. The lower reaches are easily available to the public but only poor to fair fishing for 6 to 14 inch brookies and a few rainbow with even fewer grayling, whitefish, and burbot — being dewatered in season. The upper reaches are only fair for brookies but the area is one of the most used elk and deer spots in the state.

Deerhead Lake. Fifteen acres, shoal (maximum depth 15 feet) with considerable aquatic vegetation around the shores, in lodgepole, rocky country at 7582 feet elevation above sea level; reached by jeep up the Birch Creek road. Deerhead was originally drained by Bond Creek but is now dammed and ditched to Birch Creek. It is excellent fishing for 7 to 18 inch cutthroat stocked in '70, '72, '76 and '80. The road reportedly is very bad and the USFS may soon close it. If so, there is a good hiking trail from Dinner Station Campground.

Delano Creek. A very small, 2 mile long stream in timbered mountains at the headwaters of Jerry Creek. Sometimes fished near the mouth for a few small brookies.

Divide Creek. An open meadowland stream that is followed for its entire length of 12 miles by the Butte-Dillon highway. It heads on the Continental Divide and debouches to the Big Hole River about 1½ miles south of Divide. It's nice, easy fishing for small (8 to 12 inches) brook and some rainbow trout. A good place to take the kids or a dub.

Doolittle Creek. A seldom fished, meadow and willow bottomland stream accessible by a road (through a locked gate) for 4 miles of good water above its mouth on the Big Hole River 12 miles north of Wisdom. It contains 6 to 8 inch brookies.

23

Dubois Creek. Reached at the mouth by the Willow Creek road 1 mile above the Joy Cow Camp; there is no trail and it is real rough going through down timber and brush. This one is not recommended for fishing but the lower reaches do contain a fair number of small cutthroat and brook trout.

East Stone Lake. See Stone Creek Lakes.

Elbow Lake. A high (8650 feet elevation) alpine lake reached by trail a mile from Odell Lookout, which is accessible by the Lacy Creek jeep road which can only be travelled by vehicles under 40 inches wide the last five miles or so. Elbow is fairly deep, 10.6 acres, in timbered country but open around the shore. It used to be good fishing for 8 to 12 inch rainbow and a few cutthroat, but is now (reportedly) frozen out.

Englejard Creek. About 12 miles long from headwaters to its junction with the Big Hole River 1¼ miles below Jackson and easily accessible all along by county and private roads. The lower 2½ miles are mostly dewatered for irrigation; the next 2¼ miles are in meadowland and are easily fished for fair catches of 7 to 9 inch brook and cutthroat trout.

Englejard Lake. A shallow, 2 acre pond in meadowland and scattered timber at 7503 feet elevation above sea level. It is reached by a jeep road 3 miles from the Miner Creek road, then ¾ of a mile to the edge (be sure to STOP HERE, or you'll get stuck but good) of a meadow and proceed on foot to the shore. It is seldom fished but good for 8 to 10 inch cutthroat.

Ferguson Lake. A heavily fished, 17.5 acre lake in timbered mountains (elevation 7528 feet) reached by a fishermen's trail a mile up from the Alder Creek trail. But a better way in is to take the Bryant Creek road to Foolhen Ridge and thence a ¼ mile hike to the shore. This one is 48 feet deep but with a shallow dropoff and was planted with rainbow in 1968, again in 1971, and then in '76 and '79 with cutthroat. It's now good for either species 10 to 15 inches long.

Fish (or Fish Peak, or Hicks) Lake. Take the West Fork LaMarche Creek trail by horseback (you'll need the rest later on) for 11 miles above the ranch to a little drainage coming in from the north (about 1½ miles below the Warren Lake — Cutaway Pass junction). Now strap on your climbers and make like a mountain goat up the little tributary for 1½ miles (and more than 1900 feet elevation) over talus and slide rock to the lake at 8490 feet above sea level in barren (just below the Continental Divide) country ¾ of a mile west of Fish Peak. It is impossible to get a horse

DARK HORSE CREEK
Courtesy USFS

DARK HORSE LAKE
Courtesy Bridenstine Studio

in here and is not recommended for any but the youthful, rugged type. The last recorded visitor searched for this one for 4 years, got lost 4 times and finally made it on the 5th go-around. Once there, the lake is found to be about 18 acres, deep, in a barren ice-scoured cirque with a few trees on the lower, south shore; and fair to good fishing for 10 to 12 inch rainbow trout with perhaps a lunker or two.

Fish Peak Lake. See Fish Lake.

Fish Trap Creek.
A mostly meadowland stream followed by a road from its mouth on the Big Hole River for about 5 miles upstream, real pretty, moderately popular and good fishing for mostly 6 to 14 inch brookies plus a few rainbow trout and ling. It gets dewatered in the lower stretches plus heavily grazed — could be better maybe!

Fool Hen Creek.
A real short stream flowing from Fool Hen Lake for 1 mile to Alder Creek in timbered country, crossed at the mouth by the Alder Creek trail. Although short, it is heavily fished and fair, too, for 6 to 9 inch brook and a few rainbow up to 12 inches.

Fool Hen Lake.
A heavily fished 8.1 acre by 38 foot maximum depth lake in timbered country at 7100 feet elevation, reached by a mile hike up Fool Hen Creek from the Alder Creek trail; was planted with rainbow in '68 and '71, and with cutthroat in '76 and '79. It's fair to good fishing now for 10 to 16 inch cutts and hybrids.

Fox Creek.
Drains west from the Grasshopper-Big Hole divide for 7 miles to Governor Creek and is followed by road and trail to headwaters. The lower 4 miles are mostly in open meadowland with willow along the banks, are subjected to moderate fishing pressure and produce good catches of 10 to 12 inch brook, and perhaps a few rainbow and cutthroat. An alternate route in on the Bloody Dick and Selway road exists.

Francis Creek.
Located 2 miles southeast of Wisdom, flows for 8 miles before entering Steel Creek, and is on winter range for mule deer and elk. The lower sections flow through grassland and sagebrush and the upper (USFS) through timber. Used more than a little for excellent catches of 6 to 14 inch brookies, some burbot to 10 inches, small whitefish, and a very rare grayling. The entire drainage has only 2 small improved roads so if you are willing to walk you can get that "lonesome feeling."

French Gulch (or Creek).
Crossed at the mouth by the Big Hole-Anaconda highway 10 miles above Ralston, then followed upstream for 2 miles by a jeep road through open grassland and willows. Fishing is fair for rainbow, brookies and whitefish to 11 inches — it's popular (for hunters when mule deer and elk are in season, also), although there's better angling pretty close by.

Goat Lake. See Oreamnos Lake.

Gold Creek.
A small stream that is followed by a trail through semi-open timber for 6 miles to the Wise River 1½ miles above Willow Camp. It is fished a moderate amount and is middling fair along its entire length for 6 to 8 inch brookies.

Governor Creek.
A good, easily and heavily fished stream followed by county and farm roads for 10 miles of fishing water in open meadow and willow bottomland south of Jackson — flows through grazing and hay lands with 15 of its 17 channel miles on private land wth subsequent erosion and dewatering occurring in low reaches — also requires permission for the most part. It is very popular with Butte residents for 8 to 12 inch brookies, some grayling, and an occasional ling, rainbow, or whitefish.

Granite Lake.
A high, alpine lake (elevation 8920 feet above sea level), about 6 acres, in timbered country but open around the shore. Granite is accessible to within two miles by jeep up the Cherry Creek (no fish here) road about 16 miles from Melrose. It is reportedly good fishing for 10 to 14 inch cutthroat and also contains a few lunkers and gets some usage.

HALL LAKES
Courtesy Bridenstine Studio

HAMBY LAKE
Courtesy Bridenstine Studio

Grayling Lake. Is high, 12½ acres by 33 feet maximum depth, in rock and scattered timber "goat" country at 8600 feet above sea level, reached to within a mile by the Lion Creek trail 3½ miles above the Canyon Creek Campground. It is hard to get to (but many do), supports a fair population of 8 to 12 inch rainbow and cutthroat trout and a good population of 8 to 12 inch hybrids, plus a few grayling.

Green Lake. Twenty seven acres, alpine, on the east side of Granite Mountain in good goat hunting country at 8830 feet elevation. Green Lake is reached by trail 4 miles above the Rock Creek Guard Station or cross-country 1¼ miles southwest from Cherry Lake. It is good but spotty fishing for 10 to 12 inch, maximum recorded to 3 pounds, rainbow, cutthroat and rainbow-cutthroat hybrids. Trail bikers use this area a bit.

Grouse Creek. A short, 2½ mile stream flowing through timber from the Grouse Creek Lakes to Pattengail Creek on the Lambrecht Ranch and followed all the way by trail. It is only lightly fished, but fair for 6 to 8 inch rainbow and brook trout.

Grouse Creek Lakes. Three little lakes about ¼ to ½ mile apart in alpine (about 8000 feet) timber, reached by the Grouse Creek trail 4 miles from the Wise River road. The South lake is about 5 acres and deep; the Middle lake about 2½ acres and deep; and the North lake about 5 acres and shallow. All are good fishing for 8 to 12 inch rainbow trout but are not too often visited due to the long hike in.

Hall Lake. A 6½ acre, above timberline pothole about 2 miles above the end of the Elkhorn Creek road 6 miles south from the Mono Creek campground and just below the summit of Saddleback Mountain. Used to have rainbow but was stocked with cutts in 1971 and 1976 — there is some reproduction. It is excellent for sassy cutthroat to 12 inches, receiving only moderate pressure.

Hamby Lake. At 8092 feet elevation, 37 acres, 33 feet maximum depth, in a hanging valley with alpine timber on three sides and talus on the west; it is reached by trail a couple of miles from the end of the (barren) Hamby Creek jeep trail, reached a half mile south from Jackson then 3 miles west, another mile south, another west and then south again on the trail. This one is fished mostly by local people but is good for 8 to 15 inch brookies, rainbow, cutthroat, 10 to 17 inch grayling, and apparently has a successful spawning area in the good little inlet stream.

Harriet Lou Creek. A very small stream that flows for about 6 miles through timber above and private meadowland below to the Big Hole River 2 miles west of Wise River and is followed by a jeep road to headwaters. Harriet Lou is seldom fished yet fair for 6 to 8 inch brook trout.

Hicks Lake. See Fish Lake.

26

MOUNTAIN GOATS
Courtesy USFS

Hidden Gem Lake.
Take the Wise River road for 8 miles upstream to a bridge, then the Sheep Creek road for 1 mile, and the Clifford Creek trail for another 2 miles to the lake in heavily timbered country. It is about 7 acres, shallow, and fair fishing for 10 to 12 inch brook trout yet is very seldom visited.

Hopkins Lake.
Between Saddleback and Comet Mountains in high barren country a half mile above Hall Lake and a couple of miles as the crow flies from the Elkhorn Mine at the end of the Elkhorn Creek road, 7 miles from the Mono Campground. Hopkins covers 9.6 acres, is deep with steep dropoffs and used to be good fishing for 1½ to 5 pound rainbow trout that reportedly froze out the winter of '66. So the Fish and Game fishery biologists netted it in 1972 and what do you know — it had a fair population of 7 to 11 inch cutthroat. Now how do you account for that? Stocked again in '76 and '80, it's now excellent for cutts to 14 inches — plenty of elbow room, too!

Howell Creek.
The outlet of Mystic Lake, whose lower reaches (9 miles) are followed by trail and flow through meadowland to the Big Hole River 9 miles north of Wisdom. Howell is only lightly fished and no better than fair for 8 to 9 inch brook trout, and an occasional small rainbow.

Indian Creek.
This is a very small tributary of Jerry Creek, followed by a jeep trail for 3 miles through timbered country. Fished quite a bit for such a small stream — fair catches of 6 to 8 inch trout in heavy timber.

Jahnke Lake.
A hanging valley cirque lake (elevation 8760 feet) reached by trail 2½ miles from the end of the Jahnke Creek jeep trail which takes off to the southwest about 2½ miles south of the Jahnke Campground 13 miles or so south from Jackson on the Bloody Dick (Beaverhead Valley) road. It's 11 acres, as much as 18 feet deep in places, in scrub timber but with talus and rock at the west (upper) end. Jahnke is good fishing for 10 to 12 inch cutthroat. An added attraction is the remains of a nearby abandoned silver mine that was worked out in the late 1800s.

Jerry Creek.
A clear, rapid stream flowing from the Continental Divide for 15 miles through timber above and meadowland below, to the Big Hole River a few miles east of Wise River. Jerry Creek is followed upstream for 5 miles by road and then for another 5 by a good trail. It was originally a cutthroat and grayling stream but is now heavily fished for good catches of 6 to 8 inch brookies and a few rainbow and cutthroat trout.

Johanna (or Secret) Lake.
Take the Alder Creek trail for 8 miles, then ½ mile east up the unnamed outlet of Johanna to the shore in open timber just below timberline at 8100 feet above sea level. This 5 acre lake is very seldom fished but very good for 8 to 12 inch cutthroat, and a few rainbow. Rainbow-cutt hybrids have also been reported.

Johnson Creek.
This small stream is followed by trail and road for 5 miles from its headwaters north of Little Granulated Mountain to the Big Hole River 5 miles west of Wise River. It is heavily fished in the lower, meadowland reaches for 6 to 12 inch brook, a few rainbow trout, some ling, and whitefish. The lower reaches are diverted to ditches in season causing low flows.

Joseph Creek.   A tributary of Trail Creek, 6 miles long in an open meadowland valley that is bordered by heavily timbered hills. It is crossed several times by the Big Hole highway. Joseph Creek is easily and heavily fished for mostly 6 to 11 inch brookies plus now and then a rainbow trout, and ling. Good cover, brush aplenty and beaver dams in the lower reaches sustain this good little fishery.

Lacy Creek.   There is a jeep road all the way up this stream from its junction with the Wise River 11 miles upstream through 3 miles of meadowland and then 5 miles of timber to Schwinegar Lake at the old Ibex Mine. Lacy is a fairly popular stream that is good fishing for 7 to 9 inch brook, rainbow, and cutthroat trout plus a few grayling. There are a couple of beaver dams just above the mouth. The last few miles of jeep road below the lake are closed to vehicles over 40 inches wide — at last report.

Lake Abundance.   A 3.7 acre by 35 feet deep alpine lake in scattered timber and rock-slide, mountain goat country at 8522 feet above sea level; reached by trail an eighth of a mile above Crescent Lake and 5 miles from the Canyon Creek Campground. Lake Abundance sustains a moderate fishing pressure and is generally fair for 6 to 15 inch cutthroat and some cutt-bow crosses. Cutts were planted in '80 and '81; the rainbows several years ago.

Lake Agnes.   At 7500 feet elevation, a moderately popular, red hot grayling (9 to 13 inches) lake, about 99 acres, deep with steep dropoffs and with nice sandy beaches all around. It is reached by trail 7/10 mile from the Tungsten Mining Quarry near Brownes Lake on the Rock Creek road. The grayling (¼ milion) were planted in 1959 and '60. Stay on the road on the way in (once had severe access problems only recenty alleviated), and park at Brownes Lake Campground and take the trail; or park at the bridge (below the mine) and go in by trail from there, unless posted. Prolific, gaudy, delicate, and avid feeders, grayling as caught here (easily) can almost become a spiritual thing, an obsession.

Lake Geneva.   A deep, 8 acre cirque lake in barren, rocky country at 8451 feet elevation a half mile straight up talus slopes above Hamby Lake. There is no trail and it is seldom visited let alone fished for the few 10 to 14 inch cutthroat trout that inhabit its ice cold waters.

Lake of the Woods.   A beautiful, scenic, alpine lake at 8300 feet above sea level, it was easily reached by the Lake Creek jeep road. Due to road closures being imminent here, see Schwinegar Lake and possibly check with the ranger district for the most current best route. You can take a USFS trail 8 miles from the Steel Creek Guard Station. Lake of the Woods is about 10½ acres, 30 feet deep and good fishing for 8 to 10 inch rainbow, cutthroat and hybrids.

LaMarche Creek.   A beautiful fishing stream that is followed by road and trail from its mouth at Holmes to headwaters. The lower 6 miles are mainly in willow and beaver pond country and are excellent fishing for 6 to 12 inch brook and some rainbow trout, but the creek flows through the LaMarche Creek Dude Ranch (on the site of the old Percy Storey Ranch) and in the past has been pretty well restricted to guest fishing. During irrigation season, the lower reaches are dewatered — sometimes severely.

LaMarche Lake.   A high, 3 acre lake in alpine meadows right on the top of the mountain near Boat Peak; reached by the Middle Fork trail 6 miles from the end of the LaMarche Creek road. It is seldom fished (and then mostly by accident) and was real poor for 8 to 10 inch trout. About the only thing to recommend it is its beauty. The lake is reported barren.

Land Lake.   See Rainbow Lake.

Lena Lake.   A deep, 23 acre lake in alpine cirque and talus country at about 8300 feet above sea level; reached by a good horse trail a couple of miles from the Ajax Creek trail. Lena is excellent fishing for 10 to 16 inch rainbow, cutthroat, and their hybrids. The lake up the drainage is smaller and fair for cutts. Neither one gets a ton of usage. Trail bikes have been said to make the lower (Lena Lake).

Libby Creek.   A real small tributary of Jerry Creek, followed by trail for 3 miles through timbered country to headwaters. Libby is seldom fished but contains a fair number of 6 to 10 inch brookies.

Courtesy Danny On

Lily Lake. A deep, 14 acre lake in timbered country 1½ miles southeast of Proposal Rock; reached by road 7 miles east from Wisdom and then a USFS trail for about 2 miles to the lakeshore. Lily is a pretty, easily accessible, moderately popular lake that is good fishing for 8 to 12 inch rainbow and cutthroat trout, plus a few lunkers.

Lion Lake. Reached by a USFS trail 5 miles above the Canyon Creek Ranger Station in steep (elevation 8700 feet) rocky, lodgepole country. It covers 4.2 acres with about 2 in aquatic vegetation, is 32 feet deep with steep dropoffs, and is reported to be excellent fishing for 10 to 14 inch rainbow trout.

Little Camp Creek. About 3 miles long and is reached at the mouth by the Camp Creek road 12 miles from Melrose. Little Camp contains a few trout in the lower reaches but is nothing to write home about.

Little Joe Creek. A small, lightly fished stream followed by trail for 4 miles from headwaters to its mouth at the Little Joe Campground on the Wise River. The lower 3 miles flow through open meadow and timber and contain a few 6 to 8 inch brook and an occasional cutthroat trout.

Little Lake. At 8750 feet elevation, 29 foot maximum depth, is reached by a good USFS horse trail 6 miles above the end of the Little Lake Creek road, is 13 acres in a heavily timbered mountain valley. Twenty years ago it contained goldens that all but disappeared. Planted with cutthroat trout in 1979 and last reported good fishing for 12 inchers that are still growing.

Little Lake Creek. Drains Little Lake in high alpine country near the Continental Divide for 18 miles to the Big Hole River 6 miles below Jackson. The lower 4 miles are mostly dewatered for irrigation, the upper 14 miles are crossed by road and followed by trail through meadowland and scattered timber. Over this stretch Little Lake Creek is easy to fish and a good producer of 7 to 10 inch brook, and some cutthroat trout. It's a fairly popular stream.

Little Moosehorn Creek. A small stream in heavy timber that flows to Ruby Creek and is crossed at the mouth by the Swamp Creek road 18 miles west of Wisdom. The lower 3 miles follow a ditch-like course across an upland bench, are easily accessible and fair fishing for 6 to 8 inch brookies.

Long Tom Creek. See Tom Creek.

Lost Horse Creek. Flows from Fool Hen Mountain for 5 miles to Pattengail Creek. Lost Horse is not much of a fishing stream, is seldom bothered, but does have a few brook near the mouth.

Lower Stone Lake. See Stone Creek Lakes.

May Creek. A small tributary of Trail Creek followed by a trail through meadow, willow and timber for 7 miles to headwaters. The lower reaches are fair fishing for 6 to 8 inch brook trout.

May (or Secret) Lake. A shallow, dammed, (mostly less than 10 feet deep), 5 acre lake about a 10 minute hike southeast from Peak Lake on the Birch Creek drainage. It is seldom fished but contains a few 6 to 9 inch cutthroat.

Meadow Creek. This small, open timber stream flows to Harriet Lou Creek and is reached at the mouth by road about 5 miles west of Wise River and is followed by trail for 6 miles upstream to headwaters. Seldom fished, it contains a fair number of pan-size brook trout.

Middle Fork Fishtrap Creek. A small stream followed by a good USFS trail for 6 miles from the mouth at the end of the Fishtrap Creek road to headwaters on East Goat Peak. There is some fair fishing here for 8 to 10 inch brookies and a few rainbow in the numerous beaver ponds about 1½ miles above the end of the road.

Middle Fork of LaMarche Creek. A small, timberland stream accessible by trail but hardly worth the effort as it is only poor fishing for small brookies for about 1 mile in open meadow below LaMarche Lake.

Middle Fork Lake. A shallow, 10 acre lake in timbered country reached by the Middle Fork LaMarche Creek trail 7½ miles above the ranch. It is fair fishing for 10 to 11 inch brook and rainbow trout.

Mifflin Creek. A tiny little stream —so narrow you'll have trouble getting a hook in it. The lower 4 miles flow through the Big Hole bottomlands about 10 miles south of Wisdom and are followed and crossed by county roads. It is excellent and increasingly popular fishing for 8 to 10 inch brook trout.

Miner Creek. Eighteen miles long from Little Miner Lake at the headwaters to the mouth on the Big Hole River 4½ miles below Jackson and easily accessible by road except the last 2½ miles. The lower reaches (from about 1 mile below Miner Lake to the mouth) are in open meadow and willow bottoms. This portion is heavily fished and good for 8 to 12 inch brook trout, some burbot, and now and again a grayling. The lower reaches are often split into two channels, with some erosion and dewatering occurring.

Miner Lake. A popular "campground" and fishing lake in heavily timbered mountains reached by a good road a dozen miles west from Jackson. It's 57 acres, mostly shallow but with one deep channel, heavily fished and good too for 8 to 14 inch brook trout plus an occasioal cutthroat, grayling or whitefish. It is closed to gasoline powered motor boats.

LAKE GENEVA
Courtesy Bridenstine Studio

JAHNKE LAKE
Courtesy Bridenstine Studio

UPPER MINER LAKE
Courtesy Bridenstine Studio

UPPER, UPPER MINER LAKE
Courtesy Bridenstine Studio

Mono Creek. In scattered timber and parkland, followed for its full length (3 miles) by the Wise River-Polaris road. Mono is heavily fished but only fair for 6 to 7 inch brook, a few rainbow, and a very few cutthroat trout.

Moose Creek. About 15 miles long, crossed near the mouth by the Butte-Dillon highway 6 miles north of Melrose and followed by a good gravel road, through a locked gate, for 3 miles downstream to its mouth at Maiden Rock and along the upper 5 miles from Moose Town to Burton by a pickup road. The upper reaches flow through open park country; the lower reaches are mostly in timber. It's all good· fishing for 7 to 12 inch rainbow, brook trout, and a few cutts.

Moose Creek. This very small, timberland stream flows to the Wise River just below Willow Camp. There is a trail along the lower reaches, which are seldom fished, but do contain a few pan-size brookies.

Moose Creek. A small tributary of French Gulch, crossed at the mouth by the Big Hole-Anaconda highway 7 miles above Ralston. Moose Creek is seldom, but easily, fished for small brooks, rainbow, and cutts, especially in the beaver ponds where they get to some twelve inches.

Morgan Jones Lake. Four acres, shallow, in heavy timber about ¾ of a mile east on the Big Hole Pass at around 6780 feet elevation above sea level and reached by jeep an eighth of a mile from the highway. It is seldom fished but fair for 10 to 12 inch rainbow and brook trout.

Mussigbrod Creek. Flows for 5 miles into the lake and then ten more below the lake through timber and across willow bottomed sagebrush and grassland benches to the North Fork of the Big Hole River. There is a gravel road to the lake, which is dammed and can dewater the creek at times. However, the creek is fair for 4 to 11 inch brook trout, some grayling and burbot, and gets its share of usage (when it has enough water to float a dry or sink a nymph). In the lower reaches the creek is diverted into a series of ditches.

Mussigbrod Lake. At 6488 feet elevation, a popular (there's a USFS campground) reservoir lake with 10 feet of water level fluctuation, reached by a fair car road up Mussigbrod Creek 23 miles northwest from Wisdom. It is about 100 acres, 55 feet maximum depth, mostly fished by boat (and pretty good, too) for 10 to 14 inch brook trout and 7 to 12 inch grayling at a ratio of about 3 to 1, plus hordes of suckers. Note: Gasoline powered boats are a no-no here.

Mystic Lake. An Anaconda-Pintlar Wilderness Area lake just south of the Continental Divide (elevation 7916 feet) in heavy timber, reached by a good USFS horse trail 14 miles up Howell Creek to the guard station. Mystic covers 18 acres, is about 55 feet deep at the most with a mucky bottom and perhaps 2 or 3 acres in vegetation. It is moderately popular and good fishing for skinny 7 to 13 inch rainbow trout.

North Fork Big Hole River.
A slow, placid stream formed by the junction of Trail and Ruby Creeks near the Big Hole Battlefield; flows for 17 miles through meadow and willow bottoms to the Big Hole River 9 miles north of Wisdom; easily accessible all the way by private and county roads. The North Fork is heavily fished and a consistently excellent producer of 8 to 16 inch brook trout, plus a very few whitefish and grayling.

North Fork Divide Creek.
The North Fork heads on Burnt Mountain and is followed by good logging roads for its entire length (10 miles) approximately parallel to, and a few miles distant from, the Continental Divide. It is an open, easily and heavily fished stream that is a consistently good producer of 6 to 8 inch brook, some rainbow and a few cutthroat trout.

Odell Creek.
Seven miles long, flows to the Wise River; the lower 4 miles followed by a meadowland road, the upper 3 miles by an open timber trail. The lower reaches are easily and heavily fished for good catches of 6 to 8 inch brook trout, 6 to 12 inch grayling (from Odell Lake) and some 6 to 10 inch rainbow trout.

Odell Lake.
A high lake at 8376 feet elevation in alpine timber on the eastern slopes of Odell Mountain. With shallow dropoffs along the west and north end, Odell is as much as 35 feet deep and 35.6 acres. It is easily accessible by trail a quarter mile from the end of the Lacy Creek jeep road at Lake of the Woods. Heavily fished for hordes of delicate grayling stocked in 1973, '78, and '81, which range from 8 to 14 inches and tug a fly readily. There's a good open campsite at the south end. It seems that every year there have been several new road closures — being forewarned, are you forearmed?

Old Tim Creek.
A small, mountain-meadow stream flowing to Warm Springs Creek at the Clemow Cow Camp. There is no trail for the lower 4 miles which (though seldom fished) are excellent for 6 to 8 inch brook, and some rainbow trout. A good place to take a child, or a beginner.

Oreamnos (or Goat) Lake.
At 8363 elevation, a 33 foot deep, 10 acre, timber bottomed cirque lake just below and east of West Pintlar Peak on the Continental Divide in ice-scoured country. Oreamnos can be reached by horseback about a half mile below the Highline trail and, though seldom visited, has been good fishing for mostly 8 to 10 inch rainbow, plus now and then a lunker to 3-4 pounds. Here's hoping recent reports are erroneous, since if they are right, the lake may be devoid of fish.

Pattengail Creek.
Eighteen miles long, mostly in timber but the lower three miles are in meadow just above its junction with the Wise River. Pattengail is followed upstream by a jeep road for 5 miles, or as far as Lambrecht Creek. It is fair for 7 to 9 inch brook and some rainbow. In 1927 in the lower section of the creek a dam washed out, scouring the creek channel badly. There are moose around the area — so keep an eye out.

Pear Lake.
A high, dammed lake at 8679 feet above sea level with an old CCC campground, reached by jeep at the end of the Birch Creek road. It's a good 36 acres, 45 feet maximum depth, 10 per cent shoal and then some when it is drawn away down each fall. The fishing is good for 10 to 14 inch cutthroat and is moderately popular having been stocked in '79 and '81. Now take note! If you climb on up a half mile (and about 450 feet) to the north and a little west, you will come to Anchor Lake which lies in timber, was stocked with rainbow back in '63 and '64, and again with cutthroat in '70, '72, and '76. They could be all gone by now — or big!

Peterson Lake.
A high, mountain lake in a big rock slide on the northern timbered slopes of Bloody Dick Peak, reached by a 3 mile cross-country hike south from the end of the Governor Creek-Pine Creek road. Peterson is about 8 acres, seldom fished, but fair for 12 to 14 inch rainbow, cutthroat, and rainbow-cutthroat hybrids.

Pine Creek.
A small, meadowland tributary of Andrus Creek, the lower 2 miles are accessible by road and trail and are lightly fished for the few small brookies it contains.

Pintlar Creek.
A wadeable stream flowing from Pintlar Pass between East and West Pintlar Peaks for 18 miles southeastward to the Big Hole River 11 miles north of Wisdom. It is followed upstream by a road for 10 miles past the Pintlar campground at the lake to Pintlar Falls. This is a moderately popular stream that is fair fishing below the falls for 8 to 12 inch brookies, some rainbow-cutt hybrids and ling. The creek gets dewatered at both ends — fall and winter below the lake — summer and spring in the lower reaches.

Pintlar Lake. Thirty six acres, about 20 feet deep with gradual dropoffs, a mucky bottom and much aquatic vegetation around the shores. Pintlar is a most scenic lake in the midst of a lodgepole forest and is reached by road 20 miles north from Wisdom. It is best fished by boat for fair catches of 8 to 12 inch rainbow, cutthroat and brook trout (it was last stocked in 1966 with rainbow). There's a campground and a dam — no gasoline powered boats are allowed.

Pioneer Creek. The outlet of Pioneer, Highup and Skytop Lakes, Pioneer Creek flows for 18 miles, mostly through sagebrush and meadow to the Big Hole River near Jackson and is accessible by road and trail all the way. It is seldom fished but the lower reaches are good for 7 to 9 inch brook and cutthroat trout. Pioneer Lake may have some cutts —the others are barren.

Plimpton Creek. A wading stream followed by road and trail from headwaters on the Continental Divide southeastward for 15 miles to the Big Hole River 8 miles north of Wisdom. The lower 4 miles are mostly in open meadow and are easily, though only occasionally, fished for fair catches of 6 to 9 inch brookies.

Rainbow (or Land) Lake. An Anaconda-Pintlar Wilderness Area lake just below and east of the Continental Divide reached by a good USFS trail 12 miles up the West Fork from the end of the Fishtrap Creek road. Rainbow is deep, about 18 acres, in a large cirque that is timbered below and barren above. For years it has been a consistently good producer of 13 to 14 inch rainbow, but as of late the fishing has tapered off to no better than fair and the fish are "skinnying" up; for why?

Rainbow Lake. A little to the West and above Agnes Lake, reached by 4 miles of good USFS trail from the Rock Creek Ranger Station. This one is about 8 acres, maybe 40 feet deep with gradual dropoffs, with clear green water and considerable aquatic vegetation around the shores. It is drained by Rock Creek, heavily fished for 8 to 14 inch cutthroat, and was stocked in '76 and '79.

Reservoir Creek. Six miles long, in timber with a trail following all the way to junction with Pattengail Creek. The fishing is fair (when and if, but seldom) for 6 to 9 inch brookies and a few rainbow trout.

Ridge Lake. Ten acres, 35 feet deep just south of Homer Youngs Peak at 8449 feet elevation in alpine country, and easily reached by trail 300 yards from the Rock Island Lakes road. Used to be barren but was injected with cutthroat in 1966, '70, '74, '76 and in '81 — excellent fishing for 8 to 16 inch trout. No motorized vehicles (unless on snow) are allowed on the road below the lake.

Rock Creek. Crossed near the mouth by the Butte highway 22 miles north of Dillon and followed upstream for 9 miles by a gravel road to the ranger station and another 4½ miles by a good USFS trail to headwaters. It is a high gradient stream, in lodgepole above and sagebrush and meadow below, is fair-to-good fishing for pan-size rainbow and brook trout.

Rock Creek. About 20 miles long, the upper 5 flowing through heavy timber, the lower through swamp and willow bottoms to the Big Hole River 2 miles south of Wisdom. The lower reaches are easily accessible by county road and are good fishing (with permission) for 7 to 8 inch brook and a few 8 to 10 inch cutthroat and rainbow trout.

Rock Island Lakes. Three lakes of which only the lower, and northernmost ones contain fish. Lower Rock Island is at 8500 feet elevation, 20 acres, mostly shoal around the shore with lots of vegetation, in meadow and timber; reached by a good road 12 miles west from Jackson, then 5 miles up the Miner Creek jeep road and finally 4 miles by trail to the shore. North Rock Island (a few hundred yards to the north) is only 18 acres. Both lakes are good fishing for 6 to 14 inch rainbow, plus a few cutthroat and hybrids.

Ruby Creek. A small stream heading in timbered country below the Big Hole Pass and flowing northward for about 11 miles through willow and meadowland to the North Fork of the Big Hole River near the Big Hole Battlefield (more properly termed "massacre-field"). It is easily and heavily fished for excellent catches of 8 to 10 inch brookies, a few rainbow-cutthroat hybrids and perhaps a stray ling.

Sand Creek.
Only 1 mile long, the outlet of Sand Lake, Sand Creek flows through heavy timber to Pattengail Creek west of Bobcat Mountain and is followed along the south side by a trail to the lake. It is fair fishing for 6 to 8 inch brook, some cutthroat, and fewer rainbow trout.

Sand Lake.
Reached from Wise River by the Pattengail trail, or from Wisdom by the Steel Creek-Lily Lake road, and then 2½ miles of USFS trail. This lake is 42 acres in size, 38 feet deep in spots with steep dropoffs, open around the shore but in sparsely timbered country at 8150 feet elevation. It is used mostly by horseback parties and is good fishing for 7 to 13 inch cutthroat trout — should be inasmuch as it was planted with fingerling in '76 and '79.

Sawlog Creek.
A small, seldom fished stream flowing to the Big Hole River opposite the highway 2½ miles above Fishtrap. A few brook trout are found in beaver ponds along the lower (2 miles) meadowland reaches. It is mostly inaccessible except during low water when the Big Hole is fordable.

Schultz Lakes.
Two little lakes about ¼ mile apart in barren rocky country just west of Mount Tahepia at 9000 feet elevation; reached by a good trail 6 miles up Jacobson Creek from the Mono Creek Campground which is a little better than 20 miles up the Wise River road, or, a couple of miles by pack trail down drainage and up again from Tahepia Lake. Upper Schultz is about 7½ acres; Lower Schultz is about 5 acres, and both are deep and excellent fishing for cutthroat and rainbow trout that average 1 to 2 pounds, plus a few lunkers to 5 pounds. Upper Schultz also sports some rainbow-cutthroat hybrids. Cutts were stocked in 1979 in both lakes. There are lots of bikers in this area.

Schwinegar Lake.
A 5 acre, 30 foot deep lake with shallow dropoffs, in alpine timber at 8125 feet elevation, about 1 mile north of Odell Lookout near the Ibex Mine; easily reached by the Lacy Creek jeep road. Schwinegar is fairly popular and excellent fishing for 8 to 10 inch grayling. The last few miles are closed to vehicles over 40 inches wide — so haul out a scooter, or hoof it!

Secret Lake.
See May or Johanna Lake.

Seven Mile Creek.
A small open stream flowing through Mount Haggin Game Area pastureland to Ten Mile Creek, reached at the mouth by a ranch road 9 miles above Ralston on the Anaconda-Big Hole highway. It is seldom fished but fair-to-good for small brook and rainbow trout.

Seymour Creek.
An easily fished stream flowing from Seymour Lake through timber above and meadow below to the Big Hole River a couple of miles west of Ralston. It can be reached three miles above the mouth by a jeep road from the Deep Creek highway and is followed thence to headwaters by jeep road and trail. Seymour is easy fishing — but seldom bothered — for real good catches of 8 to 12 inch brook.

MINER LAKE
Courtesy Bridenstine Studio

Seymour Lakes (Upper and Lower). Fairly deep, 35 and 15 acres, in a swampy, mountain valley at 8220 and 6750 feet elevation, reached by trail 1½ miles above the end of the road up Seymour Creek. Because of the more or less private access, they are seldom fished but the upper is real good for 8 to 11 inch cutthroat, rainbow, and hybrids, with mostly brookies in the lower lake.

Sheep Creek. A very small stream flowing across private land in the lower reaches to junction with the Wise River 8 miles upstream from the Big Hole River. It is very seldom fished but does contain small brookies.

Sheep Creek. A small tributary of Trail Creek, about 5 miles long in meadow and timberland. The first couple of miles are good fishing for 8 to 10 inch brookies. There's no trail.

Six Mile Creek. A small, open ranchland tributary of French Gulch just west of the Anaconda-Big Hole highway about 9 miles above Ralston. Six Mile is seldom fished although fair to good for 7 to 9 inch brook and a few rainbow and cutthroat trout in occasional beaver ponds and along the lower reaches.

Skinner Meadow Creek. Take a good county road for 22 miles south from Jackson to the head of this stream at Skinner Lake. It is an open meadow stream with a few beaver ponds here and there. There are about 5 miles of easily (good for the kids) and heavily fished water producing good catches of 6 to 8 inch brookies.

Slag-A-Melt Creek. A fast, mountain stream flowing for 6 miles through timber and meadow from Slag-A-Melt Lakes to Big Swamp Creek and followed by road and trail all the way. This one is fair fishing in the lower reaches for 8 to 10 inch brookies. It is too fast to support fish above.

Slag-A-Melt Lakes (North and South). North Slag-A-Melt (the first one you come to) is 8 acres, deep, in scattered alpine timber and is reached by road and trail 4 miles from the Big Swamp Creek road. It is only moderately popular but good fishing for small, skinny brookies and cutthroat. South Slag-A-Melt is about an eighth of a mile west and south, is 17 acres, good and deep, in an ice-scoured cirque in barren, rocky country. There is no trail, it's seldom bothered, only poor to fair fishing for 12 inch to 4 pound cutthroat, and small brookies.

Slaughterhouse Creek. A very small tributary of Corral Creek, seldom fished but good for 6 to 10 inch brook and some rainbow trout in beaver ponds near the mouth.

South Fork Big Hole River. After running 14 miles, this stream converges with Governor Creek to form the Big Hole River near Jackson, with improved gravel roads along and crossing it throughout its heavily used drainage. It is excellent fishing for brookies to 10 inches, a few rainbow to 12 inches and whitefish and ling to 15 inches. The lower reaches are impacted somewhat by dewatering as 10 of its 14 miles of stream bed are on private land.

Squaw Creek. Flows from Fool Hen Mountain for 10 miles to the Big Hole River about 9 miles above Fishtrap. The lower 6 miles below the mouth of Papoose Creek are followed by a road through mostly meadow and willow bottoms. This creek is seldom fished but good for 8 to 12 inch brook trout.

Steel Creek. A small stream flowing to the Big Hole River a couple of miles south of Jackson and followed by a road for 7 miles upstream to the Steel Creek Campground. The lower reaches are splendid fishing for 8 to 15 inch eastern brook trout (occasionally to 1½ pounds), plus lesser numbers of whitefish, burbot and grayling.

Stewart Lake. Take a good USFS (Stewart Meadows) trail for 9 miles from the end of the Warm Springs road to this 5 acre lake which is in a large mountain park (elevation 7500 feet above sea level) surrounded by lodgepole pine. Stewart is real shallow around the margins and there is lots of plant growth so that it is difficult to fish from the shore; however, the fish are plentiful small brookies. This one is seldom visited.

Stone Creek Lakes. East and West, or Upper and Lower, 12 and 9 acres by 30 and 47 feet maximum depth, in timbered country south of Shaw Mountain between 8000 and 7500 feet above sea level; reached by the Stone Creek trail 3 miles from the Pattengail trail, then south through the woods for a mile to the East Lake, then proceed due west for yet another mile to the West Lake. Neither one of them is fished much, but West Stone is good for 10 to 16 inch cutthroat trout, and both were recently planted with cutthroat again in '76 and '79. East Stone has been reported fair for 8 to 12 inchers.

Sullivan Creek. A small, open, tributary of Deep Creek about 4 miles above Ralston and ½ mile off the Big Hole-Anaconda highway. It is seldom fished but is good in beaver ponds along the lower reaches for 5 to 10 inch brookies and brown trout.

Sumrun Creek. An open meadow, willow bottomed stream reached by the Briston Lane road about 10 miles south from Wisdom. There are about 10 miles of easily fished water that is popular with the local residents for good catches of 10 to 12 inch brookies and grayling.

Swamp Creek. Just a little stream, about 3 miles long, flowing to the Wise River 1½ miles above the highway. Swamp Creek dries up above, but there are a few beaver ponds in the lower reaches that are fished by the local residents for pan-size brookies.

Swamp Creek. An open meadow, willow bordered stream flowing for about 20 miles northeastward across the Big Hole valley to join the main river about 4 miles below Wisdom. It is readily accessible by road for most of its length, is moderately popular and poor fishing for 6 to 14 inch brook trout, a few burbot and grayling.

Tahepia Lake. Reached either by the Jacobson Creek trail on the Wise River drainage 5 miles from the Mono Creek Campground, or by the Rock Creek trail 5½ miles from the end of the road. Tahepia is a high (elevation 8920 feet), 15½ acre by 20 foot deep lake in a great, barren, rocky cirque a mile north of Mount Tahepia. It is often and easily fished for rainbow trout that average around 10 inches but range up to 15.

Tendoy Lake. A real high (elevation 9100 feet), 30 acre lake, fed mostly by melting ice and snow, in talus and scattered timber pine country; reached to within a half mile by the Willow Creek jeep road. Tendoy is frozen most of the year but is over 100 feet deep and so does not freeze out. It is seldom fished but was stocked with cutthroat years ago and again in 1971, 1976, and 1981, and is fair to good for 8 to 12 inchers. Here you can look down on a breeched dam or look up for mountain goats — your choice.

PEAR LAKE
Courtesy Bridenstine Studio

RAINBOW LAKE
Courtesy USFS

RAINBOW LAKE
Courtesy Bridenstine Studio

RIDGE LAKE
Courtesy Bridenstine Studio

Ten Mile Creek.
Reached by jeep road on the Mount Haggin Game Range 9 miles above Ralston on the Anaconda-Big Hole highway. Ten Mile is a small tributary of Deep Creek, in open meadow with willow-bordered shores and numerous ponds along the upper reaches. It is good fishing for 8 to 12 inch brookies and some rainbow trout.

Ten Mile Lakes.
Take the Deep Creek road 4 miles north from Ralston, then the French Creek road for 6 miles and the Grassy Mountain jeep road for 3½ miles to the Grassy Mountain Lookout, thence by trail for 6 miles to six little lakes in high (between 8800 and 9000 elevation), baren country. They are seldom visited because of the long hike in but are excellent fishing for ½ to 1½ pound rainbow trout and cutts.

Thief Creek.
A small stream followed by a trail above, and road below for about 4 miles through timber and willows to Birch Creek near the USFS guard station. It is lightly fished and only marginal for 6 to 8 inch brook trout.

Thompson Creek.
Flows to the southeast from (barren) Continental Lake just below the Continental Divide for 10 miles through mostly meadowland to junction with Plimpton Creek. There is good access by road and trail all the way and it is easily, although only lightly, fished for fair catches of 8 to 10 inch brookies, plus a very few cutthroat trout and grayling.

Tie Creek.
A 12 mile long tributary of the North Fork of the Big Hole River that is followed along the north bank by a good USFS trail through timber and across open meadows to head-waters. Tie Creek is more or less a "private access" stream, but if you can get permission, it is good fishing for 8 to 10 inch brook and a few cutthroat trout.

Timberline Lake.
At 9180 feet above sea level, it can be reached up either Berry Creek or Pioneer Creek (see Berry Lake). This little 7½ acre beauty sits in rock, with scrub timber available for a campfire, and is not too often visited. Planted with cutthroat in '76 and '79, it is now good fishing for trout 6 to 16 inches long.

Tom (or Long Tom) Creek.
The outlet of Fish Lake, flows for 5 miles through fairly heavy timber to Jerry Creek and is followed all the way by a good USFS trail. Tom is very good fishing for 6 to 10 inch brook and some cutthroat trout.

Toomey Creek.
A small stream flowing to the Big Hole River opposite the highway about 7 miles above Fishtrap. The lower, meadowland reaches are the site of numerous beaver ponds which are fair fishing for small brookies but are inaccessible except during late season when the Big Hole is fordable.

Torrey Lake. Just below the summit of Torrey Mountain at 8800 feet elevation above sea level, in a barren rocky cirque that is reached by a good, but steep, trail 9 miles from the Mono Creek Campground. Torrey is 28.5 acres by 34 feet deep with shallow dropoffs and is good angling for 8 to 14 inch cutthroat planted in 1968, '71, '76 and '79. It's not overcrowded with people either.

Trail Creek. Flows along willowed-up meadows bounded by heavy timber for 25 miles from the Continental Divide (elevation 7050 feet) to the North Fork of Big Hole River (elevation 6250 feet) near the Big Hole Battlefield and is followed for 10 miles by the highway to Idaho. This is an easily fished, popular stream but fair only for 8 to 10 inch brookies, burbot, and whitefish.

Trapper Creek. Flows east to the Big Hole River near Melrose and is followed by a truck road through ranchland below and up a scattered timber and willow covered canyon above for about 18 miles to the old ghost town of Hecla at headwaters. This is a willow-bordered, beaver-ponded stream that is fair fishing for 8 inch brook trout, some rainbow, cutts, and a few brown trout. In a few places the creek flows through unreclaimed mining areas and old mine tailing piles; not an ideal situation.

Trout Creek. A very small tributary of LaMarche Creek, 3 miles above the ranch. Trout Creek is followed by a trail for 5 miles through timbered country to headwaters and, though seldom fished, is fair for 9 to 10 inch brook and rainbow trout.

Tub Lake. You backpack into this one, about an hour from Pear Lake near timberline in barren rock and scrub timber country at 9091 feet elevation. Tub Lake is about 12 acres, has a dam, is 30 feet deep but with shallow dropoffs, and drains to Pear Lake. It is pretty good fishing for 8 to 14 inch cutthroat trout planted in '80 and '81. If you keep your eye out, you may see a mountain goat as a bonus.

Twelve Mile Creek. A small, pastureland and scattered timber tributary of Deep Creek, reached at the mouth by a ranch road 1 mile off the Anaconda-Big Hole highway about 4 miles above Ralston. It is seldom fished but is good for pan-size brook and cutthroat trout.

Twin Lakes. In timbered country, reached by a good road with about a dozen gates to open and shut 25 miles southwest from Wisdom. Twin Lakes are really one hourglass-shaped lake (you can get a boat across the neck); the big (West) end is about 60 acres, the other about 15, and both are deep. It is a popular lake with a good campground and is heavily fished for nice catches of 8 to 12 inch rainbow, 6 to 10 inch brook, 18 to 30 inch lake trout (macks to 20 pounds occasionally) and 12 to 16 inch grayling. No gasoline powered boats allowed.

WARREN LAKE
Courtesy USFS

ROCK ISLAND LAKE
Courtesy Bridenstine Studio

UNNAMED LAKE, MALONEY BASIN
Courtesy USFS

Unnamed Lakes at the Head of Big Swamp Creek.
Five unnamed cirque lakes between Lena and Ajax Lakes (which are 1¼ miles apart) in high, barren, goat country just below and east of the Continental Divide. They range from 2 to 8 acres, are all deep and reportedly contain fish. There is no trail; they are hard to find and very seldom visited.

Unnamed Lakes on the East Fork of Fishtrap Creek.
A couple of shallow, 3 acre potholes ¼ mile apart in heavy timber about ¾ mile west (cross-country) from the LaMarche Creek trail from a point 1 mile above the ranch. They are seldom, if ever, fished but are reported to contain brook and cutthroat trout.

Unnamed Lake at the Head of Elkhorn Creek.
A high (elevation 9000 feet plus) cirque lake just below and ¼ mile south of Saddleback Mountain; reached by a 3 mile, cross-country hike over rocky cliffs and boulder fields, southeast from the end of the Elkhorn Creek road, 6 miles from the Mono Creek Campground. This one is deep, about 9½ acres, and not generally known. It is, however, excellent fishing for cutthroat trout that average between 1½ and 2 pounds and range up to as much as 6 pounds.

Upper Miner Lakes.
Upper Miner Lake is reached by a fair USFS trail 4½ miles from the end of the Miner Creek Road closure. Upper, Upper Miner (that's its name) is reached by going up a big rockslide from the south end of Upper Miner Lake. At 8029 feet above sea level, Upper Miner Lake is 42 acres with a 60 foot maximum depth and very good fishing for eastern brook trout from 7 to 15 inches long; it also is pretty popular. Upper, Upper Miner Lake is about 12 acres, 99 feet deep, at 8749 elevation, and not very often visited, being only fair for rainbow trout 8 to 13 inches long. Both lakes have been planted with cutthroat (years ago) that apparently did not take.

Upper Stone Lake.
See Stone Creek Lakes.

Van Houten Lake.
Thirteen miles south from Jackson by good county roads, 6950 feet above sea level, 10 acres, shallow, in sagebrush and lodgepole country. Van Houten was poisoned out in 1962 and planted with rainbow and brook trout the following year. It has been very popular ever since. There's a USFS campground, and you'll have plenty of company here. The lake is closed to all motor boats.

Vera Lake.
Four and a half acres with a maximum depth of 10 feet but mostly less than 8, open at the southeast corner but mostly in scattered timber, at 8680 feet above sea level on the northern slopes of Sharp Mountain 1 mile east of Grayling Lake and reached by trail 4¼ miles (some of which are pretty steep) above the end of the Canyon Creek jeep trail at the campground. It doesn't get fished a heck-of-a-lot but is fair for rainbow-cutthroat hybrids in the 6 to 12 inch range.

Warm Springs Creek. Heads above Stewart Meadows and flows for 20 miles down a steep, timbered valley, an open parkland above, and open meadow and willow bottoms below to the Big Hole River at Jackson. Warm Springs is followed by a good road for 4 miles upstream, past numerous beaver ponds and then by a jeep road to headwaters. It is a pleasant stream to fish and good, too, for mostly 6 to 11 inch brookies, some whitefish, and a few ling. The area is popular for hunting mule deer and elk as well as for fishing.

Warren Lake. A deep, 18 acre lake in partly timbered, partly barren Anaconda Pintlar Wilderness country at 8462 feet above sea level; reached by a good trail 9 miles up the West Fork from the end of the LaMarche Creek road, or 10 miles up the West Fork from the end of the Fishtrap Creek road. Warren is fished mostly by guests from the LaMarche Ranch and is good for rainbow and cutthroat trout that run mostly between 10 and 15 inches but sometimes to as much as 3 pounds.

Waukena Lake. Reached by a good USFS trail about a 2 hour hike above the Rock Creek Ranger Station in lodgepole and rocky cliff country near the head of the Rock Creek drainage, a mile east by trail from Tahepia Lake. Waukena is about 30 acres, 35 feet deep, dammed and drained by Rock Creek. It is good fishing for 8 to 16 inch cutthroat trout planted in '76 and '79. Motorbikers use this rough road (or trail) quite a bit at present, but rumor has it that a vehicle closure is imminent.

West Fork Deep Creek. A small stream flowing for 5 miles through open timber to Twelve Mile Creek 3½ miles above Ralston. The lower, fishable reaches are on private land and are seldom fished but they do contain a fair number of 6 to 10 inch brookies and some rainbow and cutthroat trout.

West Fork Ruby Creek. A few miles long in timber and park country, this stream is accessible for 2 miles by road and trail and is fair fishing in spots for pan-size brookies.

West Stone Lake. See Stone Creek Lakes.

Willow Creek. About 20 miles long, crossed at the mouth by the Butte-Dillon highway and accessible along the upper reaches (above the Joy Cow Camp) by road 2 miles north of the Aspen Campground on the Birch Creek drainage. Willow Creek flows through a timbered, willow-bottomed canyon above and open ranchland below. Rewarding the angler with 6 to 10 inch brookies and rainbow-cutthroat hybrids up to 12 inches, it's really not a bad little stream. Darn good mule deer country, too.

Wise River. Boy — looks can sure fool you. A clear, great looking mountain creek about 30 miles long, followed from its mouth by a fair road from the town of Wise River to the headwaters. It is really pretty, and the heaviest-used tributary of the Big Hole River (probably not warranted). Among other things, the lower five miles of river have been on occasion dewatered badly, and metals pollution from Elkhorn Creek doesn't help matters either. The lower portion (10 miles or so) flows through homesteads, willow and timber; the upper river flows mostly down a timbered valley. Wadeable, easy to fish, it is still fair (in spite of its problems) for mostly brookies to 10 inches, rainbows to perhaps 13 inches, some burbot and mountain whitefish.

Wyman Creek. Is followed for 7 miles by trail through open timber from headwaters to the end of the Anderson Meadows road up the Wise River and thence for 4 miles to junction with the Wise River. It is heavily fished in the meadows for plentiful 6 to 10 inch brook and rainbow trout.

Take No More Fish Than You Can Use

Courtesy Danny On

BOULDER RIVER
Courtesy Dr. P. Pallister

Boulder River of the Jefferson

The capability of much of the Boulder of the Jefferson river to support the high numbers of wild trout that characterize Montana's "Blue Ribbon" waterways has been affected by mans' activities within the watershed. Consequently, the Boulder offers the angler limited recreational opportunities when compared to most of the other rivers of southwest Montana.

The 17 miles of the upper Boulder above the mouth of the Bison Creek probably offers the best fishing in the entire 78 miles of river. Here, the river is stream size as it meanders through a jungle of overhanging willows. A respectable brook trout population of about 1,500 fish per mile inhabits this headwater section along with lesser numbers of rainbow trout and mountain whitefish. The population compares favorably with other high quality brook trout streams in the region. Much of the catch will be in the 6 to 10 inch class, although brook trout up to 15 inches are present. Worms and live grasshoppers are undoubtedly the best bet. The skilled fly fisherman who enjoys dapping a dry fly on a very short leader will also be amply rewarded for his efforts.

Below Bison Creek the river enters the 14 mile long Boulder Canyon and passes through the towns of Basin and then Boulder before leaving the canyon. In the canyon the river widens, straightens and loses much of the dense bank cover that hinders access. The stream gradient steepens and riffle-run areas interspersed with boulders become the common habitat type. The water quality also begins declining. The extensive hard rock mining and milling operations that occurred throughout the Basin to Boulder area in the late 1800's and early 1900's still produce toxic metals pollution that enters the river and impacts the fishery. Below the mouth of High Ore Creek, a major source of metals pollution, fish populations become severely depressed. Various State Agencies are currently attempting to solve the existing problem in High Ore Creek. Presently, only the upper ⅔ of the canyon is worth fishing. Here, rainbow trout up to 15 inches and lesser numbers of brook trout and mountain whitefish provide a fair stream fishery.

The narrow canyon could be further degraded by the present construction of I-15. Sediment yields from the project will likely have a short-term impact on the canyon fishery. In addition, portions of the river channel are being relocated to accommodate the highway. Fishermen who desire the solitude of a quiet day of stream fishing should avoid the canyon until construction is completed. Even then, a four lane highway crammed into a narrow canyon won't aesthetically enhance any recreational experience.

Below the town of Boulder, the river enters the Boulder Valley and flows 47 miles before joining the Jefferson River at Cardwell. Fish populations, which are now dominated by brown trout, remain low throughout much of the valley at about 250 trout per mile, not very good odds for the fisherman. Metals pollution, bottom sedimentation, bank and channel alterations, summer irrigation withdrawals, elevated summer water temperatures and a myriad of other problems all contribute to a depressed fishery. Towards the mouth of the river, springs and irrigation return flows help to rejuvenate the Boulder, allowing the brown trout population to recover to a respectable 1,300 trout per mile. However, the lower river is privately owned and not readily accessible to the public.

A substantial spawning run of brown trout, some in the 5-9 pound class, enters the lower Boulder River in the fall. The run is blocked in most years at an irrigation diversion dam near the mouth. The fishing season on the lower Boulder closes on September 30 to protect this highly concentrated and vulnerable spawning population.

Despite the magnitude of the problems affecting the watershed, the river endures; flowing through scenic big game country, still offering some fair fishing to those willing to take the time to seek out the better places.

Fred Nelson

Boulder River — Jefferson Drainage

Amazon Creek. Is a very small tributary of Muskrat Creek with a few 50 to 1000 foot beaver ponds in open rangeland a couple of miles north of U.S. 91 from Boulder. If it weren't for the beaver ponds, there wouldn't be any fish, but there are overcrowded, small-bodied, large-headed brookies for the skillet.

Basin Creek. Flows south from below Old Baldy Mountain for 14 miles to the Boulder River at Basin and is followed by roads all along. It's mostly in timbered country with some open parks here and there; it flows down a narrow canyon in the middle reaches and through about a mile of beaver ponds above. Here, there is some fair fishing (in a small way) for 6 to 8 inch brook trout. There is still some intermittent mining going on below the canyon with attendant siltation. There's a campground about 4 miles above the mouth, but if you see anyone fishing you'll know he's a stranger.

Bison Creek. Take U.S. 91 a mile and a half up the hill northeast from Butte to the head of this broad, open farmland creek and follow it on down for 9 miles, then through a timbered canyon for 5 more and finally through a narrow, brushy valley for another 2½ miles to the Boulder River 4 miles west of Basin. The upper reaches are quite small, accessible across open farmland from the highway and fair fishing for 7 to 9 inch rainbow and brook trout at the ratio of about 2 to 1. The canyon reaches are too narrow to fish but the lower reaches are wadeable and also pretty good, especially in the beaver ponds that come and go with their builders. The whole bit is heavily fished wherever and whenever possible. There are two campgrounds on the creek and in these areas beaver dam siltation and fishing pressure has about wiped out the native fish; so — legal size rainbow are planted here for the transient fisherman.

Boulder River School Pond. A 1 acre flooded gravel pit on the school grounds; deep enough to "stand up and drink," and stocked annually by the State Fish and Game Department with catchable rainbow trout for the kids at the Boulder River School and Hospital. This is off limits to the public.

Boy Scout Pond. An old, dammed, 10 acre pond on Lowland Creek ½ mile east of the Boy Scout Camp, 5 miles west from Trask Siding. It's bordered by steep, timbered mountains to the east, open bottomland above-below-and-to-the-west, and would be fair fishing (with permission if you could get it — which isn't likely), for 10 to 14 inch rainbow and maybe once in a while a brook trout. This pond is no longer stocked by the State Fish and Game Department but would be if public access were granted.

Buffalo Creek. Very small, only a couple of miles of fishing — by a stray hunter or two. It's crossed at the mouth by the Little Boulder River road 3¾ miles above the Elder Creek campground, but there is no trail. The fish (5 to 7 inch or smaller brook trout) are mostly congregated in ponds along the lower mile in brushy willow and lodgepole bottomland. There are too many good places to go to bother with this one.

Cataract Creek. Take U.S. 91 three quarters of a mile east from Basin (on the Boulder River) to its mouth and then a mining road up the creek for 6½ miles to about a mile above the Eva May Mine to the lower Cataract Meadows. The entire creek was once a "fisherman's dream," but the stretch you just came over has been ruined by mine pollution, although there is some spectacular scenery here. However, if you continue up the creek on your two good feet for another couple of miles, you will arrive at Upper Cataract Meadows and here, in some open meadow beaver ponds, you can catch a few small cutthroat and even fewer brook trout that are gradually invading the upper meadows from below. This beautiful meadow nestles under the eastern side of the Three Brothers and Jack Mountains.

45

Cottonwood Lake. This one is at 7305 feet elevation according to a benchmark located just to the north. There is 13½ acres of mostly shallow water here, over a muddy bottom but with a narrow "channel" down the middle, backed up behind a small earthen dam on Thunderbolt Creek 4¾ miles upstream by jeep road and trail from the Boulder River at the Whitehouse Picnic Grounds. It's long and narrow with lodgepole forest right down to the water's edge on both sides but with open, grassy (sometimes marshy) meadows at the upper end and is seldom fished because of the difficulties involved in getting past the shallow water to the channel. There is a fair population of 9 to 11 inch cutthroat in the lake and these bite nicely on flies or lures. The creek mostly contains small brook trout which drift down and populate the lower beaver ponds. Occasional moose, elk and bear are seen near the lake. Rumor has it a USFS "road closure" may be in effect here, so check area ranger office.

Elkhorn Creek. If you are picnicking, hunting, or prospecting in the area, you might fish this one — but you'd never make a special trip for it. It heads below Elkhorn Peak and (used to) flow for 11 miles down a pretty little timber-and-park canyon to the Boulder River a dozen miles downstream from boulder. But now the lower 2 or 3 miles are dewatered for irrigation and the rest of it is not in the best of condition due to poor mining practices. There are some little rainbow and brook trout left in the creek and in occasional beaver ponds. You can drive to them.

Galena Creek. Flows north down a timbered canyon for 3 miles to the Boulder River 4 miles west from Boulder by U.S. 91. There are some old brushy beaver ponds in the headwaters that are now silting up but do (or would if anybody bothered) provide some marginal fishing for small brook trout. There's a road right beside 'em.

Hoodoo Creek. Is almost, but not quite, a lost cause by way of being a recreational asset. You can jeep up Cataract Creek to ¼ mile above its mouth at the Eva May Mine when you take the right-hand fork for another ½ mile and then "shanks' mares" for a similar distance to the boggy Hoodoo Meadows. Here the creek runs slowly and supports a small population of 3 to 6 inch cutthroat trout. They haven't seen a hook in years.

Indian Creek. Come into the upper portion of the Boulder River in Lockhard meadows. It has about 3 miles of fishing, all on foot. The lower portion contains brook trout and the upper meadows contain some cutthroat rarely up to 1½ pounds. This area supports moose, elk, and bear, sego lilies, orchids and mushrooms abound. A lovely hike.

Leslie Lake. A 35 foot deep, glacial pond with steep dropoffs, 8.9 acres at 8119 feet elevation southeast of Crow Peak, reached by good gravel roads from Boulder to the ghost town of Elkhorn and thence by mining road to within 300 yards of the shore. It lies in a steep little pocket below rocky slopes that are heavily timbered to the southeast and sparcely timbered on around. It was stocked with brook trout in the '30's and is now planted with cutthroat fingerlings. Fishing is fair-to-excellent for 8 to 13 inchers (a few to 3 or 4 pounds). This is really a nice lake to visit, especially so with the fringe benefits of mountain scenery, ghost town and easy access. It is on the upper end of a tributary of Elkhorn Creek. This branch goes underground the lower 3 or 4 miles, joining the Elkhorn Creek at Queen's Siding. The fish are tough to collect because of the ultra clear water. It was stocked in 1968, 1970, 1972, 1978, and 1981 with McBride cutthroat trout and gets plenty of visitation from trout enthusiasts.

Little Boulder River. Is really a willow bottomed, beaver dammed, 14 mile long, narrow, brushy mountain canyon creek that joins the Boulder River ½ mile east of the Diamond S Ranchotel and is followed upstream by a jeep road for about 6 miles of good 8 to 10 inch brook trout fishing (especially in early season). There are also some rainbow high up in Shields and Ironsides Dams and lunker browns in the lower couple of miles, but they don't often bite. The upper creek, above the old Shields and Ironsides mining camp, where the road ends, has 3 miles or more of pan-size cutthroat habitat starting in Little Boulder Park on the other side of Nez Perce Drainage through Dirty Mike's diggings to Shields Dam. Beautiful elk and moose country, it is wild and seldom fished. You'll find a public campground at the mouth of Elder Creek, 5 miles above the Diamond S.

Lowland Creek. Ten miles long and followed all the way by road from its headwaters 2½ miles west of Trask Siding in Elk Park to its mouth on the Boulder River ½ mile upstream from Ladysmith Picnic Grounds. The upper reaches (above the Boy Scout Pond) are mostly in open meadow, the middle reaches flow through a steep walled, forested canyon, and the lower beaver

OH BOY!
Courtesy "Doc" Newberry

SAGE "HEN"
Courtesy Harley Yeager

dammed reaches are in a narrow, open, flat bottomed, placer mined canyon. The upper reaches are heavily fished, the middle and lower reaches less so — for rare catches of 10 inch rainbow in some of the old dredge ponds, and smaller (5 to 7 inch) brookies in between.

Moose Creek. Very small, of minor recreational value — as much for elk and moose hunting as for fishing for pan-size brook trout in the lower 1½ miles above its mouth on the Little Boulder River — 3½ miles upstream by poor road from the Elder Creek campground. The lower 2 miles of Moose Creek are accessible by jeep trail up its steep timbered canyon that opens at the top into Moose Creek Meadows.

Muskrat Creek. A fair-to-good fishing (for small brook trout mostly) marshy (irrigated) meadowland tributary of the Boulder River 1 mile southeast of Boulder. The lower 3 miles of fishing water are crossed and followed (along the east side) by a gravel road — but mostly people drive on by.

Nez Perce Creek. A small stream with limited potential — but is fished (reportedly) somewhat before season. It flows through timber above and meadowland below for perhaps 4 miles on public and private land to Bison Creek 4 miles south of Elk Park by U.S. 91. There's a fair road upstream, lots of willow along it and a few camp-eating rainbow and brook trout in it.

North Fork Little Boulder River. Is fair fishing (if you like 6 to 8 inch brook and rainbow trout) along the lower 3 miles in a rocky, steep walled, willow bottomed (but with lodgepole pressing in from the sides), canyon accessible at the mouth by a good gravel road 3 miles south from Boulder, and on upstream by jeep trail. The Galena Creek road is the main access route to the upper reaches. There were numerous beaver ponds here and the fishing was better with correspondingly heavier pressure — but they're gone now. Some fishing for cutthroat and cutthroat-rainbow hybrids remains on the upper 2½ miles of creek winding through a willow and beaver dam meadow. Overuse by moose helped cut down the willow and the beaver dams soon followed.

Rawhide Creek (and Reservoir). Is off limits to adults but near the mouth as it joins the Muskrat is a small reservoir that is stocked annually with catchable rainbow for kids fishing only. The creek above is barren.

Red Rock Creek. Not really a fishing stream but there is about 5 miles of fair water here, reached at the mouth by U.S. 91 three miles west from Basin, and followed upstream through open willow, placer mined bottoms by truck road. An occasional deer hunter tries it — for 6 to 8 inch brook trout.

47

WOW!
Courtesy Mike Venturino

Rock Creek. Is a very small stream just east of Indian Creek on the upper Boulder Drainage. It contains small brook trout for the campfire — largely a hunting and hiking area.

Sheep Creek. Is very small, in a steep, timbered canyon but has a few holes along the first mile above its mouth on Lowland Creek a couple of miles up from the Boulder River. Here, there are a few 6 to 7 inch brook trout. There's no trail and just as well because nobody would go there except, perhaps, for nefarious reasons.

South Fork Basin Creek. Isn't much! Very small! Steep! In heavy lodgepole timber followed to headwaters by trail along the north side for almost 2½ miles of marginal (4 to 6 inch brook trout) fishing water. Seldom if ever fished.

Thunderbolt Creek. Very small (you can jump it anywhere) with limited recreational value. It flows from Cottonwood Lake 4¾ miles due south down a steep little lodgepole canyon above — to the open, cottonwood bottoms of the Boulder River below at the elegantly titled "Whitehouse" Picnic Ground. There's a jeep road up it for about 3 miles and a USFS trail into the lake. The lower "campground" reaches get fished a little for fair catches of 6 to 8 inch brook trout.

Respect Private Property — Ask Permission **First**

BLACK BEAR CUB
Courtesy USFS

NATURAL BRIDGE FALLS
Courtesy USFS

Boulder River of the Yellowstone

The Boulder is the sort of river that makes a person wonder why there aren't more like it. Conceived in the melting snows high in the Absarokee Mountains, the river cascades over fifty miles through tall pine forests and scenic foothill ranchland to meet the Yellowstone at Big Timber. The Boulder is first and always a true mountain stream filled with rugged, fast flowing trout water so pure that it seldom clouds, even during spring runoff. It's the type of stream most fishermen would like to keep secret but can't.

The Boulder's pure water had a lot to do with its appeal for both fishermen and trout. Two main tributaries, the East and West Boulder, are rock bottomed streams in their own right and do little to compromise the mainstream's clarity. Midway in the river's northerly course, the stream passes through the scenic Natural Bridge rock formation and falls a spectacular seventy feet. The waterfall forms a barrier to upstream movement of browns and rainbow and separates the Boulder's fishing into two parts.

The lower Boulder, running through ranch land in a series of riffles broken by flat stretches and holes, harbors brown and rainbow trout in the lunker category. Although the river is essentially considered a fly fishing stream, spin fishermen with both lures and bait are not strangers to these currents. Whatever an angler's means, the chances of catching big trout in the lower Boulder are excellent. Browns and rainbow in the 12-22" range are common catches on the lower river, with browns taken, on occasion, up to 10 pounds.

Above the falls rainbow and brook trout are the only species of fish, but they live in abundance in the upper river and make the bone-jarring trip above Natural Bridge worthwhile. The upper river is a boisterous stream. There are fewer flat runs and more "pocket water" as the flow courses around instream boulders. Although much of the stream appears violent, a pattern of rapids and riffles between fishable spots remains basic. After the initial spring runoff, the Boulder becomes wadeable enough to reach the pocket water and those with agility experience superb dry fly fishing for fiesty rainbow up to 14" and firm camp fare brook trout.

The upper Boulder cuts through the heart of national forest land and access is excellent from the forest boundary thirty miles above Big Timber to the river's head. Four maintained campgrounds and several undeveloped campsites make the area popular for weekend campers. Few places in the state equal the area's offering of scenery, fishing and pure mountain air. The Boulder is an easy place to visit and a tough place to leave.

Jerry Brekke

Boulder River — Yellowstone Drainage

Alpine Lake. Drive up the West Boulder River to the Burnt Leather Ranch, then take the West Boulder trail 7 miles on up stream to (barren) Three Creeks which drains in from the west. From here you swarm up the perpendicular Three Creeks drainage for another couple of miles to Alpine Lake which is 10 acres, 20 feet deep, in timber, used to be barren but was planted with cutthroat in 1972 and 1975 and should be darned good fishing by now. At least it hasn't been fished out — it's less than heavily used.

Blacktail Lake. Is 4 acres, good and deep, partly timbered but with some steep open slopes to the south in an alpine cirque at the head of the Davis-Blacktail Creek drainage; elevation 8720 feet above sea level and 20 feet deep. It can be reached up the Davis Creek trail, but the easiest way in is up the Mission Creek (tributary of the Yellowstone River) trail a couple miles from the end of the road to Elephanthead Mountain and then another couple of miles on past the east side of the mountain to the shore. It's an isolated pothole — once there you can't go anyplace but back out the way you came in, and so very few people make the trip. It's fair for cutthroat planted in 1976 — just over a foot long at last report.

Blue Lake. Drive your hack to the end of the Boulder River road at Independence (an old mining town). Now follow the ruts (from the motor bikes and 4-wheelers who don't give a d--- what they do to the country so long as they don't have to hoist their lazy butts off the seat) for ¾ of a mile southeastward and straight up Monument Peak to this 6½ acre by 40 foot maximum depth lake with talus slopes on the southeast side and timber-rock and grass on around. It's fished a fair amount (there's lots of litter and trash brought in by the motorized "sportsmen" no doubt). There is no apparent spawning going on and it was stocked with McBride cutthroat in 1977. The Fish and Game Dept. give it a "plant" every now and again so fishing is fair-to-good for anything up to 16 inches. Let's hope it stays that way so the "rut-makers" will stay concentrated.

Bramble Creek Lakes. Drive up the Boulder River to the mouth of Bramble Creek a couple of miles below the Fourmile Guard Station. Hop out of your rig and take off like a mountain goat up the creek (no trail, and it's steep as h---) for a tough 1½ miles to the mouth of a little drainage pouring down the cliffs from the south; from here you make like a bird for another half mile in to the important lake which is about 5 acres, in timber all around except for some talus at the west end, at 8810 feet elevation. It was planted with cutthroat in 1965 and 1979 and could be darned good fishing now if anyone wants to try it. The other two lakes are barren.

BELOW CAMP MIMANAGISH
Courtesy USFS

Courtesy Craig Black

Bray's Pond (or Lost or Trout Lake). A 3½ acre by 10 foot maximum depth pond in lodgepole, spruce and marshland a couple of hundred yards east of the Boulder River and a half mile upstream (south) from the Fourmile Campground. There are a couple of cabins here, some springs in the southeast corner and a beaver dam at the outlet. It's a hard one to fish, though, and lots of folks don't have much luck, but they keep coming because the fish population is good and the fish (rainbow) are nice, to about 1½ pounds. The average is smaller, about 11 inches. There's an added bonus — very small but plentiful trout are in a nearby creek or slough.

Bridge Lake. A high (elevation 9485 feet), fairly deep, 14 acre cirque lake in rocky alpine country on the northern slopes of Crow Mountain; reached by the (poor) Bridge Creek (not a fishing stream, although it does support a small population of 8 to 10 inch cutthroat in its upper 2½ miles of meandering reaches) trail 3 miles up from the Boulder River at the Lazy Day Ranch; a half mile on up the Lake Fork until the trail takes off up out of the canyon to the north, and then a very rough, cross-country 2500 feet-in-2¾ mile climb on up the drainage to the shore. You'll not meet many people on the way and once there — well it was planted with cutthroat in 1971 and 1977. As of last year (1981), it was fair fishing for 8 to 13 inchers.

Burnt Gulch Lake. Six acres, in an old burn a couple of miles by trail (of sorts) east of Lake Kathleen, was planted with cutthroat in 1970 and has been good fishing, but froze out and is now barren.

Camp Lake. A moderately popular, excellent cutthroat lake; nice fat cutthroat that average 8 to 12 inches and range up to 2 pounds. It's a good 8 acres, deep with steep dropoffs in a glacial cirque with some scrub timber around the outlet (NE side) and is reached by the Graham Creek (no fishing here) trail 3 miles east from the Boulder River near the Falls Creek Campground to the top of the East Boulder Plateau and then a fishermen's trail 1¼ miles east to the shore. Or if you're of a mind to, you can also reach it from the Stillwater Drainage via the Picket Pin jeep road and trail to Chrome Mountain and then cross-country 1½ miles north to the shore.

Davis Creek. A small stream, the outlet of McNight Lake, it flows down a steep, rocky canyon (in timber) to the West Boulder River at the Burnt Leather Ranch. The lower 4 miles are paralleled by a USFS trail but only the first mile is fair fishing (no better than that) for 8 to 10 inch rainbow and cutthroat trout.

East Boulder River. A nice size stream about 20 miles long by an average of 20 feet or so wide in the lower reaches, clear, but with few holes. The upper reaches flow through timbered mountains and aren't much for fishing — but the lower reaches are in cottonwood "foothill" country, are readily accessible all along by road and are fair fishing for mostly 9 to 11 inch browns, some rainbow, a few cutthroat, and whitefish. They're fished a moderate amount by mostly local folks.

East Fork Main Boulder River. A small mountain stream flowing down a narrow, timbered canyon to the Boulder River just below the Box Canyon Guard Station. It's followed upstream for 1½ miles by a jeep road and on beyond the next couple of miles of fishing water by USFS trail. There are some nice meadows about 3 miles above the mouth and here this pretty, meandering little stream gets some heavy fishing pressure for good catches of 6 to 10 inch rainbow, some brown trout to 14 inches, and a few small brookies and cutts.

Elk Creek. A small, brushy stream that heads in a spring on Elk Mountain and flows (mostly through private property) for 5 miles in a semi-circle down a wide, open, mountain valley to the East Boulder River across from the school. The lower 3 or 4 miles are easily accessible (with permission) all along by road and here this nice little stream is good fishing for rainbow to around 11 inches, brown trout to about 13 inches, and some small cutthroat. Dinky but decent, Elk Creek is not heavily fished, then mostly by locals.

Elk Lake. Is (seldom) reached by a USFS trail up (above and to the north of) Elk Creek 5 miles from the Boulder River road a couple of miles above the Box Canyon Guard Station. It's right at timberline just east of and below the crest of the Absaroka Range at 9580 feet elevation, 9 acres, 22 feet deep, and is fair fishing for cutthroat planted in 1977 that are about a foot long now.

Falls Creek. Drains West Boulder Lake a half mile north to Falls Creek (or Kaufman) Lake and then flows north for 5¼ miles down a steep, narrow, brushy draw to the West Boulder River 6 miles by trail above the end of the road at the Burnt Leather Ranch. There is maybe a mile below the lake that is fair "spring" fishing for brookies and rainbow — but the trail only brings you halfway in and it's real rough the rest of the way. Those that make the trip are few and far between — not often stopping on their way to the lakes.

Falls Creek (or Kaufman) Lake. Lies partly in alpine timber just below timberline at 8942 feet above sea level (in bear country) near the head of Falls Creek a half mile below (north of) West Boulder Lake. It's 47 acres, 70 feet deep maximum, has a nice gravel bottom, used to contain some fair-size golden trout from an old plant — since gone, and has an ample population of cutthroat trout planted in 1970, 1977 and 1979 that will range in size from 8 inches to about 17 inches (but rarely). Creeled by hardy (you have to be hardy to get here) fishermen at a good clip, these are fine eating fish, the surroundings spectacular, the total trip a memory maker. A few local guides come in from the West Fork of the Boulder River over 13 miles of poor horse trail. Strangers mostly get their rear in gear (more try than you'd think) and follow the creek up for 2½ miles above the end of the "trail."

Fish Lake. In high (elevation 9472 feet above sea level), open, alpine country just at timberline; reached by a 9 mile ride up the Upsidedown Creek trail from the Boulder River at the Lazy Day Ranch; or 6 miles by trail from the end of the East Fork logging road 4 miles above the

WEST BOULDER RIVER
Courtesy USFS

GORGE ON THE BOULDER
Courtesy USFS

BOULDER RIVER
Courtesy USFS

ranch; or from the Stillwater River drainage via the Wounded Man Creek trail. It's good fishing for 7 to 10 inch cutthroat. Few people bother to make the trip to this 18 acre; 45 feet deep lake to try for its small "wild" trout.

Fourmile Creek. Drains Silver Lake 2 miles east down a steep, rocky gorge and then another couple of miles in fairly open country to the Boulder River at the Fourmile Guard Station. It's crossed at the mouth by a USFS road and followed by trail upstream for 2 miles of fair 9 to 11 inch rainbow and some cutthroat fishing — by few parties.

Helicopter Lake. So named because that's about the only way you can get there. It's away-and-heck-and-gone at the head of (barren) Hawley Creek, a good 5 miles above the end of the trail where it turns off up the North Fork, 4 miles by road and trail above Hells Canyon on the West Boulder River. It's 6 acres, 25 foot maximum depth, in very scenic alpine country, used to be barren but was planted with cutthroat in 1970 and 1976 and may or may not have fish in it now depending on whether they did or did not freeze out. If it does not, it should be good inasmuch as nobody but a wild man would go there.

Horseshoe Lake. Take the (barren) Upsidedown Creek trail east from the Boulder River road a quarter of a mile below the Lazy Day Ranch buildings for about 4 miles to this 16 acre, horseshoe-shaped lake in open grass and some timber at about 9500 feet above sea level. It used to be barren but was planted with cutthroat in 1970, is good fishing now for 6 to 16 inch fish that are wild and sassy, and gets a surprising amount of use considering the name of the trail in.

Kaufman Lake. See Falls Creek Lake.

Lake Kathleen. Is reached by jeep and foot about 4½ miles up the East Fork of the Boulder River above the Box Canyon Ranger Station (on the East Fork). It's only a couple of acres below talus slopes and lodgepole, maybe a couple of hundred yards or so through the trees to the north of the trail. It used to be barren but was planted with cutthroat in 1971, and is now barren again.

Lake Raymond. Is unnamed on most maps but is about a mile southeast of Horseshoe Lake a half mile south of the trail. It's maybe 11 acres, at a timber line, was planted with cutthroat in 1970 and is presently barren.

Lost Lake. See Brays Pond.

McNight Lake. About a mile east, a little north and over the divide from Pine Creek Lake (in the Yellowstone drainage) is McNight Lake in the above-timberline headwaters of Davis Creek (in the Boulder River drainage). It can be reached by a rugged 2½ mile scramble up the creek from where it leaves the trail — but the easiest way in is as just described. McNight is 9½ acres, deep enough to keep from freezing out most winters, but has no fish. At 9120 feet above sea level and 60 feet maximum depth, plus being tough to get to — this lake makes one wish!

Meatrack Creek.
A small, mountain stream flowing northeastward to Fourmile Creek ½ mile above the Boulder River road, paralleled upstream by a good USFS trail. The first 1½ miles are too steep for fish but the next couple of miles are in a partly open, more-or-less flat bottomed canyon with a few meadows along, and here it is good fishing for 6 to 10 inch cutthroat. Few folks ever see it, however, because the lower reaches are a fooler, and there are no lakes above.

Rainbow Lakes.
Three lakes, one above, another a few hundred yards apart, on a high (elevation around 9400 feet above sea level), alpine plateau with some scattered timber and lots of beautiful campsites; reached either by a good pack trail 6 miles up Rainbow Creek from the end of the East Fork Boulder River road or 5½ miles by a many switchbacked trail from the end of the Upsidedown Creek logging road which takes off to the east from the Boulder River road near the Lazy Day Ranch. The lowest (as you come to them) lake is about 15 acres, the middle one 12 acres, and the upper one 25 acres. The lower two are shallow (you can wade way out into them); the upper one is fairly deep (especially along the east side) and all three are fished a fair amount for good catches of 10 to 14 inch rainbow, cutthroat and rainbow-cutthroat hybrids. There are a few 2 to 3 pounders in all three lakes. Four other small lakes in the immediate vicinity may or may not have fish — they may winterkill.

Silver Lake.
A pretty, little, alpine lake that is really a wide spot near timberline in Fourmile Creek, with a house-size island in the middle. It's reached by trail 7 miles up the creek, is good fishing for good-size rainbow that will average a foot long and run up to a recorded 6½ pounds — I hope to shout! It's thirty feet deep, ten acres, at 9046 feet elevation with successful spawning (apparently). Is the long trip in keeping the pressure down?

Speculator Creek.
Is seldom fished and really not worth fussing with, but does support a very few pan-size cutthroat in the lower mile. If you are still interested, it's crossed at the mouth by the Boulder River road just below the Hells Canyon Ranch.

Trout Lake.
See Brays Pond.

Unnamed Lake.
Follow the outlet of McNight Lake ½ mile east down to Davis Creek, then up Davis for a few hundred yards, and finally ¾ mile up another small tributary coming in from the south and you will come to a shallow 3 acre lake that is all in the open just above timberline. It is very seldom visited but is good fishing for 12 inch cutthroat trout stocked a few years back.

Unnamed Lake Half Mile East of Horseshoe Lake.
Across the high, rocky plateau, no trail. Believe it or not there is a little shrubbery around its 3 or 4 acres of ice cold water. It was planted with cutthroat (heavens knows why because surely no one will ever visit it) in 1970 and has been and probably still is pretty good fishing for camp-fare trout. Good thing too because it's too high and too rugged to pack much food into.

West Boulder Lake.
Lies in a high (elevation 9628 feet above sea level), barren cirque reached by a rough climb straight up the mountainside ½ mile south and 686 feet above Falls Creek (or Kaufman) Lake. It's 13 acres, quite deep on the southwest end, is real good fishing (once in a blue moon when somebody gets there to try it) for 8 to 10 inch cutthroat trout, was stocked in 1979, and used to have goldens but they finally died out.

West Boulder River.
Heads in timbered mountains at the junction of its East and West Forks a mile above Beaver Meadows and flows north-northeastward for 25 miles to the Boulder River about 15 miles south of Big Timber by State Highway 298. It's followed upstream for 15 miles by road (to the Burnt Leather Ranch) and on to headwaters by a USFS trail. The lower reaches are in pasture-hayland-foothill country with cottonwood and some brush along it; the upper reaches flow down a timbered canyon. The lower reaches are no better than fair fishing for 9 to 12 inch fish, mostly browns with a scattering of rainbow, cutthroat, and whitefish in the winter. The upper trail reaches are fair-to-good for 8 to 10 inch cutthroat trout, especially on a fly rod.

Woolsey Lake. Take the Ennos Flume maintenance road 1½ miles or so east from East Boulder to this fairly shallow, 3 acre lake in a small partly open, partly timbered coulee. It is private but good fishing, if you get the chance, and if it isn't fished or frozen out, for rainbow that run around 2 pounds or better.

Put Your Campfire Dead Out

STRICTLY VEGETARIAN
Courtesy Ernst Peterson

PILOT PEAK
Courtesy USFS

Clark's Fork of the Yellowstone

This fork of the Yellowstone River heads on the Beartooth Plateau in a small lake at the junction of the West Fork Broadwater River and Sedge Creek – 3 miles east of Cooke City where it flows (a brawling little stream) for 3 miles through dense timber into Wyoming. It recrosses the line back into Montana about 25 miles above (south of) Bridger and is followed for 40 miles by State 310 to the Yellowstone River (and U.S. 10) at Laurel. The Montana head-waters are reached all along by short ¼ mile hikes northeast from the Cooke City-Beartooth highway and are fair to good fishing for 6 to 10 inch brook trout. There are about 6 miles of stream in the upper reaches above Bridger to the Wyoming line that are fair fishing for 8 to 10 inch rainbow and a few cutthroat trout and good fishing for 12 to 16 inch mountain whitefish. The lower reaches below Bridger are badly silted from irrigation practices and are poor to fair fishing at best for brown and rainbow trout, sauger, ling, and an occasional catfish.

Clark's Fork of the Yellowstone Drainage

Aero Lake (Lower).   See Lower Aero Lake.

Aero Lake (Upper).   See Upper Aero Lake.

Albino Lake.   A very high (elevation 10,160 feet above sea level) Beartooth Plateau lake; about 40 acres, deep with steep dropoffs, talus slopes on the northeast side and grassy slopes on around. To get there you leave your car at Island Lake (a few hundred yards north of the Red Lodge-Cooke City highway 2½ miles east of Camp Beartooth in Wyoming) and take off by trail up the drainage for about 5 miles as the crow goes. You'll recognize Albino Lake when you get there by its roughly rectangular shape and because the trail brings you in at its southeast corner. There are a moderate number of fishermen who make this one, and it is good for 10 to 14 inch cutthroat trout. 'Twas planted in 1974, 1975 and 1978 with 2 inchers. There may be some (very limited) reproduction here also.

Aquarius Lake.   Twelve acres with a little island in the north end, mostly in timber but with some talus slopes on the north side. If you've a compass (and you'd better have), it's a cinch ½ mile cross-country hike through the timber northeast from Sedge Lake. Once there you'll find the fishing fair and the cutthroat ranging all the way from fingerling to maybe 14 inches. The lake was stocked in 1970 and 1977, has some natural reproduction, is 65 feet deep, located 9180 feet above sea level, and although off the beaten path, gets some visitation.

Arctic Lake.   Straddles the Wyoming line on the Beartooth Plateau at just a shade under 10,000 feet above sea level, a mile southeast of Lonesome Mountain and ½ mile east and just off (north of) the Beartooth-Green Lake trail 4½ miles as the crow flies from Camp Beartooth. Arctic is a deep 4 acres, is bordered by rock and a little grass and is barren.

Bald Knob Lake. Sixteen acres, 38 feet deep, way up there (elevation 9420 feet above sea level) in open alpine country right at the edge of the timber with talus slopes all around the north side. It is reached by trail 1¼ miles north from Russell Lake along the small connecting stream. The fishing is good for mostly 4 to 12 inch brook trout averaging about 6 inches. Maybe they'd grow up if more people passing through stopped to catch their supper.

Basin Creek Lakes. Upper (4 acres, 8900 feet elevation) and Lower (2 acres, 8350 feet elevation) on the lower, timbered slopes of Silver Run Plateau. Lower Basin is reached by 2¼ miles of pretty steep trail from the West Fork Rock Creek road 7½ miles west from Red Lodge. Upper Basin is a mile further west by trail. Both lakes are shallow and the lower one has frozen out in the past. It has been moderately popular in recent years, and if it's O.K. now, it should be fair fishing for 10 to 11 inch brookies. The Upper lake, good in early season, is only about 5 feet deep, but at last report was full of small brookies.

Big Butte Lake. Thirty five acres, on the barren Beartooth plateau a mile north and some east up the drainage from Jordon Lake. No trail. It was planted with cutthroat in 1968 and is barren now. Look for a plant (this coming year or so) of golden trout — rumor has it.

Big Hellroaring Lake. See Hellroaring Lakes.

Big Moose Lake. Is 84 acres, at 8000 feet elevation, in timber right on the Montana-Wyoming line a quarter mile below (south) of Widewater Lake by way of Crazy Lakes pack trail. Fact is — some of the game wardens honor fishing licenses from either state, but I wouldn't bet on it. It's good fishing too, for 6 inch to a couple of pound brookies, rainbow and grayling, but most anglers pass it by.

Black Canyon Lake. Take the Lake Fork Rock Creek trail 3 miles above Broadwater (the little one) Lake to 60 acre Black Canyon Lake in a high (elevation 9400 feet above sea level) rocky canyon between Mount Rearguard and Thunder Mountain. There are talus slopes all around this lake, which is very deep (185 feet) and greenish colored from glacial silt (Grasshopper Glacier lies just above it to the south). It is seldom visited and fair fishing although they run large — cutthroat to 3 or better pounds from time to time. Stocked in '75 and '79, the "usual catch" is 8 to 13 inchers. There are mountain goats on the ridge to the south, a very rugged climb.

Bluewater Creek. Is followed by a good county road from headwaters at Bluewater Springs northwestward for 13 miles through open rolling hills to the Clarks Fork of the Yellowstone a mile east and across the river from Fromberg. The Bluewater fish hatchery is located near the head of this creek, which, by the way, is fairly brushy along much of its course. The lower reaches are only poor fishing because of excessive siltation from poor irrigation practices, but the middle and upper reaches are good fishing for 1 to 2 pound browns plus quite a few that will go to 5 pounds or better. Nevertheless, it's not fished much in the summer, due to the presence of large numbers of ever lov'n rattlesnakes. It is, however, fairly popular in the spring and fall.

Bob and Dick Lakes. Two, moderately deep 3 acre lakes joined by a shallow east-end neck at 9700 feet above sea level on a barren rock and meadow plateau reached cross-country ½ mile northwest (up the outlet) from Long Lake. It is heavily fished for good catches of 8 to 10 inch brook trout.

Bowback Lake. Is perhaps 6 acres, a quarter of a mile over the hill north and a little west of Triangle Lake on the barren rocky Beartooth Plateau. It used to be barren but was stocked with cutthroat in 1968, '71 and '80, is good fishing now but seldom sees a hook. At 10,380 feet elevation, 40 feet at its deepest, this little gem gives up an occasional 3 pounder to the tenacious angler.

Broadwater Lake. Is just above Curl Lake to which it is joined by a 200 yard long, 30 foot wide — and too deep to wade neck. It is about 80 acres, deep, in timber except for a large and beautiful meadow at the upper end and is fair fishing for 12 to 14 inch brook, plus an occasional 12 to 16 inch cutthroat trout.

Broadwater River. Is really only a creek formed by the junction of Zimmer and Star Creeks; it flows south across the Beartooth Plateau for 2 miles to Broadwater and Curl Lakes, thence for 2½ miles to the Clarks Fork of the Yellowstone 3 miles east of Cooke City. It is more or

CATHEDRAL SPIRES
Courtesy USFS

less paralleled by a trail all the way up its fairly steep timbered reaches below the lakes and across a mile or so of grassy meadows, above which there are lots of nice holes. It is moderately popular and good fishing for 6 to 8 inch brook trout.

Burnt Fork Creek. A very small tributary of West Red Lodge Creek. The lower ½ mile is easily accessible by road (and supports a few 6 to 8 inch brook trout).

Canyon Lake. Is mistakenly called Crazy Lake on some maps. It is ⅛ of a mile wide by a mile long in an east-west direction below rocky cliffs on the north side and timber to the south; is reached (by darned few) by the Farley Creek trail 1½ miles east from the upper (north) end of Fox Lake, and is only fair fishing, but the rainbow and cutthroat you'll find here will average a foot long and range up to seven or eight pounds — a self sustaining fishery.

Cliff Lake. A deep, 5 acre, irregularly-shaped lake with a small island in the southeast corner. It lies in alpine timber 9200 feet above sea level, ¾ of a mile west and a little north by game trails from Moccasin Lake. It is not fished often, but the fishing is good just the same for nice, fat, 12 to 16 inch brook trout that can be a little temperamental at times. Try small dry flies or nymphs — and a prayer!

Cliff Lake. Is so-named from the steep, rock cliffs along the north side; it is about 10 acres, deep, with timber on the south side and very good fishing for 8 to 10 inch grayling. To get there (which few do) you take the Farley Creek trail ¾ of a mile past (east of) the north end of Fox Lake and then strike out cross-country through the low saddle southward through scrub timber for another ½ mile to the shore. Good luck! If you're there, fish the outlet creek downstream (on through a little pothole) with a light action fly rod. Just plain fun!

Cloverleaf Lakes. Between 18 and 31 acres in size, 3, reached cross-country about a mile west from Jasper Lake (the other 3 or 4 lakes nearby don't have fish). Sitting right on the glaciated bedrock a mile northwest of Lonesome Mountain at just over 10,000 feet above sea level, the lakes were planted with cutthroat in 1968 and in 1975. The trout now average 10 inches or so, and when hitting are easy enough to catch; a fella could land a fair sized one (to 3 pounds) but not often.

Cole Creek. A small, "farmland" tributary of Harney Creek; the lower 3 miles are accessible by road and are fished a moderate amount (mostly by kids) for 8 inch brook trout. It's not a bad stream but the lower reaches are heavily dewatered for irrigation.

Companion Lake. At 9040 feet above sea level, this one is ¼ of a mile east (200 yards from the jeep road) from Long Lake; is 6 acres, fairly deep, in timber except for some meadows at the north end, and is excellent fishing for 6 to 12 inch brook trout. The combination spells for nothing less than moderate to heavy fishing pressure.

Cooney Reservoir. A 640 acre open rangeland reservoir about 20 feet deep behind an earth-fill dam, with mostly shallow dropoffs. Drained now to allow repairs to the dam and spillway, it will be chemically rehabilitated and planted with small rainbow trout. It is reached by the Red Lodge Creek road about 9 miles west of Boyd. Hard hit and good for small rainbow in the past (and occasionally a 3 or 4 pounder), the reservoir should be even more popular and better fishing soon. Look for annual stocking of rainbow which could grow well with most of the competing suckers gone.

Copeland Lake. Subcircular, 41 acres, only 8720 feet above sea level, 125 feet deep, in timber all around but with open grassy shores to the north and west; Copeland lies just north of the Montana-Wyoming line and is reached by the Elk Park-Big Basin trail 8½ miles from the Cooke City Highway. There are lots of 6 inch brook trout here — good enough for camp fare.

Corner Lake. Ten acres, fairly shallow, in timbered country but with grassy banks; reached by the (barren) Goose Lake jeep road maybe 4 miles up from the Cooke City Highway and fished way more than somewhat for 10 to 14 inch cutthroat. A natural population exists which the MDFWP enhances with a small plant once in a while (last in 1980).

Crazy Lake. See Canyon Lake.

Crescent Lake. See Hellroaring Lakes.

Curl Lake. Elevation 8400 feet above sea level 30 acres, 45 feet deep, in dense timber just below Broadwater Lake; reached and followed around the east side by the Broadwater Creek (its outlet) trail 2½ miles up from the highway (U.S. 12). It's fished quite a lot and is excellent for 12 to 14 inch brook trout, plus a very few 14 to 16 inch cutthroat trout.

Daly Lake. See Hellroaring Lakes.

Derchemaker (or August) Pond. A private farm pond accessible by road a few miles west from Boyd (on Rock Creek near the mouth of Red Lodge Creek). It's about 100 by 150 feet, 8 to 10 feet deep, very seldom if ever fished by the public — but has been very good for rainbow and brown trout to 4 pounds in the past.

Dollar Lake. One acre, full of 6 to 12 inch grayling, a quarter of a mile below Aquarius Lake in small timber, 12 feet deep, at 8920 feet above sea level, with a few small cutthroat given up to a moderate amount of takers.

BOULDER FIELD
Couretsy USFS

PILOT AND INDEX PEAKS
Courtesy Bridenstine Studio

WATCH IT, HE'S EVIL TEMPERED
Courtesy USFS

Courtesy Dave Line

Dude Lake. Take a pack trail 4 miles above the end of the West Fork Rock Creek road and then head off across country for about a mile (and a thousand foot climb) up a small unnamed creek coming in from the west past (barren) Senal Lake to Dude Lake in a barren rocky cirque just below Elk Mountain at 10,200 feet above sea level. It is about 12 acres, 20 feet deep, and has a small population of cutthroat planted in 1968, '75 and '80. It's fair fishing, not hit much.

Elaine Lake. Take the USFS pack trail north from Granite Lake for 2½ miles to Elaine Lake in timbered country but with several open parks around for horse pasture. It is 101.6 acres, has a little islet on the southeast side, is good and deep, excellent fishing for 6 to 9 inch brook trout and is seldom bothered. The trail follows around the west side and on to perhaps bigger trout.

Estelle Lake. In timber but with enough meadow for the horses, 1 mile east of Elaine Lake and ½ mile south of (little) Green Lake, by USFS trail; about 18 acres, 30 feet deep, excellent fishing for 8 to 10 inch brook trout — seldom visited.

Farley Lake. Is reached by foot trail 1 mile west from the upper end of Elaine Lake; elevation 9800 feet (it's getting up there), in open alpine country with some scattered scrub timber here and there. It's 24 acres, 35 feet deep with steep dropoffs, and is seldom visited, although excellent fishing for nice 10 to 12 inch brook trout.

First Rock Lake. In timber (but partly open on the north side), reached by a fishermen's trail a mile above Keyser Brown Lake at 8800 feet above sea level on the northern slopes of Thunder Mountain. This lake is about 18 acres, fairly shallow, and good fishing for 8 to 9 inch brook trout and 10 to 11 inch cutthroat. It is fairly popular and the nice little stream that connects it to Keyser Brown is an added bonus; it's excellent fishing.

Flat Rock Lake. Is 35 acres, on the barren Beartooth Plateau, reached 1½ miles northeast of Summerville Lake. (Note well: Don't go UP the drainage due NORTH from Summerville.) It was planted with cutthroat in 1968 and 1978, and is reported to be really good fishing now for 6 to 14 inchers. The wind blows (and nothing grows) here at 9990 feet above sea level. The lake is 85 feet deep — and needs to be — to keep from freezing out.

Fox Lake. At 8055 feet elevation, about 1 mile long with irregular shores, 120 acres, 75 feet deep, in timber all around except for some nice open meadows at the upper end; it is connected to Widewater Lake by a few hundred yards of stream (over some little rapids), and the lower end lies 100 yards or so off (northeast of) the Cooke City Highway 10 miles east of town. It is moderately popular for mostly 10 to 12 inch rainbow plus some 10 inch or so grayling and brook trout. The best fishing is in the channel at the lower end. Stocking isn't necessary here.

63

Gertrude Lake. Drive your car up the West Fork Rock Creek road about 11 miles west from Red Lodge to within a mile of Camp Senia, and then take the Timberline Creek pack trail 3½ miles south to Gertrude Lake, which is ½ mile below Timberline Lake at 9520 feet above sea level. It is 5 acres, fairly shallow but doesn't freeze out and is good fishing for 8 to 9 inch brook trout. Quite a few summer folks come here.

Glacier Lake. A nice, 180 feet deep, 177 acre lake on the Wyoming line, at 9702 feet above sea level, in scattered alpine timber, with barren talus and scree slopes and cliffs along the sides and meadows at each end. It is fed by snowmelt from a small glacier at the northwest end and by an inlet stream from a small lake (northwest about 300 yards) above it. Used to be only whoppers here and there are still some nice fat brookies to an occasional (but rare) 6 pounds and some nice cutthroat rarely to 2½ pounds. Planted with cutthroat in 1971, '78, and '79, the usual catch is 8 to 13 inches — but you never know. That's what brings the crowds. Lots of anglers take the Rock Creek road up the canyon past the old burn and on up the creek for another 4 miles to a deadend parking area, and then a steep trail (about a mile) on in to this sparkling clear scenic lake.

Golden Lake. Is very irregular in outline, sort of resembles a ruptured duck with an arrow (a small island) through its gizzard; it's about 50 acres, at 10,100 feet above sea level, deep enough (90 feet) to keep from freezing out. You can get there by trail around Lonesome Mountain (north) from Albino Lake. It gets "middling" usage for a migrant population of 10 to 12 inch cutthroat.

Granite Lake. Park your car 4 miles west of Camp Beartooth on the Cooke City Highway (20 miles east of town) on Muddy creek and take the trail up this stream for 8 miles to 250 acre Granite Lake, at 8625 feet elevation. It's 125 feet deep, partly in Montana and partly in Wyoming. It has a very irregular shoreline, is mostly in timber but with cliffs to the water on the east side and some open shores on the north (head) end. Quite a few folks take advantage of the good fishing here for 8 to 14 inch rainbow plus an occasional brook trout.

Green Lake. An excellent lake for 10 to 12 inch brookies; also the little stream above it (Lake Creek) for about ¾ of a mile. It's about 36 acres, 129 feet deep, in scattered timber at 9350 feet above sea level, and is reached by trail a mile east of Elaine Lake 6 miles by trail from Camp Beartooth on U.S. 12, or by trail from Wright Lake. It gets its share of usage.

Green Lake. About 3 acres, in a high (elevation 9700 feet above sea level) alpine meadow a mile south of Mount Zimmer. You take the Goose Lake jeep trail about 6 miles up from the Cooke City highway (U.S. 12) to ½ mile above Star Lake and thence through a low saddle to the east for another ½ mile on foot to the shore. It's fished quite a bit and is usually good for tiny brook trout.

Greenough Lake. At 7280 feet elevation above sea level, shallow, about 9 foot maximum depth, 1 acre, has a good population of brook trout and some rainbow trout and is fished more than somewhat for good catches of small trout. You can drive to it about 15 miles southwest of Red Lodge a couple of miles up the Rock Creek road.

Courtesy MDFWP

Harney Creek. A small farmland stream flowing to East Red Lodge Creek 3½ miles above Castagne and crossed upstream by the East Rosebud road 9 miles west from Red Lodge. There are about 3 miles of fair fishing along the middle reaches for 6 to 7 inch brook trout. It's mostly frequented by kids.

Hellroaring Lakes. Twelve in all, of which about ½ freeze out and only ½ support fish. To reach them take U.S. 12 (the Cooke City Highway) twelve miles south from Red Lodge to the Parkside Campground on the "yon" side by Black Pyramid Mountain. From here you can drive your car, if you don't value it highly, 5 miles farther on to the south and west across the plateau to a large snowfield that will always be there no matter what the season. Now unload, gather your tackle and take an easy half mile hike north to shallow, subcircular, 9 acre Wapiti Lake which lies in grassy alpine meadows but has a small rock cliff above its northwest side. Lots of folks stop at this one for good catches of 8 to 9 inch brook trout. A quarter mile hike northwest across open alpine country brings you to Big Hellroaring Lake which has a most irregular shoreline, is about 75 acres, good and deep and good fishing for 8 to 10 inch cutthroat planted in the late '60's and '70's and fair fishing for nice size (2 to 3 pound) trout. Now follow the drainage east for 1¼ miles (still no trail but you are down in a canyon) past 3 shallow ponds to shallow 5 acre Smethurst Lake — all of which freeze out. From here you hike north cross-country for ⅛ mile to deep, long, 8 acre Crescent Lake below ice-scoured bedrock except for some talus on the northeast end. It supports a moderate to heavy fishing pressure for good catches of 9 to 10 inch brook trout. Now hike southeast up over the ridge and down through some scrub timber for a quarter mile to Daly Lake on the creek once more. It also is good and deep, about 6 acres, and lies below sliderock along the north side and timber pine to the south. It is heavily fished for plentiful 10 to 12 inch brookies. Some of the lakes were stocked with cutthroat in 1977 and are scheduled again for the mid 80's.

Hileman Pond. A posted, 100 by 300 foot, shallow pond on the Rock Creek flood plain a mile south of Red Lodge. It's good fishing for 8 to 10 inch rainbow and brook trout. It's sponsored by various local men's clubs and is stocked every year for crippled and handicapped children.

Hogan Creek. A small tributary of West Red Lodge Creek 3 miles above Castagne; in willow-bottomed farmland, crossed here and there by county roads and heavily fished for about 4 miles along the middle reaches for pan-size brook trout. The lower reaches are pretty well dewatered for irrigation.

Hunter (or Robin) Lake. Used to be that almost nobody got to this one, but it is visited a bit nowadays even without a trail. Perhaps the best way in is to follow the outlet of Little Falls Lake downstream (west) for about ¼ of a mile through scrub timber and alpine parky country to the shore at 9520 feet above sea level. It is about 8 acres, deep (58 feet), and is excellent fishing for 6 to 12 inch brook trout and a very few rainbow; AND the inlet stream can be a nice surprise.

Jasper Lake. Deep, 107 feet maximum, at 10,150 feet above sea level in barren alpine country, about 55 acres, about 300 yards north of (above) Golden Lake or ½ mile north of Albino Lake. A very limited natural reproduction here is supplemented by periodic (1968 and 1974) stocking of cutthroat. The fishing is slow, but husky 1 to 4½ pound cutts are not really that uncommon if you stay at it. Needless to say, more than a few come here to try.

Jorden Lake. A fairly heavily fished, 120 feet deep, 36 acre lake in high (elevation 9600 feet) alpine, grass and scattered timber plateau country reached by trail a couple of miles west from Elaine Lake. The fishing used to be real slow but the fish large. It was planted with cutthroat in 1968 and they are plentiful although smaller than in days of yore.

Kersey Lake. Here's one you can drive to by jeep road 1½ miles east up Sedge Creek from U.S. 12 three miles east of Cooke City. It is on a rolling, timbered plateau, is 118 acres, deep (68 feet), used to be heavily fished for good catches of small brookies that were poisoned out in 1968, and is now excellent for 6 to 14 inch brook trout and some cutts. The rehab wasn't 100% effective. Lake trout were stocked in 1980 — this could become an interesting place right after ice-out.

Keyser Brown Lake. At 8720 feet elevation, 88 feet deep, Keyser is a popular, fairly shallow, 10 acre lake in timber all around but with mostly open shores. It's good fishing for 6 to 8 inch brook trout and a few cutthroat. The best way in (short of wings) is by the Lake Fork trail 6½ miles up from the end of the road. As long as you've come this far you might as well fish on up the creek to First Rock Lake — it's better.

Kidney Lake. See Question Mark Lake.

Lady of the Lake. A beautiful, 43 acre, 29 feet deep, scenic lake that lies at 8800 feet above sea level in an ice-gouged canyon reached by USFS trail 2¾ miles north up Lady of the Lake Creek trail from State Highway 12 just east of Colter Pass. It is mostly in timber except for a large meadow at the upper end (good horse pasture here), is fished quite a lot and is excellent for 8 to 16 inch brook trout and some 8 to 12 inch cutthroat.

Lady of the Lake Creek. A small stream that freezes out below the lake but there is about a mile above (in flat, timbered country, no trail) that is good fishing for 6 to 9 inch brook trout. It is seldom bothered.

Lake Creek. Originates as melt-water from Castle Rock Glacier at 11,000 feet above sea level and flows for 4 airline miles across open, alpine upland through Long View, Flat Rock, Queer, Green and Estelle Lakes and finally for 2 miles down a timbered canyon to Granite Lake on the Montana-Wyoming line. It is seldom fished but very good in places (especially in the rocky canyon between Green and Queer Lakes) for 8 to 12 inch brook trout and a few rainbow. It is fairly well known but a tough place to get to — lightweight waders help.

Lake Fork Rock Creek. Heads at 10,000 feet elevation above sea level below a large glacier on the slopes of Beartooth Mountain and flows for 11 airline miles east through Second Rock, First Rock and Keyser Brown Lakes to Rock Creek at Richel Lodge. It is reached at the mouth by U.S. 12 ten miles south from Red Lodge and is followed by trail up its wide timbered canyon for seven miles of poor 8 to 9 inch brook trout fishing.

Lake of the Winds. Gird your loins and take off due north across barren rocky alpine terrain for a long ¼ mile from the lower (north) end of Mariane Lake to this 41 acre, 186 feet deep, correctly named lake at 9910 feet above sea level, lying below cliffs on the north side and talus and scree on around. It had golden trout in the '50's and '60's and now only nice (to 1 lb.) cutthroat planted in 1977 as 2 inchers (4,000) today averaging about 10-12 inches.

Lillis Lake. At 8140 feet elevation, is reached by trail through dense timber ½ mile below Kersey Lake. Lillis is 4 acres, fairly shallow and almost completely covered with lilies. It is moderately popular and very good early season fishing (before the lilies get too thick to fish and before the mosquitos carry you away) for 11 to 12 inch brook trout.

THE BEAR'S TOOTH
Courtesy Phil Farnes

Courtesy John and Frank Craighead
Montana Co-operative Wildlife Research Unit

TOURING NORTH OF COOKE CITY
Courtesy USFS

KEYSER BROWN LAKE
Courtesy USFS

Line Lake. Park your car on U.S. 12 a half mile north of the Montana-Wyoming border, then hike east for 1½ miles across Wyoming Creek basin to this little, mostly shallow (26 feet deep maximum) lake that sits right on top of the plateau at 9680 feet elevation with no protection from any direction. It is windy! Poisoned out, then planted with cutthroat in 1969, 1970, 1977 and 1980, it is slow fishing for 10 to 14 inchers (average). Now hear this! Lunkers (to 6 pounds) can dance on the end of your line and however infrequently hooked, the possibility will keep your palms sweaty. Chances are you won't be alone here.

Little Falls Lake. At timberline (9620 feet elevation), it is on the Beartooth-Green Lake trail in open alpine meadows and a little scrub timber 1¼ miles below (southeast of) Green Lake ¼ of a mile beyond Trail Lake. It is about 11 acres, deep and excellent fishing (if you can call it that) for overpopulated, skinny, 6 to 8 inch brook trout. Most folks pass it by.

Little (or Washtub) Lake. At 9190 feet elevation, on a rock bench with open meadows to the north and scrub timber on around; ¼ mile cross-country by game trails south from Cliff Lake. Little Lake is only a couple of acres in size but is fair fishing for nice fat 12 to 16 inch brook trout. You won't have much company here either.

Lone Elk Lake. Lies in an open grassy swale, is 18 acres, 40 feet deep, and has a small island just west of center at 10,000 feet above sea level. Quite a few people hike 3½ miles in up Sky Top Creek, 2 miles by trail above Broadwater Lake. There are 8 to 17 inch grayling and some really nice (2 to 5 pound) brook trout — both in limited quantities. Fishing here will either be fun or frustration.

Long Lake. About ½ mile long by 100 to 200 yards wide, it's on the open plateau and reached by the Goose Lake jeep trail 5 crooked miles from the Cooke City Highway. Lots of people come from town to fish this one for excellent catches of 6 to 12 inch brook trout — a real social event.

Lost Lake. Confined by a lateral moraine in a rocky, timbered, glaciated canyon a few hundred yards south of Lake Fork Rock Creek 4½ miles by easy pack trail from the end of the road. Planted in 1971 and 1975 with cutthroat (due again?) that run between 11 and 15 inches, the fishing is good. Lost Lake is at 8520 feet elevation, has a 25 foot maximum depth, and is 11 acres in size.

Lower Aero Lake. 9995 feet up in the air, 190 acres, 185 feet maximum depth with sharp dropoffs and two small islands in its southeastern and southwestern corners. Too bad it's a popular place. Take the Broadwater River trail on up Zimmer Creek a mile beyond the mouth of Star Creek, then climb 750 feet while going a mile east to the lake — if you really want to. Used to be really good for 1 to 3 pound brook and cutthroat (the cutts drift down from Upper Aero) but is now only fair fishing with fewer and smaller fish the rule.

Margaret Lake. There is no trail but if you take the Lillis Lake trail a quarter mile north from Vernon Lake to a good sized opening in the timber, and then proceed due east for ⅛ mile you will hit lonesome, 5 acre Margaret right on the nose. She lies in a small clearing, is surrounded by a floating bog, has a few lilies in her upper end, froze out in the '60's, was replanted with cutthroat in 1972 and 1978, and is fair fishing for 8 to 12 inchers.

Mariane (or Morqaine) Lake. Seventy feet deep, 50 acres, is reached by trail ⅓ mile up the drainage from the "unnamed lake east of Russell Lake," at 9500 feet above sea level. Mariane is an oddly shaped lake, about ¾ of a mile long and looks sort of like a drunken salamander with two little islands at the north end for eyes. Very few fishermen ever get here but it is excellent for 6 to 12 inch brook trout.

Marker Lake. 10,870 feet above sea level, 15 acres and 155 feet deep (maximum) in extreme high rock country. This jewel has cuts from 8 inches to a couple pounds (planted in 1972 and 1978) and is good fishing. You won't have much company here. It's ¼ mile southwest from Ship Lake — see Triangle Lake for route.

Martin Lake. At 9660 feet elevation, 42 feet deep, a shallow lake that has a small island with a few trees on it smack dab in the middle of its 31 acres. There is also some sparse timber on the lower (south) end where it attaches to Wright Lake but the upper end is in alpine meadows. It is seldom fished but good for 6 to 8 inch brook trout.

Mary Lake. Take the West Fork Rock Creek trail 4 miles above the end of the road to Quineabaugh Meadows, and then a steep switchback trail for another (airline) mile and a thousand foot climb to the shore. Mary is just shy of 10,000 feet above sea level, behind a terminal moraine on the south end of Grass Mountain. It has some sparse scrubby timber on the east side, is about 8 acres, deep, and good fishing for 10 inch brook trout. That last mile of switchbacks really cuts down on the number of folks coming in to this one.

Moccasin Lake. A high (9500 feet above sea level), 30 feet deep, 7 acre lake in scattered timber but with a large open meadow on the west side, on a rock bench west of Oxide Mountain reached cross-country ¾ of a mile east from Little (or Washtub) Lake around the north side of Middle Mountain. It is seldom fished but fair for fair-sized (12 to 16 inch) brook trout.

PILOT AND INDEX PEAKS
Courtesy Phil Farnes

FROM SUNDANCE PASS
Courtesy USFS

Moon Lake. At 10,400 feet, reached cross-country up the drainage (north) a quarter mile from the Unnamed Lake antigoglin to the west between Shelf and Moon Lakes. It is maybe 80 acres, deep, with talus on the east and west and meadows below, was planted with cutthroat in 1969-72 and 1975 and supports a moderate amount of fishing pressure for good catches of 12 to 18 inch fish. At times it can be a cold and windy spot.

Morqaine Lake. See Mariane Lake.

Otter Lake. At 9620 elevation, it occupies a steep grassy canyon ¼ mile up the drainage from Mariane Lake — or can also be reached by trail a couple of miles north and west past (barren) Jordan, Shrimp and Picket Lakes — from Farley Lake. Otter is about 60 acres, very deep with many cliffs along the north shore and steep grassy canyon walls to the south. It is seldom fished and excellent for 6 to 8 inch brook trout — hordes of 'em.

Ovis Lake. On a shelf below Sheep Mountain and easy to get to — a half mile jeep trek west from Long Lake. It's 9 acres, 45 feet deep, with nice open banks and a good population of cutthroat planted in '70, '76, and '79 — all of which enhances its popularity. Expect good catches of 8 to 12 inchers if you "join the crowd."

Queer Lake. So named for the inlet that splits just above it and then flows around a small butte to enter at separate corners of this 26 acre, seldom fished but excellent lake for 6 to 8 inch brook trout. A game trail ⅛ mile cross-country northwest from Summerville Lake gets you to it. P.S. The creek above is also good if you are satisfied with little ones.

Question Mark (or Kidney) Lake. A seldom fished but good (using the term advisedly) 6 to 8 inch brook trout lake just east of the Beartooth-Green Lake trail ⅛ of a mile below (south of) Little Falls Lake. It is only a couple of acres and so shallow it ought to freeze out — but doesn't.

Red Lodge Creek. Is followed by good roads from its head at the junction of East and West Red Lodge Creeks, 30 miles northeast to the Clarks Fork of the Yellowstone 6 miles east of Joliet. Most of its course is within a broad open valley but with quite a few cottonwood and much brush along the banks. The upper reaches (for about 15 miles above Cooney Reservoir) are heavily fished for good catches of 10 inch to 4 pound browns. The lower reaches (below the reservoir) are poor fishing at best for a few scattered browns, some whitefish, and rough fish.

Robin Lake. See Hunter Lake.

GRASSHOPPER GLACIER
Courtesy USFS

Rock Creek. Heads on the Beartooth Plateau in Wyoming and is followed northward by State 12 for 13 miles to Red Lodge, and then another 27 miles to junction with the Clarks Fork of the Yellowstone 6 miles below Joliet. Above the National Forest boundary (6 miles south of Red Lodge) the stream is too fast for really good fishing but still has quite a lot of rainbow and a very few cutthroat trout. Between the National Forest boundary and Roberts it flows down a wide flood plain where it is bordered by cottonwood and willows (past 5 public recreation areas) and is excellent fishing and heavily fished, too, for rainbow plus a few brook, brown trout, and whitefish. Between Roberts and Joliet the stream is still good fishing where it hasn't been channeled. Below Joliet it is poor at best for mostly browns.

Rock Island Lake. This lake is 110 feet deep with a couple of little islands in each end, 137 acres, at 8166 feet elevation, in timber all around except for a large swampy meadow at the upper (north) end. Reached by the Crazy Lake trail 7½ miles from U.S. 12, ten miles east from Cooke City and ¼ mile west of Fox Lake. Cutthroat stocked here in 1970, 1972, 1974, 1977 and 1980 grow fast and now generally run to about a foot long,but can go to a boisterous three pounds. There are small brookies also, and an infrequent large brook to 4 pounds or so has been reported. Good fishing and nothing less than popular. Bring your bug dope!

Round Lake. At 9340 feet elevation, a deep, 30 acre lake in timber all around, right on the (barren) Goose Lake trail 4½ miles north from Cooke City. It is very popular and excellent fishing for 10 to 14 inch brook trout.

Rough Lake. An irregularly-shaped isthmus almost divides this irregularly-shaped lake in two — hence the name, Rough Lake. It lies in high (10,200 feet above sea level) alpine meadows ½ mile cross-country up Sky Top Creek from Lone Elk Lake; is 90 acres, 110 feet deep, and provides good fishing for 6 inch grayling plus ½ to very occasional 4½ pound brook trout for the more than a few intrepid souls that try it.

Russell Creek. A small stream (in the Montana reaches), it is followed by a USFS pack trail from Russell Lake to Fox Lake and has a lot of nice holes along the lower ½ mile or so — that are good fishing for 8 to 10 inch brook trout. It's worth the trip in just to see the cascades at the head of the fishing water just below Russell Lake.

Russell Lake. This 95 foot deep, 28 acre lake at 8780 feet elevation, is surrounded by timber and rock but with some open banks along the west side, and is reached by a new USFS trail to the creek (Russell, that is) 2 miles above Fox Lake. Trails take off in 4 different directions from the lake and it is fished quite a bit by folks passing through — for excellent catches of 8 to 10 inch brook trout. An added attraction is a large and beautiful cascade just below the outlet.

Second Hidden Lake. Take the Beartooth-Green Lake trail to a point ¼ mile south of Kidney Lake — then hike east for another mile across rolling alpine country to this Second Hidden Lake (1½ miles north of the Wyoming line). Seeing that it's hard to find, its waters seldom see a hook but are fair fishing nonetheless for 10 to 12 inch brook trout, plus an occasional lunker up to 2½ pounds.

Second Rock Lake. At 9110 feet elevation, a little larger (26 acres) than First Rock Lake and ¾ of a mile up the boulder strewn creek bottom above it. Second Rock Creek Lake is good and deep (50 feet) below talus slopes on the west side, has some scrubby timber on the east side, is moderately popular and good fishing for 1 to 1½ pound brook trout plus a fair number of 1 to 1¾ pound cutthroat.

Sedge Lake. At 9100 feet elevation, 28 feet deep, a 4 acre lake in alpine timber at the head of Sedge Creek. If you want to get there and avoid that "lost" feeling, the best way in is to follow the drainage 2¾ miles upstream east and north from the upper end of Kersey Lake. It's not too often fished for good catches of campfare cutts drifted down from Aquarius Lake.

September Morn Lake. If you've been to Keyser Brown Lake, it's a cinch to get to this one. If not, go to Keyser Brown, then backtrack ½ mile east to a trail which bears off to the north up out of the canyon for one steep mile to September Morn, which is all in alpine meadow, 12 acres, deep, at 9696 feet elevation, and has lots of 10 to 11 inch brook trout that are real skinny early in the season and don't really fatten up until late summer. It is probably not fished more than a dozen times a year.

Shelf Lake. Can be reached from either above or below. From above, take the trail from off the jeep road maybe ⅛ of a mile south of the Hellroaring Lakes snowfield, east across open alpine meadows for 1½ miles by trail above (north of) Glacier Lake. It is about 51 acres, deep, with steep dropoffs below talus slopes, at 10,120 feet elevation, and is fished quite a lot for good catches of 10 to 13 inch brookies.

Ship Lake. At 10,480 feet above sea level, on a barren rocky bench a quarter of a mile south across alpine meadows from Triangle Lake. It's 29 acres, good and deep (55 feet max) and excellent fishing for 8 to 10 inch brook trout that get real skinny along in mid-August.

Skytop Lakes. Six, that from a north-south trending string about 2 miles long in alpine country ranging in elevation from 10,500 to 10,600 feet above sea level. The lower 4 are almost hung together, the upper two about ¼ mile on up the drainage. There is no trail but an easy ½ mile hike up the creek from Rough Lake gets you to them. The lowest one is 20 acres, very irregularly shaped, and deep. The second one is only 15 acres, long and narrow and deep. The third (and largest) is 45 acres and has a nice little island near the center. The upper lake is really two conjoining 2 acre lakes that are good and deep. All of them are devoid of fish. Not that it makes much difference because few fishermen or anyone else ever gets to the Skytops. They were planted with grayling in the 1950's, but that didn't take.

Sliderock Lake. Hike around the contour north and west for 1 mile from the Hellroaring Lakes perennial snowfield to Sliderock in a big barren cirque below steep, thousand foot talus slopes of Rearguard Mountain (12,204 feet above sea level). It is a big lake (all of 81 acres), and deep all over which is just as well inasmuch as it's heavily hit for good catches of 12 to 14 inch brook trout. At 10,480 feet elevation, the lake needs all its 245 foot maximum depth, being free of ice only in the very short summer.

Sodalite Lake. Is reached by a packers trail 3 miles northeast up Sodalite Creek from Curl Lake to the shore just above timberline at 9840 feet above sea level. Sodalite is 30 acres, deep (90 feet) and provides some good fishing for the few anglers who try it for mostly snakey 12 to 14 inch brook trout.

Star Creek. Drains (the little) Green Lake 1½ miles down a narrow timbered canyon to Zimmer Creek just above that stream's junction with Skytop Creek at the head of Broadwater River. It's reached by jeeping to Star Lake and hiking down the intermittent outlet ¼ mile east to the main creek. There is no trail but it's very good fishing for 6 to 8 inch brook trout. Very few folks bother to try it.

Star Lake. Lies on bedrock 9700 feet above sea level on the Beartooth Plateau a mile by jeep trail above (north of) Long Lake. It is about 8 acres, deep, has a few scrubby old limber pine around it and is fished a fair amount for 8 to 14 inch cutthroat trout. Used to have albino but they died out. Cutts were stocked in 1964, 1970, and 1976 and good catches can be made, although a bit "spotty" at times.

Summerville Lake. A deep (50 feet), 43 acre lake at 9560 feet elevation in high alpine meadows with a rocky cliff a short way back from the northwest side — one of the most scenic lakes on the Beartooth Plateau with some beautiful 20 foot falls at the outlet. To get there (and few do) take a game trail north from the northeast corner of Green Lake (don't follow up the inlet at the northeast corner) 1 mile to the shore. It is excellent fishing for 6 to 10 inch brook trout.

Thiel (or Tiel) Creek. A small farmland stream flowing northeastward to East Red Lodge Creek 2¼ miles above Castagne. The lower reaches are mostly dewatered for irrigation but there are a couple of miles above that are fished by kids for pan-size brook trout.

Thiel (or Tiel) Lake. Is named after an old-time forester who fished these waters when there were no trails. It lies mostly in timber but has some good meadows along the north shore, is seldom fished or even visited but can be reached cross-country 1 mile east from Granite Lake or ¼ mile west of the Beartooth-Green Lake trail ⅓ of a mile on the Montana side of the Wyoming line. Once there you will find it is about 18 acres in size and excellent pan-fishing for 6 to 8 inch brookies.

Timberline Lake. Is right at timberline (9660 feet above sea level, 31 acres, 85 feet deep, and ½ mile above Gertrude Lake by trail. There is considerable scrub timber (and talus) on the north side, and some open grass on the south but there are no good camping spots here. It is good fishing for 7 to 8 inch brook trout. You can do better on a windy day if you'll hike a couple of hundred yards southwest up over a 40 foot moraine to a small (2 acre) pothole full of 10 to 12 inchers that really go for a dry fly.

Triangle Lake. Take the West Fork Rock Creek trail about 7 miles above the end of the road to an unnamed drainage coming in from the west 2 miles above Quinnebaugh Meadows. Then strike out west for sort of an up and down climb a mile to Triangle which is in barren alpine country maybe an eighth of a mile north of Ship Lake at 10,440 feet above sea level. It is about 6 acres, 35 feet deep, and in earlier days used to be slow fishing for good-size brook trout. However, it was planted with cutthroat in 1971, 1977, and 1979, and is excellent now for anything up to 14 inches.

Unnamed Lake ½ Mile North of Russell Lake. Take the Russell Creek trail a half mile north from Russell Lake, and then hike an eighth mile west through scrub timber to this 4 acre lake in a little barren cirque. It was planted with cutthroat in 1967 and is good fishing now although seldom bothered. The fish are apparently reproducing okay.

BEARTOOTH PLATEAU
Courtesy USFS

ROCK CREEK
Courtesy USSCS

Unnamed Lakes (8) Above Bald Knob Lake.
Follow the Bald Knob inlet ¾ of a mile by trail to a shallow, 5 acre lake in open, grassy, alpine meadows 9700 feet above the ocean. Few if any ever fish it, but it's full of 6 to 8 inch brook trout. If you continue on up the inlet (no trail now — it bears off to your right to Fossil Lake) for another ½ mile, you will reach an irregularly-shaped deep, 30 acre lake that is crawling with skinny 6 to 12 inch brook trout. There are 6 other unnamed lakes in the vicinity, but all are barren.

Unnamed Lake East of Russell Lake.
Take the trail due east up the drainage (be sure to stick to the south fork) from the north end of Russell Lake for 1 mile to this 5 acre lake in a big alpine meadow just above timberline (elevation 9325 feet). It is neither fished nor known by many folks but is good for 8 to 10 inch brook trout. Being a very pretty little lake makes an added reward.

Unnamed Lake Midway Between Flatrock and Martin Lakes.
Reached cross-country about a mile north or south from Martin or Flatrock lakes as the mood strikes you. It's about 25 acres, in barren rocky country, and was planted with cutthroat in 1968. They're nice size running 8 to 14 inches. Occasionally a nicer one (to about 2 pounds) is taken. Report has it that fish here are relatively hard to catch.

Unnamed Lakes North and Northwest of Glacier Lake.
The lowermost of these three lakes almost attaches to Glacier Lake. The upper two are a half mile and 500 feet above. They range from 5 to 15 acres, were planted with cutthroat in the 1970's and provide fair-to-middling good fishing for those who find them. If you like stark glacial scenery it's terrific here.

Unnamed Lake Southwest of Timberline Lake.
See Timberline Lake.

Upper Aero Lake.
At 292 acres and 195 feet deep at its maximum, in a huge alpine glaciated cirque at 10,140 feet elevation below Glacier Peak a mile north-northeast up the drainage cross-country from Lower Aero, this lake is a so-called "trophy" fishery. Cutthroat trout caught here will run from a foot to about 18 inches (a few) and are fished for more than somewhat with a fair number taken. They were planted in 1969 and 1976 by the many thousands as 2 inchers.

Vernon Lake.
Moderately popular, in dense timber ¾ of a mile by pack trail south from Lillis Lake. It is larger than Lillis (8 acres) and deeper, but also has lots of lilies that rim the shore for 30 feet or so out. The fishing is good in early season before the lilies choke it up for 10 to 14 inch brook trout, and some small cutts.

Wall Lake.
A deep, 14 acre Beartooth Plateau lake at 9900 feet above sea level, reached by following up the inlet to Martin Lake ½ mile to the east. It is fairly often visited and good fishing for camp-fare brook trout.

Wapiti Lake.
See Hellroaring Lakes.

Washtub Lake.
See Little Lake.

West Fork Rock Creek.
The municipal water supply for Red Lodge, only the lower 6 miles are open to fishing. The West Fork flows down a broad timbered canyon, is followed by a good road all along the lower (open) reaches and is fished quite a bit by tourists as well as local folks for good catches of 8 to 10 inch rainbow, brook and brown trout. The MDFWP just recently planted cutthroat trout.

West Red Lodge Creek.
A small stream in brushy, "parky" country above. About 3 miles of the middle and upper reaches are moderately popular, fair fishing for 8 to 9 inch brook and a few brown trout to 16 inches. It's accessible by county and USFS roads 15 miles or so west from Red Lodge.

Widewater Lake.
Is reached by the Crazy Lakes trail ¼ of a mile above Big Moose Lake ½ mile below Fox Lake, 6½ miles up from the Cooke City Highway 10 miles east from town. Widewater lies in dense timber (the trail follows the west shore), is 110 acres, deep (100 feet), is visited more than somewhat by man and mosquitos, is fair to good fishing for 6 inch to 2 pound rainbow, and a few grayling and brook trout.

Willow Creek.
Heads below the Palisades a few miles west of Red Lodge and flows north for 20 miles to Red Lodge Creek. The lower 5 or 6 miles are badly silted but the middle reaches (accessible here and there by county roads) are good fishing for 6 to 8 inch brook trout. As the name implies, there is lots of willow along its banks.

Wright Lake.
Seven acres, 40 feet deep, 9400 feet above sea level, in mostly alpine meadows but with some scrubby timber on the west end, it's just north and on the other side of the Green Lake-Beartooth trail from Little Falls Lake. An occasional party will fish it on its way through for excellent catches (using the term loosely) of good eating 6 to 8 inch brookies.

Zimmer Lake.
Is about 26 acres, good and deep (55 feet), and lies at 10,000 feet above sea level in a barren cirque just below (south of) Iceberg Peak. It can be reached (and quite a few do) by way of a 5 mile hike up the Broadwater River-Zimmer Creek trail north from Broadwater Lake — or, you can jeep almost to Long Lake, then take the Lady of the Lake trail east for ½ mile to a large meadow on your left hand (north) side, at which point you bear off to the north by trail and in about 1 mile you'll come in on the Broadwater-Zimmer Creek trail 2½ miles below the lake. The fishing is good for cutthroat planted in 1976. These few thousand 2 inch fry are now 10 to 16 fiesty inches long.

Pack It In — Pack It Out

Keep Your Wilderness Clean

ROCK CREEK LAKE No. 2
Courtesy USFS

THE DEARBORN
Courtesy Bill Browning

Dearborn River

The headwaters of this river originate near Scapegoat Mountain on the Continental Divide. The river flows southeasterly for nearly 61 miles before emptying into the Missouri River about 45 miles southwest of Great Falls. The mountainous portion of the river above the Diamond Bar X Guest Ranch is accessible only by foot. Here the crystal clear water is fair fishing for rainbow and cutthroat trout that weigh up to about a pound. Below the Diamond Bar X the river is heavily dewatered for irrigation and fishing is spotty for 6 to 12 inch rainbow and brook trout until it enters a mountain canyon below Highway 287 north of the town of Wolf Creek. Here, the last 15 miles of river twists and turns, with deep pools and a few boulder strewn rapids providing homes for 2 to 5 pound brown trout and fair numbers of rainbows up to 3 pounds. This portion of the river is only accessible by floating, however, by mid-summer river flow drops to unfloatable levels.

Al Wipperman

Dearborn River Drainage

Bean Lake. This excellent fishing lake has neither inlet or outlet and is becoming eutrophied. Its future is problematical. To get there you drive good county roads through rolling foothills about 15 miles so. from Augusta a mile north of the Dearborn River midway between the Diamond Bar X and Mosher ranches. Bean's gravel and mud bottom is roughly saucer shaped; mostly about 20 feet deep with fairly steep dropoffs below its partly willow-fringed shores. It's fed by some springs in the southwest end and by runoff. A very nice State Fish Wildlife and Parks campground is heavily used by mostly pleased and successful fishermen. It is planted every spring with rainbow trout that grow a sensational 10 to 12 inches in length by late fall, providing the bulk of the catch the following summer. Trout caught average about 13 inches long with the chance of a 3 pounder or so adding to the thrill and excitement of fishing Bean Lake.

Falls Creek. Is named for the picturesque 75 foot falls ½ mile up from its mouth on the Dearborn River at the Diamond Bar X Ranch 3 miles upstream on the Dearborn road from the Bean Lake turnoff. The lower reaches (below the falls) and the fast, cold water above for about 3 miles to the junction of the East and West forks and a short way on up each of them are poor to fair fishing for 6 to 8 inch brook and an occasional rainbow trout. There is a trail all the way up the creek, horses are available at the ranch and the scenic beauty of this timber and park country is well worth the ride even if you don't care to fish.

YOUNG RED FOX
Courtesy USFS

A STUDY IN CONCENTRATION
Courtesy Montana Fish, Wildlife and Parks

Flat Creek. Heads in open grazing land 10 miles south of Augusta and meanders east and south for maybe 25 airline miles (about twice that counting all the crooks and turns) through grassy meadow and hayland to the Dearborn River about 5 miles east of the State 287 bridge over the river 45 miles north from Helena (or 25 miles south from Augusta). It's a small stream, mostly only 5 to 10 feet wide but fairly slow with undercut banks and lots of nice holes and some beaver ponds. It sustains only a slight to moderate amount of fishing pressure but (although there are lots of rough fish) it generally produces good catches of 10 to 12 inch (a few to 2 or 3 pounds) rainbow, 6 to 12 inch brook and nice-size brown trout (up to 5 or 6 pounds). Although crossed here and there by state and county roads, access is mostly across private, posted farmland.

Middle Fork Dearborn River. This is a brushy stream flowing northeastward from Rogers Pass on the Continental Divide for 12 airline miles to the Dearborn River about 35 miles southwest from Great Falls — and is more or less paralleled all the way by Montana 20. The upper reaches are in a timbered canyon but the lower 4 miles (all of the fishable water) are in open grazing land and occasional hay meadows. This section is mostly 8 to 12 feet wide, fairly slow with undercut banks and lots of nice holes. It's moderately popular (with permission only) and fair fishing too — for 6 to 12 inch rainbow, brook and a very few cutthroat trout.

South Fork Dearborn River. Heads on the Continental Divide below Rogers Pass and flows northeastward for 12 airline miles (past Montana secondary road 434) to the Dearborn River about 4 miles downstream from the Montana 20 bridge 35 miles or so southwest from Great Falls. The upper 9 miles (above Montana 434) are followed all along by a gravel road; the lower 3 miles (below Montana 434) are accessible by a private "hay meadow" trail. The upper reaches are in beautiful coniferous country, the middle and lower reaches are lined with quaking aspen and cottonwood. A moderately popular stream, the South Fork is pretty good fishing for 8 to 10 inchers — for about the first 9 miles up from the mouth. It is easily wadeable (is mostly only 8 to 12 feet wide) with lots of nice holes, meanders and beaver ponds the entire length. Added attractions are Rittel's Blacktail Ranch about 4 miles upstream from Montana 434, which has an interesting Indian artifact museum, tourist accommodations and an annual muzzle-loading rifle meet and, near the mouth of the stream, an occasional rattlesnake to keep you company.

Whitetail Creek. A small, easily wadeable, muchly beaver dammed and therefore fairly slow stream that heads on the Continental Divide and flows eastward down a wide canyon through timber and park country (but with lots of aspen along the banks) to the Dearborn River about 7 miles above the end of the road, 9 miles above the Diamond Bar X ranch. Only the lower mile is (very seldom) fished for fair catches of 6 to 12 inch rainbow. It's followed alongside by a good USFS pack trail.

PUT YOUR FIRE DEAD OUT!

Courtesy Danny On

SPANISH PEAKS PRIMITIVE AREA
Courtesy USFS

Gallatin River

The Gallatin River is part of southwestern Montana's rich resource in "blue ribbon" wild trout streams, overshadowed by its more famous neighbors, the Madison and Yellowstone Rivers. But the Gallatin River is an excellent wild trout stream, with the first 67 miles in one of the most beautiful canyons in the West. Gallatin anglers commonly catch rainbow and brown trout between 10-16 inches, with good possibilities of catching even larger trout, 2-5 pounds. Occasionally a very large brown trout over 8 lbs. is taken.

The Gallatin River originates in Yellowstone National Park as an outflow of Gallatin Lake. Upon leaving Gallatin Lake, it flows approximately 115 miles in a northerly direction where it joins the Madison and Jefferson Rivers forming the Missouri River. Although the Gallatin originates in the Park, it is unlike the Madison and Yellowstone Rivers in that it passes through no major thermal areas which would warm and add additional nutrients to its waters. The Gallatin River can be divided into four major reaches depicting differences in stream channel morphology, water velocity, scenery and fish populations.

The upper 45 miles of the Gallatin from its source to the mouth of the West Fork (Big Sky) has the poorest wild trout fishery. It is a typical low productivity high mountain stream in which water temperatures seldom exceed 60°F. Also, the channel is wide and shallow with most of the river being a long riffle. These are characteristics of wild trout streams where fish are small with slow growth rates, numbers are low, and the primary trout species are rainbow or cutthroat. The average size caught in this reach are rainbow between 7-12 inches, although an occasional rare brown trout may reach 2-4 pounds. This reach is excellent for fly fishing because of the open channel and the presence of rainbow.

The next reach of river (37 miles) lies between the mouth of the West Fork and Shedd's Bridge near Bozeman. This is the most productive and scenic section of the Gallatin River. The upper 22 miles flows through scenic Gallatin Canyon and the remaining 15 through the fertile Gallatin Valley. The Gallatin Canyon is relatively narrow, forested with lodgepole pine and Douglas fir. The conifer forest often reaches to the streambank providing a pleasant atmosphere in which to fish. Many cold mountain streams feed the river in this canyon adding to its atmosphere. Big game animals such as elk, deer, moose and bighorn sheep use the immediate area and during certain times of the year are visible to the angler. The lower fifteen miles flow through the beautiful Gallatin Valley where streambank vegetation is primarily cottonwood and willow. The channel becomes more braided with the heavily brushed banks providing more brown trout habitat than found in the faster pool-riffle, boulder-strewn canyon section. Rainbow trout are the predominant species, ranging in size from 8-16 inches. Brown trout, more common in the lower fifteen miles, range up to five pounds. Since this portion of the Gallatin River has special angling regulations, current regulations should be examined before fishing.

The third reach lies between Shedd's Bridge and the mouth of the East Gallatin River, the largest tributary to the Gallatin River. The entire reach lies within the Gallatin Valley and historically had the best trout population on the Gallatin. But due to dewatering from irrigation, extensive channel manipulation, and sediment loads from the upper river drainage, trout populations are very low with rainbow numbers almost non-existent. During most years, 80-90% of the potential stream flow has been removed in some sections allowing little water to maintain a trout fisheries. Sediment and past instream activities have left the channel unstable causing many pools to become filled with gravel and banks left raw and eroding. Brown trout is the predominant trout species comprising over 90% of the numbers. Whitefish is also quite common in this reach. Even with these severe habitat problems, brown trout may be caught up to 2 or 3 pounds. An occasional rainbow trout may also appear in the creel.

The main Gallatin River is formed by the confluence of the East Gallatin and Gallatin Rivers (locally known as the West Gallatin). The two streams converge immediately upstream from Nixon Bridge, north of Manhattan. The Gallatin then flows west for about half of its twelve mile length, and then northwest for the remaining distance to the Missouri River.

The Gallatin River's character in this reach resembles that of the East Gallatin, on a large scale. The trout population is divided approximately 60-40, browns to rainbows. North of the river are dry land hills used almost exclusively for grazing land. The land bordering the river on the south is mainly irrigated hay land. The stream is usually low in late summer and runs very high each spring. It is this force, coupled with the limestone cliffs on the north bank, that has created the unique, very deep pools.

The fishing opportunity is exceptional in this reach of the river. Public access is good with points at Nixon Bridge, county access west of Logan, and a boat ramp at the Headwaters State Park (on Missouri River just below the Gallatin's junction). Wade fishing or float fishing are both productive here. One word of caution to floaters: downstream from Logan there has been a main channel obstruction (cottonwood) that completely blocks the stream. This requires a portage.

Use of this fisheries resource has been very low compared to other nearby streams, but recently shows signs of changing.

There are abundant rainbow in this excellent fishery, although few exceed 16 inches. Rarely, a rainbow will be taken in the 6 to 7 pound range. Brown trout are quite another story; catches usually include 15 to 17 inch specimens, and much larger ones are not uncommon. Browns in the 8 pound range have been taken and others much larger have been observed. As a bonus, there is a substantial whitefish population characterized by fish of excellent size. During April, numbers of rainbow move up the Gallatin, probably from the Upper Missouri, and October marks similar movements of brown trout.

The quality of fishing is quite variable. The best times to fish are, 1) early spring to runoff, when water is adequately clear; 2) early summer after run-off, while the water is cool and there is sufficient depth to assure floating; and 3) fall, when the water has cooled. The Gallatin in this area is open to fishing year-round.

Actual methods for successful angling are the same as in other area rivers. For bait fishermen, deep pools offer special interest and potential. Brushy banks and debris piles intrigue lure and fly fishermen. The Gallatin has numerous seasonal hatches where such dry flies as the elk hair caddis, humpy, Adams and Wolff's can be used. For larger fish, patterns such as the spruce fly, muddler minnow, bitch-creek and wooly worm will be productive.

Richard Vincent & Bruce Rehwinkel

MIRROR LAKE
Courtesy USFS

Gallatin River Drainage

Arden Lake. Is the southernmost of the Palace Lakes (the others are all barren) in a high rocky cirque, 9420 feet above sea level on the south side of Hyalite Ridge about 4 miles due south of the Middle Creek (Hyalite) reservoir. The best way in is up the West Fork Hayalite Creek trail about a mile beyond the end of the road, and then take off cross-country to the west up an unnamed rivulet over Twin Falls for about 1½ miles to Middle Palace Lake and then turn due south for another half mile to Arden Lake which — you can believe it — is very seldom fished. It's about 4 acres, deep enough to keep from freezing out and spotty fishing for cutthroat, if they haven't died off.

Asbestos Lake. Cross the West Gallatin at High's Bridge (13½ miles south of the Squaw Creek Ranger Station on U.S. 191), hike north up the river for about a mile to the mouth of (barren) Asbestos Creek and then 2½ miles up the creek (keep to the right, north fork) to the lake. It's only a couple of acres and no more than 15 feet deep with shallow dropoffs. It's very clear and may be barren — no fish seen in 1978.

Bacon Rind Creek. A very small stream flowing east from Cone Peak for about 7 miles to the West Gallatin River, 4 miles above Specimen Creek. The lower 1½ miles meander through Yellowstone Park meadowland, the upper reaches are mostly in an open canyon that is slicked off clean (willows, brush and all) by browsing elk and moose. There is about a mile of fair 7 to 9 inch rainbow, and some cutthroat fishing outside the Park. It is accessible by trail.

Baker Creek. A small "irrigation pickup" farmland stream on the south side of the West Gallatin River between Belgrade and Manhattan; accessible all along (for about 10 miles) by county and private roads. It's fished a moderate amount by mostly local folks for good catches of 6 to 16 inch brown and rainbow trout. A few nice browns to 4 pounds have been reported.

Bear Creek. The outlet of Bear, Crystal and Pine Lake, Bear Creek flows northward for about 6 miles through a timbered canyon above, and 5 miles across open ranchland below to Rocky Creek. It's crossed near the mouth by U.S. 10, three and a half miles east of Bozeman and is followed by a gravel road below and a poor jeep trail above for 10 miles to the lakes. There are quite a few summer homes along the lower reaches. The upper 4 miles sustain moderate fishing pressure for poor catches of 6 to 10 inch rainbow trout.

BREAKING CAMP AT JEROME LAKE
Courtesy USFS

BRIDGER BOWL
Courtesy Max Hunke

Bear Lakes. Two, 3 acre lakes ⅛ of a mile apart in scattered timber and grazing land at the head of the steep, timbered, Bear Creek canyon reached by 10 miles of real rough excuse for a logging road southeast from Mount Ellis on U.S. 10. They're fished quite a lot for such small lakes and are fairly good for 8 to 12 inch cutthroat planted in 1972, 1976 and 1979.

Beaver Creek. A fast, clear, mountain stream crossed at the mouth (at Ophir) by State 191 and followed upstream by road for about 2½ miles — and then by a USFS trail for 3½ miles to headwaters. The lower reaches are in open ranchland but the upper reaches flow down a timbered valley and are fair fishing for 4 to 7 inch rainbow trout. The lower are a little better but posted.

Beaver Creek (or Secret) Lakes. Two little lakes a hundred yards or so apart in dense timber across the creek from the trail 2 miles up Beaver Creek from the end of the road. The upper lake is evidently too shallow to support fish. The lower lake is about 100 yards long by 50 yards wide, quite deep with steep dropoffs and was planted years ago with rainbow trout that are now mostly hybridized with the native cutthroat. The result is some fair fishing for 8 to 12 inchers for the few people who know how to find it.

Beehive Lake. A deep (over 70 feet in spots) 3 acre lake with steep dropoffs all around, in grassy alpine country 9440 feet above sea level and reached by an unmarked trail a mile above (east of) Upper Spanish Creek Lake. It's good for cutthroat planted in 1969 and 1976 that are 8 to 15 inches and it gets hit hard.

Benhart Creek. Heads in some springs about 3 miles above (southeast of) the East Gallatin River about 3 miles north and a mile west of Belgrade. Is almost identical to Thompson Creek in terms of its fishing potential and a very popular fly fishing stream with local anglers.

Big Bear Lake. You can get to this 2 acre pond via logging roads about 5 miles from the end of the Little Bear Creek road, in timber all around and only 10 or 12 feet deep. It was even shallower but the loggers shoved some fill across the outlet and raised the water level a couple of feet. On this basis (and because they were lost) some State Fish and Game personnel dumped in a bunch of cutthroat — along in the summer of '65. If you can find your way in, you might have some fun since it was stocked again in 1979.

Big Brother Lake. A high 5 acre lake in an old burn 8340 feet above sea level at the head of Camp Creek reached by 5 miles of USFS trail from the new North Fork Spanish Creek road. It is very shallow, mostly less than 5 feet deep except in the southwest corner, but is fed by a year-around inlet and so does not freeze out. It's seldom fished but fair for snakey 8 to 10 inch cutthroat and rainbow trout.

85

Bluff Lake.   Take the Taylor Fork road a couple of miles above the Wapiti Creek road, then the Eldridge trail 3½ miles south by (within a few hundred yards west of) this 1½ acre, 21 foot maximum depth lake in partly open — partly timbered mountains. It was planted with cutthroat in 1968 and 1972 and is good fishing now, although not many folks will hike in to try it.

Bozeman (or Sourdough) Creek.

Flows from Mystic Lake for 7 miles down a timbered canyon above, and for another 7 miles across open range and farmland below to the East Gallatin River at Bozeman. From its mouth for 4 miles upstream to the mouth of Limestone Creek it's known as Bozeman Creek; the upper reaches are called Sourdough Creek. The lower 10 miles are paralleled by roads, the upper reaches by trail. The upper 10 miles support a good population of small brook and rainbow trout. The stream is part of the Bozeman City water supply and is closed to fishing — for just a 1000 foot section that is clearly signed POSTED — above the settling basins 5 miles south of town. The lower reaches (right in town) are heavily fished by kids for 8 to 9 inch brook and a few rainbow trout.

Bridger Creek.   About 15 miles of good fishing here for mostly 8 to 12 inch rainbow, plus a few brown, fewer brook, and cutthroat trout. This small stream flows west to the East Gallatin River at Bozeman and is accessible all along by county roads. It is heavily fished (especially by kids), although much of it is on posted farm and ranch land. The Bozeman Fish Hatchery is located about 3 miles above the mouth. Once in a blue moon this creek gives up a lunker.

Buck Creek.   Heads on Flattop Mountain and flows east for 10 miles to the West Gallatin River a couple of miles above Rainbow Ranch. It's crossed at the mouth by State 191 but the lower 3½ miles are in a real steep canyon and there is no road or trail. There are about 2 miles of open meadows above the canyon and here the slow, meandering stream is good fishing for 8 to 10 inch rainbow and a few cutthroat. The best way in is by the Cinnamon Creek trail and "over the hill" into Buck Creek Basin — a total distance of about 6 miles from U.S. 191 at Almart Mountain Lodge.

Buffalo Horn Creek.   The outlet of Ramshorn and Buffalo Horn Lakes, it is followed upstream by road for 2 miles above its mouth on the west Gallatin River at the 320 Ranch, and then by a USFS pack trail for 5 miles to headwaters. The upper reaches are mostly in timbered mountains but there are some meadows a couple of miles above the end of the road. The stream is poor fishing for 4 to 8 inch rainbow trout. It's seldom bothered.

Buffalo Horn (or Fish) Lakes.   In mountainous timbered country, reached by trail 3½ miles from the end of the good dirt road 1½ miles up Buffalo Horn Creek from the 320 Ranch on State 191 and the West Gallatin River. The upper lakes never supported fish, although they were once planted. The lower lake (which is 1½ acres and mostly less than 10 feet deep with a maximum of 16 feet) was good cutthroat fishing until 1955 — marginal since and seldom bothered.

Cache Creek.   A small stream that heads on the east side of Shedhorn Mountain and flows east for about 14 miles to junction with Lightning Creek to form the Taylor Fork of the West Gallatin River. The lower 1½ miles flow through a steep canyon above which are some nice meadowland reaches and beaver ponds. A road takes you to the head of them and they are fished for fair catches of 6 to 12 inch cutthroat trout.

Camp Creek.   Flows north for 25 miles to the West Gallatin River about 1½ miles northeast of Manhattan. The upper reaches are quite small but the lower 7 or 8 miles, within the Gallatin Valley, are larger due to pickup flow from irrigation seepage. The lower reaches are all on private farmland, are quite brushy, accessible here and there by county roads and good fishing for 6 to 12 inch brown and rainbow, plus now and then a brook trout. It's fished a fair amount by mostly local folks, posted heavily, and requires permission.

Cascade Lakes.   Take off to the north from the Deer Creek trail (about ½ mile below the lake) out around Table Mountain to the east and north for maybe a mile and there is (a rugged half mile to the north below nearly vertical 600 foot cliffs) the middle and largest (3 acres) of three lakes (the other two are barren). It's in alpine timber but with open marshy shores and is mostly shoal but there are a few spots as much as 16 feet deep, or deep enough to keep from freezing out at this high (elevation 9180 feet) altitude. It was stocked with rainbow years ago, is seldom visited now, is an unknown, and presently a mystery.

Courtesy Montana, Fish Wildlife and Parks

Chilled Lakes. Upper (barren) and Lower, in an alpine meadow below a rock face to the northeast and reached 440 yards up the outlet where it crosses the trail just below (southwest of) Thompson Lake. It's about 3 acres, deep with steep dropoffs, and very good fishing for 8 to 14 inch cutthroat planted in 1970 and 1973. Most folks don't know it's there and hike right on by.

Chiquita Lake. Is very seldom visited, no trail; Chiquita lies below steep talus slopes right on the edge of the timber ½ mile west from Marcheta. It's about 4 acres, was planted years ago and is reported to (sometimes) be fair-to-good fishing for 8 to 10 inch cutthroat trout.

Crystal Lake. A three-quarter acre pond in scattered timber and open grazing land ⅛ mile south above the upper Bear Lake in a wide swale at the head of Bear Creek. It's deep enough to keep from freezing out, has been planted with cutthroat and is fished a fair amount for 8 to 12 inchers.

Deer Lake. A 7 acre lake, fairly deep with steep dropoffs on the north and west sides. It lies in a glacial cirque at about 9300 feet, is in timber all around except the west side where there are talus slopes to the water. To get there take the Deer Creek trail 5 miles from the West Gallatin River and State 191, twenty miles south from Gallatin Gateway. This is a real temperamental (but sometimes excellent) grayling lake that is fished a moderate amount for 8 to 14 inchers.

Diamond Lake. Lies at 8900 feet above sea level in a glacial cirque with steep rocky slopes all around. It's 9 acres in size, over 80 feet deep with steep dropoffs and some grass and scattered trees around the shore. To get there you drive up the South Fork Spanish Creek to the Spanish Creek Ranger Station, then take a USFS trail 5 miles south on up the South Fork and finally a "way" trail for 2 miles east up the unnamed outlet to within 500 yards of the lake. Note: this last stretch is all on "shanks' mare." It's too steep and rocky for horses. Once there you'll not find many people but it's slow fishing for rainbow that'll go up to 7 pounds, really hard to catch.

Dry Creek. A small stream flowing south for 15 miles through hilly juniper and sagebrush country to East Gallatin River 6 miles north of Belgrade. It's more or less followed all along by a county road but is all on private (mostly posted) farmland. The lower ¾ of a mile is pretty well dewatered for irrigation. The next 8 miles above are poor fishing for 7 to 9 inch brook, some rainbow, and few brown trout — rattlers aplenty, though.

Dudley Creek. A small, rapid, clear stream flowing from (barren) Dudley Lake down a timbered draw to State Highway 191 and the Gallatin River about ½ mile below the confluence of the West Fork Gallatin River. Not many people fish it but the lower couple of miles are fair in the summer for small brook trout.

East Fork Hyalite Creek. The small, fast, hard to fish outlet of Heather and Emerald Lakes flows down a rocky, timbered canyon to the upper (southeast) end of Hyalite Reservoir and is followed all the way by a good USFS trail. It's seldom fished and no better than poor-to-fair for small cutthroat, brook and grayling. Watch the regulations here, since this is a spawning stream — it opens later.

87

East Gallatin River. The East Gallatin River drains portions of the Bridger and Gallatin mountain ranges. Its technical beginning is just north of the City of Bozeman with the junction of Rocky and Sourdough Creeks. From this point, it flows approximately 37 miles in a westerly direction joining the main Gallatin River near Manhattan. It has four major mountain stream tributaries, plus numerous large and small spring creek tributaries, and flows within the northern portion of the fertile Gallatin Valley. It is a low gradient, meandering river rather than a high velocity stream such as the main Gallatin, Madison or Yellowstone. Since it flows through primarily agricultural land, over 95% is private with little public access.

The East Gallatin River is potentially a highly productive trout stream due to nutrient enrichment from fertile valley soils plus numerous brushy bank areas favorable for good trout harvest. Good wild trout populations exist in several sections of the river with the upper thirteen miles showing the highest trout numbers. This is primarily due to more stable stream banks with heavy brush cover and a smaller sediment problem. In this reach rainbow trout predominate, comprising 95% of the trout numbers with brown and brook trout making up the remainder. Few whitefish live in this reach. Rainbows range in size from 8-18 inches, with 1 to 2 pounders not uncommon. As one moves downstream, the channel becomes more unstable, brushy banks decrease and the sediment load is high, making the stream turbid much of the year. Brown trout become the dominant trout species here with total trout numbers diminishing. Brown trout range in size from 10-16 inches with an occasional 2-4 pounder being caught. Fly fishing can be excellent during clear water periods with bait fishing peaking during the spring runoff period (March-May).

Emerald Lake. A 25 acre, fairly shallow lake in a high open basin 7750 feet above sea level half a mile below Heather Lake at the head of the East Fork Hyalite Creek. It is reached by a good USFS trail 4½ miles up the East Fork from the end of the road and is heavily fished — very good at times for 9 to 11 inch grayling and small cutthroat.

Falls Creek Lake (Upper). Two and a half acres, in open alpine country a mile northeast by trail from Lake Solitude, 12 devious miles from Ennis. It was stocked with cutthroat in 1953 and still has a good population of 6 to 8 inchers.

Fish and Game Headquarters Ponds. Three, out in the open a few hundred yards north of the Bozeman office building of the Montana Fish, Wildlife and Parks Department, all about 25 feet deep and all good fishing. The East Pond has a spring, the Middle and West fed by seepage. All three are self sustaining perch fisheries, and are stocked regularly with rainbow and cutthroat that will run up to a husky 5 pounds. Eastern brooks in all three ponds will average 8 to 14 inches. They're also good ice fishing. Surprisingly they are not overrun with people.

Fish Lakes. See Buffalo Horn Lakes.

Flanders Lake. Lies in a small cirque with some scrubby timber at 8600 feet elevation near the head of Flanders Creek, reached by a poor unmarked trail 2½ miles from the East Fork Hyalite Creek road. It's been planted with rainbow, should be good fishing and is virtually unknown. The last report was in 1975 — no fish seen.

Godfrey Canyon Creek. A small stream flowing north to Baker Creek 5 miles southeast of Manhattan in the West Gallatin valley. The lower 3 miles run through a shallow, dirt-walled so-called canyon. All of it, (about 8 miles), is in farmland (dairy) country, is accessible here and there by county and private roads, not fished much, supports a poor population of 6 to 8 inch brook and a few 8 to 10 inch brown trout, and is grossly polluted.

Golden Trout Lakes. From State 191 in the West Gallatin Canyon 2 miles above the Karst Ranch, take the Portal Creek road for about 2½ miles east and then a steep USFS foot trail for another 4 miles to the (3) Golden Trout Lakes at about 9100 feet elevation above sea level on the northern timbered slopes of Eaglehead Mountain. The first one you come to on the trail has a nice open shore all around, is fished a fair amount and is good for skinny 8 to 10 inch goldens. The other two lakes, about ⅛ of a mile to the east and west, are barren.

Grayling Lake. From State 191 about a mile south of the Squaw Creek Ranger Station, take the Hellroaring Creek trail 4½ miles upstream, then the North Fork trail for about 1½ miles to the outlet stream of Grayling Lake where you strike out west aross country for a steep 1¼ mile climb to the seldom visited shore at 8550 feet elevation above sea level. The lake is about 4 acres, fairly shallow, in timber at the lower end, and excellent fishing for skinny 6 to 10 inch grayling that will hit anything.

GALLATIN RIVER
Jim Derleth photo

JUMP SHOOTING
Courtesy H.L. Hasler

Heather Lake.
A deep, 20 acre lake in a high (elevation 9000 feet above sea level) open basin reached by a fishermen's trail ½ mile above Emerald Lake at the head of the East Fork Hyalite Creek. The fishing is good here for cutthroat up to a foot long and small grayling. People are not uncommon here.

Hellroaring Creek.
A small stream, the outlet of (barren) Hellroaring Lake, Grayling and Thompson Lakes (on the North Fork). It is crossed at the mouth by State 191 a mile above the Squaw Creek Ranger Station and is followed upstream by a USFS trail for 10 miles along its steep-walled, timbered canyon to headwaters. The upper reaches are torrential and cold but 8 miles are fair fishing for 8 to 14 inch rainbow trout.

Hermit Lake.
Elevation 8560 feet above sea level, 2½ acres and all under 8 feet deep, in rocky timbered country about 500 yards north and 350 feet below Lake Solitude. It was planted with cutthroat in 1953 and although very seldom fished it is reported fair for little ones.

Hidden Lakes.
Eight in all, little alpine lakes at about 8800 feet above sea level in the headwaters of Hidden Creek (too small for fish). To get there take State 191 eleven miles south up the West Gallatin River from the Squaw Creek Ranger Station, then the Portal Creek Forest Service road 2 miles up to your left (east), and finally a foot trail 2½ miles (and 1700 feet up) south to the lakes. First you will come to a barren lake on your right. Skip it. Almost directly to your left (south) you will see Epsilon and Delta, close together and about 5 acres each. Most folks camp and do their fishing here, for fair catches of 4 to 7 inch goldens (if you can call any number of 4 to 7 inchers a fair catch). Now proceed on up the trail 230 yards west to Beta, which is 12 acres, drops off on a rock shelf for about 25 feet out from shore and then gets deep. It's pretty slow fishing, but they're larger (in the 16 to 18 inch class). A hundred yards above (south of) Beta is Alpha, which is 21 acres, over 100 feet deep and slow fishing for big goldens — recorded to 5 pounds. A hundred and fifty yards below (north of) Beta is Gamma, about 5 acres and perhaps the best of the lot for 8 to 10 inch goldens. The two lakes below are barren. The rest were planted in 1959.

Hyalite (or Middle) Creek.
Flows from Middle Creek Dam (Hyalite Reservoir) for about 7 miles down a narrow timbered canyon, and then for 16 miles out across a broad alluvial fan through farming country to the West Branch East Gallatin River 2½ miles east of Belgrade. The upper (canyon) reaches are known as Middle Creek and are followed all along by a logging road. The lower reaches are known as Hyalite Creek and are crossed here and there by county roads. It's a clear, rapid stream above and good fishing for rainbow plus quite a few cutthroat, some brook trout and grayling, and a few browns. The murky lower reaches are drawn way down for irrigation, are brushy and hard to fish for only poor-to-fair catches (locally) of brook, rainbow and a few brown trout, excepting the first 4 miles out of the canyon, which are good.

Hyalite Lake.
A cirque lake at the base (north side) of Hyalite Peak at 8900 feet elevation above sea level, reached by a good USFS trail 5½ miles above the end of the West Fork Hyalite Creek road. It's in open alpine country with a little scrub timber around, is about 3 acres and so shallow it sometimes freezes out. It had small cutts and rainbow but may be barren now.

Hyalite Reservoir (or Middle Creek Dam).

Sets up in beautiful timbered mountains with some open shores up Middle (Hyalite) Creek 15 miles south of Bozeman. It's a good sized body of water, about 1¼ miles long by a ¼ mile wide with about 30 feet of water level fluctuation and is reached by a somewhat bumpy road which runs along the northeast side of the reservoir past a USFS campground and a boat ramp. In 1976 MDFWP began stocking long loved McBride cutthroat here and they are now spawning in the tributaries, along with the grayling. The fishing is excellent for 8-14 inch cutthroat and grayling with a few small brookies taken also. The cutts can run to 5 pounds and the grayling to about 2½. Some feeling exists that the State record grayling will come out of here soon. August is generally slow fishing, otherwise, winter included, it's splendid year round. There is a move about to try to fund the plowing of the road in winter. To top it off, the lake is not over used, especially in winter.

Jackson Creek. See Rocky Creek.

Jerome Rock Lakes.

Three — Lower, Middle, and Upper. At 8750 feet to 9000 feet elevation above sea level just east of the crest of the Madison Range in sparsely timbered alpine country at the head of (barren) Falls Creek 1½ miles northwest of Lake Solitude. It can be reached either from the Madison River drainage 2½ miles by logging road and 4 miles by trail up East Hammond Creek, or over the Divide from the Jack Creek campground, or from the Gallatin River side 3 miles by trail up the South Fork Spanish Creek above the end of the road at the Spanish Creek Ranger Station and then 4 steep miles up the Falls Creek trail and another ½ mile on past Second Lower Falls Creek Lake. Lower Jerome is 4 acres, mostly shallow but with a maximum depth of 22 feet, has lots of aquatic vegetation around the shore and is good fishing for 12 to 14 inch cutthroat. Middle Jerome is only 3 acres, is also mostly shallow with a maximum depth of 21 feet, and is fair cutthroat fishing. Upper Jerome is the largest of the three (5 acres), mostly less than 22 feet deep, and fair-to-good fishing for cutthroat trout. They're all fished mostly by tourists — and not much at that. Old timers tell me of a few lunkers taken now and again.

Kelly Canyon Creek.

A very small stream with about 1½ miles of fishable water in willow-bottomed farmland near its mouth at the head of the East Gallatin River 3 miles east of Bozeman. It's seldom bothered but does produce some small rainbow and cutthroat trout.

Lake of the Pines. See Pine Lake.

Lake Solitude.

A very shallow lake (mostly less than 6 feet deep), at about 8900 feet elevation above sea level, 3 acres, bordered by trees on the north side, with steep rocky slopes reaching for ½ mile to the crest of the Madison Range on the south. It's about 500 yards south and 250 feet above Hermit Lake, 1½ miles southeast of Jerome Rock Lakes, and about the same distance northwest of the Spanish Lakes. The shortest way in is by a logging road 2½ miles up East Hammond Creek from the Jack Creek campground (on the Madison drainage), and then a pack trail for about the same distance on up the creek and over the Divide to the lake which is good fishing for 8 to 14 inch cutthroat.

HELLROARING CREEK
Courtesy USFS

90

MOUNTAIN SHEEP
Courtesy USFS

PINTO FISHING
Courtesy Bill Browning

Lava Lake. A clear, deep, 20 acre land in steep timbered mountains, reached by trail 2 miles up Cascade Creek from the West Gallatin River and State 191 about 3½ miles up (south) from the Squaw Creek Ranger Station. It has steep dropoffs below equally steep, rocky banks and is heavily fished but fair for 10 to 12 inch rainbow, plus a few that will go to maybe 4 pounds.

Lightning Creek. A small creek flowing north to Taylor Fork about 9 miles above the mouth (a mile above the end of the road) and is followed by a USFS trail for about a mile upstream through a timbered draw and then for another mile across some open meadows. The meadow reaches are poor fishing for 6 to 10 inch cutthroat and rainbow trout.

Little Hellroaring Creek. A very steep little stream flowing down a narrow timbered canyon for 6 miles from the northeastern end of Indian Ridge to the South Fork Spanish Creek Ranger Station; reached at the mouth by the South Fork road. There are maybe 2 to 3 miles of very poor brook trout fishing here.

Little Wapiti Creek. A small tributary of Wapiti Creek, the lower 2 miles (in the vicinity of the Wapiti Ranger Station) are in open rangeland, are followed by a jeep road and trail and are moderately popular and fair fishing for 6 to 10 inch rainbow — especially in the lower end where there are a few beaver ponds.

Lizard Lakes. Upper Lizard (½ acre and barren) and Lower Lizard — about ½ mile apart and reached by 3 miles of steep USFS pack trail north from the end of the Cache Creek road at the Cache Creek Ranger Station. Lower Lizard is 8860 feet above sea level, 4 acres, 32 feet deep at the maximum and has fairly steep dropoffs and a muddy bottom. It is fair-to-good (although spotty) for 8 to 14 inch cutthroat. There's quite a bit of marshy area around the shores. Dudes use the lake fairly often. It was stocked in 1972, '75, '77 and '80.

Lower Falls Creek Lake. About 4 acres, in a sparsely timbered cirque at 8200 feet above sea level ½ mile north by trail "over the hill" and a short steep climb down from Lower Jerome Rock Lake. It's all under 20 feet deep, was planted with cutthroat years ago, and is fair-to-good fishing now — mostly by dudes.

Marcheta Lake. No trail and very few people know of it but if you happen to be up around Jerome Rock Lake —it's easy to get to. Just take the trail north for ¼ mile to (barren) Second Lower Lizard Lake, then west for ½ mile when it swings due north and you stay with it for another ¼ of a mile — and then strike off west up across reasonably gentle alpine slopes for a few hundred yards and then finally down over steep 300 foot cliffs and talus for a last rough ¼ of a mile to Marcheta — right on the edge of the timber. It's a cirque lake, about 3 acres, was planted with rainbow years ago and is reported to be good fishing for 8 to 13 inchers now.

Meadow Creek. Here is a small stream that has been pretty good fishing in the lower 2 or 3 miles for small rainbow and cutthroat trout, but is very seldom bothered now. It flows north down its willow-bottomed canyon to join Rocky Creek 4 miles west of Bozeman Pass and should you want to try it, it's accessible all along by a good county road — it's posted, however.

Middle Creek. See Hyalite Creek.

Middle Creek Dam. See Hyalite Reservoir.

Mirror Lake. A seldom fished, triangular-shaped 5 acre lake, no more than 20 feet deep aywhere and mostly less, in timber all around but with nice open shores except on the west side where it's steep and rocky, at 8460 feet elevation above the ocean on the northeastern slopes of Blaze Mountain. It's reached by a Forest Service trail 7 steep miles above the end of the South Fork Spanish Creek road at the Ranger Station and is good fishing for 8 to 10 inch rainbow-cutthroat hybrids.

Moon Lake. Three and a half acres, about 500 feet below and ¼ of a mile south of Deer Lake on a timbered shelf (but with open grassy shores). It's moderately popular and good for 10 to 12 inch rainbow.

Mystic Lake. The mile long by eight mile wide city of Bozeman water supply; via the Sourdough (Bozeman) Creek drainage; used to be closed but is now open to fishing. It's in a timbered canyon with an earth-fill dam at the outlet, has about 35 feet of water-level fluctuation, and is reached by an impassable (closed) road up the creek, or by trail 3 miles over the Divide from Bear Lakes. It is good fishing for 8 to 14 inch cutthroat (some bigger) and reportedly, Lake trout up to 6 pounds and brookies 6 to 10 inches.

North Fork Spanish Creek. The outlet of Chiquita Lake, the North Fork flows north for 8 miles down a steep timbered canyon and then for 2½ miles across the (posted — no trespassing) Spanish Creek basin to join the South Fork at the head of the main stream. The lower couple of miles are excellent fishing for skinny 8 to 12 inch brook trout. The upper reaches are followed most of the way by trail and there is some good beaver pond fishing about half way in to the lake.

Palace Lakes. See Arden Lake.

Pass Creek. A small stream followed by a jeep road for a couple of miles down its narrow timbered canyon from headwaters in the Bridger Range, and then out across open hilly farmland for 7 miles to Dry Creek. The lower 3 miles or so are quite brushy, hard to fish and no better than poor-to-fair for small brook trout. It does get fished some though, mostly by local folks.

Pine (or Lake of the Pines) Lake. Take the Squaw Creek road 5½ miles to the Blanchard Sawmill, then a logging road south for ¼ mile up Orchid Gulch, then west "around the hill" for about a mile and finally south for another to the end of it. From here you hike due south for ¾ of a mile down a small draw to the seldom visited lake. It lies in lodgepole and down timber, is about 1½ acres, fairly shallow with lots of weeds and grass around the edges and is excellent fishing for 8 to 12 inch rainbow-cutthroat hybrids and a few to maybe 16 inches or so.

Pioneer Lakes. Take the Garnet Mountain trail 2½ miles southeast (and 1900 feet up) from the mouth of Squaw Creek to these two little lakes on a timbered shelf high above the Gallatin River. The upper one is 2½ acres, a good 30 feet deep in the middle, and is reported to be fair cutthroat water, being stocked in 1976 and 1979. The lower one is only a shallow ½ acre and freezes out.

Porcupine Creek. This one isn't fished much. It's a small stream flowing to the West Gallatin River at Ophir. The lower 3 miles are in fairly open rangeland, are followed by a USFS trail, and are good fishing for 6 to 10 inch rainbow, whitefish and a few browns 10 to 14 inches.

Ramshorn Lake. Elevation 8440 feet above sea level in timbered country just south of Fortress Mountain (west of Ramshorn Peak), 3 acres, bout 20 feet deep with steep dropoffs and a mucky bottom; Ramshorn is reached by a good Forest Service pack trail 4 miles above the end of the Buffalo Horn Creek road and 8 miles from the 320 Ranch on State 191, fifty two miles south from Bozeman. The fishing is good here for 10 to 15 inch cutthroat and gets hit hard.

EAST GALLATIN
Courtesy Phil Farnes, SCS

HYALITE CREEK
Courtesy SCS

Rat Lake.
Take a poor logging road (road closes due to mud slides often) about 3½ miles up Squaw Creek and then a right turn for 2 miles to this real shallow, 18 acre lake. It's in timbered mountains but half of the shore is often meadow, and ⅔ of the lake is covered with aquatic vegetation. Tons of folks give her a whirl. There's good fishing here for rainbow that'll average 10 inches and range up to 7 pounds. Cutts were stocked in 1980.

Ray Creek (or Rey or Rae).
Here's a fooler — a 10 mile long pastureland "pickup" creek that flows to the Gallatin River about 3½ miles northeast of Three Forks, is crossed by U.S. 10 near the mouth and is accessible all along by county roads. It doesn't look like much and is seldom fished, is fair for 10 to 14 inch brown and a few 6 to 8 inch rainbow, but it's private.

Reese Creek.
A real small, open ranchland tributary of Ross Creek (of which the less said the better) in the East Gallatin drainage about 4 miles north by county roads from Belgrade. The lower 3½ miles are reached by a quarter mile hike south across the fields from the paralleling Reese School road and are fished once in a while with good success for 9 to 11 inch brown, rainbow and some brook trout. The stream is heavily posted — no trespassing.

Rocky (or Jackson) Creek.
Junctions with Kelley Creek to form the East Gallatin River about 3 miles east of Bozeman, and is followed upstream by U.S. 10 through Rocky Canyon for 8 miles to the mouth of (barren) Timberline Creek from which point it changes its name to Jackson Creek and is followed by county and logging roads for 5 miles north to headwaters. It's a small stream but good fishing and moderately popular too, for 7 to 10 inch rainbow, cutthroat, brook and a few brown trout — some of which can go to a whopping 5 pounds, although rarely.

Secret Lakes.
See Beaver Creek Lakes.

Slide Lake.
Take the Lightning Creek trail 2¼ miles upstream to the mouth of (barren) Alp Creek and then take off to the southeast through the timber for a couple of hundred yards to this fairly deep, 1 acre lake which lies below a big slide and has a nice little stream running in and out of it. It's not generally known, is not named on many maps (including the USFS), but is fair-to-good fishing for small rainbow trout.

Smith Creek.
Is only a couple of miles long, a small valley-flat stream in the East Gallatin area 5 miles north by good county roads from Belgrade. Several ditches run into it and it's almost always "murky." It's sometimes good in late summer and fall for 6 to 14 inch browns — plus a scattering of rainbow.

Solitude Lake.
See Lake Solitude.

Sourdough Creek.
See Bozeman Creek.

South Cottonwood Creek.

A real clear nice looking stream, the upper reaches are followed by a USFS pack trail for about 5 miles down a narrow timbered canyon; the lower reaches are followed by a county road for about 3 miles out across open pastureland towards the West Gallatin River near Gateway, but it's all taken for irrigation before it gets there. It's fished a moderate amount below and a little above for 6 to 8 inch rainbow. There are a few beaver ponds alond the middle reaches. It's mostly all private.

South Fork Spanish Creek.

The outlet of Summit Lake in the Spanish Peaks, the upper reaches flow for a steep 1½ miles across barren alpine rocky country to Mirror Lake, then for about 7 miles down a narrow grass and timber-bottomed canyon, and finally for another 3 miles above the West Gallatin River. The lower reaches are accessible by a logging road (to the Spanish Peak Ranger Station and campground at the mouth of Little Hellroaring Creek), and the upper reaches are followed all the way by trail. There are quite a few beaver dams below the mouth of the canyon and from here on down it's good fishing for 8 to 10 inch brookies.

South Fork of West Fork Gallatin River.

Is reached at the mouth by the West Fork road and followed upstream by a good USFS road for 3½ miles to Ousel Falls and thence by trail for 4 miles to the Big Springs Ranger Station. The lower reaches (below the falls) are along the edge of open meadowland, are heavily planted and fished for 8 to 12 inch (and some good ones) rainbow. The stream flows through timbered country above the falls. The first 1½ miles are fairly open but the next ½ mile is in a steep canyon and the creek gets pretty small above. These upper reaches are only lightly fished but fair in places for mostly native cutthroat.

Spanish Creek.

A clear, swift, willow-bottomed, wadeable stream followed by a logging road for 2½ miles eastward from its head at the junction of the North and South Forks, to   Gallatin River where it is crossed by State 191 nine miles above Gallatin Gateway. Public access is generally withheld by the Spanish Creek Ranch, but there's excellent summertime fishing here if you can get it — for mostly 8 to 10 inch brook trout and some browns and rainbow trout.

Spanish Lakes.

Two relatively large lakes a few hundred yards apart, with a couple of ponds in between, in open alpine meadows right at timberline. They are fished mostly by guided parties who reach them either by 7½ miles of good trail above the end of the Spanish Creek road at the Ranger Station, or 1½ miles by trail southeast from Lake Solitude. The lowest lake (first one you come to) is 4 acres, as much as 37 feet deep in a couple of places, below cliffs around the south side but with a nice shore to the north. It is good fishing for 10 to 15 inch cutthroat — plus an occasional BIG one. On the next bench up (20 feet and 100 yards or so from the east end of the lower lake) is a 1½ acre pond that is shallow — but connected to the outlet from the large lake above, so does not freeze out. It's fair fishing for 8 to 14 inch cutthroat. The upper, and largest lake,

HYALITE RESERVOIR
Courtesy USFS

GALLATIN RIVER NEAR SAGE CREEK
Courtesy Phil Farnes, SCS

MIRROR LAKE
Courtesy USFS

is 9 acres in size, as much as 46 feet deep with steep dropoffs all around, lies below steep rocky slopes to the south and east and timber to the north, and used to be good fishing for cutthroat and some rainbow but is very poor now.

Spring Branch of the South Fork Ross Creek.
Very small, about 4 miles long in flat grassland (with some cottonwood and brush along it) reached by county roads 9 miles north from Bozeman. For such a small stream the fishing is excellent for small rainbow, brook trout and some late summer early fall browns up from the river but it's all closed up and posted.

Spring Creek.
A swift, clear mountain stream above, the lower 3½ miles flow west across open rangeland to Bridger Creek ½ mile south of the Upper Bridger School and are paralleled by the Bridger Canyon Cutoff Road. This section is fished by local ranchers for fair catches of brook trout, along with a few rainbow and cutthroat too.

Squaw Creek.
Take State 191 for 10 miles above Gallatin Gateway to the Squaw Creek Ranger Station, then cross the West Gallatin River over a concrete bridge to the east (left) side of the river and follow a dirt road on upstream for 1½ miles to the Squaw Creek campground at the mouth of the creek. There's a logging road on up its heavily timbered canyon for about 11 miles and then a USFS trail for another 3 miles to headwaters on the western slopes of Divide Peak. This creek is fair fishing for rainbow, some cutthroat and brook trout, and a few browns 8 to 12 inches.

Summit Lake.
Here is a real spotty but sometimes good lake for nice fat cutthroat that will average 10 to 18 inches and sometimes run up to better than 2½ pounds — if you know how to catch 'em. It's 1½ acres in size, mostly between 10 and 14 feet deep with steep dropoffs, and is surrounded by talus slopes in a narrow saddle between the heads of the South Fork Spanish Creek and the North Fork Hellroaring Creek drainages at 7540 feet above sea level. It can be reached by trail up either drainage but the Hellroaring is the closest — about 10 miles from State 191. Summit Lake is fished quite a bit in spite of the long pack in, probably because it's only a mile from Thompson Lake which is one of the best in this region.

Swan Creek.
A clear, swift, mountain stream flowing due west from Hyalite Ridge for ten miles down its narrow timbered canyon to the West Gallatin River and State 191, seven and a half miles above the Squaw Creek Ranger Station. There are some summer homes near the mouth, a poor dirt road by a couple of miles upstream to a public campground, and then a USFS pack trail to headwaters. The lower five miles are poor fishing for 5 to 8 inch rainbow and cutthroat trout — but are very seldom bothered.

Taylor Fork Gallatin River. A rapid trout stream flowing east to the West Gallatin River (and State 191), seven miles below the Yellowstone Park boundary. It is followed upstream by a USFS road for 7½ miles and then 2½ miles by trail to Taylor Falls at the head of the fishing water. All but the upper mile or so is in open, hilly rangeland and is heavily fished (in the middle reaches, above and below the Nine Quarter Circle Guest Ranch) for fair catches of 8 to 14 inch rainbow and an occasional cutthroat or brown trout, a few to about 2 pounds.

Tepee Creek. A very small stream, only about 3 miles long in "elk rangeland," it is crossed at the mouth by State 191 a couple of miles above the Taylor Fork and produces a few 5 to 8 inch rainbow for even fewer fishermen. Pass it by!

Thompson Creek. Heads in springs, is 4 miles long, debouches to the East Gallatin River 3½ miles north of Belgrade, parallels a county road for most of its length in open farm land, was moderately popular for good catches of browns, rainbow and brook trout in the 10 to 16 inch class, mostly by local fly fishermen. Note: this is a nice little meandering stream with lots of good holes but is private, posted, and being subdivided. What a shame!

Thompson Lake. A moderately popular lake, one of the best in the Spanish Peaks area, Thompson lies at 9140 feet above sea level on the northwestern slopes of Gallatin Peak at the head of the North Fork Hellroaring Creek and is reached by a USFS horse trail up that stream about 9 miles above the West Gallatin River and State 191. It's 5 acres maybe 20 feet deep with a steep dropoff below talus slopes on the southeast side but is mostly shallower, and is bordered by scattered timber and grass on around. The fishing is good-to-excellent for cutthroat that will run between 8 to 10 inches and range up to a couple of pounds.

Upper Falls Creek Lake. A long, narrow and shallow (all under 10 feet deep) 3½ acre lake ⅜ of a mile east across sparsely timbered barren country from Lower Jerome Rock Lake. It's not fished much but was stocked with cutthroat away back in 1953 and is now spotty but sometimes still fair fishing for 10 to 11 inchers.

Wapiti Creek. A small clear (except in the springtime) mountain stream flowing north from timbered mountains for about 3 miles across open rangeland to the Taylor Fork of the Gallatin River, 3½ miles upstream, about a mile below the Quarter Circle Guest Ranch. The lower reaches are followed by a good USFS logging road, are moderately popular, and are fair fishing for 6 to 10 inch rainbow trout.

West Fork Hyalite Creek. A clear rapid stream with lots of falls in it that flows down a timbered canyon for 6 miles from Hyalite Lake to the Middle Creek (Hyalite) Reservoir. The lower couple of miles are followed by a logging road, the upper reaches by a USFS trail. It's not fished much, but there is some poor-to-fair fishing (especially in the lower reaches) for 7 to 8 inch brook trout, grayling and cutthroat. Watch the regulations here.

West Fork of the Gallatin River. Is formed by the junction of its Middle and North Forks and is followed (within a few hundred yards or so) by a USFS road through mostly flat meadowland to the Gallatin River and State 191, fifteen miles above the Squaw Creek Ranger Station. It's a nice stream, heavily fished, good for mostly 8 to 12 inch (and a few up to 2 pounds) rainbow trout, plus a few brown trout. It's mostly all on "Big Sky" resort land.

West Gallatin River. See Gallatin River.

DON'T BE A LITTERBUG

Courtesy Bill Browning

JEFFERSON RIVER
Courtesy US Fish & Wildlife

Jefferson River

The Jefferson River gained fame with white man's first observation of the river. The Lewis and Clark expedition's struggle up the swift clear water in August, 1805 was impeded by brushy banks which made the task of pulling the "toe line" very difficult. Other problems included hordes of mosquitoes, beaver dam obstructions, hot days, cold nights, strong winds and anxiety about the coming winter.

Today, many of these first observations are still true. A hundred and seventy-five years of development has made its mark, but the heartbeat of this great river continues. The spectacular scenery varies from a beautiful canyon setting to peaceful, cottonwood-encased meanders full of wildlife. The water is presently somewhat off-color, probably due to irrigation return flows. During peak irrigation demands from mid-July to mid-September, water shortages and an increase in water temperatures are cause for concern, but the mighty Jefferson perseveres with amazing resiliency.

The Jefferson is formed by the confluence of the Big Hole and Beaverhead Rivers just north of Twin Bridges, Montana. The river first flows north and then east for a total of 77 miles before joining the Madison and Gallatin Rivers to create the Missouri. The Jefferson is predominantly a brown trout fishery, but rainbow are not uncommon. The fish population is good to excellent and is comparable to that of the lower Gallatin and upper Missouri. Fish average about one pound, but occasional 7-9 pounders are pulled from its deep holes. One must remember to direct his angling effort toward the banks, since brown trout here are strongly cover-oriented.

The Jefferson is one of the few major rivers in the area that still offers uncongested float-fishing. In addition, minimal skill will usually suffice in navigating the river during the non-runoff period. Due to its size, the Jefferson is most easily fished from a boat, but one can manage from the bank as well. Public access sites are available at a number of points and additional sites are being pursued for the future. At convenient points (usually bridges) where public access is not yet available, permission can usually be procured from the land owner.

The River is open year round with winter fishermen usually directing their attention to whitefish. While the best time for trout is April through July and early September through November, mid-summer fishing can be productive in early morning or late evening. The water then is sufficiently cool to encourage more aggressive trout activity.

Access to the uppermost reach of the Jefferson River is usually by way of the Beaverhead River at the Madison County Fair Grounds in Twin Bridges. The last two miles of the Beaverhead are floated above the mouth of the Big Hole, which marks the actual beginning of the Jefferson River. The upper portion of the Jefferson is characterized by numerous large, deeply scoured holes which stimulate the imagination of any angler. Gradually, as one proceeds downstream, the single channel stream evens out into longer pools, runs and riffles.

The picturesque Tobacco Root Mountain Range is on the right and snow covered highlands on the left. Access to the river in the Hell's Canyon to Ironrod portion of the stream can be made from private land via a parallel county road. Approximately one mile above Ironrod Bridge (State Route No. 41 between Silver Star and Twin Bridges) several large irrigation withdrawals appear. From here to just below Silver Star several more large diversions occur. It is in this area that severe flow reductions exist during low flow years and peak demand periods.

By this time, the Jefferson begins to flow northeast. The current velocity is now slowing, a factor which can create problems for floaters, especially if a head wind is encountered.

At Guy George Bridge (county bridge to Waterloo) there is another major irrigation diversion spanning the Jefferson. Portaging around this diversion is recommended. This structure furnishes water for the land immediately south of Whitehall.

After Guy George Bridge the river heads more easterly as it passes the northwestern edge of the Tobacco Root Mountains. Within this reach the scenery is inspiring and the area's history hauntingly intriguing. Ancient Indian caves, visible to the floater, are seen immediately above the river with a hot spring at river grade. Abandoned buildings and the foundation of the Parrot Smelter send one to the days of the warring copper kings. The Jefferson in this area produces most of its finest catches of trout.

Passing under the Kountz Bridge (county road 4 miles S.E. of Whitehall) more braiding of the channel appears. Every undercut willow growth beckons the angler to stop and try for that lunker certain to lie there. Here, too, the mouth of the Jefferson Canyon becomes visible to the east. The powerful Jefferson, part of its strength returning due to "return" flows, must still boil and churn its way under Mayflower Bridge (named for an inactive gold mine in the area), past Cardwell (crossed by State Route No. 359), and be joined by the North and South Boulder Rivers before entering the canyon. Within this reach, there are several very large, deep holes that have generated numerous monster trout stories.

Once in the canyon (paralleled by U.S. 10), the Jefferson River is again a single channel stream with its velocity regained. First, one will see a gaping hole in the left canyon wall. This is the sight of the now abandoned limestone quarry locally known as limespur. On the right hand walls (more difficult to observe) are the remains of a wooden flume. This flume was constructed in the early 1900's to supply water to the Chinese Placer Gold diggings immediately below London Hill.

The river continues past the site of the Lewis and Clark Caverns, one of the most visited state park facilities in Montana. This canyon area is a particularly good spot to fish in the evenings during the warm mid-summer, since it has earlier shade. The Jefferson then passes under the Sappington Junction Bridge (State Route No. 287) and turns northeast toward its ultimate destination.

In the lower reach, the river still maintains its fishing potential. As William's Bridge nears, the town of Willow Creek is negotiated and Willow Creek itself joins the Jefferson and a colorful past is all around. Any place one steps or guides his boat could be the very site where some larger-then-life drama occurred during the beaver trade period. Names like John Coulter, George Drouillard, and Jim Bridger are all around. As one passes the Three Forks Bridge (U.S. 10) he enters an area of braided channels and only a handful of signs of development are noticeable all the way to the Jefferson's end (and the mighty Missouri's origin) at Headwater State Park. Here the Jefferson maintains its wildest appearance. Wildlife is abundant and usually visible. Access in and out is almost completely limited to boats. Top fish habitat exists everywhere and no matter how one tries, it all passes too rapidly.

Although the fishing, scenery, and the history of the Jefferson River is our special heritage, the story would be incomplete without mentioning tributaries and back-country alpine lakes. The tributaries to the Jefferson are not abundant but they do merit a fisherman's investigation. Pan size cutthroat, brook, rainbow, and brown trout are all available. Some streams have amazing numbers while others will yield occasional trophies. High mountain lakes in the Jefferson drainage are mainly limited to the Tobacco Root Mountain range. The fishing can be as challenging as the scenery is spectacular. Lakes offer McBride cutthroat, rainbow and brook trout.

One can only conclude that the Jefferson River with its rich fishery resource is a very fitting river to bear the name of the man responsible for its discovery. We can only hope it will always remain that way.

Bruce Rehwinkel

Jefferson River Drainage

Albro Lake.　This is an earth dammed, 12 acre reservoir at 8620 feet above sea level but away below (northwest of) Potosi Peak in the Tobacco Root Mountains. The best way in short of a helicopter is by a good circuitous USFS trail 10 miles in all directions but eventually to the west from the South Willow Creek road at the Potosi Ranger Station. Once there you'll find it lying beneath great open talus slopes to the southwest, in lodgepole to the northeast, with relatively shallow dropoffs and maybe a few aged cutthroat from an old plant — if they haven't frozen out or died off.

Bell Lake.　An 18 acre lake in a partly timbered pocket 8760 feet above sea level below (east of) Long Mountain and Thompson Peak. It's over 70 feet deep in places with mostly steep dropoffs, open around the east shore and accessible by USFS pack trail 3 steep miles up its outlet from the South Willow Creek road 2½ miles above the Potosi Ranger Station. It used to be barren but was planted with fingerling cutthroat trout the summers of 1967-1969, again in '78 and '81, and has provided some good fishing since. Cutts 8 to 13 inches are regularly seduced here by more than a few enthusiasts.

Big Pipestone Creek.　Heads in Delmo Lake and is more-or-less followed along the northeast side by USFS and county roads for 20 crooked miles to its mouth on the Jefferson River a mile southeast of Whitehall. The upper third is in timbered mountains but is so small it has little potential. The middle "canyon" third is "big enough to float a fish and clean enough to keep him alive." It used to provide some fair fishing for 10 to 11 inch brown trout, plus a few rainbow and cutts. The Fish and Game Dept. rehabilitated the upper reaches of this creek in 1971 but did not replant it, although they did plant Delmo Lake wth cutthroat and some of them have migrated on down during spring peaking flows. The lower third (valley reaches) provide some marginal brown trout (better in late fall) fishing despite flow problems associated with irrigation and livestock.

Bismark Reservoir.　A shallow, silty bottomed, 5 acre pond in timber on one side and open on the other, just east of the South Boulder River road 4 miles above Mammoth. Not many people fish it which is just as well because the few small brook trout that are here are hard to come by. It is a good "jumping off" point though — for better waters. The road in isn't the best — pretty nearly a four-wheeler.

Brannan Lakes.　Two, upper and lower, 20 and 16 acres, maximum depths 20 and 18 feet in hummocky moraine below great talus slides to the north and sparse scrub timber to the east, at 9250 feet elevation, 400 feet up and 300 yards north with a good jeep from Sailor Lake — north of Lake Shore Mountain in the Tobacco Roots. They're not fished much but were spotty producers of good sized brook trout — up to 10 pounds recorded. The last three trips produced a few foot long rainbow in the lower lake — zilch in the upper. Unless you want to trade in that jeep, park just below Sailor Lake and hike in.

Camp Creek Reservoir.　There's not a tree around it, only sagebrush and grass at 6950 feet elevation in the Tobacco Root foothills a mile northeast by steep, switchback trail from the South Willow Creek road at the Potosi Ranger Station. It's roughly rectangular, about 5 acres with mostly shallow dropoffs except at the face of the dam on the north end and was excellent fishing for ½ to 2½ pound rainbow trout. Reports have it that the dam was breeched, leaving only two feet of water and no fish.

Cataract Creek Reservoir.　On Cataract Creek, 160 acres, reached by road 2 miles southwest from Pony. The creek (which is too fast for fish) flattens out a bit here and was dammed in 1959 for irrigation. The resulting reservoir is from 20 to 30 feet deep, mostly in open foothill rangeland and good for rainbow trout that used to average between 1½ to 2½ pounds and run upwards of 10. Most folks (lots of them) catch mostly "wee" brookies and an occasional rainbow or brook to 2 pounds. The road in is not the best some years.

CAMP FARE
Courtesy Bridenstine Studio

FAWN
Courtesy Craig Black

Deep (or Upper Hollow Top) Lake. Lies at 8870 feet above sea level in a small glacial cirque below (just east of) Hollow Top Mountain, 200 yards southeast and below Sky Top Lake, 300 yards northwest and 40 feet above Hollow Top Lake at the head of North Willow Creek. It's 10 acres, open on the west but with timber right down to the water's edge on around, deep enough to keep from freezing out most winters, but it finally did in 1971. Although there's no record of a plant, the fishing has been fair for 8 to 11 inch cutthroat and it's not overcrowded.

Delmo Lake. Take U.S. 10 three miles west from Whitehall to the far side of the Great Northern overpass where you take the Big Pipestone Creek (Delmo) road 11 miles north to the lake shore at 6095 feet elevation, or you can also come in 7 miles from Homestake Lake via Pappa's Place. This is a 44 acre irregularly shaped, partly artificial lake behind a concrete dam on Big Pipestone Creek. It has 3 inlets (Haney, O'Neil and International Creeks), is open on the north side and timbered on around. The maximum depth is around 70 feet and it needs it because the draw down is sometimes as much as 50 feet. Lots of people hit it, some also coming in from north of the Continental Divide. There is a boat ramp and a darn good population of cutthroat stocked in 1980 and 1981 averaging 7 to 12 inches, and some rainbow stocked in '77, '78, and '79 that may run up to 2 pounds or so.

Fish Creek. Heads way up in the Highland Mountains, is followed along the upper 5 or 6 miles by a USFS road, and is crossed every few miles from here on down for 11 miles eastward to its mouth on the Jefferson River at Parson's Bridge. The upper reaches are in timbered mountains, the next 4 miles in mostly inaccessible canyons, and the lower 7 miles in arid grazing land. The upper and middle reaches (where you can get to them) provide some beautiful scenery and fair fishing for 8 to 9 inch brook and a very few cutthroat trout. Quite a few picnickers take advantage of the combination. The lower reaches are mostly dewatered for irrigation — don't bother. You can drive a car up to the campground at Pidgeon Creek.

Globe Lake. Lies below steep, open slide-rock talus slopes to the north, in timber to the south, at 8760 feet above sea level in the Tobacco Root Mountains ½ mile by steep trail from Sailor Lake. It's 4 acres, fairly deep with moderate dropoffs and is packed with zillions of small brook trout. Perhaps if more people would fish it, there would be enough food per fish to let 'em grow.

Hanson Lake. See Sky Top Lake.

Harrison Lake. See Willow Creek Reservoir.

Hell Canyon Creek. Heads below (south of) Table Mountain in the Highland Mountains south of Butte, and flows to the southeast through steep, partly timbered foothills for 10 miles to the Jefferson River at the Ironrod Bridge. It's in an inaccessible canyon for the first 5 miles upstream, but the next 3 are followed by road, are full of beaver dams, mostly wadeable and excellent fishing for 6 to 10 inch cutthroat trout. Lots of picnickers come here.

103

Hollow Top Lake. Is 17 acres, fairly shallow but with some deep spots, in a partly dammed — 8550 feet above sea level — alpine hollow 300 yards below Deep Lake at the headwaters of North Willow Creek on Hollow Top Mountain. To get there take a USFS road 3 miles up North Willow Creek southwest from Pony, and then a trail that gets steeper by the minute for another 2½ miles on in. Once there you'll find it's in timber all around except at the northeast corner, and good fishing for 8 to 10 inch rainbow trout. Chances are you'll have company.

Homestake Creek. A very small creek flowing east from just below the Continental Divide for 7 miles to Big Pipestone Creek (pan-sized brook trout fishing in some headwater beaver ponds) and for about 3 miles above (north of) the new Interstate, 10 miles east from Butte. You take the Radar Creek-Moose Creek-Delmo Lake road 6 miles north from the Toll Mountain campground (which is reached by a good dirt road 3½ miles north from the Nineteen Mile House, 13 miles west from Whitehall on U.S. 10 south) to about the middle section of the creek — and then a left hand fork on upstream through willow, meadowland type bottoms interspersed with lodgepole pine. There may be a little mediocre fishing downstream, but not many would bother fishing down it to find out.

Homestake Lake. Is an old Northern Pacific ice pond in an open canyon but with willow and lodgepole around the shore — right beside the new Interstate just east of the Continental Divide — six miles east of Butte. It is fairly shallow, no motors are allowed and it's stocked annually with a couple of thousand 8 to 10 inch rainbow trout making for good fishing. Every year Butte puts on a "Kids Fishing Derby" here.

International Creek. A small mountain stream in a rough rocky canyon, one of three inlets to Delmo Lake. There is a series of cataracts about 100 yards above the mouth, and from here down it's good fishing for 10 inch (and up to 3 pounds) rainbow and brook trout. You have to hike above and there's nothing much when you get there — so most folks don't.

Little Whitetail Creek. An open pasture, meadowland stream formed by the junction of Bigfoot and Beaver Creeks, with a good county road along the east side for about 10 miles south to its mouth on Whitetail Creek, 5 miles north of Whitehall. The lower reaches are pretty good duck hunting in season, but are poor fishing, having recently been dewatered. The middle and upper reaches are good for mostly brook trout (up to 14 inches), a very few rainbow to 11 inches, and in the middle reaches, browns to a foot long. It gets a fair amount of pressure.

Lost Cabin Lake. An old USFS trail takes off from the Bismark Reservoir and climbs 3 steep miles up to Lost Cabin at 9100 feet above sea level below (east of) great rock slides from the crest of the Tobacco Root Mountains. This 7 acre lake cuts squarely across an outwash gravel train to the south and is bordered by scrub timber on the north and west. It is as much as 30 feet

BULL ELK DURING RUT
Courtesy Phil Farnes

deep in places with steep dropoffs to the south and west, is seldom fished and really spotty for 8 to 13 inch rainbow trout. In 1981 MDFWP planted tiny cutthroat trout in this scenic lake — enough said.

Louise Lake. See Mary Lou Lake.

Lower Boulder Lake. You can jeep to it up Dry Boulder Creek 10 miles east from State 41, six miles north from Twin Bridges in hummocky, rocky country at 8520 feet above sea level just below (west of) the "backbone" of the Tobacco Roots. It lies below small scrub-timbered hills to the southeast, is mostly open to the north and east, is 12.7 acres with shallow dropoffs on the east but steep on around, and is good fishing for 8 to 10 inch cutthroat and some brook trout. The cutts were planted in 1979 and 1980 as fingerling.

Mary Lou (or Louise) Lake. Two steep miles up from the South Boulder River road at (almost) the Bismark Reservoir will bring you to 12½ acre Mary Lou at 8900 feet above sea level, below high talus and scree slides on the east. It is west and south from Middle Mountain, with alpine scrub timber to the north. With icy water, perpetual snowbanks along the west shore, and steep dropoffs to its 40 foot deep bottom, this little jewel was at one time a slow producer of golden trout to 7 pounds. Now, planted with cutthroat in '67, '69, '72, '76, and '79, it is a spotty but respectable producer of trout in the 8 to 14 inch class (best early summer or late fall), and gets heavy usage for its size. There is no apparent reproduction here.

Mason Lakes (Upper and Lower). Go to Pony. Take the Willow Creek-Cataract Creek-Mountain Meadow Mine road 4½ miles that get steeper by the minute into the Tobacco Root Foothills west of town, and finally a good USFS foot trail on in to Lower Mason at 8140 feet above sea level. From here you proceed another half mile up the drainage (south) to Upper Mason at 8730 feet above sea level. Both are dammed and about the same size (4.9 and 4.7 acres). Lower Mason lies in tmber on both sides but there is a large marshy meadow at the upper end. The shoreline is quite shallow all around making it difficult to fish. Upper Mason lies in a little timbered pocket below steep talus slopes to the south. It's fairly deep with good dropoffs and a very rocky shore. Upper Mason is good fishing for 10 to 12 inch rainbow and is fished a lot by locals. Lower Mason blows hot and cold but is sometimes also fair. Both can be affected by lower water levels any given year.

Mill Creek. Used to be fair fishing but is no longer. It heads below Brownback Mountain in the Tobacco Roots and flows west down a steep, rocky, partly timbered canyon for 3 miles to the bench on the east side of the Jefferson River valley, east of Waterloo. The lower reaches are all diverted for irrigation. The first couple of miles in the canyon still produce a few small brookies. There's a jeep road along the south side.

Moose Creek. In the Moose Creek Meadows there are 3 small, nice (⅓ to 1 acre) beaver ponds. There is one on each of the forks a few hundred yards above the Moose Creek-Delmo Lake road crossing 4½ miles above (north) of the Toll Mountain campground which is reached 3 miles north of the Nineteen Mile House — 13 miles west of Whitehall on U.S. 10 south. The third is on the mainstream a few hundred yards below the crossing. All are in marshy meadowland with willow and brush along the water's edge. It's not a place you would go expressly to fish but does produce some camp-fare brook trout for an occasional picnicker.

Mullin Lake. Go west from Whitehall on U.S. 10 south for 13 miles to the Nineteen Mile House where you turn north and drive 3½ miles north up the (dirt) Toll Mountain road to this 3½ acre lake on the North Fork Little Pipestone Creek. It's in timbered mountain country but with perhaps 10% of the shoreline in open grassland. The water is rust colored, drops off shallowly, but is deep enough to keep from freezing out due to an 8 foot dam at the outlet. It's excellent fishing for mostly 10 to 11 inch brookies, plus some rainbow and cutthroat trout. There are several summer homes here, but the lake could stand a great deal more pressure.

North Willow Creek. Drains Deep and Hollow Top Lakes down a steep wooded canyon for 5½ miles to Pony and another 3½ out across its broad open grazing land fan to junction with the South Fork 2 miles southwest of Harrison. There's a good gravel road along the lower stretches, a USFS access road 3 miles up the canyon above Pony and finally a trail on to headwaters. It's a small stream and easily fished for good catches of mostly 6 to 10 inch brook trout, some 12 to 14 inch rainbow and a few brown trout.

105

Norwegian Creek.
Pretty small but deep and good fishing. It's all in open grazing foothills from its mouth on the Willow Creek Reservoir for 8 miles upstream to headwaters. There are some old placers and beaver ponds here that are truly excellent fishing for 8 to 10 inch rainbow and brown trout that migrate up from the reservoir, plus quite a few indigenous brook trout. There are lots of willow along the banks and the grass grows right out over the water. A good place for night crawlers! The stream is accessible by county road at its mouth, but lots of people prefer to take State 1 four miles southeast from Harrison to its middle section, and then fish either up or down. Watch for closures (regulations) in early season to protect spawners — strictly enforced here.

O'Neil Creek.
One of the very small inlets to Delmo Lake — so small there wouldn't be any fishing if it weren't for some beaver ponds about 1½ miles up the creek in thick willow bottoms — moose country! There is no trail — you have to fight your way in from the Delmo Lake road, but if you make it, you can catch your supper of small cutthroat trout, plus zillons of redside shiners.

Sailor Lake.
You can jeep to this one 7 miles up the South Boulder River from Mammoth. It's 12 acres, 40 feet maximum depth, lies below open slide rock at the northwest end and timber around, at 8870 feet elevation a half mile north of Lakeshore Mountain in the Tobacco Roots. Often and avidly fished for excellent catches of mostly small brook trout planted in the 50's. In '61, '62 and '63 cutthroat were planted but apparently are all gone now. By the way, not very often, but now and again, colorful brookies up to 18 inches long attack a bait or whatever, ending up in someone's creel.

Sappington Ponds.
A couple of old railroad borrow pit ponds about a mile east of Sappington at the south edge of the Jefferson River flood plain, reached by a dirt road off (east of) State 1 just south of the railroad tracks. Only the larger pond (about 2½ acres) amounts to anything. It's spring fed, drains to the river and is reportedly stocked now and then by private parties. Permission is needed.

Sky Top (or Hanson) Lake.
Lies below scrub timbered talus slopes on the north and west with scattered rock and alpine timber on the east and is mostly open on the south at 8850 feet above sea level, just east of Hollow Top Mountain, 200 yards northwest and 200 feet above Deep Lake. It's only 7 acres of sparkling water and a steep climb in, but the scenery is beautiful, the air crisp and invigorating, and the fishing is reportedly good at times for 10 to 12 inch rainbow trout.

South Boulder River.
Is a fast, white-water creek paralleled by a good gravel road 17½ miles from the headwaters (near Bismark Reservoir) northward to its mouth on the Jefferson River a mile east of Jefferson Island. The upper reaches are in open park and timber public land, the lower reaches flow through private rangeland. It's a neat little creek, good for mostly 6 to 14 inch rainbow and brook trout with an occasional brown to about 16 inches maximum caught in the lower reaches. Plenty of anglers give it a whirl.

South Willow Creek.
Heads in (barren) Granite Lake away up near the top of the divide in the Tobacco Root Mountains and flows for 6 miles down a steep narrow canyon to the Potosi Ranger Station where it flattens out for a couple of miles and the canyon widens a bit. It next flows for 2½ miles through an out-and-out steep-walled rocky gorge, and finally flows for 3 miles out onto the Willow Creek floodplain to join with the North Fork 2 miles southwest of Harrison. The lower reaches are in farmland and the middle reaches (all followed by road to and beyond the Ranger Station) are in timber and meadow. It's a dandy little creek and is fair fishing for mostly 7 to 13 inch rainbow and some brook trout.

Sunrise Lake.
Take the Ziegler Reservoir (which is drained) road 3 miles up from the Wisconsin Creek road to the end — and then "shank's mares" ½ mile on in to the shore. Sunrise lies 9300 feet above sea level in a great barren rocky cirque just west and below the crest of the Tobacco Root Range. There is some alpine timber around its 4 acre shoreline. The water has a maximum depth of 15 feet and was planted with cutthroat trout the summers of '67, '70, '72, '75, and '78. More than a few are successful here for 7 to 14 inch tasty trout. It still had fish as of last year (81) but could freeze out each winter.

Upper Boulder Lake.
A shallow 10 acre cirque lake a mile up the inlet of Lower Boulder Lake (you can jeep to Lower Boulder Lake), at about 9000 feet elevation. It was stocked with cutthroat in 1976, 1979, and 1980. If it hasn't frozen out, should be good for 6 to 13 inchers and some rainbow-cutt crosses (hybrids).

106

Upper Hollowtop Lake. See Deep Lake.

Whitetail Creek.
Heads in the Whitetail Reservoir up in the hills 11 airline miles east of Butte and flows for 7 miles through a series of steep, rocky, brushy canyons, and then for another 9 miles of open foothill and valley rangeland southeastward to the Jefferson River at Whitehall. The upper (canyon) reaches are mostly inaccessible except on foot up the creek bottom from the "sheep camp" at the end of the road 7½ miles north from the east end of the Burlington Northern viaduct 3½ mills west from Whitehall. There are some beaver ponds here (and others at intervals up the creek) that are excellent fishing for eat'n size brookies, fair size browns, and a few rainbow. There's a substantial brown trout population to 15 inches or so. They're easier caught in the fall but not many people try their luck.

Whitetail Reservoir.
A large (1149 acre), high (elevation 7249 feet), State Water Conservation Board irrigation reservoir that has drowned out half of Upper Whitetail Park, 11 miles up in the mountains east of Butte. You can jeep to it but not many do because: (A) It's swampy all around, is difficult to get to the water. (B) It has very shallow dropoffs — when the wind blows, the water changes to mud. (C) The fishing at last report — none. It used to have small brook trout but has always been poor fishing. There's a cow puncher's cabin a mile below the outlet.

Williams' (or Steiver) Sloughs.
Go east on U.S. 10 one and a quarter miles from the Ennis turnoff and then continue straight on (on a gravel county road while U.S. 10 turns to the north) for another mile and you'll be right on top of these old cut-off oxbow sloughs on the Jefferson River floodplain. They have some cottonwood and willow around them, are spring fed but also receive some water from an irrigation canal, and they discharge into the river. They provide a little mediocre largemouth bass and yellow perch fishing — mostly to locals — and some fair duck hunting in season.

Willow Creek.
Is formed by the confluence of its North and South Forks a couple of miles south and west of Harrison, and soon splits into several channels which more-or-less parallel each other northeastward (past Harrison) for 4 miles to rejoin in a narrow open draw at the head (east end) of the Willow Creek Reservoir. Upon leaving the reservoir it flows through a steep, rocky, brushy rattlesnake-infested canyon for a few miles and then down a broad open valley for another 5 miles to the Jefferson River 7 miles southwest of Three Forks. It's easily accessible above and below the canyon by county and private roads. The upper and lower (farm and rangeland) stretches are easily fished (with permission), moderately popular and fair for mostly 10 to 16 inch rainbow, some brown and a few brook trout. The canyon stretch is harder to get to, or rather through. There's no road or trail, and as might be expected, less popular but better fishing, and great rattlesnake hunting (it's all yours). Read fishing regulations on this creek.

Willow Creek (or Harrison) Reservoir.
A big, 4 mile long by a maximum of one mile wide but very irregularly shaped 880 acre State Water Conservation Board irrigation reservoir in the open foothills of the Tobacco Root Mountains, 4 miles east of Harrison by good county roads. It is ponded at a maximum of 4750 foot elevation behind a dam on Willow Creek and is fed by Willow, Norwegian and Dry Creeks. There is about 15 feet of draw down and much of the lake gets pretty warm in hot summers (especially in Norwegian Bay). However it does not freeze out, is planted now annually with Lake DeSmet rainbow, a wild Wyoming strain (since 1978) that run up to 4 pounds already, and spawn successfully in the creeks entering the reservoir (watch regulations). Fishing is now excellent for 10 inch to 4 pound trout which are long-lived and already vigorous jumping brawlers. Now and then a brown trout is caught averaging over a pound, but up to ten. Spring and fall (from shore or boat) is best, with usage increasing now that the word is out. There's a boat ramp and public camping is provided for, although there is very little shade. The reservoir is also used a great deal for waterskiing but with caution because of hazardous conditions resulting from strong gusty winds. P.S. Thanks to the innovative stocking program of the MDFWP in a few years this lake may not have to be stocked.

BIG SPRING CREEK
Courtesy USSCS

The Judith River

The Judith River drains much of the north and east slopes of the Little Belt Mountains. The Judith River, formed by the confluence of the South Fork and Middle Fork, flows in a northeasterly direction after leaving the mountains picking up tributaries which drain the north and west slopes of the Big Snowy Mountains and the southwest corner of the Judith Mountains. Near Lewistown the river swings north picking up tributaries draining the south and west slopes of the Moccasin Mountain range. Continuing on north the river passes through steeply eroded breaks to its confluence with the Missouri River.

Trout inhabit the upper reach of the Judith River while the lower reach is inhabited primarily by warm water species typical of those found in the Lower Missouri River.

Upper Missouri cutthroat, once native throughout the upper river system and its forks, are now present only in the small headwater tributaries. Rainbow trout from eight to twelve inches are the dominant fish species found throughout the South Fork, Lost Fork and Middle Fork as well as the main Judith River upstream from Utica. From Utica to Hobson brown, brook and rainbow trout make up the fishery. The larger brown trout grow to around eighteen inches in length.

The middle portion of the river, from Hobson to the mouth of Big Spring Creek, is a transition zone where trout become less abundant and warm water species more abundant as we proceed downstream. Sauger, goldeyes and an occasional trout are taken by fishermen near the mouth of Big Spring Creek, which is the largest tributary in the river system. Species commonly taken by fishermen at the mouth of the Judith River include sauger, burbot, channel catfish, and shovelnose sturgeon.

Much of the upper Judith River is adversely affected by severe fall water shortages and spring flooding. The South Fork flows through a steep limestone canyon where the stream often goes dry during late summer and fall. This naturally occurring low flow coupled with irrigation withdrawals puts a severe limitation on the trout fishery potential in the main river from where it leaves the mountains downstream for about twenty-five miles. Unstable banks resulting from overgrazing, channel changes, highly erosive soils and frequent spring flooding are all factors contributing to channel instability and widespread destruction of fish habitat along much of the upper and middle reaches of the river. Considering the severity of the problems and the relatively good fish population that persists one cannot help but wonder at the tenacity and adaptability of wild trout populations.

In spite of the problems, the Judith River drainage has a wide range of fishing opportunity including hike-in fishing for wild cutthroat and rainbow trout, fishing for catchable hatchery trout stocked near several Forest Service campgrounds, angling for wild brown, brook and rainbow trout along the brushy prairie river bottom, or angling for sauger, catfish, burbot or sturgeon along the lower reaches of the river. No matter what your preference for fishing, something is available for nearly everyone.

For hunters, the mountainous portion of the Judith River drainage supports one of the state's finest elk herds. The mountains and brushy river bottoms support good populations of mule deer, whitetail deer, black bear, blue grouse and ruffed grouse. For sightseers, many of the beautiful mountains, rivers and prairie panoramas of the area are recognizable in the western classics of Charles M. Russell. The famous cowboy artist spent some of his happiest years in the Judith Basin area.

Michiel Poore

RESTING
Jim Derleth photo

Judith River Drainage

Ackley Lake. In open farmland 4½ miles southwest from Hobson by gravel roads, behind a 400 yard long by 40 feet high earth dam, this lake is fed by a 5 mile long canal from the Judith River. It has a surface area of 247 acres, a muddy bottom and mostly gradual dropoffs into the clear water. It's used heavily by water skiers (keep an eye out) and fishermen alike, has some picnic tables, toilets, two concrete boat launching ramps, and the State is currently involved in upgrading recreational facilities here. Planted annually with 20 or 30 thousand rainbow trout and in 1978 and 1980 with kokanee (full of suckers naturally), the reservoir surrenders both at a decent rate, the rainbow between 11 and 17 inches (to 2 pounds), and the kokanee now about 14 or 15 inches long. As an added bonus brown trout to 5 pounds are netted once in a while.

Barta Pond. On the Judith River bottoms a couple of miles by county and private (there's 3 or 4 gates to open — and shut) roads from Danvers. It's 3½ acres with some low brush around the shore, 15 feet maximum depth, mossy in the shallows, gets pretty warm in the summer and is fished now and then for rainbow trout that mostly average around 9 inches but range up to as much as 4 pounds. It's planted yearly with 5 inch trout.

Big Spring Creek. Fabulous, one of the best (according to the Lewistowners it IS the best) fishing stream in Montana or any other state. It heads in the Big Spring at the Lewistown Fish Hatchery and is paralleled by an oil road for 5 miles through low, rolling hills dotted here and there with aspen and juniper — to Lewistown where it flows under the town and picks up a bit of pollution in transit (too bad), and then twists and turns for another 15 miles to its mouth on the Judith River. It gets real muddy during the spring runoff, is mostly 15 to 20 feet wide and wadeable but has some terrific holes that will "float your hat" and do float some huge browns (recorded to better than 20 pounds) and rainbow trout in the 10 ro 14 inch class. The above town stretch is heavily fished by both in-and-out-of-staters, but is now being urbanized and this will no doubt have an adverse effect on it. How about a zoning district? The lower reaches, below town, are also followed by road for about 7 miles — but because of the pollution problem are not fished much.

Buffalo Creek. A half dozen people could fish this one out in a day (mostly 6 to 8 inch brookies), but it's closed and posted. It's only a few feet wide and has perhaps 3 miles of fishable water crossed here and there by county roads west from Straw — and followed along by cow trails.

Carter's Ponds. Both the upper and lower ponds have washed out, and the MDFWP is attempting to locate a way to get the dams repaired, or give up the fishery for good. Located on the east side of U.S. 191 six and a half miles north of Lewistown, it has public access and some facilities and in the past has been a popular (although muddy-bottomed, and at times warm and mossy) place to rainbow trout fish. Let's wait and see...

Casino Creek. Has a few small (6 to 8 inch) brookies and is fished a little in early season from its mouth on Big Spring Creek on the south side of Lewistown for about 1½ miles upstream where it's followed by a county road through open farmland. In case you're interested it's also "home" to an active beaver colony.

Castle Creek. A very small, short-term-early-season-fishing for 8 to 10 inch rainbow trout, meandering farmland stream with about 1½ miles of "kids'" fishing above (south of) its mouth on Big Spring Creek ¼ mile below the hatchery. The Fish and Game Dept. stocked it with 2-inch brookies the spring of '75 and they gave the rainbow a "run for their money," with good catches to 10 inches reported.

Cottonwood Creek. Heads below Greathouse Peak in the Big Snowy Mountains and flows to the north down a timbered canyon above, and brushy coulees below to Big Spring Creek near Hanover, 7 miles northwest of Lewistown. It's mostly accessible by gravel roads and the upper 10 miles are moderately popular and fair fishing for small rainbow and brook trout, and a few cutthroat. Some sections may go dry during the summer and fall.

Crater Lake. See Rhoda Lake.

Crystal Lake. A most beautiful spot, the prime recreation site in the Big Snowies. It lies in a steep-walled, timbered mountain valley at just over 6000 feet elevation, is an elongated 40 acres with a nice USFS picnic area about midway up the east side, and a 30 unit campground at the upper end — all in lodgepole and ponderosa pine with a few open glades here and there. It's spring fed, but — here is the clincher — it has a leaky bottom and goes practically dry in the winter; however the recreational attributes are so evident that the State Fish and Game Department plants it each spring with 8 to 9 inch rainbow trout that grow like mad and provide excellent summertime fishing for beautiful fat 10 to 14 inchers. All in all this lake is a valuable and quite popular recreational asset, readily accessible by the Rock Creek road about 30 miles south from Lewistown.

Dry Wolf Creek. Heads way up in the Little Belts below Tepee Butte and flows to the northeast for 25 miles — rapidly down a rocky timbered brush-and-deadfall canyon above — and more slowly out across open rangeland below to Running Wolf Creek 4½ miles west of Stanford. The lower reaches dry up but the upper 15 miles (paralleled by a USFS road to Dry Wolf camp and trail above) produce fair messes of 7 to 8 inch rainbow trout, along with a few small cutthroat in some of the headwater beaver ponds. It's a popular weekend stream.

East Fork Big Spring Creek. Heads below Greathouse Peak in the Big Snowy Mountains and is followed for most of its length (about 20 miles) to the north and across open range, meadowland and grainfields to junction with the main stem about a mile below the Big Spring. It's real brushy in places, mostly clear, fairly fast with some nice holes but generally wadeable, and sustains a moderate pressure for fair catches of 8 to 9 inch rainbow trout, quite a few brookies, and a few browns.

East Fork Creek Reservoir. Built in the 70's for flood control, located southeast of Lewistown about 8 miles taking the Big Spring Creek highway and turning east on the East Fork road. Stocked annually by the State, it is good fishing for small rainbow up to about a foot long and is moderately popular.

Elk's Country Club Pond. Is not much more than a marsh, reached by hiking a foot trail half-a-mile southeast from the Club house (southeast from town) along a dammed coulee next to the Lewistown Country Club Golf Course. There's a little timber here, some moss around the edges and 2½ acres of fair fishing for 10 inch rainbow that were planted there by the Fish and Game Dept. Quite a few kids fish it cause it's handy, and stocked every year.

Hanson Creek Reservoir. A flood control, built in the 70's, 12 acre, reservoir behind an earth dam in foothill country a quarter mile east of the Big Spring Fish Creek Hatchery. It's planted heavily each year with pan-size rainbow, is full of 'em, red hot fishing, and correspondingly popular.

Harlow Reservoir. See Reimer's Pond.

Harrison Creek. Very small, in a timbered, rocky, Little Belt Mountain canyon reached by trail a couple of miles down Weatherwax Creek, or you could (once upon a time) jeep to it down (barren) King Creek a half mile north. The USFS recently closed the road. 'Tis tough, but it looks like you'll have to walk to this one. There's about 3 miles of fair fishing here in and around the brush, deadfalls and what-have-you for camp-fare cutthroat and rainbow. It's not often visited.

Hidden Lake. See Rhoda Lake.

Holgate Reservoir. Is stocked annually by the Montana Department of Fish, Wildlife and Parks and is moderately popular in this area. To get there, take the county road south from Denton 1½ miles to the Holgate Ranch then turn west and follow the road through pastureland for 3 miles, and the pond is located in a little coulee. It is 1¾ acres in size, 17 feet deep and fair to good fishing for 8 to 10 inch rainbow trout.

Kingsbury Pond. This pond is privately owned but is stocked each year by the State. It lies in an earth-dammed wheatland coulee, is about 5 acres with mostly steep dropoffs, to a maximum depth of 18 feet, and provides fair-to-good fishing for put-and-take 10 to 14 inch rainbow. Anyhow,

CRYSTAL LAKE IN THE BIG SNOWIES
Courtesy USFS

you can get there by taking a county road due north from Denton for 8 miles, then a cross road to the east (right) for another couple of miles and, although you can't see it from here, the pond sits down in a Coffee Creek drainage coulee off to the south about a half mile by dirt road.

Lost Fork Middle Fork Judith River. Heads below Ant Park in the Little Belt Mountains and is followed by a closed jeep trail down its partly-timbered-partly-open valley for 10 miles to junction with the Middle Fork. There are a few (mostly silted up) beaver ponds here and it's fair fishing for small cutthroat above and rainbow below — but doesn't attract much of a following.

Louse Creek. Has a very limited recreation potential — a few days only of fair early season fishing in the open farm and grazing land reaches just north of Moccasin. They get a few pretty good rainbow and brook trout (up to a couple of pounds) here but it peters out quickly.

Middle Fork Judith River. A nice, clear, Little Belt Mountain canyon creek that would be accessible at its mouth except-that-it's-closed-to-traffic by the Judith River road 12 miles southwest from Utica. Here you back up a mile, detour to your right (west), come in on the Middle Fork a couple of miles upstream and follow it along a closed jeep trail for another mile to the Middle Creek Ranch at headwaters. It's pretty good fishing for cutthroat in the upper reaches; rainbow, cutthroat and rainbow-cutthroat hybrids on down. Some of the more easily accessible reaches are fairly popular with weekenders, but mostly it isn't overrun with fishermen.

North Fork Running Wolf Creek. Is very small and not fished often but provides camp-fare brook trout on occasion. It's followed up its timbered canyon by a USFS logging road for about 3 miles (all of the fishable water) from the head of Running Wolf.

O'Brien Pond. Is no longer stocked by the State because it was closed by the land owner, but if you receive permission then take the Lewistown highway about 5 miles east from Hobson till you cross Ross Fork Creek and then for another half mile (upon a little bench) beyond. Now park your car and hike a quarter mile south across a small open meadow to the shore of this private 3-acre by 20-foot deep with mostly gradual dropoffs, seldom visited reservoir that is fair fishing for 10 to 16 inch rainbow trout (last stocked in 1977) and a few brookies.

113

Old Folks Ponds. Two, about an acre each, separated by a dike on Little Casino Creek (pretty brushy on the upper end), and located south of and below Spring Street in Lewistown. The ponds and stream give up mostly small brook trout and a few small rainbow here and there. Unofficially "kids' fishing" which is just as well because the water gets quite warm in summer and the fish correspondingly soft.

Pecks Pond. A few old timers from Lewistown come here once in a while in the winter and catch a few 10-14 inch rainbow trout. They drive first to Judith Gap, then 4 miles west, a mile south and another 5½ miles west again and there it is (if you haven't gone astray), in a small draw that you can't see till you're on top of it. A couple of mossy acres, and only mediocre fishing.

Reimer's Pond (or Harlow Reservoir). Is in the old Harlow Ranch barnyard on Rock Creek about half a mile below the Lewis and Clark National Forest Boundary, and reached by the Rock Creek road 25 miles south from Lewistown. It's 2½ acres with a little timber on the far side but mostly in grass above shallow dropoffs to a maximum depth of 15 feet on a muddy bottom. There's lots of moss in the summer when the water warms up but it's good fishing all season for rainbow and brook trout in the 10 to 12 inch class. Not too many stop here, though, because most prefer to go on to Crystal Lake. Fact is, the owner would just as soon they did too. It's been off limits since 1973.

Rhoda (or Crater or Hidden) Lake. A beautiful 9800 foot elevation, 2 acre alpine lake below almost vertical walls of granite to the northwest and south, but partly open and partly forested to the east; reached by a steep horse-and-foot trail 3 miles "straight up" from the end of the Big Baldy jeep road in the Little Belt Mountains 12 miles from the Kings Hill turnoff on U.S. 89 about 70 miles south from Great Falls. It's mostly less than 10 feet deep but has a couple of 12 foot holes in its steep sided boulder strewn bottom. The State Fish and Game Department stocked it with golden trout in 1959 but they died out. It was planted every year from 1970 to 1979 with cutthroat trout and is now good fishing (if it hasn't frozen out) and moderately popular, considering the steep climb in, for 12 to 14 inchers.

Rock Creek. The outlet (during the spring runoff) of Crystal Lake and a small tributary of the Ross Fork of the Judith River crossed by U.S: 87 eleven miles west of Lewistown and followed upstream by gravel roads to headwaters. The lower reaches go dry, but the middle reaches (for 3 miles below Reimer's Pond) are fair fishing for 8 to 10 inch rainbow trout (down from the lake) and brook trout. This section of the creek is partly in timber, some cottonwood and quaking aspen and lots of brush, and is a really nice little stream and quite popular in early season only as it is too small to hold up under the pressure it gets.

Ross Fork Judith River. Heads in the western foothills of the Big Snowy Mountains east of Judith Gap and flows 6 miles west and then 25 miles north to the main stream near the town of Ross Fork. It's quite small (you can almost jump it even in the lower reaches), gets real low in summer, and, conversely, high in the spring, runs mostly through open farming country where it's crossed now and again by county roads, and is mediocre fishing for 6 to 16 inch rainbow trout along the lower reaches 5 miles or so up from the mouth. With all the good water around, plus the small local population, it doesn't get fished much.

Running Wolf Creek. Is formed by the junction of the North and South Forks in the northern foothills of the Little Belt Mountains 15 miles southwest by gravel road from Stanford, and flows out across the open prairie for 60 tortuous miles to the northwest and the Judith River about 15 miles west-by-north from Winifred by gravel, dirt and jeep roads. It's a nice little creek in the upper foothill reaches (above Stanford) where there are lots of willow-fringed beaver ponds, a good access road along the south side, and it's fished a lot for mostly 6 to 8 inch brook trout and an occasional rainbow trout. The fish habitat below Stanford is only marginal (the water gets a little warm and silts in the summer) and the fishing is fair-at-best for 8 to 10 inch rainbow and brook trout, except for about 2 miles where it flows by the north side of Denton. Here it is stagnant and muddy but is stocked annually with catchable rainbow trout and is hit hard by the local youngsters.

Sage Creek. A slow meandering open farmland tributary of the Judith River, mostly accessible by roads (paralleling it above Windham and crossing here and there below). It's fed along the lower reaches by overflow from private reservoirs and picks up a few fish now and then along with the water. Not many fish it, a boy now and then and perhaps a few locals.

114

FROZEN WATERFALL
Courtesy USFS

GOT 'IM
Courtesy Bill Browning

South Fork Judith River.
Heads in Hoover Springs away up in the Little Belts and flows to the east and northeast for 18 miles to junction with the Middle Fork at the head of the Judith River. It's accessible here by a good gravel (the Judith River) road 12 miles southwest from Utica and is more or less paralleled upstream by private and USFS (some of them closed) roads to the Springs. It's pretty fast above, flows through some mountain meadows in the middle reaches and a canyon below. The fishing is fair-to-good for 8 to 10 inch put-and-take rainbow trout, and small cutthroat in the headwaters that you really have to work for. Lots of people do too. There are several USFS campgrounds here but the creek gets so low in the fall that you can't find it — from "Hay" canyon on down.

South Fork Running Wolf Creek.
Heads below Bandbox and Sheep Mountains (in the Little Belts) and is followed by a USFS jeep road down its small timbered canyon for the lower couple of (fishable) miles to its mouth on the North Fork at the head of the main stem. It's not visited much but does produce some camp-fare brookies on occasion.

Warm Springs Creek.
Heads in the Judith Mountains 9 miles east of Brooks and is followed by county roads out across farm and meadowland in the Judith Basin for about 25 miles to within a couple of miles of its mouth on the Judith River 14 miles west by oil, gravel, and dirt roads from Denton. The fishing is excellent here at times for 8 to 10 inch rainbow (a few up to a couple of pounds) and it's moderately popular, especially in the early season before the fish get soft and the multitudinous rattlesnakes get feisty. The stream also contains sauger which move up into it during the spring and summer, and smallmouth bass which have been planted several times, both of which can run up to a couple pounds, the better fishing for them being in the lower reaches (nearer the mouth).

Weatherwax Creek.
A very small stream flowing east through open parks above, down a steep-walled timbered canyon with lots of deadfalls below, for a couple of miles from Kings Hill Pass in the Little Belt Mountains east to Harrison Creek. It's seldom fished but is really good (for such a small stream) for 6 to 12 inch cutthroat trout. Not really much of a recreational asset in the regional aggregate but easy to get to inasmuch as the USFS has run a road down most of its length except for a little way just above the mouth.

West Fork Lost Fork Middle Fork Judith River.
Is reached at the mouth by jeep trail (or would be except that it's closed) 7½ miles up the Lost Fork and is followed on upstream by a closed jeep trail for about a mile. It's pretty small and its timbered, brushy canyon is so steep that trout from the Lost Fork are apparently unable to work their way up into it. It's seldom fished for the small native cutthroat that swim in its chuckling waters or the even fewer rainbow trout near the mouth.

Wolverine Creek.   A very small, brushy creek that flows to Big Springs Creek just west of Lewistown and has a few small brookies in the lower reaches (¾ of a mile) between Yaeger Pond and its mouth. If it weren't for the pond — this one you could forget.

Yaeger Pond.   A semi-private (but the owner used to let a few in) 7 acre by 15 foot maximum depth stock reservoir on Wolverine Creek ¾ of a mile above its mouth and 2 miles northwest of Lewistown by gravel road. It's a clear-water reservoir in open country. Was stocked with rainbow trout back in '66 but is mostly home to a burgeoning population of suckers now and it's just as well that it's closed — and no longer managed.

Yogo Creek.   Take the Judith River road 8½ miles south from Utica, where you turn to the right (west) for ¼ mile, then take the left hand fork for 6 miles west to the creek about 4 miles above its mouth on the Middle Fork Judith River. From here you can drive about a mile downstream, and/or 5½ miles upstream to headwaters. The old ghost town of Yogo is about half way up. Three to four hundred gold miners used to winter here back in the '80's, but there's nothing much left now. The creek is partly in timber and partly in open rangeland, has quite a few beaver ponds and is heavily fished for its size (which isn't much) for small cutthroat trout above, and brook and rainbow trout below.

A BIG SPRING CREEK KEEPER
Courtesy Bill Browning

Madison River

Southwestern Montana is rich in quality trout streams and boasts some of the finest wild trout waters in the nation. Many anglers feel the premier river in this group is the nationally famous "blue ribbon" Madison River. Two factors have built this reputation, one being the unusual natural beauty surrounding the river and the other the high quality fishing available on most of the river. Anglers commonly catch 10 to 15 inch rainbow with excellent possibilities of catching larger trout (2-5 pounds) and occasionally the five pound and larger trophy trout. Excellent hatches of midges, caddis, stone and may flies which occur most of the summer stir trout into active feeding, providing for some excellent fly fishing. Where allowed, good bait fishing occurs throughout the fishing season, but the best results occur during the heavy spring runoff period. Lure fishing is good during most of the clear water periods.

The Madison originates in Yellowstone National Park with the union of the Gibbon and Firehole Rivers. From a beginning in numerous thermal hot springs and geysers, the Madison River flows 140 miles in a northerly direction to join the Jefferson and Gallatin Rivers to form the Missouri River. The Madison can be divided into four main reaches depicting differences in stream channel, water velocity, trout populations, trout sizes and scenery.

The first reach begins in Yellowstone National Park and ends in Montana at Hebgen Reservoir. This is probably the most scenic section of the Madison. This portion of the river slowly meanders through mountain meadows and stands of lodgepole pine, with abundant wildlife, especially elk, utilizing the immediate floodplain. The river water within this reach is unusually warm for this altitude due to numerous geysers and hot springs which feed the Madison and its tributaries. Water temperatures during July and August occasionally reach into the low 80's F. Game species present are brown trout, rainbow trout, mountain whitefish and an occasional cutthroat trout. Fishing in this reach generally peaks in the fall (October-November) focusing on spawning runs of brown trout migrating out of Hebgen Reservoir. The brown trout range in size from one to three pounds. Several campsites are available in the area, such as Madison Junction in the Park and Baker's Hole in Montana.

The next reach includes the river between Hebgen Reservoir and Varney Bridge (13 miles south of Ennis). This 35 miles of the Madison is the premier fly fishing area, as a wide open channel and water depths less than six feet facilitate this sport. Here the river is swift with many large boulders in the channel, making wade fishing more difficult. But with proper equipment and care, wade fishing is both productive and practical. Wild rainbow trout are the most commonly caught trout, averaging 10 to 15 inches in length. An occasional large brown can be taken, with a few exceeding five pounds.

The third reach (15 miles in length) lies between Varney Bridge and Ennis Reservoir. The Madison River changes considerably upon entering this reach. The stream gradient lessens somewhat and the channel begins to split into numerous channels. Many of these channels have a heavy, brushy bank cover which provides excellent brown trout habitat. Because of this habitat change, brown trout become the predominant trout species. Because of better habitat and more favorable water temperatures, both brown and rainbow trout grow faster and larger here than in any other section of the Madison. Trout in the two to four pound size class are not uncommon. Many anglers choose to float this reach of the Madison to improve access, but since float fishing restrictions vary from year-to-year, current regulations should be checked if a float fishing trip is planned. Bank access points are available within this reach with five campgrounds spaced appropriately along the fifteen miles in this section.

The fourth reach extends from Ennis Reservoir to the mouth near Three Forks. The first seven miles lie within the Bear Trap Canyon Primitive Area and can be reached only on foot. The canyon area, which is a narrow gorge, has unusually high velocity rapids separated by deep pools and is not recommended for float fishing. The remaining twenty-eight miles is much calmer and easily navigated by the less experienced floater. Wading is easier because the channel is wide and shallow, with large vegetation beds. The water within this reach is much warmer than upstream reaches during the summer due to warming by the shallow Ennis Reservoir. Water temperatures commonly reach into the high 70's and occasionally into the low 80's. This results in very poor fishing during the hot summer months of July and August. Wild trout are somewhat smaller in this reach, due to these high summer water temperatures. The best fishing occurs during the spring period (April-mid-June) or late fall (mid-Sept.-Oct.), when the water is cooler. Wild brown and rainbow trout average 10 to 15 inches with few taken over two pounds. Most of the larger trout are taken in May or early June. Mountain whitefish are very abundant. Access is good in the first fifteen miles, as almost 90% is in public ownership. The last twenty miles is almost entirely within private land and the best access to this stretch is by float fishing. Public access sites are at the beginning and middle of this area (Graycliff and Cobblestone Fish, Wildlife and Parks Access).

One of the most famous fishing periods on the river is the salmon fly hatch. This consists of the emergence of the large pteronarcys stone fly which often signals the beginning of heavy feeding by larger trout. Timing of this hatch varies with the section of river, as stone flies first appear near the mouth in early June and then progress upstream. By late June or early July, the hatch usually has reached the Varney-Quake Lake area. Since the Madison River has various special angling regulations, one should consult current regulations before fishing.

The Madison River is a valuable national resource, deserving its blue ribbon status. Hopefully, this valuable asset to Montana will be maintained or enhanced through the efforts of concerned anglers. Adequate water flows, quality fish habitat and good water quality must be maintained to insure the Madison's future as a premier national trout water.

Richard Vincent

KOHANA LAKE
Courtesy USFS

Madison River Drainage

Alpine (or McKelvey) Lake. Is 2 miles by a marshy trail up the North Fork Meadow Creek from the end of the Twin Lakes jeep road; about 7 acres, fairly shallow, in timber all around at 9000 feet elevation above sea level, and good fishing for 10 to 13 inch cutthroat trout planted there by the State Fish and Game boys in 1971, 1976 and 1979.

Antelope Basin Lake. See Conklin Lake.

Antelope Creek. A small, easily wadeable stream that heads high on Saddle Mountain (elevation 8343 feet above sea level) and flows north for 8 miles to the Antelope Prong (at the upper end) of Cliff Lake. The lower mile flows down a steep little canyon in open rangeland (there's some timber along the bottom); is accessible by trail and is fair early season fishing for 7 to 15 inch rainbow trout.

Antelope Lake. Is posted but permission to fish is usually granted upon request. It's a shallow, long and narrow 7 acre reservoir behind an earth-fill dam on Antelope Creek; in an open basin reached by trail 2 miles upstream from Antelope Prong of Cliff Lake; is heavily fished and good, too — for 9 to 18 inch rainbow trout and rainbow-cutthroat hybrids.

Avalanche Lake. Take the highway 1½ miles from Hebgen Dam to Beaver Creek, and then a USFS access road 3 miles north almost to the Ranger Station where you leave the car and proceed by trail 4½ miles up the West Fork to Avalanche in high glaciated country at 8960 feet elevation above sea level. It's 12 acres, over 75 feet deep (and needs to be to keep from freezing out), is spotty but sometimes good fishing for 8 to 14 inch cutthroat trout, and was planted in 1976 and 1979.

Axolotl (or Twin or Crater) Lakes. Five, between 6860 and 7350 feet above sea level in mostly open hill country at the head of Moran Creek. They are reached by a poor county road 5 miles southeast from Virginia City, (on the Ruby River drainage) or by a not-so-good jeep road 5 miles west from Varney on the Madison River. The largest (southernmost lake) is a long narrow 10 acres below a sparsely timbered ridge to the south. A little over a mile to the north is the next in size, a subcircular 8 acres. The remaining 3 lakes lie in a half mile long northeast-southwest string between the first two just described. The upper and lowermost are each about 5 acres, the middle one only about 1½ acres. All but the smallest lake are excellent fishing at times for 11 to 12 inch rainbow trout — and not a few lunkers to 6 or 8 pounds, or even better. Could be they feed on the axolotl. In 1979 and 1980 cutthroat trout were stocked in 3 of the lakes and should start showing up in creels about now.

Bear Trap Creek. Is quite small and steep, flows to the main river from the east, provides lots of rattlesnakes and about a mile of poor fishing for 8 to 10 inch rainbow trout. If you're interested, it can be reached by trail 4 miles down the east side of the river from the Madison Power House, or up 4 miles from the road barricade by trail up into Beartrap Canyon from the Norris Bridge across the Madison River.

Beaver Creek. Flows for 11 miles from the Taylor-Hilgard Mountains before discharging into Quake Lake. The drainage is important to wildlife of many forms including moose and elk, but only fair fishing for small rainbow trout, and not fished that much. There's a fair road up it for several miles.

Blaine Spring Creek. A hard to fish, very brushy creek that drains from Blaine Spring a half mile to the Ennis Cultural Station and then for another 3½ miles down a little draw through (mostly posted) open rangeland to the Madison River near Varney — and is followed all the way by a good county road. The stream is seldom fished, but below the hatchery it's real good for ½ to 2 pound rainbow and brown trout, plus a few that will run upwards to 4 pounds.

LARGEST OF THE AXOLOTL LAKES
Courtesy Bridenstine Studio

AVALANCHE LAKE
Courtesy USFS

Blue Lake. A beautiful blue water, deep 10 acre lake in a steep timbered pocket at the head of Elk River; reached in several ways but most folks drive 7 miles up the West Fork Madison road, cross Elk River, make a right turn from the West Fork Madison and head straight up the mountain for about 8 miles (by jeep). It was stocked in 1977, 1978 and 1981 with Yellowstone cutthroat trout and is good fishing for 10 to 14 inchers.

Blue Danube Lake. A fair fishing, moderately popular, 8 to 10 (and a few to 18 inch) golden trout, alpine lake in a 9000 foot elevation cirque; reached by trail 5 miles up the West Fork from the Beaver Creek Ranger Station near the end of the road 1½ miles west and then 3 miles north from Hebgen Dam. It's 14 acres, 40 feet deep with fairly steep dropoffs, and a rock bottom.

Blue Paradise Lake. See North Fork Hilgard Lakes.

Brentin Lake. A private dammed reservoir on Leonard Creek 3 miles above its junction with South Meadow Creek; reached by a private road a mile north from the South Meadow Creek Ranger Station. It's about 8 acres, in open rangeland but with timber on the south side and willows at the lower end, and it provides some good fishing for 6 to 12 inch rainbow, plus a few brown and brook trout.

Cabin Creek. Cascades down 2000 feet in only 10 miles from the Taylor-Hilgard Mountains entering the Madison River between Hebgen and Quake Lakes. Fair fishing and only lightly used for small rainbow, cutts and brown trout. There are only trails up it, no roads. It is also important moose, elk, deer, black and grizzly bear habitat.

Cameron Lake. From Ennis drive 11 miles south to Cameron, then take the Bear Creek road 8 miles to the Middle Fork, and finally a good USFS pack trail 4 steep miles to this 20 foot deep, 4 acre lake at 9020 feet above sea level. There's timber on the south and east sides, talus to the west and a meadow on the north side. Not many people make the trip because of the rugged climb — but it was stocked in 1976, 1979, and 1980 and is excellent fishing for 10 to 14 inch cutthroat trout.

Cataract Lake. See South Fork Hilgard Lakes.

Cedar Lake. Forty acres, 22 feet deep, planted with cutthroat in 1976 and 1981, at 9500 feet elevation above sea level, this mountain cirque lake is good for 8 to 13 inch fish, and has a nice falls in the outlet below the lake. From Ennis go a half dozen miles south, then east up Cedar Creek about 8 miles (by horse, bike or foot) and then a couple of miles below the lake the trail is closed to all vehicles.

Cherry Creek. Heads on the eastern slopes of Red Knob at the crest of the Madison Range and flows in a 20 mile half circle, first to the east, then south, and finally west to the Madison River 2½ miles below the Bozeman Bridge. The upper reaches are in timbered mountains, the middle and lower reaches in posted rangeland. About 14 miles are good to excellent fishing for skinny 8 to 12 inch brook trout, and some nice 3 to 4 pound browns come up into the lower reaches in the spring. The lower couple of miles are accessible by road, but posted tight, allowing no trespassing on most of the creek.

Cherry Lake. Lies in an open flat in timbered mountains at the head of an unnamed tributary of Cherry Creek at 8490 feet above sea level. It's about 4 acres, with mostly shallow dropoffs below nice open shores, and is fair-to-good fishing for 10 to 12 inch, and a few to 16 inch, cutthroat trout. You can just barely get there with a good jeep — or a mountain goat, 5 miles southeast from the Cherry Creek Ranger Station, or take the old Indian trail from near the Ennis Lake Dam.

Clear Lake. See South Fork Hilgard Lakes.

Cliff Lake. Hike ⅓ mile south from Alpine Lake (no trail) to 9 acre Cliff Lake (8940 feet elevation and 30 feet deep) in a rocky cirque below the steep cliffs of Belle Point which rises to 10,085 feet above sea level. It's not too often fished but is good for 8 to 14 inch cutthroat that were stocked in 1977, 1978 and 1981.

Cliff Lake. Is 4 miles long by as much as ⅓ of a mile wide — and real deep; right down in the bottom of a steep-walled canyon (heavily timbered on the west side) 30 miles west by road from West Yellowstone. There are three inlets: Horn Creek from the west, Antelope Creek and the short unnamed outlet of Otter and Goose Lakes up Lost Mine Canyon from the south). This is a very popular recreation area; there are tourist camps here and a tiny public campground on the northwest end of the lake (maybe 6 sites) — and, a 10 day camping limit. The fishing ??? It's good for 10 to 12 inch rainbow trout (reported up to an occasional 3 or 4 pounds) and mountain whitefish. It's tough to launch a fair-sized boat here — it needs a decent ramp.

Coffin Lakes. Upper and lower, 1500 yards apart in high (elevation 8500 and 8100 feet above sea level) spruce bottomed cirques; reached by a USFS pack trail 4 miles above the end of the Watkins Creek jeep road. Upper Coffin is about 10 acres, Lower Coffin 20 acres, and both are fairly deep, rocky bottomed and good fishing for 6 to 8 inch cutthroat trout.

Conklin (or Antelope Basin) Lake. Elevation, 6680 feet, 41 acres, an earth-dammed shallow hollow in an open sagebrush flat with the water ditched around to it about a mile from Antelope Creek. It's reached by a private road on the Vujovich Ranch and provides good fishing (for family friends) for rainbow-cutthroat hybrids that will average 1½ pounds and commonly weigh in at 4 pounds or better.

BLUE PARADISE LAKE
Courtesy USFS

THE BLUE DANUBE
Courtesy USFS

LOWER ECHO LAKE
Courtesy USFS

MOOSE IN THE MADISON
Courtesy USFS

Cougar Creek. Heads in Yellowstone National Park and flows west across the boundary for about 3 miles through flat, swampy, willowed-up country in Montana to Duck Creek about a mile above Hebgen Lake. It's crossed by roads in a couple of places, but there is no trail and it's quite brushy and hard to fish although fair along the lower couple of miles — for mostly 10 to 12 inch brookies, some cutthroat, grayling, rainbow, rarely a 4 to 5 pound brown trout probably up from Hebgen Lake, and a few whitefish.

Crag Lake. See North Fork Hilgard Lakes.

Crater Lakes. See Axolotl Lakes.

Crater Lake. In a little pocket below Ramshorn Mountain, with timber on the east, talus on the west, cross-country a thousand feet due north and 200 feet above the upper end of South Meadow Creek Lake. It's about 4 acres and deep with steep dropoffs. The fishing was poor but the fish real nice — in the 3 to 5 pound class. Seldom visited, may now be barren, my last visit — zip (1978).

Darlington Creek. A small, spring-fed hay meadow stream on the Darlington Brothers Ranch in the Madison Valley about 8 miles south of Three Forks. It was practically an unknown quantity because there's no brush along it and you just don't see it from the road — but it's excellent fishing for nice fat 1 to 5 pound brown trout. MDFWP's ¼ mile long cobblestone access gets its share of visitors now.

Denny Creek. Flows from the vicinity of Targhee Pass for 4 miles eastward through timber above and (posted) pastureland below to the South Fork Arm of Hebgen Lake. It's crossed here and there by roads and the lower (posted) couple of miles are fair fishing (when the opportunity arises) for small brook trout.

Duck Creek. Is a small, marsh and willow bordered stream that flows from Yellowstone Park about 3 miles across flat, swampy meadowland to the upper end of the Grayling Arm of Hebgen Lake. There is no trail, but it's approached and crossed by private roads and is moderately popular and easy to fish for fair catches of mostly small brookies, a few small cutthroat, grayling, rainbow and some really nice (rarely) brown trout up to 5 or 6 pounds probably migrating up from Hebgen Lake.

East Fork Denny Creek. Heads in some beaver ponds on the big flat about 8 miles west of West Yellowstone and is followed by a logging road for 4 miles down its timbered canyon to the main stream. It's moderately popular and fair fishing in the ponds for 8 to 12 inch brook trout.

123

Echo Lakes.
Two, Upper and Lower, about 10 acres, deep wth steep dropoffs, in grassy pockets with some scattered timber, about 400 yards apart and a mile west of Echo Peak below the crest of the Madison Range (elevation 9550 and 9800 feet) in really scenic, mountain goat country reached a couple of miles cross-country from the Moose Creek Trail along the top of the Madison-Gallatin Divide. Both lakes are snowed in until mid-July. Both are excellent fishing for 8 to 14 inch rainbow trout, with once in a while, a winner to 3 pounds.

Elk Creek.
Heads below Ruby Mountain and is followed here and there by roads and trails as it flows west for 15 miles to the Madison River and State 287, twelve miles north of Ennis. It's a small, mostly open rangeland stream that is poor (full of sediment) for pan-size rainbow and brook trout — and is only lightly fished.

Elk River.
Take the West Fork Madison River road 7 miles upstream to the mouth of this small "river" in brushy, grassy country — and then jeep up it a couple of miles to the canyon which you bypass for 3 miles to the end of the trail in timbered mountains. It's moderately popular and easily fished below the canyon, where it's fair for 6 to 8 inch rainbow, plus a few cutthroat and brown trout. The canyon reaches are pretty rough, but the next 3½ miles above are also fishable.

Ennis (or Meadow) Lake.
Elevation 4820 feet above sea level, subcircular, about 3 miles in diameter, in open grassland 5 miles below (south of) Ennis and followed all around the north and east sides by a good county road. Ennis Lake is really a flooded hay meadow and is mostly quite shallow except for the old stream channels through it. It's full of weeds in summer and underated but tough fishing (chiefly in the deepest water along the old channels) the year around for rainbow, brown and a very few whitefish and grayling. Some real whoppers have been caught here and still are. However, 20 years from now there likely won't be anything left. The water is just too warm, could damage the Madison River below too if something drastic isn't done about it, like removing the dam. In the meantime, occasional rainbow to 6 pounds and good sized grayling (to 2 pounds) can be caught here, especially in the spring, and often on a fly rod — surprisingly.

Expedition Lake.
See North Fork Hilgard Lakes.

Falls Creek Lake (Upper).
Two and a half acres, in open alpine country a mile southeast by trail from Lake Solitude, 12 devious miles from Ennis. It was stocked with cutthroat in 1953 but nothing since — and — is nowhere over 8 feet deep and they may have frozen out, although one packer reported seeing fish jump in the summer of 1964 and a hiker "thought" he saw one rise in '68 — probably barren now, huh?

Finger Lakes.
See Moose Lake.

NOT FOR BEGINNERS
Courtesy Bill Browning

CRAG LAKE AND EXPEDITION LAKE
Courtesy USFS

UNNAMED LAKE ON SOUTH FORK
Courtesy USFS

QUAKE LAKE
Courtesy Ernst Peterson

Freezeout Creek. The small outlet of (barren) Freezeout Lake, flows down a sagebrush and willowed-up draw for 6 miles from the southern slopes of Flatiron Mountain to the West Fork of the Madison River where it's crossed by the West Fork road. There's no trail up this creek and it's seldom fished, the first 1½ miles are poor for 6 to 8 inch rainbow and cutthroat trout.

Gazelle Creek. Take State 287, ten miles north down the Madison River from "Quake Lake" and across that stream to the West Fork Cow Camp, and from there a pack trail 5 miles (in an erratic zig-zag fashion) to the middle reaches of Gazelle Creek — in a narrow, timbered canyon — and another 4 miles to headwaters. It's a very steep, almost torrential stream, very tiny, but the lower couple of miles (as far up as the rapids) are fished a little bit for 7 to 8 inch rainbow and a few brown trout.

Gnome Lake. See South Fork Hilgard Lakes.

Goose Lake. A half mile by trail below Hidden Lake and ⅛ mile by trail above Otter Lake, at 6600 feet elevation above sea level, in timbered country near the head of Lost Mine Canyon 2½ miles above Horn Arm of Cliff Lake. It's about 10 acres in size, shallow, is fished a fair amount and is good for rainbow and rainbow-cutthroat hybrids that average about 12 to 14 inches and range up to 4 or 5 pounds.

Grayling Creek. Only the lower 3½ miles of this small stream are outside Yellowstone Park in Montana, and only the lower mile (above the mouth of Grayling Arm of Hebgen Lake) is on public land. The "Montana" reaches are in a swampy willowed-up area and are hard to fish (mostly by tourists with access through dude ranches along the way) with only fair success for a little bit of everything — that is — mostly 6 to 10 inch rainbow, a few brooks, cutts, some browns to an occasional 18 inches, and whitefish. It was planted with cutthroat in 1979 and 1980 to enhance the Hebgen Lake "cutt" fishery.

Grayling Lake. See Wigwam Reservoir.

Ha Hand Lake. See North Fork Hilgard Lakes.

Haypress Creek. The very small outlet of Haypress Lake, flowing for a couple of miles eastward across private (closed) rangeland to Wigwam Creek about ½ mile above the end of the road at the Shining Mountains ranch. It's seldom fished, but the first mile below the lake is fair for nice-size rainbow.

Haypress Lake. See Wigwam Reservoir.

Hebgen Lake. A very popular, commercialized, tourist resort, summer home, waterskiing, picnicking, swimming, and fishing area. Hebgen is a most irregularly shaped body of water, 16 miles long by as much as 3 miles wide in the timbered, mountainous, "quake" area 6 miles west of State 287 from Yellowstone Park. There are roads (and people) all around it. In spite of all the "traffic" the fishing holds up to good-or-better for 10 to 13 inch rainbow trout (a few to 4 pounds), plus a fair number of the biggest browns in Montana (in the 6 to 22 pound class) in the winter. It is now being stocked (200,000 in 1981) with McBride cutthroat, a long-lived vigorous trout that should be 1 pounders in the summer of 1982, and if they spawn successfully in the future, may eventually negate the further stocking of the reservoir — establishing a "wild" fishery.

Hidden Lake. A very popular, excellent fishing lake at 6600 feet elevation above sea level in a timbered canyon ½ mile above Goose Lake by a good trail, or 2½ miles north from Elk Lake (by jeep) on the Red Rock drainage. It is 149 acres in size, deep with steep dropoffs, and has a camp and boat livery at the north end. There is a really good population of hungry 13 to 18 inch rainbow and rainbow-cutthroat hybrids here and the fishing pressure is extreme.

Hilgard Lakes. See South Fork Hilgard Lakes.

Horse Creek. Heads on Monument Ridge and is followed by a USFS horse trail for 10 miles eastward down its narrow canyon to an unimproved road (6 miles south from the Wall Creek Guard Station) at the head of a short narrow gorge which ends a mile above the stream's mouth on the Madison River. A tiny creek, the lower 4 miles are fishable, although very brushy, and support fair numbers of 6 to 8 inch rainbow and cutthroat trout — especially in some beaver ponds along the lower reaches.

Hot Springs (or Warm Springs) Creek. A small, beaver-dammed stream that flows through open rangeland eastward for 9 miles right through the town of Norris — and on to the Madison River — and is followed by State 287 most of the way. It's fished quite a lot by kids (and grownups too, for that matter) for mostly brown trout 10 to 12 inches long, but up to 2 pounds, and rainbow trout 10 to 14 inches.

Indian Creek. A small stream flowing west from the Madison Range to the Madison River about 18 miles above Ennis. It's crossed at the mouth by State 287, and the lower reaches are accessible by county and private roads across open rangeland to the mouth of its canyon about 6 miles upstream, but this part is almost completely dewatered for irrigation. The next 4½ miles are

HA-NANA LAKE
Courtesy USFS

126

UNNAMED LAKE ON SOUTH FORK
Courtesy USFS

followed by a USFS trail up its timbered (and quite brushy in places) canyon past lots of open spots and nice clear holes that are excellent fishing for 10 to 13 inch rainbow trout. You'll not be bothered by an over supply of company, either. In the past access to the forest land has been a problem and needs to be resolved.

Jack Creek. Take the east side Madison River road about 3½ miles north from Ennis to the mouth of Jack Creek, then a good county road 4 miles east up its broad, open rangeland fan; from there a logging road for another 3½ miles up its narrow, timbered canyon to the mouth of Hammond Creek and finally a USFS foot trail and cross country hike for 6 miles to its head in Ulreys Lakes. The lower reaches are mostly dewatered for irrigation, but the road and trail reaches, especially in some little grassy basins about 2 miles above the end of the road, are heavily fished for 8 to 15 inch rainbow trout, and a rare brown.

Lake Creek. Is fed by underground drainage from Wade Lake and flows north through open rangeland for a mile and a half down its little, flat-bottomed canyon to the West Fork Madison River across from the road. It's a small stream without many holes, but there are some nice riffles and it's fished a lot for 8 to 10 inch (a few to 14) rainbow and brown trout.

Lily Lake. Is accessible by trail right on timberline in scenic mountain country about midway between Alpine and Lupine Lakes. It is about 14 acres, 20 feet maximum depth, has 8 to 14 inch cutthroat and was planted with cutthroat fingerling in 1971 and 1977, and with the fry of McBride Lake cutts in 1981 — excellent fishing.

Lost Lake. I hope someone finds this one — and reports on it. From Shadow Lake strike out to the southeast up a little draw for 2 miles through, over, under and around standing and down lodgepole to the lakeshore in a deep cirque at about 8890 feet elevation above sea level on the west side of Lone Mountain. It's about 3 acres, with talus slopes to the water at the upper (east) end and has, supposedly, provided some red hot fishing some 10 years back. P.S. Don't confuse it with the Lost Lake about 1500 yards east of Shadow Lakes. That one is barren.

Lupine Lake. Lies in a beautiful timbered basin (elevation 8400 feet above sea level) formed below the 10,000 to 15,000 foot sheer rock walls of Ward Peak to the east, Porphyry Mountain to the south, Belle Point to the west and Kid Mountain to the north; 1¼ miles by trail (past Lily Lake) southeast from Alpine Lake. Lupine is 7 acres in size, fairly shallow but doesn't freeze out and contains 8 to 10 inch cutthroat trout. It is very seldom visited. The lake above (about the same size), ½ mile in the cirque, reportedly is fair fishing also.

McKelvey Lake. See Alpine Lake.

Meadow Lake. See Ennis Lake.

CANOEING ON THE MADISON
Courtesy US Fish & Wildlife

ONE OF THE "BARREN" SUNSET LAKES
Courtesy USFS

Moose (or Finger) Lakes.

A couple of 2 acre "wide spots" in (barren) Moose Creek, moderately deep but with shallow dropoffs, in timber with rock and meadows along the sides; a most scenic camp site reached by 4 miles of good trail above the end of the Moose Creek jeep road which takes off from State 287 about 30 miles above Ennis. It's heavily fished by mostly dudes — for fair catches of 6 to 12 inch cutthroat trout, stocked in 1976 and 1981 as 2 inchers.

No Man Creek.

A small tributary of Indian Creek about 31 miles above the end of the road. There's a trail all the way up its timbered canyon to the lake (No Man), but only the lower couple of miles are mediocre fishing water — for 8 to 10 inch cutthroat. It's not fished much!

No Man Lake.

Is reached by 3 miles of good USFS pack trail (the last ½ mile steepens up quite a bit) in a glacial cirque at the head of No Man Creek at 9200 feet above sea level. It's about 10 acres, timbered around the north (outlet) side with talus and rock elsewhere, is over 75 feet deep, planted in 1971, 1976, and 1981, is excellent fishing for 9 to 14 inchers (cutthroat), and uncommonly, One to 3 or 4 pounds.

North Fork Hilgard Lakes.

Nine lakes and a few potholes, reached by trail 1 to 3 miles south-southeast of Expedition Pass, reached by trail 7 miles from the end of the Beaver Creek road up Sentinel Creek. The first one you come to is Expedition Lake, which is in a high mountain meadow, is about 3 acres, fairly deep with a rock and mud bottom, and good for cutthroat and rainbow to 14 inches. The next lake is ¼ mile east down the drainage, Crag Lake, which is about half in timber and half in open meadow, about 5 acres in size, fairly deep, fair fishing for 6 to 14 inch rainbow trout, easy to fish and fairly popular inasmuch as there is a dude camp setup here. Ha Hand Lake, ½ mile to the south and right on the trail, 6 acres, 29 foot maximum depth, used to contain BIG rainbow, now is good for cutts 7 to 16 inches and gets quite a play. Blue Paradise, a mile south by trail from Ha Hand and the southernmost of the North Fork Hilgard lakes, is in a timbered cirque, about 5 acres, good and deep with steep dropoffs below talus slopes that reach to the shore along the west side, and is real spotty but sometimes fair fishing for 10 to 16 inch rainbow, golden trout, cutts, and crosses. The remaining 5 lakes are reportedly all barren or nearly so at this writing.

North Meadow Creek.

Heads below Alpine Lake at 8500 feet elevation above sea level, and flows 16 miles southeastward to Ennis Lake at 4825 feet elevation above sea level. It also drains Twin Lakes by a mile long tributary, and is paralleled by a jeep road for most of its length. The upper reaches flow down a timbered canyon, the lower reaches across open rangeland but with lots of willow along its margins. There are a series of cataracts a couple of miles below Lower Twin Lake and from here down the fishing is good for 6 to 10 inch cutthroat, rainbow, and an increasing pecentage of brook trout. The lower reaches are on private land and fair for brown trout to 14 inches and small rainbow.

128

BUGLING ELK
Courtesy Ernst Peterson

MOOSE IN THE MADISON
Courtesy USFS

Odell Creek. A spring-fed "pickup" creek, almost a channel of the Madison River which it joins 1½ miles north of Ennis. It heads about 8 miles south of town in open rangeland and is crossed just east of town by State 287. Although it's small, the banks are often undercut and there are lots of nice holes which are excellent fishing (with the owner's permission) for browns that run all the way up to 7 or 8 pounds and a few small rainbow. It's pretty brushy in spots and hard to fish — unless you've got an "in," it's almost totally "private!"

Otter Lake. Is reached by a good trail ½ mile below Goose Lake, or 2½ miles through timber up Lost Mine Canyon from the end of the Horn Arm of Cliff Lake. Otter is about 10 acres, not more than 35 feet deep anywhere with fairly shallow dropoffs and lots of snags around the shore, and is extremely clear and difficult to fish although fair-to-good at times for 12 to 14 inch rainbow. You'll have plenty of company here.

Painted Lake. See South Fork Hilgard Lakes.

Quake Lake. After all the notoriety a few years ago, this one needs little description. It is about 4 miles long by a maximum of ⅓ mile wide, quite deep with lots of "drowned" timber to snag your line, and was, of course, formed behind the famous Madison Canyon Slide. It's accessible all along the south side by State 287, a few miles below the outlet of Hebgen Lake. A popular tourist spot in the summer, the fishing is good for 10 to 14 inch rainbow trout (sometimes to 3 pounds), some pretty nice 10 to 20 inch browns (to 5 pounds fairly often), and 12 to 14 inch whitefish. Although not "found" yet, it's a good ice fishing lake.

Ruby Creek. There's about 6 miles of fair fishing here, for mostly 8 to 10 inch rainbow and a few cutthroat and brown trout above, and rainbow, cutthroat and brook trout (in some beaver ponds) below. Take a county road west from State 287 (at the mouth of Indian Creek) across the Madison River, and then turn south for 3 miles to the mouth of Ruby Creek and follow jeep roads for about 5 miles on upstream. There's lots of beaver ponds, brush and swamp for the first 1½ miles, and then a very narrow, timbered canyon on upstream.

Shadow Lakes. Two, in timber maybe 100 yards apart and 500 yards east of the South Fork of Jack Creek 6 miles by a good USFS trail from the end of the Jack Creek road at the campground. The Lower Lake is about 6 acres, the Upper one about half that and neither is more than 20 feet deep with lots of shoal water. There are quite a few campers who come here for the good rainbow trout fishing — 10 to 12 inchers.

Sheep Lake. From State 287 about 5 miles west of Quake Lake, take the "good" Cliff Lake road 2 miles south, then the Horn Creek road 4 miles southwest to the Shaw Ranch, then a jeep road 3 miles north to Sheep Creek, and finally a USFS trail 5 miles up the creek to this 25 acre lake in a deep mostly barren cirque (although there is some timber around the shore). It is seldom fished but reported to be fair-to-good for 6 to 8 inch cutthroat trout.

Smith Lake.
A quarter of a mile long, not so very wide spot on Lake Creek; fished more than somewhat for good catches of 8 to 14 inch rainbow and brown trout (now and then up to 2 pounds).

Soap Creek.
A pretty little mountain stream flowing east through timber and brush for 6 miles to the West Fork of the Madison River, 2½ miles by good road from the West Fork Forest Service Camp. It's seldom fished but does support a few small rainbow and brown trout.

South Fork Hilgard Lakes.
Six (Hilgard, Cataract, Gnome, Painted, Clear and Talus) alpine lakes between 9200 and 10,000 feet elevation above sea level on the northern slopes of Hilgard Peak; reached by an old, abandoned (largely impassable) trail up the South Fork of Hilgard Creek, or you can come in ¾ of a mile "over the ridge" south from Blue Paradise. All were stocked years ago and were once fair-to-excellent fishing, but there was no reproduction, some had the habit of freezing out, and all of them are now reportedly either fair fishing at best or barren. More people than you'd suspect — try.

South Fork of Indian Creek.
Joins Indian Creek at the end of the road and is followed upstream by trail for 3½ miles, or a mile beyond the "top" of the fishing. This is a snow fed, open rangeland (with some scattered timber, brush and willows), high gradient stream that used to have lots of beaver dams that slowed it down and the ponds were real nice to fish. There are some 10 foot falls at its mouth and these act as a fish barrier so that only native cutthroat trout were caught — 10 to 12 inches and lots of them. However, the beaver are now gone and most of the fish with them. There are only a few 4 to 6 inchers left.

South Fork of the Madison River.
A good fishing creek in timbered hill country with lots of water in the lower reaches (4 miles), which are followed by a jeep road from its mouth at the head of the South Fork Arm of Hebgen Lake. There is a USFS public campground (the South Fork camp) about 2 miles upstream and tourists fish the stream a fair amount for 12 to 18 inch "wild" brown trout (especially in the lower reaches), some rainbow which averge smaller, and a very few brookies and whitefish. Cutthroat were recently planted here to enhance the Hebgen Lake fishery by using this as a spawning stream, hopefully, when mature. Note: Some of the fall brown trout spawners from Hebgen Lake will tip the scales at 5, 6, 7, 8 or what-have-you pounds.

South Meadow Creek.
The small outlet of South Meadow Creek Lake, about 11 miles long to its mouth on Ennis Lake ¾ of a mile below Meadow Lake Camp. It is crossed by State 287 a mile and a half upstream and is followed along the south side past the 7 mile point, which is as far as there is fishing. The lower 5 miles are in open rangeland, the next couple of miles in timber — and fair fishing for mostly 7 to 10 inch brook, rainbow, and some cutts. It's not fished much, though, because there is better water close at hand.

HA NANA LAKE
Courtesy USFS

ECHO PEAK
Courtesy USFS

BEAVER DAM ON NORTH MEADOW CREEK
Courtesy USSCS

HILGARD LAKES
Courtesy USFS

South Meadow Creek Lake.
Seventy-nine acres and 42 feet deep; an earth-dammed reservoir below talus slopes on the south side and scattered timber on the north side, at 8800 feet elevation above sea level on the eastern slopes of Ramshorn Mountain; reached by a jeep road a couple of miles above the "Missouri Mine." It is good fishing here — rainbow trout that will average 10 to 14 inches and range up to 16 or better, and was "replanted" in 1978 with 4 inchers. You will not be alone here.

Spring Branch.
Heads on the northern slopes of Deer Mountain where it is crossed by a jeep road 6½ miles southeast from State 287, and then flows north for 5 miles down a shallow draw across mostly open grassland to Antelope Creek just above its mouth at the end of Antelope Prong of Cliff Lake. The lower mile is fair early season fishing for 7 to 8 inch rainbow trout.

Squaw Creek.
A fast stream flowing southwesterly for 10 miles before joining the Madison River near the West Fork Campground (opposite Standard Creek). Access is severely restricted, permission needed, but if granted, the creek is good for rainbow trout to 11 inches and browns to 15 inches. Lots of luck.

Standard Creek.
Heads at 9300 feet above sea level on the crest of the Gravelly Range in good elk hunting country just "over the saddle" from the headwaters of Cottonwood Creek on the Ruby River drainage. Standard Creek flows east through timber and open sagebrush country for 12 miles to the Madison River a couple of miles north of the West Fork Campground. The lower reaches are in a steep little canyon with no trail, but a jeep road 9 miles south from Ruby Creek crosses Standard at the head of the canyon and a trail takes you on up to headwaters — and to the Cottonwood Creek and Gravelly Ridge roads. There are a half dozen or so beaver ponds for about a mile up above the head of the canyon and they are fair fishing for small (6 to 12 inch) rainbow, brook and cutthroat trout. The lower end is posted.

Sureshot Lakes.
Upper and Lower; 5 acres each with shallow dropoffs and maximum depths of 37 and 15 feet respectively; ¼ mile apart on the timbered eastern slopes of the Tobacco Root Muntains at 7100 and 7240 feet above sea level and reached by a poor dirt road 2 miles northwest from the North Meadow Creek road at a point 2½ miles above the Washington Creek junction. These lakes are not dammed but have been formed by diverting water from Sureshot Creek into natural depressions. The Upper one is heavily fished (heaven knows why) for zillions of 4 to 6 inch brook trout. The Lower one is good fishing now for small cutthroat.

Talus Lake.
See South Fork Hilgard Lakes.

Teepee Creek.
Is seldom fished, very small, in timbered country, crossed at its mouth on Grayling Creek a few miles up from the lake by State 191 just within Yellowstone Park. The lower mile is fair, fishing (if you could call it that) for 4 to 6 inch cutthroat.

Teepee Creek. Flows from off Lobo Mesa for 6 miles eastward to the West Fork of the Madison River just above the end of the North Fork Road. The lower mile is in rolling sagebrush and grass covered hills and, although it is not much of a creek and is seldom bothered, it does support a few 6 to 8 inch rainbow and brook trout.

Three Forks Ponds. Three, with fish, borrow pits side by side in open fields just south of U.S. 10 a mile east of Three Forks. The westernmost pond is a half mile long but quite narrow and only 12 acres, 12 feet deep with steep dropoffs. The middle, and largest pond, is 22 acres, 14 feet maximum depth, also with steep dropoffs all around. The oval shaped easternmost pond is 1.3 acres, fairly shallow but steep off from the shores. The U.S. Fish and Wildlife Service and the MDFWP are going to plant trout in the spring to monitor growth rates and success ratios (ponds middle and west have been rehabilitated). The east pond reportedly has largemouth bass and cutthroat. All are heavily fished.

Trapper Creek. Is quite small, crossed at the mouth by the west side Hebgen Lake road and followed upstream by a jeep road for about a mile of so-so fishing for 8 to 10 inchers. It's seldom bothered.

Twin Lakes. See Axolotl Lakes.

Twin Lakes. Are shallow, earth-dammed reservoirs reached by the North Meadow Creek jeep road at 8000 feet elevation above sea level in timber and talus 9 miles northeast from McAllister. Upper Twin is about 30 acres with some marsh at the upper end; Lower Twin is about 10 acres and they are both moderately popular and very good fishing indeed — for 8 to 10 inch cutthroat trout, stocked again in 1978. The road is in a mess, and may be impassable some years.

Upper Falls Creek Lake. See Falls Creek Lake (upper).

Upper Haypress Reservoirs. See Wigwam Reservoir.

Ulreys Lakes. Three (Lower, Upper, Upper-upper) in timbered pockets a mile and a half northeast of Lone Mountain and reached by pack trail 4 miles east from Shadow Lakes, or ½ mile from the end of a good dirt road up the Middle Fork of the West Fork of the Gallatin River. Lower Ulrey is about 7 acres in size, 17 feet maximum depth, is more or less covered with lily pads, used to be a fish hatchery, and was planted with cutthroat in 1981. Upper Ulrey is 150 feet above and ½ mile east by trail. It is 6 acres, nowhere over 10 feet deep, and excellent fishing for 10 to 12 inch rainbow trout. Upper-upper Ulrey lies 80 feet above and 1000 yards to the east (cross-country but easily negotiable with horses) from Upper Ulrey. It is only 3 acres, deep but with mostly shallow dropoffs, and had a few BIG rainbow trout in it — up to better than 8 pounds recorded. Who knows?

Wade Lake. A very popular, 1½ mile long by ¼ of a mile wide, deep lake, in a steep-walled canyon ½ mile below (north of) Cliff Lake by a good gravel road. As at Cliff Lake, there's a small public campground here (with a 10 day limit), plus a tourist resort and boat livery. The lake is heavily fished — for mostly 10 to 13 inch rainbow and an occasional good-size brown trout. A 29 pound brown (largest caught by hook and line in the state) was caught the summer of 1967. Ten pounders are not uncommon. The rainbow (10,000 or so 5 inchers) are stocked annually. They can run to 5 pounds or more on occasion. The boat launch is gravel — not for your larger craft. It's good ice fishing here (by snowmobile).

Wall Creek. The lower 1½ miles of this little stream flow through a steep walled brushy little canyon to the Madison River across that stream from State 287 — 7 miles below (north of) the West Fork Madison River Campground. The first mile above the canyon is in open rangeland and above that there are another 6 miles or so of canyon. There are lots of beaver ponds in the rangeland stretch and fishing is fair here for 6 to 8 inch brookies, plus a few rainbow and cutthroat trout. It's not really much of a stream though, and even if it were — it's posted!

Warm Springs Creek. See Hot Springs Creek.

Watkins Creek. A small stream flowing to the southwest side of Hebgen Lake where it is crossed by a good USFS road. The lower (willow-bordered) open grassland reaches are followed for a couple of miles by a jeep road and support a small population of 5 to 6 inch rainbow trout. It's seldom fished.

WADE LAKE
Courtesy Bridenstine Studio

MADISON RIVER
Courtesy Ernst Peterson

West Fork Madison River.
Joins the Madison River 9 miles below Quake Lake and is reached at the mouth (at the West Fork Campground) by a bridge across the river from State 287. From here it is followed upstream by a jeep road for 14 miles of good fishing. It mostly flows down a narrow, flat-bottomed but steep-walled little valley (almost a canyon), in timber along the lower reaches and open rangeland and timber above. There are lots of side channels along the West Fork, with numerous beaver ponds that support good populations of mostly 8 to 11 inch rainbow, some 10 to 16 inch brown trout and a few whitefish. The stream sustains a moderate amount of fishing pressure. Due to natural conditions and overgrazing, it carries a heavy sediment load. Moose winter in its willow covered bottomland.

Wolf Creek.
Crosses mostly private land in its lower reaches, with plenty of Forest Service land above. It is small but good for 5 to 10 inch rainbow, coming into the Madison River from the east a mile south of the South Madison Campground. A nifty little creek but mostly "posted."

Whits Lakes.
From the junction of State 191 and 287, drive west on State 287 for 2 miles and then take a jeep road to the northeast for another 2 miles to these 1 and 3 acre, 15 feet or so deep lakes in rolling timbered country east of Graycroft Ridge. There are some small openings around the lower lake, but the upper one is timbered right to the shore all the way around. They were reportedly only poor-to-fair fishing for 18 to 20 inch rainbow trout — may have died out.

Wigwam Creek.
Five miles long, in timber above and open rangeland below; reached near the mouth by road 1½ miles south from Varney and followed upstream for a couple of miles. The lower reaches are in open (posted) rangeland and just as well, too, because they are poor fishing at best for 6 inch or so cutthroat trout.

Wigwam Reservoirs (or Haypress Reservoirs or Grayling Lake).
Two shallow, 3 acre lakes a few hundred yards apart in open rangeland with a spring between them, reached by jeep 2 miles up Wigwam Creek from the end of the road and then another mile up a small tributary to the northwest. The upper reservoir (or Grayling Lake) used to have grayling in it — naturally — but both lakes now contain only 1 to 1½ pound rainbow trout, and are private — permission needed.

Release Fish Carefully

Marias River

The Marias River heads at the junction of the Two Medicine River and Cut Bank Creek a dozen airline miles south of Cut Bank. The river then flows east and south for approximately 130 miles through open range and farmland to the Missouri River 50 miles northeast of Great Falls on U.S. 87. It's crossed by three bridges above and four bridges below Tiber Reservoir. Other access is by trails mostly through private land. The river is sluggish above and below Tiber Reservoir; however, for the first 10-15 miles below the dam the river flows over clean sand and gravel and has many good runs, pools and riffles.

The entire drainage above the reservoir was rehabilitated prior to closure of the gates of Tiber Dam to eradicate goldeye and carp. The rehab project was successful in getting rid of the goldeye but carp have again invaded the system. The upper reaches above the reservoir are fair to poor fishing for rainbow, brown and whitefish. The lower reaches on down to the reservoir are very good at times for northern pike, walleye, channel catfish and burbot.

A variety of species provide an excellent fishery immediately below Tiber Dam for at least the first 10-15 miles. These include rainbow (up to 5 pounds), brown, sauger, walleye, northern pike (up to 20 pounds), burbot, yellow perch and goldeye. A large population of mountain whitefish also inhabit this stretch with some approaching state record size. Occasional paddlefish have been reported, especially during years of extremely high flows such as the 1964 flood. The remainder of the river, beyond the first 10-15 miles below the dam, to the mouth, gradually increases in turbidity and water temperature. Few trout are found in this section but the same species listed below the dam do occur. The lowermost reaches are popular for channel catfish, burbot, and shovelnose sturgeon. Several species of rough fish are found throughout the river, both above and below the reservoir.

Bill Hill

Marias River Drainage

Big Badger Creek. Heads below Half Dome Crag at the junction of the North and South Forks 6 miles east of the Continental Divide and flows generally northeastward for 35 airline miles to Two Medicine Creek. The upper 7 or 8 miles flow down a steep, rock-walled, timber and brushy-bottomed canyon in the Lewis and Clark National Forest. The lower reaches are all on Blackfeet Indian Reservation grazing land. The upper 5 miles are accessible by horse or bike trails 2½ miles over the pass from the head of the South Fork Two Medicine Creek. The lower reaches are crossed by U.S. 89 seventeen miles southeast from Browning and are accessible all along to within a few hundred yards by private and county roads. It's moderately popular; the upper reaches are fair fishing for 8 to 15 inch cutthroat and some brooks; the lower reaches are fair-to-good for 8 to 12 inch cutthroat, rainbow and brook trout in the summer, and also for whitefish in winter.

Big Spring Lake. A half-mile long by a couple of hundred yards wide, private (posted) lake in open Blackfeet Indian Reservation rangeland at the very base of the Rockies, with some scattered cottonwood and willow around it; reached by road 3 miles south and east from East Glacier. Time was when it was very good fishing indeed (although seldom visited) for 18 to 20 inch brook trout. They're all gone now.

Birch Creek. Marks the southern boundary of the Blackfoot Indian Reservation from its head at Swift Reservoir for 17 airline miles to its mouth on Two Medicine Creek, 6 airline miles north from Lake Francis. It's reached by U.S. 89 ten miles north from Dupuyer and is crossed here and there and followed the full length to within ½ mile or so by county and private roads. An open rangeland stream with scattered patches of timber along the flood plain, it's not fished often but used to be fair-to-good for 8 to 9 inch rainbow, cutthroat and brook trout but was flooded and scoured badly when the Swift Reservoir went out in '64 and hasn't recovered too well.

Blacktail Creek. A small Indian Reservation grazing land stream flowing northeastward 3 to 4 miles (to the northeast), more or less parallel with, and eventually to, Birch Creek 11 miles due north of Dupuyer. U.S. 89 crosses it a couple of miles above the mouth and you can jeep along it (but few do) 16 miles to headwaters. The lower, meandering reaches are poor fishing for 6 to 10 inch rainbow, brook trout, and rough fish. The upper reaches flow down a little coulee, are considerably faster than below and fair-to-good fishing for more of the same.

Cameron Reservoir. Lies behind a 30 foot dam in moderately steep hilly country south of Mosquito Coulee below Gold Butte; reached by a few fishermen, 35 miles northeast by first paved and finally dirt roads from Sunburst. It's about 30 acres, 20 feet deep with grassy banks, and fair-to-good fishing for 12 to 16 inch rainbow stocked annually by the Fish and Game.

Chester Pond. An old railroad water supply pond of maybe 3 acres right in Chester; planted with rainbow at times (when water levels are up) and can be fair to middling fishing before it winterkills.

Cooper (or Minnie Whitehorse) Lake. A lightly fished, Blackfeet Indian Reservation lake reached by jeep road 2½ miles up the South Fork Little Badger Creek. It sits almost on the top of a hill in scrub pine, is 19½ acres, has a maximum depth of 15 feet, lots of aquatic vegetation, and is on-again, off-again water. It used to be planted annually with cutthroat, was thought to have frozen out in the early '60s, but was good fishing in the mid-'60s and early '70s and if it hasn't frozen out should still be. It was last planted in 1975.

Cut Bank Creek. Heads among the ice-scoured peaks of Glacier National Park and flows east from the Park for 65 miles across pastureland and the Blackfeet Indian Reservation to the mouth of Two Medicine Creek at the head of the Marias River 12 airline miles south from Cut Bank. It's crossed by U.S. 2 near Cut Bank and a dozen times here and there by county roads and is accessible all along (where you can get permission) by roads and trails. It's heavily fished, where available, for good catches of 6 to 16 inch rainbow, brook, and some cutthroat trout and ling in the upper reaches, and ling and brown trout below, plus whitefish in the winter.

KEEPERS
Courtesy Bill Browning

Dawson (or Dog Gone) Lake. A 20 foot maximum depth, 80 acre by a mile long, Blackfeet Indian Reservation lake reached by a fair secondary road in open rangeland-foothill country at the eastern edge of the Rockies 20 miles south and west from Browning. Used to be "doggone" good for rainbow, was stocked with eastern brook in 1978 and 1979 and at last report, was "doggone" good for small trout, and used accordingly.

Deep Creek. A very small, very brushy, foothill creek draining into and out of Dog Gone Lake for 10 miles northeastward to Two Medicine Creek. The upper reaches are followed by trail (on posted land but with access generally given on request) and are good fishing for 8 to 10 inch brook and a few cutthroat trout.

Dog Gone Lake. See Dawson Lake.

Dry Fork Sheep Creek. Drys up in dry years, but there are about 6 miles of good fishing when it doesn't for 6 to 10 inch brook trout. It's mostly on private rangeland; there is no trail but it's all accessible to within a mile by county roads just west from Dupuyer; there are some nice springs, pools and beaver ponds along its meandering course — it's only lightly fished.

Dupuyer Creek. Heads at the junction of its North, Middle and South Forks at the edge of the Rockies below Old Man Of The Hills Mountain, and flows for 12 miles as the crow flies northeastward to Dupuyer, and for another 9 to junction with Birch Creek 7 miles north of Lake Francis. It's an open rangeland stream, pretty brushy, mostly paralleled by county roads (except for about 4 miles northeast from Dupuyer), and fair-to-good fishing for 8 to 10 inch rainbow, brook, and a few cutthroat trout in the upper reaches.

Elizabeth Lake. See Fish Lake.

Fish (or Elizabeth or Patrick) Lake. A private dammed (earth-fill) lake below Split Mountain 3 airline miles east of Swift Reservoir — with little access allowed and very light fishing pressure. It's 5 acres, as much as 25 feet deep in spots, pretty well up on a hillside in scrubby limber pine, and can be reached, with permission, 15 miles west by fair secondary roads from Dupuyer. It's been privately stocked and is reported to be fair-to-good for middling size rainbow, brook, and some cutthroat trout.

Fish Creek Lake (or Spring). A half-acre beaver pond on Birch Creek about a mile above the Swift Reservoir reached by the Birch Creek trail; seldom fished and only poor at best for small brook trout.

Fitzpatrick (or Hutterite) Reservoir. From Sunburst drive ten miles west, then a couple of miles south and finally three more west to the shore of this 75 acre, mud-bottomed reservoir that is stocked with rainbow (20,000/year); pretty good fishing much of the time and as a result, moderately popular, with access and parking lot on state land on west shore.

136

Courtesy USSCS

Flat Iron Creek. A very small, brushy, grazing land tributary of Cut Bank Creek reached by county roads 4 miles north and west from Browning. There are only about 2 miles of fishing (on posted land with permission required) but is pretty good as quite a few local people will attest — for 8 to 10 inch brook and rainbow trout. Access is easy — there are cow trails all over the place. Quite a few beaver ponds here too.

Four Horn Lake. You need both a State and Indian license for this 300 acre, 35 foot maximum depth, mile-long reservoir in open rolling rangeland 6 miles by a good secondary road due south from Piegan on U.S. 87. It's drawn wav down in dry years but is stocked annually with 4 inch rainbow and is fair-to-good for 10 to16 inchers, plus an occasional small brook trout.

Frances Lake. See Lake Frances.

Heath (Dale) Pond. A 5 acre, private farmland pond on Buckley Coulee reached by farm road off U.S. 81 about 20 miles north from Sunburst. It was once good for half-pound rainbow and brook trout but is seldom if ever fished now.

Hope Lake. Take U.S. 2 twelve miles west from Cut Bank, then turn north on a county road for about 3 miles and finally east again for another mile to this 40 acre, 12 foot maximum depth, farmland lake that was stocked with brook and rainbow trout in the early and middle '60s and should still be excellent fishing. You'll need a Blackfeet Indian tribal permit here.

Hutterite Reservoir. See Fitzpatrick Reservoir.

Kipps Lake. Take the Cutfinger School gravel road 7½ miles east from Browning to the shore of this mile long by a third of a mile wide, earth-dammed reservoir in open grazing land. Although 12 feet deep, there are water-level fluctuations of as much as 6 feet. Usage is moderate but it is fair for mostly 10 to 20 inch rainbow (planted every year in the 4 to 6 inch class), and lesser numbers of eastern brookies up to 16 inches long.

Kiyo Lake. An abandoned 4½ acre, fairly shallow beaver pond in an old burn below 1500 foot snow rimmed cliffs on the headwaters of Little Badger Creek ¾ of a mile northwest from Kiyo Crag. You can jeep to the lake, not too many do, although it's fair fishing for cutthroat stocked in 1975 and 1977, running now between 10 and 15 inches long.

Lake Frances (Frances Lake). A 5,500 acre, open farmland lake, 5 miles long by 3 miles wide on the "doorstep" of Valier. It has a maximum depth of about 45 feet; is drawn down at least 20 feet in dry years, but usually has only 6-8 feet of water-level fluctuation. There's a good picnic area with boat ramp near the airport. It is good fishing for husky northern pike (to 25 lbs.) and nice walleye (2-4 lbs.) and occasional yellow perch, rainbow and ling, and small kokanee were planted in 1979. At last report, it could stand more usage.

SOME TOMSCHECK RAINBOW
Courtesy USSCS

FARM POND FISH
Courtesy SCS

Lenington's Reservoir. A private, 5½ acre, 20 to 25 ft. maximum depth with mostly steep dropoffs and mud and gravel bottom, earth dammed reservoir in rolling plains (and some cultivated land) about 10 miles by crow flight north from Fort Benton, the last couple of miles by dirt trail from a gravel county road. Used to be stocked with eastern brook trout til '78, but in 1979 and 1980 rainbow were planted and provide fair fishing for 9-15 inchers, along with small brookies mostly but up to a couple pounds.

Little Badger Creek. Heads on the slopes of Kiyo Crag and Mt. Baldy on National Forest land (see Kiyo Lake) and flows northeastward for 7 miles through a pretty timbered and brushed-up draw to Palookaville (nothing there now) and then for 10 miles across open rolling grazing land below to Two Medicine Creek about 15 miles by U.S. 87 and secondary roads southwest from Browning. The lower reaches are followed by trails, are only lightly fished, but are reported to be very good for 8 to 9 inch rainbow, brook and some cutthroat trout. The upper 4 miles or so (sometimes called the North Fork) are followed by a road and are fair-to-good for pan-size cutthroat and brook trout.

Lower Two Medicine Lake. See Two Medicine Lake (lower).

McCracken (Woody) Reservoir. Is posted, 3 acres, maximum depth about 25 feet with steep dropoffs, in open farmland reached by a private road half a mile past the owner's home, 8 miles east of Fowler Siding which is 15 miles north, up the Great Northern Railroad, from Conrad. It used to be wonderful fishing but is poor now and seldom bothered — for a few 12 to 15 inch brook and rainbow trout.

Middle Fork Dupuyer Creek. A very small, very brushy hay meadow stream that is very seldom fished and very poor at best for 8 to 10 inch brook and cutthroat trout. There are about 2 miles of fishable water reached by secondary roads along Dupuyer Creek 12 miles southwest from Dupuyer.

Midvale Creek. Heads at around 8500 feet above sea level on Mount Henry, Mount Ellsworth and Bearhead Mountain in Glacier National Park and flows east for 10 miles through the community of East Glacier to Two Medicine Creek. There are only about 3 miles of brushy, beaver-ponded, open rangeland fishing water here. It's seldom bothered but is followed all along by trail and is fair fishing for 8 to 10 inch rainbow and brook trout.

Minnie White Horse Lake. See Cooper Lake.

138

Mission Lake. A mile long by half a mile wide, 20 feet deep, Blackfeet Indian Reservation open rangeland lake in Flat Coulee. Take U.S. 87 one mile southeast from Browning, then a secondary road down the north side of Two Medicine Creek and then swing over into the coulee for a total of another 8½ miles northeast to the shore. It's heavily fished and very good, too, for 10 to 18 inch (maximum recorded to 6 pounds) rainbow, and is stocked annually in quantity.

North Fork Birch Creek. Heads at about 7000 feet elevation below Badger Pass on the Continental Divide, and is followed by a good USFS horse trail 5 miles east down its fairly flat-bottomed, timbered canyon to the Swift Reservoir at the head of the main creek. It's seldom bothered for the few cutts it contains.

North Fork Dupuyer Creek. A moderately popular little stream that heads below Bum Shot Mountain and flows east for 5 miles out across brush-and-grass covered hills to the head of the main stream 12 miles by secondary road southeast from Dupuyer. It's accessible by roads below and trail above, and is good fishing for 9 to 10 inch cutthroat and rainbow above, and some brook trout in the lower reaches.

North Fork Little Badger Creek. See Little Badger Creek.

O'Haire Reservoir (or Lake). Six miles south of the Canadian border in rolling grassy hills; reached by a good gravel road 7 miles east from Sunburst. It's about 20 acres with dirty brown water, 15 feet maximum depth behind a 5 foot earthfill dam. On private land (access is now questionable), it used to be good for rainbow trout, nice size (recorded to 7 pounds).

Patrick Lake. See Fish Lake.

Railroad Creek. Heads on Red Crow Mountain in Glacier National Park and flows 7 miles eastward to Midvale Creek a mile southeast of East Glacier. The lower couple of miles outside the park are mostly accessible by U.S. 2 but on private and Blackfeet Indian Reservation lands. They used to be fair fishing but were reportedly ruined by highway construction and now are poor indeed for 6 to 7 inch brook trout.

Romain Lakes. Three small earth-dammed farm ponds about 28 miles by county roads south from Chester (and a couple of miles by trail northwest from the owner's house). Only the one fartherest to the west has fish. It's about 3 acres, as much as 20 feet deep with very steep dropoffs and is posted and therefore seldom fished, but used to be fair for 15 to 18 inch brook and rainbow trout.

Scoffin Creek. A small tributary of Dupuyer Creek flowing eastward from its headwaters for 4 miles through a narrow, steep walled canyon on the eastern flanks of Walling Reef and then for another ½ mile across an open hay meadow to the main stream. The lower 1½ miles are accessible by a jeep trail from the Dupuyer Creek road 10 miles southwest from Dupuyer, and the whole creek is fair-to-good fishing (in the wet years) for 8 to 10 inch brook trout and a few small cutthroat. It is, however, seldom bothered because its just too d----- brushy.

Shee-Oole Lake. The Shelby watershed dam with a park below it, one mile north of town. It's 50 acres, stocked annually with rainbow and good for trout up to 19 inches and 3 pounds (on occasion).

Sheep Creek. A small, brushy creek that heads on Walling Reef, flows northeastward for 2½ miles down a timbered canyon, and then out across open rolling rangeland for 14 airline miles past the town of Dupuyer for a couple of miles to Dupuyer Creek. You can jeep down to it in several places and the upper reaches are fished a little for 6 to 13 inch brook and some rainbow trout, but access in general isn't too good.

South Fork Birch Creek. A small stream, only 7 miles long from its headwaters at Gateway Pass on the Continental Divide to its mouth at the head of the Swift Reservoir, and all accessible by a good USFS pack trail. The lower couple of miles (from the Reservoir up to the falls near the mouth of Phone Creek) are in an old burn. There are lots of beautiful holes here that are easily, but very seldom fished, although cutthroat planted in 1974 appear to be doing well and are between 4 and 12 inches long now.

Courtesy Danny On

South Fork Cut Bank Creek. A small stream reached near the mouth by a fair secondary road 6½ miles west from Browning and more or less followed by roads and jeep trails for 8 miles west through open grazing land to its headwaters on Two Medicine Ridge near Kiowa. It's heavily posted but access permission is usually given, and quite a few folks fish it for good catches of mostly 10 to 12 inch brook, and some rainbow trout.

South Fork Dupuyer Creek. This creek heads on National Forest land between Old Man of the Hills and Mount Frazier and flows northeastward down a timbered canyon above and out across rolling range and farmland below for 6 miles to the main stem, 14 miles southwest by county roads from Dupuyer. There's an irrigation diversion 2½ miles upstream from the mouth and the lower reaches sometimes go dry. They are, however, usually fair fishing for small rainbow and brook trout — and are moderately popular too. The first couple of miles above the irrigation diversion are seldom fished but do support a small population of cutthroat. The whole section is accessible by jeep road and a trail.

South Fork Little Badger Creek. A little bitty creek, the outlet of Minnie White Horse Lake; reached at the mouth by the Little Badger road 15 miles southwest from East Glacier on the Heart Butte road. There are 2½ miles of fishing water accessible all along by jeep trail up its wide bottomed valley. It's fished once in a while and is pretty good too for 6 to 15 inch cutthroat trout and a few brooks.

South Fork Two Medicine River. Heads in a little mountain meadow between Kiyo Crag and Bullshoe Mountain a few miles east of the Continental Divide, and flows northwestward for 7 miles, and finally northeastward for 15 miles to the main stem. It's crossed by the Heart Butte road about 5 miles above the mouth (5 miles southeast from East Glacier) and is accessible on USFS land by bike or horse only. The headwater reaches flow through some big swampy beaver ponds in brushy, timbered mountain country, and (although only lightly fished) are good for 6 to 10 inch, plus a few to 15 inch, cutthroat. From here on down, through the middle and lower reaches, there are lots of riffles and it's fair fishing for 6 to 10 inch brook, cutthroat, whitefish and rainbow in that order of plentitude.

Summit Creek. Is followed by U.S. 2 northeastward for 5 miles from Marias Pass on the Continental Divide to where it enters the South Fork Two Medicine River. It was once good but has been ruined by excessive straightening in conjunction with road construction — and is seldom fished now and poor at best for 6 to 8 inch rainbow and cutthroat trout. Its chief claim to fame is its position as the boundary marker between Glacier National Park and the Lewis and Clark National Forest.

140

Courtesy Danny On

Swift Reservoir. A good sized diamond-shaped reservoir over a mile long by ¾ of a mile wide; the west (upper) end in a timbered canyon, the lower end in an open valley. You can drive to it across Indian Reservation land (there's a fee) or walk to it up the south side on USFS land and there are trails all around it. The dam you're looking at is new. The old one washed out in the spring of '64 and spread umpteen cubic yards of boulders and gravel down the creek for a mile or so. The fishing is only moderately good for 8 to 16 inch rainbow planted in 1976 and the pressure is minimal.

Tiber Reservoir. A dammed up section of the Marias River reached by U.S. 2, thirty-six miles east from Shelby to the Tiber siding and then another 14 miles south on gravel roads to Tiber Dam. It was built in 1955 supposedly for irrigation — but the price was too high for the farmers and no irrigation use has been made of its water yet with the exception of individual private pumps. It's in open range and farmland almost 30 miles long, mostly narrow but with a large arm projection 7 miles from the lower end up Willow Creek, and is about 190 feet deep (at full pool) at the dam. There is an airfield at the dam and several boat ramps and campgrounds. The boat ramps can be used only when the reservoir is at the right elevation. Most of the campgrounds are in need of repair with the exception of one at the dam on the south side of the lake. Initially, it was good for 10 to 16 inch rainbow but poor in later years due to a shortage of food. Northern pike presumably entered the system in the late 60's via drainage from Lake Frances. Walleye were introduced in 1971. Mostly walleye, northern pike and yellow perch have produced good fishing in recent years. Other species caught include ling, rainbow trout to 2½ pounds and channel catfish. A few lake trout have been reported taken, which probably migrated down the Marias from Lower Two Medicine Lake. Some of the northern pike get really big — up to 37 inches long.

Tomscheck (Robert) Pond. A private (but the public is welcome) 10 acre pond, as much as 12 feet deep with steep dropoffs, in open farmland ¾ of a mile north by ranch road from the owner's home about 14 miles east and a little north of Kevin. It used to be heavily fished and good too for brook trout that averaged 14 inches and rainbow that ran around 18 inches and ranged up to 5 or 6 pounds; but is no longer managed and the fishing has suffered accordingly.

141

LONE BULL
Jim Derleth photo

Two Medicine Creek.
The outlet of Lower Two Medicine Lake, it flows southeastward for 6 miles (past East Glacier) and then eastward for 45 airline miles (actually twice that far counting all the crooks and turns) to junction with Cut Bank Creek at the head of the Marias River 12 airline miles south of the town of Cut Bank. It's mostly in rolling grassy rangeland, with some steep canyon stretches in the lower reaches and is all on the Blackfeet Indian Reservation. It's all either followed or crossed here and there by gravel county roads, is fairly heavily fished near the roads but seldom elsewhere, and is fair for mostly 9 to 12 inch rainbow, some brook, and a very few cutthroat trout. On many maps the upper and middle reaches are labeled "Two Medicine Creek" — the lower reaches "Two Medicine River," but there seems to be no agreed demarcation point.

Two Medicine Lake (Lower).
Drive 3½ miles north on a good road from East Glacier to the lower (south) end of this deep, 3 mile long by a third of a mile wide "canyon" reservoir lake whose upper end lies within the boundary of Glacier National Park — the bulk of it on the Blackfeet Indian Reservation. The spring flood of 1964 washed the dam out and lowered the water level about 20 feet. However, the dam was subsequently rebuilt and the water level restored to its preflood (natural) level. There is a good campground, boat launching facilities, and heavy fishing pressure here for good catches of brookies from 6 to 14 inches (stocked as 2 inchers, many thousands, annually), 9 to 14 inch rainbow planted in 1980, whitefish and a few (very) lake trout.

Weter (Roy) Lake.
A heavily fished, 7 acre, shallow kids' (under 13 years) pond in open rangeland with some rushes around it, right on U.S. 2 a couple of miles west of Browning, stocked periodically with rainbow and excellent fishing for 6 to 8 inchers.

Whitetail Creek.
Heads in scattered timber on Major Steele Backbone and Feather Woman Mountain but flows mostly across open rolling rangeland for 15 miles northeastward to Badger Creek. It's crossed near the mouth by the Badger Creek road 6 miles upstream from U.S. 89 and is more or less accessible all along by jeep — with permission from the Blackfeet Indians. The lower reaches sometimes go dry, but there are about 10 miles or so of very good early spring fishing for mostly 8 to 9 inch brook, plus a few cutthroat and rainbow trout — and whitefish in season.

Willow Creek.
A posted, open rangeland — real brushy in places — creek that heads just east of Two Medicine Lake on Two Medicine Ridge and "flows in all directions" but generally east-northeastward right through the town of Browning, by the Cutfinger School and Kipps Lake and eventually to Cut Bank Creek 15 miles east of Cook's Ranch. There are about 15 miles of fishable water in all (accessible by state highway, county roads, jeep roads and trails), that are heavily fished for good catches of 10 to 12 inch brook and rainbow trout.

142

EVENING RISE
Courtesy Bill Browning

Courtesy Danny On

Milk River

The lazy, meandering Milk River is one of the longest tributaries of the Missouri. Its South Fork originates in Glacier National Park, flows 30 miles into Canada, returns to Montana just above Fresno Reservoir, and then meanders easterly for 250 airline miles to its mouth on the Missouri River just below Fort Peck Dam. If you included all of the meanders, it would be at least twice that distance. From Havre eastward it occupies a broad floodplain built by the Missouri River during pre-glacial times. In order to irrigate this floodplain with the modest water supply of the Milk River, two storage reservoirs and a diversion of water from the St. Mary's drainage are utilized.

The sluggish, turbid Milk River is deceiving at first appearance and is frequently dismissed as an uninviting stream from an angler's point of view. The reverse is the case, however, and if an angler carefully picks the time and place to exert his effort, some excellent fishing can be found.

One of the best places to fish the Milk River is at its mouth. The best time to angle here is when the river is rising, either during spring runoff or following a rainstorm that may swell the river's discharge. At this time, particularly when the water discharged from the river is warmer than that of the Missouri River, some excellent catfish, sauger and walleye fishing can be experienced. A similar situation exists when its tributaries carry runoff into the mainstream. Such tributaries as Whitewater, Frenchman, Rock and Beaver Creeks, to mention just a few, provide excellent walleye, sauger, and channel catfish fishing at their confluence with the Milk. Spring, of course, is the best season for this type of fishing. In addition to good fishing at the mouths of tributaries to the Milk there are three irrigation diversion dams that serve as barriers to upstream fish movement and are good sites to find fish concentrations. These are Vandalia Dam, Dodson Dam and Paradise Dam.

There are many picnic spots up and down the river, and public parks at Hinsdale and Malta. But if the search is ever made for a sportsman's paradise within a five mile radius few areas could compete with the Milk River area near Nelson Reservoir. A 5 mile radius in this region would include Nelson Reservoir with its excellent walleye, perch, crappie, and northern pike fishing; McNeil Slough with bass, northern pike and walleye; Cole Ponds with rainbow trout; and the Milk River itself with good walleye, sauger and catfish. For the hunter there is the nationally famous Nelson Reservoir goose hunting; two state-owned waterfowl development and hunting areas; some of Montana's finest pheasant and Hungarian partridge flocks; sharptailed grouse, sage grouse and sleek, grain-fed whitetailed deer. All of this is packed into a small area not much larger than a township. So don't let the lazy Milk fool you at first sight; you are getting close to a sportsman's paradise.

Jim Pozewitz

HILL COUNTY

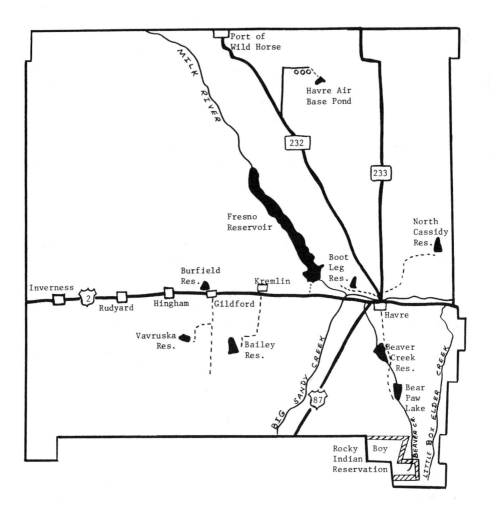

Hill County Fishing Waters

Fresno Reservoir	F	Walleye, northern pike & yellow perch
North Cassidy Reservoir	S	Stocking discontinued
Bear Paw lake	FWP	Rainbow & Brook trout
Beaver Creek Reservoir	C	Rainbow trout
Burfield Reservoir	P	Not open to public fishing
Vavruska Reservoir	P	Stocking discontinued
Boot Leg Reservoir	FWP	No fishing at present
Bailey Reservoir	P	Rainbow trout
Havre Air Base Pond	S	Rainbow trout
Milk River (below Fresno Res.)	F&S	Rainbow trout, walleye, sauger northern pike & yellow perch
Beaver Creek		Rainbow & brook trout some brown trout in lower poirtion
Little Box Elder Creek		Brook trout
Big Sandy Creek		Rainbow & brook trout

F — Federal Land   FWP — Fish, Wildlife and Park Land   P — Private Land
S — State Land   C — Hill County Land

Respect private property — ask permission **first**

Milk River Drainage

Arnold Creek. A small spring-fed beaver dammed, brushy creek that flows slowly north-ward down a broad open rangeland basin to junction with the South Fork Milk River about 1½ miles upstream from the mouth of Livermore Creek. It's crossed by a road about 1½ miles above its mouth and is fair-to-good fishing for about the same distance in both directions — for brookies that'll average 6 to 8 inches and now and then run upwards to a foot. It's mostly fished by locals — and not by too many of them because they generally fish Livermore, which is larger.

Baileys Reservoir. About 5 miles south of Kremlin by county road, about 70 acres, with no motors allowed and restrictions on shoreline vehicle usage. First stocked in 1978, again in 1979 and 1980 with 3 to 5 inch rainbow (about 35,000 each year). Good access and picnic facilities, is heavily used and rightfully so as it is superlative fishing for 13 to 18 inch trout, plus many in the 2 or 3 pound class. Lacking shoreline brush, it is good fly fishing, and is excellent ice fishing in season.

Bearpaw Lake. About 50 feet maximum depth, 55 acres, long and narrow, behind an earth-fill dam built by the State Fish and Game in open grassy foothill country (but with some ponderosa pine back from the water) on the northern flanks of the Bearpaw Mountains; it is reached by oil and gravel roads 16.5 miles south from Havre. There is a well maintained public campground, shelters, fireplaces, tables and restrooms. The lake was overrun with suckers so was drained and poisoned in 1979, and subsequently restocked with rainbow and cutthroat (hoping that the cutts will show some reproduction) that are now growing fairly fast (despite numerous suckers again). It is good fishing for all sizes of fish; cutts 11 to 13 inches, rainbow up to 2½ pounds, and some brook trout to 1½ pounds; and is heavily used by anglers summer and winter. By the way, no motors are allowed here.

Beaver Creek. Is over 150 miles long, heads in the Little Rocky Mountains, wanders every which way, eventually flows to the Milk River a mile north of Hinsdale (on U.S. 2). The upper 15 or 20 miles splash through mountains, meadow, brushy canyon, foothill country, are crossed in the upper reaches by State 19, thirty nine miles south from Malta, and are more or less accessible by dirt roads and cowpaths. Little and pretty, wadeable, easy to fish, fairly easy to get to in most places, it gets some usage in this area for small rainbow and brook trout, and lesser amounts of same in the middle reaches. The lower reaches offer fair to good fishing for walleye, northern pike and some smallmouth bass and are used by both "locals" and "city" dwellers (mostly Montanans) more than somewhat.

Beaver Creek. A small stream flowing north for 32 miles east from the Bearpaw Mountains to the Milk River a couple of miles west of Havre. The lower reaches of this stream are dewatered for irrigation and thus have very limited recreational potential. The upper reaches, from about 5 miles below Bearpaw Lake, 11 miles south from Havre, for 15 miles to headwaters, are paralleled by oil and gravel roads, and are mostly in a wide bottomed, forested, brushy canyon. The reaches above (upstream of) Bearpaw Lake are good fishing for small brookies and rainbow, and occasionally a fairly large brook trout is taken. Between Bearpaw Lake and Beaver Creek Reservoir the stream is only fair for rainbow. A current water quality study is underway to determine flows for adequate spawning and survival of trout. The results of the study could lead to improved stream flows and better fishing in years to come. The lower section below Beaver Creek Reservoir is fair for rainbow up to a pound or so at times. Brown trout have been planted here in l981 and are growing... By the way, good public facilities, restrooms and picnic tables are maintained by the State on the stretch below Bearpaw Lake.

Beaver Creek Reservoir. About 180 acres, 6 miles north of Bearpaw Lake, built for flood control and recreation with pretty steep banks except for the upper end, and full of suckers. Stocked with rainbow every year, it gives up good catches of 10 to 11 inch trout (they don't grow well here). However, largemouth bass were stocked in 1981 to control suckers and minnows (which compete with trout for food), and should be about a foot long in 1982. Maybe if the bass "take," the rainbow will grow faster, huh?

BEARPAW LAKE
Courtesy SCS

Bonneau Reservoir. A 55 acre (35 foot maximum depth with 15 feet of draw-down behind an earth filled dam) reservoir in timbered Rocky Boy Indian Reservation country about 4½ miles northwest of the Agency Headquarters and reached by a county gravel road 8 miles east from Box Elder (on U.S. 87, twelve miles south from Havre). A $5.00 "scalp insurance" fee has been required in the past, but the fishing is fair-to-good (and the pressure moderate for this neck of the woods) for rainbow trout that average about 8 to 10 inches but occasionally run upwards of 4 pounds — along with an overabundance of suckers. The rainbow are stocked as catchables every year.

Box Elder Creek. A small, real brushy, willowed, mountain meadow, Rocky Boy Indian Reservation creek in the western Bearpaw Mountains. The lower "foothill" reaches are mostly dewatered for irrigation but the upper 8 miles or so (mostly above Bonneau Reservoir) maintains a good flow, is readily accessible by gravel road east from Box Elder (on U.S. 87, twelve miles south from Havre); supports a fair population of 6 to 8 inch (a few to maybe 14 inches) brook trout, and provides pleasant piscatorial pastime in pursuit of the finny tribe — for multitudinous recreationists from Havre and the vicinity. Note: The Rocky Boy Indians have at one time or another required a special "fishermans" fee for all, and/or various agency waters. It would be wise to inquire at the Agency Headquarters for information as to the present status — lest you send the tribe on the warpath.

Clear Creek. A dandy little creek flowing across numerous beaver dams northwest through mountains, meadows, the lower foothills of the Bearpaw Mountains and finally the Milk River breaks, for 35 miles to the Milk River at Lohman (12 miles east of Havre on U.S. 2), and paralleled more or less all the way by gravel roads. It supports heavy fishing pressure by picnickers and campers for, in the upper mountainous reaches, good catches of 6 to 10 inch brookies; in the middle foothill reaches, good catches of 6 to 12 inch rainbow trout; and in the lower "breaks" reaches, fair-to-good catches of sizeable brown trout which occur as smaller fish occasionally in upstream areas. Also, some dewatering occurs in the lower reaches.

Cole Gravel Pits. A pretty little oasis of 6 nice clear-water steep-sided ponds from 2 to 8 acres in size in old Great Northern Railroad borrow pits astride the tracks with cottonwood shade trees, picnic tables, barbeque pits and restrooms a couple of miles by gravel road north from Saco. Here's a nice place to stop for a swim or overnight camping if you're traveling through on U.S. 2. The ponds east of the tracks contain largemouth bass and northern pike. Two out of three ponds west of the tracks have largemouth bass and the biggest of these two ponds has as an added bonus, a few nice walleye. One pond west of the tracks has rainbow trout. All of these can be "really good at times" but during mosquito season — beware.

PHILLIPS COUNTY

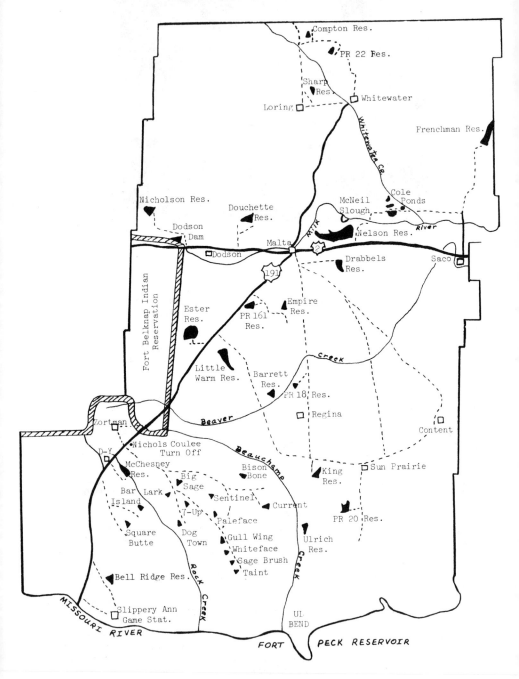

Phillips County Fishing Waters

PR 22	F	Rainbow trout
Sharp Reservoir	F	No fishing at present
Compton Reservoir	P	Rainbow trout
Nicholson Reservoir	P	Rainbow trout
Cole Ponds	FW&P	Three west of RR: rainbow trout, bass, and walleye. Ponds east of RR contain northern pike and bass
Drabbels Reservoir	P	Not open to public fishing
King Reservoir	F	Rainbow trout
Bell Ridge Reservoir	F	Rainbow trout
Lark Reservoir	F	Rainbow trout
Sentinel Reservoir	F	Rainbow trout
Current Reservoir	F	Rainbow trout
Pale Face Reservoir	F	Bass stocking scheduled 1979
Whiteface Reservoir	F	Rainbow trout; some largemouth bass
Taint Reservoir	F	Rainbow trout
Sagebrush Reservoir	F	Rainbow trout
Big Sage Reservoir	F	No fish at present
Square Butte Reservoir	F	Stocking discontinued
Bar Island Reservoir	F	Rainbow trout and largemouth bass stocked, but unsuccessful
Bison Bone Reservoir	F	Northern pike
Dog Town Reservoir	F	Largemouth bass stocked, status unknown
7-Up Reservoir	F	Largemouth bass stocked, status unknown
Gull Wing Reservoir	F	Largemouth bass stocked, status unknown
McChesney Reservoir	P	Northern pike
PR 20	F	Largemouth bass and a few crappie
Ulrich Reservoir	F	Largemouth bass and bluegill
PR 18	F	Largemouth bass
Little Warm Reservoir	P	Northern pike, yellow perch
Barrett Reservoir	P	Northern pike, bluegill, sunfish, pumpkinseed, yellow perch
Ester Reservoir	P&S	Walleye, northern pike, yellow perch, and crappie
PR 161	F	No fishing at present
Empire Reservoir	F	Largemouth bass
Douchette Reservoir	F	Rainbow trout
Nelson Reservoir	F	Walleye, yellow perch, northern pike
McNeil Slough		No fishing at present
Frenchman Reservoir		Yellow perch, sparse walleye

F — Federal Land   P — Private Land   S — State Land

VALLEY COUNTY

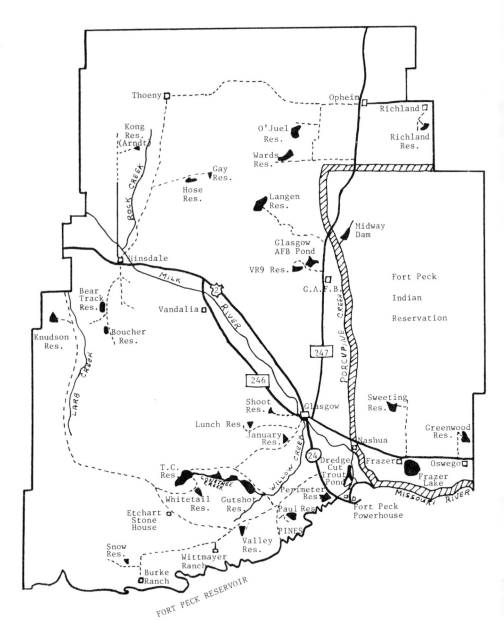

Valley County Fishing Waters

O'Juel Reservoir	P	Rainbow trout
Shoot Reservoir	F	Rainbow trout
Glasgow AFB Pond	S&P	Rainbow trout
VR 9 Reservoir	F	Rainbow trout & yellow perch
Kong Reservoir	F	Rainbow trout intro. in 1976
Greenwood Reservoir	P	Rainbow trout
Valley Reservoir	P	Rainbow trout
Snow Reservoir	F	Largemouth bass stocked 1978
Hose Reservoir	F	Rainbow trout
Gay Reservoir	F	Rainbow trout
BearTrack Reservoir	P	Channel catfish stocked 1978
Perimeter Reservoir	F	No fishing at present
Boucher Reservoir	P	Rainbow trout
Dredge Cut Trout	F	Yellow perch, northern pike largemouth bass, and walleye
Wards Reservoir	F	Northern pike & black bullheads
Richland Reservoir	P	No fishing at present
Midway Dam	Tribal	Northern pike
Gunshot Reservoir	F	Northern pike
Lone Tree Reservoirs	F	Northern pike
Triple Crossing Reservoir		No fish
Langen Reservoir	F	Largemouth bass
Knudson Reservoir (Helen)	F	Largemouth bass
Paul Reservoir	F	Largemouth bass
Whitetail Reservoir	F	Largemouth bass stocked twice but unsuccessful; channel catfish stocked in 1978
January Reservoir	F	Largemouth bass stocked, but unsuccessful
Sweeting Reservoir		Northern pike stocked, status uncertain
Frazer Lake		Bullheads
Lunch Reservoir	F	Largemouth bass
Milk River		Walleye, sauger, catfish and northern pike

F — Federal Land   P — Private Land   S — State Land

Dry Fork Milk River.   A small spring-fed, slow flowing stream that heads on St. Mary's Ridge and flows 10 miles to the northeast to the North Fork Milk River about 7 miles upstream from its junction with the South Fork. It's crossed by a county road 1½ miles above its mouth and has limited recreation potential, but the lower 4 or 5 miles through brushy beaver ponds are fair-to-good fishing (although seldom bothered) for pan-sized brookies.

Ester Lake.   A 150 acre reservoir with mostly gradual dropoffs to a maximum depth of 14 feet behind an earth-fill dam up on a bench in open prairie grassland about 30 miles southwest of Malta; reached by first the Lewistown highway (State 19) for 25 miles and then gravel and dirt county roads on in. There are a few cottonwood for shade but no camping facilities; however it is a moderately popular fishing and swimming hole due to the presence of fair populations of walleye in the 1½ to 2 pound (maximum recorded to 7 pounds) class and ¾ to a pound yellow perch — as well as a pretty good population of northern pike. The walleye and northern were stocked as fry in 1977.

Faber Reservoir.   Sitting right at the base of the Bear Paw Mountains 1 mile south of Cleveland in Blaine County with a park-your-rig-and walk-in policy, about 30 acres in size, this reservoir is a consistent producer of rainbow from 12 to 20 inches (averaging about 1½ pounds). Fly fishing is especially good here. It is stocked annually with 3 to 5 inch trout (between 8-10,000) that grow fast.

Fox Creek.   Drains a big brushy basin on St. Mary Ridge 8 miles eastward to the South Fork Milk River about 8 miles upstream from the mouth of Livermore Creek. To get there you take the East Glacier (Blackfoot) highway (State 20) about 6 miles south from St. Mary and then follow a dirt road east for a couple of miles to the middle reaches of the creek. From here to its mouth (maybe a couple of miles) it's slow-flowing with lots of beaver ponds that are easily fished (although very seldom) and fair-to-middling good for 6 to 8 inch brookies. It wouldn't stand much pressure.

Frenchman Creek.   Rises in Canada and flows south across the line for about 35 miles to the Milk River, 7 miles east and north by oil, gravel, and dirt roads from Saco (on U.S. 2, twenty eight miles east from Malta). From Frenchman Dam down to the Milk River walleye and northern pike are present; the stretch immediately below the dam and the lower (east) couple of miles of stream (bordered by cottonwood, willow, and some brush) are the best fishing. But any spot in this 50 mile or so stretch of stream that has good deep pools is good, too. The northern pike average about 4 pounds and run up to 7 and the walleye 1½ and up to 4 pounds, with no reports in yet on the smallmouth bass planted in the late 1970's. The mosquitos "will carry you away" at times which partially accounts for fishermen "being conspicuous by their absence"; the stream meriting more usage than it gets.

Fresno Reservoir.   Has a surface area of 5757 acres on the Milk River bottoms backed up behind the Fresno Irrigation Dam built by the Bureau of Reclamation in 1939 — nine miles west and a little north of Havre. It's mostly quite shallow for its size with a maximum depth of 30 feet at the dam. The fishing has been good in the past but the water level fluctuates widely in accordance to drawdown, which in some years is next to complete. Reproduction here for perch and northern pike has been excellent, and fair to good for walleye. Smallmouth bass planted in 1976 do not appear to have survived. By the way, northern pike to over 20 pounds have been taken here in the past. It has and can again support heavy sport fishing pressure for good catches of northern pike and walleye — and there are a few crappie along with lots of yellow perch planted in 1974, also good duck hunting in season. The Havre Boat Club maintains a picnic area here with shelters, toilets and boat launching facilities.

Gay Reservoir.   Five miles east of Hose Reservoir and also located on Bureau of Land Management land. Fair to good fishing for small rainbow trout.

Glasgow Air Force Base Pond.   Seven acres of dammed coulee reservoir, freezing out in bad winters, reached by the Air Force Base road away out on the open prairie about a mile north and another west of the main base gate (now operated by Valley Country) and is used more than somewhat by area fishermen to take 9 to 12 inch rainbow trout stocked mostly as 3 or 4 inch fingerling. Some "catchables" are also stocked following winterkills to re-establish spring fishing. The Kiwanis club put in a park, the Department of FWP has taken it over, enhancing the maintenance of the facility for visitors.

Grasshopper Reservoir.

Right by the Lloyd Highway 15 miles south from Chinook in an earth-dammed coulee in open grazing land at the northern edge of the Bearpaw Mountain foothills. It covers about 20 acres, has a couple of little islets in the middle and south end, is deep with a muddy bottom, somewhat weedy around the margins, and fair fishing for rainbow that will average about a foot long and run up (some of the old lunkers) to around 2½ pounds. Because of its easy access and fair fishing, it receives heavy pressure. A few of the conveniences here would greatly enhance its recreational potential. Although planted annually with 3 inch trout, it is full of suckers, and fishing has "fallen off," causing talk of possible rehabilitation (poisoning).

Hick's Reservoir (Upper).

Eight acres, with mostly steep dropoffs to a maximum depth of 15 feet behind an earth dam in open grassy Bearpaw Mountain foothill country reached to within ½ mile by gravel and dirt county and private roads a mile north from Lloyd (which is about 25 miles south from Chinook), then 4 miles east and finally 1½ miles south. There's nothing much here but fish — a fair population of 12 to 16 inch rainbow — and an occasional local fisherman trying his luck. Note: Don't confuse this with Lower Hick's Reservoir 6 miles down the creek — it's barren and the upper one might as well be too because the owner has closed it due to "people" problems.

Hose Reservoir.

Located about 15 miles north of the town of Hinsdale on BLM land this is a nice, fertile prairie reservoir about 10 acres in size and 25 feet deep — and a darn good rainbow fishery with some good ones taken on occasion.

Kuhr-Newhouse Reservoir.

A hard one to find — on People's Creek in grassy foothill country on the northeastern flanks of the Bearpaw Mountains, reached by county and private roads about 12 miles east and a little north from Cleveland. It might be a good idea to ask for detailed directions there. It's about 20 acres with moderate dropoffs to a maximum depth of 25 feet behind an earth dam, is somewhat weedy about the margins, has a muddy bottom, and (considering its relative isolation) supports a moderate fishing pressure for excellent catches of 15 to 16 inch rainbow plus a few that will range up to 4 pounds. A real recreational asset, but there is a "people" problem here and the owner has closed it to the public.

Lenhart Ponds.

Five of them, ranging from 2 to 15 acres in dammed up coulees scattered over about 6000 acres of open prairie, reached by gravel roads and jeep trails about 25 miles north and a little east from Havre. All are private, 2 or 3 have been stocked with rainbow and/or brook trout, and they provide some fishing for the family and a few neighbors.

Livermore Creek.

This small, brushy, muchly beaver-dammed, open prairieland, heavily fished tributary of the South Fork of the Milk River is crossed near the mouth by a graded gravel road about 20 miles north-northeast from Browning, and is followed upstream by a dirt road for about 6 miles of very good fly fishing for mostly 6 to 10 inch brook trout — plus a few rainbow trout.

LENHART POND
Courtesy USSCS

Lodge Pole Creek. A small Little Rocky Mountain "foothill" stream flowing north down a burned over, brushy canyon to eventual junction 15 miles downstream with the South Fork People's Creek. The lower 3 miles of clear flowing meandering water provide a limited amount of surprisingly good fishing for small brookies to a few stray fishermen who pick up some "better ones" in quite a few large, deep beaver ponds.

McNeil Pond or Slough. Is a sub-circular cutoff oxbow about 15 feet wide by ¼ of a mile long with an average depth of about 15 feet and lots of cattails, fed by seepage from Nelson Reservoir, in beautiful cottonwood bottoms of the Milk River reached by a jeep road off the Nelson Reservoir road about 12 miles northwest from Saco. Used to be one of the best (foot long average) largemouth bass areas in the state, was also good for northern pike up to 20 pounds, small bluegill, crappie, perch and an occasional walleye to 3 or 4 pounds, also a fair goose and duck hunting spot. At the mouth where it enters the Milk River it is noted for good catches of walleye and sauger. The bordering Milk River bottoms are excellent hunting for whitetail deer, sharptail grouse and huns. At present there is no fishing at all as the dam washed out but there are plans to rebuild the dam in the near future. Maybe then it'll get the usage it could stand. There is an old fish hatchery here, since transformed into a Boy Scout camp.

Middle Fork Milk River. From its headwaters below Hudson Bay Divide (St. Mary Ridge) the Middle Fork meanders eastward across open prairie rangeland for 15 miles to ultimate junction with the (much larger) South Fork. It is crossed near the mouth, and again in the middle reaches, by graded county roads about 20 and 25 miles north, or north-northwest from Browning. The lower 10 miles or so are followed along by dirt roads and, although it's a brushy stream with lots of beaver ponds, it's easily wadeable, fair fishing for 8 to 12 inch brook and cutthroat trout — and therefore moderately popular with both local people and Canadian visitors.

Nelson Reservoir. In the open prairie about a mile north (by road) of U.S. 2 five miles west of Saco. A 4560 acre Bureau of Reclamation irrigation-recreation reservoir, it has shallow dropoffs and lots of sandy beaches. It's a darn decent recreational asset with a couple dozen private cabins around it and a MDFWP campground. Gave up the state record (14 pounds) walleye, and is still one of the best for 1 to 3 pounders; also several 10 to 14 pounders are taken every year. A mess of perch size 9 to 12 inches and on up to a pound is a common catch (a self sustaining population), with crappie and goldeye also caught pretty regularly (up to 4 years ago, goldeye were netted here commercially and sold to Canada). Northern pike to an exceptional 30 pounds (say that again?) can bust your tackle here. There is a good population of all sizes here, though no apparent reproduction, and the theory is they maybe come in from the Milk River. Whether you spear them in the winter (several 20 to 30 pound northern taken every winter) or baitfish or troll for them in the summer, these brawling pike will add excitement to your trip. To top it off, for a lake this size, it's not overcrowded.

North Faber Reservoir. A 10 acre pond about 3 miles north of Zurich that presently has low water levels but should be fair to good fishing when full for 10 to 13 inch rainbow trout, with an occasional 3 or 4 pounder taken.

North Fork Milk River. An excellent fishing stream but seldom bothered because of its remoteness; the North Fork heads in some small prairie potholes just east of Goose Lake (in the St. Mary River drainage) and flows east-northeastward down a narrow, brushy, steep-walled, 200 foot or so deep canyon for about 20 airline miles to Canada. It's crossed near the middle (at the Galbreath Ranch) by a graded county road about 35 miles north from Browning, and is followed downstream by an old excuse for a road along its north bank to the border. It's a slow, brushy but easily wadeable creek with scattered beaver ponds here and there and the lower 10 miles or so are full of 8 to 12 inch brook and cutthroat trout.

People's Creek. Heads in the Bearpaw Mountains about 15 miles southwest of Cleveland and flows eastward out through the northeastern foothill country and eventually across the open prairie for 70 miles to the Milk River where it crosses U.S. 2 about midway between Malta and Harlem. The upper 8 to 10 miles or so flow through brushy, beaver-dammed canyons in places, across open bottoms in others, are more or less accessible by gravel and dirt roads, are mostly easily wadeable, and are moderately popular with local residents for picnicking and fishing — (especially in the occasional beaver ponds) for good catches of brookies that mostly average between 6 to 8 inches but sometimes run up to a foot or better.

BEAVER CREEK VALLEY
Courtesy USFS

Reservoir 82. See Ward's Dam.

Rieve Reservoir. Is a 15 acre, 15 foot deep, mud-bottomed stock reservoir behind an earth dam on private land (and just possibly behind a locked gate) in the northern Bearpaw Mountain foothills 1½ miles up Rieve Creek from its mouth on People's Creek 3 miles south by county road from Cleveland. It's in open grazing land with a few conifers scattered about, was stocked with rainbow and brook trout years ago and still contains a small population of brookies that run around 2 pounds or so but is seldom fished and has relatively few attractions in terms of recreation which is just as well because it's been put "off limits" by the owner.

Rock Creek. Heads in Canada and flows 45 miles south to the Milk River 1½ miles north by dirt road from Hinsdale. The lower couple of miles are on the brushy, buffalo berry, cottonwood, and willowy Milk River bottoms and, although seldom visited, are good fishing in the spring for walleye, sauger and smallmouth bass up from the river. Boat access to the better fishing at the mouth is good from the city park in Hinsdale (on the Milk River).

Ross's Reservoir. Is 12 acres in size with a maximum depth of 20 feet with mostly steep dropoffs and muddy bottom behind an earth dam on Wind Creek in a narrow brushy canyon below Barber Butte in the Northern Bearpaw Mountain foothills, "50 miles from nowhere" and reached by an unimproved dirt road 2 miles south from a point of the Warrick-Chinook road midway between those towns, or six miles south from the Ada school. Despite its location this little reservoir provides a lot of sport for local anglers who take good catches of 12 inch or so cutthroat (a few to maybe 3 pounds) from its waters — the trout being planted yearly as 2 inchers. Note: don't confuse with the next reservoir a mile down stream; it's barren.

Salmo Reservoir. Located 6 miles northwest of Chinook with a maximum depth of 12 feet, with dam seepage problems, about 6 surface acres, and very weedy and hard to fish. The BLM has plans to fix the dam which would correct present low water levels, 'cause when full this reservoir is fair fishing for 8 to 12 inch rainbow with a fair number of 3 to 7 pounders taken out every year. It was first planted in 1978.

South Fork Milk River.
The easily wadeable South Fork is reportedly "the best fly fishing creek" in this entire region. It heads on the eastern slopes of White Calf and Kupunkamint Mountains (a couple of miles within the borders of Glacier National Park) and flows northeastward across rolling prairie country for maybe 30 miles to the Canadian line. The upper (headwater) reaches are crossed by the Blackfeet highway about 20 miles northwest from Browning; the middle and lower reaches by graded county roads about 20 miles north-northwest, and/or north from Browning. It is also accessible by old unimproved roads in numerous areas in between. The upper reaches, above the mouth of Livermore Creek, are very brushy but there are lots of beaver ponds that are very good fishing, indeed, for mostly 6 to 10 inch brookies plus a scattering of rainbow trout. The lower (meandering) reaches are not so brushy and there are some beaver ponds here, too, and lots of beautiful deep holes that produce excellent catches of 10 to 14 inch cutthroat and rainbow trout at the ratio of about 3 to 2. The entire stream is heavily fished — for this way out neck of the woods.

South Fork People's Creek.
Heads below (south of) Twin Buttes in the northern foothills of the Little Rockies and flows for 18 tortuous miles to eventual junction with People's Creek. The upper 3 miles or so of clear flowing stream wind through a burned over, brushy canyon and are crossed at the lower end of this stretch by a bituminous road 11 miles north from Hays. It doesn't amount to much in terms of recreation but does provide an occasional angler with fair-to-middling fishing for pan-size brookies.

Thornley Dead River.
Is a sub-eliptical cutoff oxbow about 1½ miles in circumference in the brushy, cottonwooded Milk River bottoms a mile south by dirt "road" from U.S. 2 at a point 3 miles west of Harlem. It is mostly 10 feet or so deep with a muddy bottom, has a few northern pike and some bullheads, and is seldom visited by fishermen but does see an occasional duck hunter in season.

Toad Creek.
A little bitty, clear, spring fed creek heading in an open basin on St. Mary Ridge between Fox and Livermore Creeks and flowing (slowly) for about 3 miles to the South Fork Milk River. It's full of brushy beaver ponds, and they are full of pan-size brookies that are seldom bothered because this one is only available via shank's mares up the South Fork.

VR9 Reservoir.
Valley Reservoir No. 9, built in 1939 just below the Glasgow Air Force Base Pond; is maybe 5 cres and good fishing for planted rainbow and yellow perch.

Ward's Dam (or Reservoir 82).
Take U.S. 2 a mile east from Glasgow, then the oiled Opheim road 33 miles north where you turn off to the west through open prairie rangeland on a graded gravel road that after about a mile gives way to 3 miles of gumbo which in turn terminates in 200 yards of absolute hell at the reservoir shore. It's a beautiful 16 acre by 15 feet deep body of water impounded behind an old WPA earth dam across a small tributary of the West Fork Porcupine Creek. There are lots of cottonwood and willow around the upper end, campground facilities, and it has supported good populations of rainbow that attracted hosts of local fishermen, but there was so much winterkill that the Montana Department of Fish, Wildlife and Parks may only (maybe not even, if they give the fishery up completely) stock bullheads in the future. There has been no fishing available here for 3 years due to winterkill followed by poor runoff and drought the last two summers, suggesting poor chances of success and a low priority for any stocking program.

White Water Creek.
Heads in Canada and flows to the south-southeastward for 40 airline miles across the open prairie to the Milk River 10 miles north and west by county roads from Saco (on U.S. 2 forty three miles west of Glasgow). Only the first mile above its mouth (in the brushy, cottonwood and willow Milk River bottoms) has much recreation potential (in the form of good walleye and sauger fishing in the spring).

Wind Creek.
The Clearwater Creek road about 25 miles south from Chinook crosses the lower reaches of Wind Creek and an unimproved road takes you about 2 miles upstream to Ross's Reservoir in the northern foothills of the Bearpaw Mountains. It's a small, mostly open hay meadow and agricultural land stream, pretty good fishing for 6 to 10 inch brook trout, and visited a moderate amount below the road but seldom if ever above, where it is posted and closed to fishing by MDFWP's commission.

Respect Private Property — Ask Permission First

BEAVER DAM
Courtesy USFS

TYING UP FOR THE NIGHT
Courtesy Bill Browning

Missouri River (Lower)

The Missouri is the nation's longest river, 2475 miles from its origin at Three Forks, Montana, to its confluence with the Mississippi River near St. Louis, Missouri. A 207 mile reach of the Missouri from Great Falls to Fort Peck Reservoir in Montana is unique because it is the last major free-flowing portion of the river. This remote and inaccessible part of the Missouri River has kept most of its primitive character. Through a gorge-like valley bordered by rough breaks and badlands, the river has carved its course between the Little Rockies, Bearpaw and Highwood Mountains.

Because of its exceptional recreational, historic, scenic and natural values, a 149 mile segment of the Missouri from Fort Benton to Robinson Bridge (roughly the lower ¾ of the free-flowing reach) bacame part of the National Wild and Scenic Rivers System in October, 1976. In rubber rafts, canoes, and in motorized crafts, people today float this stretch and enjoy many of the same scenic vistas that Lewis and Clark described in 1805-6. From that time until the coming of the railroads, the Missouri River was the major route to the Rocky Mountain west.

History buffs can relive much of the excitement of early explorers. An excellent museum at Fort Benton with a reproduction of an early keel boat helps tell the story of the river's past. With a little searching to find the rotting timbers and broken glass, one can find the unmarked sites of several early military posts· – old Fort McKenzie near the mouth of the Marias, Fort Cook, Fort Chardon and Fort Clagett near the mouth of the Judith. Crumbling woodhawker cabins and homesteads can spark the imagination of the roving historian. Fur trade flourished briefly in the early 1800's at the riverside trading posts of Forts Lewis, Benton and Piegan. Steamboats plied the shallow waters as far as Fort Benton, bringing gold seekers and materials for an expanding economy. Some exceptionally scenic landmaks along the river recall those days of long ago. The names of Labarge Rock, Hole-in-the-Wall, Dark Butte, and Citadel Rock echo the romance of our westward expansion.

161

The free-flowing river, protected as part of the National Wild and Scenic System, preserves not only scenery, solitude and recreational opportunities, but also a bountiful Fish and Wildlife resource. Canada geese nest along the river in the spring. Pelicans can be seen feeding and bald eagles nest in the vertical cliffs above the water. Thousands of cliff swallows build their mud nests on the rock walls. Game animals such as deer, coyote, bobcat, beaver and muskrat abound along this entire stretch of the river. There are a few elk and bighorn sheep along the lower portion below Cow Island, and in some places prairie dog towns line the banks.

Fishing along this stretch of the Missouri is as varied as the wildlife. The Missouri changes in character as it emerges from the mountains near Great Falls. Below the confluence of the Sun River, the Missouri widens, the water is warmer, and it carries a heavy silt load through the summer months. While some trophy-sized trout (rainbow as large as 5 pounds and brown trout as large as 10 pounds) are caught in the Missouri below Great Falls, it is primarily a warm water fishery. Sauger, northern pike, channel catfish, sturgeon, freshwater drum (sheepshead), paddlefish, goldeye, burbot (ling) and rough fish make up the bulk of the population. A spring run of sauger and northern pike move into the reach of river between Morony Dam and Fort Benton and offer excellent sport fishing in season. Sauger are native to the Missouri and make fine eating. Northern pike up to 10 and 15 pounds are taken each year. Loma, Virgelle and the mouth of Belt Creek also offer some fine chances to take these fish.

The spring runoff triggers a spawning run of prehistoric paddlefish up the Missouri from Fort Peck Reservoir. Fish up to 120 pounds have been caught around James Kipp State Park and near Slippery Ann Ranger Station on the C.M. Russell Game Range. April and May is the best time to catch paddlefish here. They are plankton eaters and are rarely taken by conventional bait fishing – most anglers snag them in murky waters with large, weighted, treble hooks. Channel catfish abound throughout the entire length of the Missouri River below Fort Benton. Set or trot line fishing for catfish is a favorite sport at the mouths of tributaries or in deep pools with moderate current and a firm bottom. Often shovelnose sturgeon are taken while catfishing and they may weigh up to 14 pounds. In recent years king-size northern pike up to 20 pounds or better have been taken upstream from Fort Peck Reservoir. Goldeye are considered trash fish by most Missouri River fishermen but they will strike a fly or lure readily and put up a fine tussle on light tackle.

There are six major access points on the Missouri River between Great Falls and Fort Peck Reservoir. A gravel road will take you to the uppermost access at Carter Ferry. Fort Benton has a fine all-weather concrete boat ramp used by many floaters as a launching site. Another take-off point is at the Loma Ferry about eleven miles north of Fort Benton. Sixty miles downstream from Coal Banks at Judith Landing there is another access just below the mouth the Judith River. Roads lead there from Big Sandy to the northwest and from

Winifred to the southeast. The last access, and usually the take-out point for boat trips, is at the Fred Robinson Bridge in James Kipp State Park on U.S. Highway 191. The head of Fort Peck Reservoir is a dozen miles downstream.

The modern day "explorer" should take insect repellent, rain gear, drinking water and a paddle or oars in case of motor trouble. There are rattlesnakes in the area, but with normal caution they can be avoided. Stay out of high grass and slab rock unless you have high rubber boots. Although there are many rapids they are not dangerous. Water levels are lower after mid-summer. This is a stretch of river filled with good fishing and scenery besides, so load up your gear and head for the Missouri. It is an outdoor adventure you will remember for years to come.

Rod Berg

CRUISING THE MO
Courtesy Bill Browning

Fort Peck Dam to North Dakota Border

Deep releases of cold water from Fort Peck Dam keep this stretch of the Missouri River relatively cold and clear, although the water does warm and become more turbid by the time it reaches Wolf Point. There is public access below the dam to the tailwaters and the nearby dredge cuts, formed when earth was removed to build the dam. This area provides the most popular fishing, although there are good catches made downstream too.

Sauger is probably the most abundant game species. Others present are walleye, northern pike, channel catfish, shovelnose sturgeon, burbot (ling), paddlefish and rainbow trout. The state record burbot came from the Missouri River near Wolf Point and 5 to 10 pound burbot are common. Best fishing for this species is during early spring and late fall, and at the mouths of tributaries during winter. Lately some large rainbow spawners have been caught in the Fort Peck tailwaters.

Much of the river bottom is wooded and makes for pleasant camping and picnicking. There is very little public access downstream from the tailwaters, so you may need to request permission from private landowners. The north side of the Missouri River from the Milk River to Big Muddy Creek is the southern boundary of the Fort Peck Indian Reservation.

Phil Stewart

Missouri River — Lower

Arrow Creek. Heads just north of Geyser and flows for 50 miles in a large semicircle to the east and north around the Highwood Mountains to the Missouri River 7 miles upstream from the mouth of the Judith River. It's a big drainage but a small stream in an eroded brushy-bottomed draw. The upper 4 miles are accessible by road 5 miles north and then 2½ miles west from Geyser. It's generally pretty good fishing for 8 to 12 inch brookies here and sometimes also for escapees from various ponds and reservoirs on the headwaters, but these don't last long.

Bainville Pond No. 1, 2. See Great Northern North Reservoir, South Reservoir.

Bear Creek. See Big Otter Creek.

Belt Creek. Heads away up in the Little Belt Mountains below Kings Hill and flows north to the Missouri River 10 miles east of Great Falls. The upper 12 miles are mostly in timber, the lower 40 miles in open foothills and prairie. It's mostly wadeable but there are some deep pools in some upper "canyon" reaches called "the Sluice Boxes." At one time this was the hottest, most popular fishing stream in Montana. In fact, the Great Northern Railroad ran a "Fisherman's Special" on Sundays all the way from Great Falls to Neihart. They'd drop you off here and there on the way up in the morning and pick you up on the return trip come evening. In 1957 the stream was polluted from the mines at Neihart up Carpenter Creek and there is still some trouble there, although the workings are closed. All together there is now about 40 miles of good fishing for 8 to 10 inch (plus-a-few-to-14) rainbow, 3 to 17 inch whitefish and brown trout — all accessible by U.S. 87 and county roads.

Big Coulee. Not really a fishing stream, but it does have a fair population of 6 to 8 inch brook and cutthroat trout for maybe a mile above its mouth (accessible by jeep road) on Highwood Creek at the headwaters.

Big Horn (or Brockton) Reservoir. Take the Redstone road 11 miles north from Brockton, turn right at the crossroads and drive 5½ miles east and the reservoir will be off to the south on the Spring Creek drainage. It washed out in '66 but was repaired and replanted with rainbow fingerlings that grow like mad here and should be good fishing now for 2 to 4 pounders. If so, folks 'round and about will know about it.

Big Muddy Creek. Occupies the prehistoric bed (deserted now for about 12,000 years) of the Missouri River. It rises in Canada and follows a twisting, cottonwood-lined course at the eastern boundary of the Fort Peck Indian Reservation through fertile agricultural land for about 65 miles past Daleview, Redstone, Archer, Midby, Plentywood and Reserve to the Missouri River 4 miles east of Fort Kipp (and 13 miles east of Brockton by U.S. 2). It's an intermittent stream with a mucky bottom (you wouldn't want to wade it) that is very popular and excellent fishing in the spring, for about a mile up from the mouth (between U.S. 2 and the Missouri) for 1½ to 2, plus a few to 10 pound walleye, and 10 to 20 pound northern pike that are taken in the lower 15 to 20 miles of the creek. Sauger, ling, and catfish are also picked up here mostly as migrant fish.

Big Otter (or Bear) Creek. A nice slow, deep little creek, with about 6 miles of good ½ to 1½ pound (maximum recorded to 3 pounds) brown trout fishing, mostly in an open haybottom valley paralleled by a good county road up from its mouth on Belt Creek a mile south of Armington. It's also crawling with rattlers, but they don't seem to bother the fishermen much.

Big Timber Gulch. Drive upstream 1 mile from the Logging Creek campground to the mouth of Big Timber, and then on up it for about ½ mile of mediocre 6 to 8 inch brook trout fishing in a few brushy, ¼ acre beaver ponds scattered along.

Birkeland Lake. A private, long narrow 7½ acre by 25 foot maximum depth lake with steep dropoffs and a muddy bottom in open wheatland 5½ miles by improved road northwest from Skonkin. It's used mostly for fishing, is planted annually with rainbow trout and is pretty good for 8 to 9 inchers.

BELOW FORT BENTON
Courtesy U.S. Fish and Wildlife

Bowdoin Lake. The Bowdoin National Wildlife Refuge, one of the Nation's valuable wildfowl sanctuaries is in northeastern Montana, 8 miles east of Malta. The refuge was established in 1936 to preserve suitable habitat for migratory birds and is administered by the Bureau of Sport Fisheries and Wildlife, U.S. Fish and Wildlife Service. The refuge comprises about 15,500 acres and contains Lake Bowdoin, Dry Lake, Drumbo Lake, Lakeside Marsh and Lakeside Marsh Extention.

This area is in an extensively used flight path of the Central Flyway and is overlapped somewhat by the Pacific Flyway, both of which extend from Canada to Mexico. Large numbers of waterfowl, marshbirds and shorebirds either nest here or stop to rest and feed during migration.

Canada geese, mallards, pintails, gadwalls, American widgeons, blue-winged teal, shovelers, ruddy ducks, redheads and canvasbacks nest by the thousands within the refuge. During migrations, especially in the fall, myriads of northern ducks and thousands of geese find safe resting and feeding conditions on the waters and marshes of Bowdoin. Seven breeding pairs of Canada geese — a remnant of the once-great flock of years gone by — remained in the area by 1935. These geese increased and by 1943, about 75 broods were reared. More than 150 broods are now normally produced annually.

White pelicans, California gulls and ring-billed gulls nest by the thousands on the islands in Bowdoin Lake. Woody Island has the greatest numbers of colonial nesting birds. It is also the largest with a surface area of about 5 acres. In addition to pelicans and gulls, this island is used for nesting by double-crested cormorants, great blue herons, and common terns. The numbers of these birds on the islands are so great that duck and goose nests are often destroyed by trampling. Colonies of nesting Franklin's gulls and black terns are present in some areas of the marsh. In summer the marshes literally teem with young and adult coots and eared grebes. Soras and American bitterns can often be seen or heard throughout the marshes on summer evenings.

Many species of nesting shorebirds are common during the summer and lage concentrations of common snipe, yellowlegs and dowitchers stop during migration. Upland game birds and songbirds are abundant during the spring, summer, and fall. These include the ring-necked pheasant, sage grouse, gray partridge, sharp-tailed grouse, yellow warbler, Bullock's oriole, blue grosbeak, redstart, and many others. A bird list containing about 160 species is available at refuge headquarters.

The best times to observe the abundant birdlife on the refuge are late in spring, during early summer, and in the fall. In late March and April, the summer resident Canada goose flocks of the entire region return to the refuge and congregate here for long periods. Massive flocks of mallards and pintails also congregate here before dispersing to continue north or remain to nest. From May through mid-July, resident waterfowl nest and raise thousands of young. The first Canada goose broods can be observed shortly after the middle of May, depending on the season. Many thousands of canvasbacks start congregating on Lake Bowdoin during late August and early September. The largest waterfowl concentrations occur during September and early October when the vast migrating flocks stop on their return from more northern nesting areas.

The refuge is easily reached from U.S. Highway 2 which borders the north and west boundaries for a distance of about 7 miles. Refuge headquarters are located one-fourth mile off the highway about 1½ miles east of Malta and 20 miles west of Saco. Travelers from the north or south driving on State Highway 19 should leave this highway at Malta and proceed east on U.S. Highway 2 in order to reach the refuge. Persons wishing to visit the refuge should communicate with the Refuge Manager, Bowdoin National Wildlife Refuge, Malta, Montana. Visitors to the refuge can find ample hotel, motel, and tourist camp accommodations in Malta or at the American Legion Health Plunge 12 miles northeast.

Box Elder Reservoir.
This 90 acre tadpole-shaped earth-dammed reservoir is within the northern city limits of Plentywood and easy to find. It has a shallow head end and steep dropoffs to its deepest 27 feet, has boat ramps, picnic tables, toilets and fireplaces, and is in a town that will not tolerate litter, period. It's pretty good fishing, loaded with mostly stunted perch, some northern pike, and some crappie. Rainbow trout have been stocked here on and off but they haven't been growing well the last few years. The MDFWP is working with the city to try to get either a chemical rehabilitation or a total drawdown to start all over. Plans are then to stock rainbow. This has traditionally been a busy, popular reservoir, and a real asset to the community.

Briggs Creek.
Flows to the west for a couple of miles down a rocky timbered canyon to the North Fork Cottonwood Creek at the Thain Campground. It's followed by a USFS trail and is fair fishing for camp-fare brook and cutthroat trout, but most people fish the main stream.

Brockton Reservoir.
See Big Horn Reservoir.

Candee Reservoir.
About 6 acres — was initially stocked with rainbow fingerling in the spring of '68. Has indications of becoming a good rainbow fishery for all sizes. Access is 22 miles of gravel road north of Richey, or across the Missouri River on a bridge east of Poplar — then about 6 miles south.

Cecil Coulee.
Is very seldom fished, even by the local residents. It's just too small, but there are a few 6 to 8 inch brook trout in a couple of 50 to 100 feet-across beaver ponds about 2 miles upstream by an old jeep road from the Shonkin Creek road a mile below the National Forest boundary. If you're still interested, they're in a timbered draw with more than their share of brush around them.

Chabot Reservoir.
Eight acres of fairly clean water, 16 feet deep on a dammed little tributary of the Poplar River south of the Carbert road about 6 miles northwest of Scobey. It's planted each year with rainbow fingerlings but is only so-so fishing and not very popular.

Childers Dam.
Is in the Missouri River "breaks" 10 miles south of the Fort Peck Reservoir on the Indian Creek Drainage, reached by fair-to-middling good county roads 50 miles northwest (past the Brusett Post Office) from Jordon. It's in a steep-walled coulee, is 14 acres, 25 feet deep behind an earth dam with ponderosa pine all around, and was good but is now poor fishing for northern pike — and zillions of bluegill. You'll need permission but won't be bothered much by the crowds.

Clark Reservoir.
About 20 acres by 25 to 30 feet deep with shallow dropoffs on a garlic-smelling mud bottom in the Missouri River Breaks 10 miles south of Fort Peck Reservoir, reached by gravel road 27 miles northwest (7 miles beyond Brusett Post Office) from Jordan. It was planted with rainbow in '65 and is excellent for 14 to 16 inchers now — mostly fished by local fishermen.

Cottonwood Creek.
Take the Geyser road 14 miles southwest from Geraldine to a crossing on the middle of this creek. Here you turn right (west) upstream for a couple of miles right through a rancher's yard and finally a USFS trail about 4 miles to headwaters below Prospect Peak in the Highwood Mountains. It flows down a rocky, timbered canyon and a little valley above the ranch and is fished a little here for camp-fare brook and cutthroat trout. Below the ranch it flows out across open foothill grazing land for about 8 miles and is heavily fished (for this region) for 8 to 10 — perhaps a few to 12 — inch brook trout.

Cow Creek.
A small, southern Bearpaw Mountain-to-foothill-to-open-prairie-to-the Missouri River Breaks stream. The upper 6 miles (from the junction of its North and South forks to the mouth of Al's Creek) is mostly in open rolling hills but with a few patches of timber here and there, is crossed in the middle reaches (one and a half miles below headwaters) by a gravel road 13 miles south from Lloyd and is more or less accessible elsewhere by jeep roads and cow trails. There are a lot of beaver dams from the headwaters downstream for about 6 miles to the mouth of Al's Creek.

DAM! They never told us about this when they built the dam.
Courtesy MDFWP

It's good fishing here for brookies (with permission from the McLeisch Ranch), some of which have been recorded up to 1½ pounds. This creek is quite popular with weekend campers from Havre and Chinook. The lower reaches go dry.

Danelson Reservoir.
Seven miles south of Scobey and 7 miles east or 7 miles south of Madoc. Six and one-half acres — stocked with fingerling rainbow in 1967 and are reproducing well. No fancy picnic area but a good spot to fill your creel with fast growing rainbows. Good during all seasons of the year.

Dredge Cut Trout Pond.
Is in the Missouri River bottoms right below Fort Peck Dam. About 60 acres, has a concrete boat ramp and overnight camping facilities. Good for nice size yellow perch, northern pike (up to a now and then 20 pounds), some largemouth bass, bluegills, and walleye. This pond used to have rainbow trout but appears to be a more versatile fishery now and rewards anglers more consistently. The "dredge cuts" all through the area below the dam can be good for various species including sauger, walleye, northern pike, lake trout, and channel cats. Inquire locally and see Fort Peck Reservoir listing.

Dry Fork Belt Creek.
You might do just as well to skip this one. It used to be a nice little cutthroat creek — before mining wastes befouled its waters. Now it's seldom fished for the few pan-size trout that survive up around Oti Park. There's a gravel road up it 10 miles east from Monarch, and then jeep trail 3 miles on in.

Dyba Reservoir.
The closest of 3 stock reservoirs to the ranch buildings (in open pasture and a couple of miles west from the house by a dirt road), about 16 miles south from Cohagen. It's 25 acres and pretty good walleye fishing for 2 to 4 pounders but — the owner closes it while the "cheat" grass is in head because the sheep then congregate around the reservoir and he doesn't want 'em spooked.

Eagle Creek.
Heads in the Bearpaw Mountains, and flows south for 25 miles through open rolling foothills and the Missouri River Breaks to the Missouri River 16 miles east of Virgelle. It doesn't have much recreation potential in the lower reaches, but there are quite a few beaver ponds above (in the stretches above the mouth of Dog Creek) and there is good fishing for mostly small brookies plus an occasional 1 to 2 pound lunker to keep you guessing. It's readily accessible by gravel road 20 miles east and south from Big Sandy and is popular with weekend campers.

Edwards Ponds.
Two — a couple of miles apart in shallow earth-dammed coulees way out in the open prairie about 18 miles west (via a big south-to-west-to-north half circle on gravel and dirt roads) from Cohagen. They're only a couple of acres each, maybe deep enough to keep from freezing out, were stocked with rainbow years ago and are not now overrun with either fish or fishermen.

Engdahl's Reservoir.

A 35 acre by 20 foot maximum depth stock reservoir reached by a county road (dirt) 15 miles out in the open prairie north of Jordan. It was built in 1961 and has been stocked every other year since with rainbow fingerlings. The earlier plant now averages around 1½ to 2 pounds, but they don't get fished much.

Fort Peck Reservoir.

"The place that has it all" is perhaps an apt description of Fort Peck Reservoir, Montana's largest body of water located about 20 miles from Glasgow and surrounded by the 800,000 acre Charles M. Russell National Wildlife Refuge. This 134-mile long lake, with roughly 1,600 miles of shoreline, probably offers more outdoor recreation opportunities than any other area in Montana. Whether it's fishing, hunting, camping, boating, swimming, sightseeing or just a place to get away from it all, Fort Peck definitely provides the recreationist with many varied options.

Fort Peck is probably best known for its variety of fish and fishing. Although there are over 40 species of fish inhabiting the reservoir, the most popular ones are walleye, sauger, northern pike and lake trout. Contrary to some rumors, it's not always easy to fill your stringer with 3-pound walleye and 20-pound pike but there are those times and places when the fishing's really great.

The Big Dry Arm is probably the most popular fishing area of the reservoir, especially for walleye and northern pike. This arm is about 35 miles long and has several fair-to-good access roads along its length. Numerous bays, islands, sandstone ledges, rocky outcroppings and graveled beaches make this an ideal and interesting area to fish. Public boat ramps are available at the Nelson and Rock Creek areas and gas, groceries and fishing tackle may be purchased at the Lakeview Resort which is near Rock Creek State Park. Cabins may also be rented there.

Other popular areas for walleye and northern pike are in lower parts of the reservoir near the dam and in Bear and Duck Creek bays and the Pines. There are shelter houses, picnic tables, toilets and a concrete boat ramp at the Pines. Concentrations of walleye are more difficult to locate towards the head of the reservoir but sauger become more abundant as one progresses in this direction. Northern pike are present throughout much of Fork Peck but also tend to become scarce towards the head of the reservoir. Areas in and around Hell Creek Bay, located about 45 miles from the dam, provide excellent fishing at times for northerns and sauger. There is a marina in this bay with gas, groceries, cabins and docking space available. A state park is also located here with fee overnight camping, picnic tables, running water, and flush toilets for public use.

Lake trout (Mackinaw) are primarily caught during two periods of the year, with the face of the dam being the most popular area. May is the best month in spring, and from late September into November is also a prime time to catch lakers. Trolling along the face or casting lures from the rocks which line the dam are the most effective methods of catching these fish. A full-service marina is located near the west end of the dam with good boat ramps available for public use. The Corps of Engineers maintains several shelter houses and fee campgrounds in the area.

The upper third of the reservoir is noted for good populations of sauger, channel catfish, freshwater drum and both black and white crappie. One of the best fishing areas is around the UL Bend and in Musselshell Bay. Both sauger and catfish are abundant but access to this area is poor and requires driving many miles on unimproved roads to reach this destination. There is a concrete boat ramp located at the Crooked Creek campgrounds on Musselshell Bay but you must haul in all supplies as none are available in this area — you're a long way from any town. Yet the scenery and fishing make this a worthwhile trip.

Many other species of fish inhabit Fort Peck Reservoir which provide both action and a tasty meal to fishermen. Yellow perch, burbot, sturgeon, carp, suckers, goldeye and an occasional brown or rainbow trout are all possibilities at the end of a rod. Also, smallmouth bass were introduced during 1981 and should provide additional action in the years to come.

Paddlefish, Montana's largest fish (state record is 142½ lbs.), while rarely taken in the reservoir, are caught by snagging in the Missouri River near the head of Fort Peck as they begin their annual spring spawning run. May and June are usually the best months to try this method. As you can imagine, stout fishing tackle is needed in order to hook and land one of these monsters, which commonly weigh between 60 and 100 pounds.

Besides the reservoir, excellent fishing opportunities exist below the dam in the river and adjoining dredge cuts. The tailwaters are especially good for sauger and lake trout most of the year and some areas of the river and dredge cuts also provide good fishing for sauger and walleye. The dredge cuts offer the opportunity to shoot paddlefish with a bow and arrow which is a unique experience. Summer months are the best time to try this sport when these fish lie near the surface, generally in the early morning and evening hours, and at night. The archer usually stands at the bow as the boat slowly cruises shoreline and bays and must be ready for a quick shot as the frightened fish move away. Twenty- to forty-pounders are common but occasionally much larger ones are taken.

Jim Liebelt

FORT PECK LAKE SUNSET
Courtesy Jim Derleth

Great Northern North Reservoir (or Bainville Pond No. 1).

Drive 3 miles west from Bainville on U.S. 2 — and you're there, at an old bathtub-like, 10 acre reservoir dug in the prehistoric Missouri River bottoms to water the old-time Great Northern steamers. Originally so shallow as to freeze out, the water level has now been raised to a maximum of 12 feet and the fishing (which used to be poor at best) is pretty good for walleye, northern pike and bullheads. The pond is weedy around the edges, has a few Cottonwood (and Russian Olives planted by the Bainville Rod and Gun Club) back from the shore, and one Chick Sales.

Great Northern South Reservoir (or Bainville Pond No. 2).

Is about 50 yards south of the Great Northern North Reservoir and is connected to it by a small ditch. Its history, setting and recreation potential are similar to No. 1.

Groh Reservoir.

From Circle take the Horse Creek road 5½ miles northwest and then turn due north for another mile to the ranch. You can see the buildings from the road and once there you can see the reservoir east of the house. It's a real nice 110 acre, 20 foot deep, irregularly shaped, dredged pond away out in the badlands so far back, they say, there's still a range war going on and the ranchers carry licenses to hunt Indians. It was originally built for irrigation (in a nice green grassy coulee) but is not used for that purpose at present. It gets its share of use, and is fair fishing for northern pike, bullheads, a few largemouth bass and some bluegills.

Hassler Pond.

This one is pretty good fishing (especially with flies) for rainbow that run up to 3 pounds but average less — more like 10 to 13 inches is usual. It's 3½ miles east of Hilger on State 19 and then a short ¼ mile hike across open grazing land to the left (north). It's 3½ acres and maybe 12 feet deep, strictly a runoff reservoir and gets pretty warm of summers. However, it supports lots of pressure, especially in the winter when the creeks are closed.

Hatfield Reservoir.

Six and one-half acres filled only several years ago — was stocked with fingerling rainbow in 1968. Looks good and should be a top fishing spot in the area. One-half mile south of the old community of Navajo — or 5 miles east of Flaxville.

Highwood Creek.

The most heavily fished stream in Choteau County. Its upper, timbered mountain canyon reaches in the Highwood Mountains flow for 10 miles downstream from its headwaters between Middle and Lava Peaks. Here it is easily wadeable and pretty decent fishing for 6 to 10 inch brook trout and 8 to 12 inch rainbow. The lower 10 to 15 miles of Highwood Creek contain a good population of large-sized resident trout. Rainbow trout as large as 2 pounds, brown trout up to 4½ pounds and a few brook trout as large as 1½ pounds are found in this reach year round. Average catches will, of course, be smaller but it's still a prolific fishery. Before dumping into the Missouri about 20 miles below Great Falls, it is crossed by county and farm roads here and there, and is paralleled by county and USFS roads for 20 miles from Highwood upstream to its headwaters.

Hoffman Reservoir. Stocked in 1968, looks promising, about 7 miles northeast of Culbertson, 6 acres, has fair-to-good picnic facilities provided by the Rod and Gun Club of Culbertson. Scenic setting in prairie country just at the head of drainage of Missouri Breaks. A consistent rainbow fishery.

Homestead Lake. See Medicine Lake.

Hoover Creek. There's about 1¼ miles of mediocre fishing for pan-size brook and some cutthroat trout here in this small mountain tributary of Belt Creek. It's crossed at the mouth by U.S. 89 a mile north of the Belt Creek Ranger Station and followed up its narrow timbered valley by a road. There's some logging going on in the vicinity, and a few summer cabins.

Hutterite Reservoir. See Surprise Creek Reservoir.

Jefferson Creek. Here is a clear, steep, pretty little mountain stream in a narrow timbered valley with a logging road all along its north side from headwaters below Teepee Butte west to Belt Creek 2½ miles south of Neihart. There's lots of picnicking and a little incidental fishing here — but it's too small to amount to much.

Killenbeck Reservoir. Drive 8½ miles west from Scobey out across open rolling grassland on a paved road to Four Buttes, then 5 miles north and finally 5½ miles west on gravel roads, right smack through the farmyard (Nash Bros. Inc.) to the lake; permission obtained, of course. The northern pike here are in the one to two pound class and on up to four or five, and are fairly abundant but the crappie and largemouth bass are sparse. The fishing is fair. There are benches, tables, and toilets that the Scobey Jaycees and the former owner, highly regarded locally, collaborated on.

King Reservoir. About 5 acres, an excellent rainbow trout producer in rolling prairie country. Go 20 miles southwest of Malta on Highway 191, then 30 miles southeast on graded roads. Hard to find but locals know the way. Picnic facilities are your own.

Kirby Creek. Provides a couple of miles of good fishing for 6 to 8 inch brookies in a lot of beaver ponds up its narrow timbered Highwood Mountain canyon, accessible by jeep from its mouth on Shonkin Creek.

Kolar Reservoirs 1, 2, 4, 5, 6. From Geyser take good county gravel roads north for 1 mile to Reservoir No. 1 (Lower Kolar) on the right hand side of the road, then backtrack ½ mile and turn left (east) for ¼ mile to Reservoir No. 2 on the right hand side of the road, now continue east for about 5 miles and then turn off to the left (north) on an old dirt farm road for 1½ miles to Reservoir No. 3 which is, alas, no more, and finally for another 1/6 mile to Reservoir No. 4. From here on in to Nos. 5 and 6 you'd best stop and ask directions. All of them are in the Arrow Creek drainage pasture and farmland. They were all built for stock and irrigation supply and range from 8 to 11 acres in size behind low earth dams. All provide fair to good fishing depending entirely upon Fish and Game Dept. management practices. They're generally planted each year with rainbow and brookies except when they're poisoned out now and then to get rid of the suckers. When they are producing they are really hit hard — but — word has it that the (justifiably) irate owner is in the mood to kick everybody off his property by reason of excessive littering. Don't be a litterbug! If you can carry your trash there from home, you can lug it back again.

Kuester Reservoir. Five and a half miles northeast on State 20 from Richey, in a steep little badland draw — dammed up to provide recreational opportunity for and by the local residents. It's about 80 acres by 30 feet maximum depth with mostly steep dropoffs. The Richey Rod and Gun Club has installed picnic tables, Chick Sales, and a boat launching area. It's already paying recreational dividends, is very popular and provides pretty good fishing for mostly yellow perch along with some largemouth bass and fair size northern pike.

Kuhn Reservoir. See Lisk Creek Reservoir.

Lipke Pond. Is 4½ acres, 15 feet deep in a dammed up coulee in open grazing land. You can drive right to it, 2 miles south from Hilger on a country road, and then 2 more east from the ranch building. It is planted in wet years and is then good for awhile and heavily fished for 8 to 12 inch rainbow put-and-takers in winter and early spring before the creeks open.

PADDLEFISH
Courtesy MFWP

Lisk Creek (or Kuhn) Reservoir. An irrigation reservoir 17 driving miles by fair-to-good gravel and dirt roads southwest from Brockway on the Lisk Creek drainage across the wide open prairie. It's about 25 acres with mostly steep dropoffs to a maximum depth of 18 feet behind an earth dam, is planted annually with rainbow trout and they're growing like mad. The fishing is excellent for two pounders (a few recorded up to 7 pounds) and the pressure is phenomenal. A real boon to the local fishermen.

Little Belt Creek. Heads at the junction of its North Fork (which is too small to worry about) and South Fork in the Highwood Mountain foothills and flows 13 miles west to Belt Creek 4 miles south of Belt by a good gravel road. The upper reaches are paralleled by road, but the lower reaches are in hay bottoms and grazing land accessible only by foot or jeep. There are a few beaver ponds along it and it's generally good fishing (in nice clear water) for 7 to 8 inch brook, rainbow and some cutthroat trout in the headwaters. Quite a few local urbanites come here.

Little Otter Creek.   There is a little limited trout fishing here, in beaver ponds on posted grazing land 3 to 4 miles by county roads up from the mouth on Big Otter Creek 11 miles south from Armington. What with one thing and another it is seldom fished.

Logging Creek. This is a popular tributary of Belt Creek with lots of summer homes, cabins and a USFS campground 6 miles by road above its mouth, easily accessible by road 22 miles south from Armington. There is about 4 miles of easily waded, fast, clear water here that used to provide some good cutthroat fishing, but is now planted annually with rainbow (right around the campground). There is also a small population of 6 to 8 inch brookies.

Lone Creek Reservoir. See Surprise Creek Reservoir.

Martin Creek. A very small tributary of Davis Creek (which has very little recreation potential) in the southern foothills of the Highwood Mountains. There are a lot of small beaver ponds ½ mile above and below the Geyser-Geraldine county road 8 miles north of Geyser. They could produce some good catches of 6 to 8 inch brookies — if anybody bothered to fish them.

McChesney Reservoir (or Robinson Reservoir). Drive 7½ miles south by county road from Zortman to the Malta-Lewistown Highway (State 19), then 2½ miles west and finally about a mile south out across the rolling prairie to this dammed little 20 acre, 16 feet deep with gradual dropoffs and a mud bottomed reservoir on Rock Creek. It's too far from civilization to attract much attention but has been good fishing for northern pike that averaged around 15 inches and ran up to 20 pounds. It's just so-so now.

Medicine Lake.

The Medicine Lake National Wildlife Refuge lies on the heavily glaciated rolling plains of extreme northeastern Montana, between the Missouri River and the Canadian border. It was established as a waterfowl refuge in 1935, under the management of the Bureau of Sport Fisheries and Wildlife, U.S. Fish and Wildlife Service in the Department of the Interior. Located in the Central Flyway, it might be considered a "Port of Entry" for south-bound ducks and geese in the fall. In addition to providing a stopover for migrating birds, it also serves as an important breeding ground for waterfowl and other water birds, including many shore birds.

The refuge consists of two tracts. The north tract contains several impoundments, including 8700 acre Medicine Lake proper, five smaller lakes, and numerous potholes. The smaller south tract has a single impoundment, the 1280 acre Homestead Lake. Overall, 40 percent of the 31,457 acres comprising the refuge is lakes and ponds, 57 percent is pasture and meadowland, and three percent is in farming plots.

Waterfowl are most abundant on the refuge during the spring and fall migration periods. Nesting begins as early as late March, or as soon as the ice is gone, and continues on through July and into August. The most common nesting species are the western subspecies of Canada geese, mallards, gadwalls, pintails, blue-winged teal, American widgeon, shovelers, redheads, ruddy ducks and canvasbacks. Since all the water areas freeze over, no waterfowl remain over the winter.

In early summer, large colonies of double-crested cormorants, white pelicans, great blue herons, California and ring-billed gulls, and common terns nest on islands in Medicine Lake. Grebes and other types of water and marsh birds nest abundantly in the marsh areas. The birder will be intrigued by the interesting grassland birds found on Medicine Lake Refuge. Among them are the burrowing owl, Sprague's pipit, lark bunting, Baird's and Le Conte's sparrows, and chestnut-collared and McCown's longspurs. A birdlist containing over 200 species found on the refuge is available at headquarters.

Substantial numbers of pronghorn (American) antelopes and white-tailed deer are present, as are a few mule deer. Muskrats inhabit the marshes and furnish income to local trappers working on a share basis. Striped skunks and badgers are quite common. During summer, Richardson's and thirteen-lined ground squirrels, known locally as "gophers," are common along all refuge roadways. Two mammals usually associated with forested areas, beaver and porcupine, are also refuge residents.

Fishing (for northern pike introduced in the spring of '68) and hunting are allowed on the refuge in accordance with applicable State and Federal regulations. Game fish are quite scarce. Waterfowl and deer hunting are allowed in designated areas during open season. Boating, swimming and water skiing are permitted in the Public Recreation Area which is equipped with bath house, rustic toilets, fireplaces and tables. There are no overnight camping facilities.

Wildlife photography and observations are encouraged. Guided tours for organized groups may be arranged in advance. The months of May through October provide the most favorable opportunities for observing the varied wildlife of the Medicine Lake Refuge. Refuge headquarters is located 1 mile south of the town of Medicine Lake and 2 miles east of State Highway No. 16. Accommodations are available at towns within 30 miles of the refuge. Visitors are requested to check at refuge headquarters for current information about regulations, routes of travel and road conditions before entering the refuge.

Recent reports indicate "red hot" northern pike fishing at Medicine Lake. Good for 4 to 6 pounders, with a husky battler in the high teens or possibly over 20 pounds taken on occasion. Gaffney Lake was stocked in 1978 with northern pike and both smallmouth and largemouth bass. Lake No. 12 was stocked with northerns in 1978. For details be sure to stop at the refuge headquarters for applicable regulations and maybe a fishing tip. Refuge waters are low from drought — hope is they don't winterkill.

North Fork Cow Creek.

Heads in the mostly open (but with scattered patches of timber) rolling southern foothills of the Bearpaw Mountains and is readily accessible by trail and gravel roads 15 miles south from Lloyd. There are small beaver ponds up and down the lower 5 miles of water and it's good fishing here for 6 to 9 inch brookies with permission only — it's all on the Moore Ranch. It's quite popular with weekenders from Chinook and Havre.

North Fork Highwood Creek. You can drive up it for a couple of miles above its mouth (past the Thain Creek campground) about 13 miles above Highwood and there's a USFS trail on up for a couple of miles to headwaters and on over the top of the divide to Cottonwood Creek. It mostly flows between timbered ridges and gravel banks, is fair fishing in the upper 2 or 3 miles for 5 to 8 inch brook and cutthroat trout that almost never see a hook, and likewise along the lower reaches for 7 to 9 inch brookies that look well in a frying pan.

North Winifred Reservoir. See Stafford Reservoir.

O'Brien Creek. A very small creek, the Neihart city water supply — and closed water. It does have a few small brook trout, though, if you want to risk it.

Olson Pond. Belongs to Steve Watt, is only about 3 acres, 19 feet deep at the deepest with mostly gradual dropoffs, has some weeds around the shallows, and is fished a lot (for this sparsely populated area) for 8 to 12 inch rainbow, and a few "good" ones. It's on the old Chris Olson Ranch reached by the Jordan-Brussett road 18 miles north from Jordan, then the Smoky Creek road 5½ miles north and finally 2½ miles on across country by jeep.

Peer Reservoir. A 10 acre by 16 foot deep open prairie reservoir on the (barren) Timber Creek drainage 7 miles due west and a mile north from Girard by good county road. It's fair-to-good fishing for largemouth bass up to 1½ pounds, but they mostly run smaller. It is closed to the public.

Phillips County Reservoir No. 20. A WPA dam built on BLM land, reached by a dirt road about 4 miles southeast of King Reservoir. Very good fishing for largemouth bass up to 2 pounds and some nice crappie.

Pilgrim Creek. Heads on Mount Pilgrim and flows down a rocky ridge and timber valley for 9 miles to Belt Creek a mile upstream from the Logging Creek road. Pilgrim is a nice open stream with a good horse trail up it, and has been a real fine fishing stream, clear, easily wadeable and with lots of nice holes that used to produce good catches of 6 to 8 inch cutthroat, and a few rainbow out in the lower reaches. Unfortunately it is now being overfished and overrun by cyclists who are using it as a cross-country racetrack.

Pohlod Creek. Is a very small headwaters tributary of Highwood Creek followed up its rocky, timbered, and in places brushy, little canyon by an old jeep road for about 1½ miles of mediocre pan-size brook trout fishing. It's not bothered much.

GATES OF THE MOUNTAINS
Courtesy USFS

FLOATING THE WILD MISSOURI
Courtesy MFWP

Poplar River. Meandering across 80 miles of open rolling prairie from Canada, this slow, mostly wadeable creek slides to the Missouri River at Poplar. It is good for walleye pike, ling, and northern pike and fair for sauger and catfish in the 1 to 4 pound class, plus a few smallmouth bass. Some of the better fishing is between Scobey and the mouth of the West Fork, but certain lower stretches are hard to get to unless you leave the road and drive out across the prairie. The upper reaches, including the Middle and East Forks, contain mostly walleye and northerns. The more accessible reaches, for about 20 miles south from Scobey and 15 miles or so north from Poplar are fair to good fishing and popular also for swimming and canoeing. Northern pike often reach 10 to 20 pounds in the lower few miles and burbot are relatively abundant.

Prairie Elk Creek. Heads on the open prairie just west of Weldon, and is more-or-less followed by county roads northward for 29 miles (through the best whitetail hunting country in the world) to the Missouri River about 1½ miles south of Oswego (on U.S. 2, seven miles east of Frazer). It's good early spring sauger and walleye fishing for about a mile above the mouth, but isn't bothered much — mostly by locals. When the northern pike and/or catfish run up it, the creek gets a little "play."

Raymond Dam. Next to the baseball park southeast of Raymond (7 miles north by oiled road from Plentywood) in flat prairie rangeland about 25 miles from the absolute northeastern corner of Montana. It's about 12 acres but only 9 foot maximum depth so that it freezes out in rough winters (like for instance '64-'65). It has been good fishing for 3-5 pound northern pike and nice size yellow perch, ½ pound or so, was restocked in '66, has been and should still be excellent fishing now — in which case it no doubt is getting its share of attention unless winterkilled.

Redwater River. A small prairie stream emptying into the Missouri River near Poplar, flowing north from below Circle through rangeland and some dryland farmland. Some fishing for northern pike exists as far south as Circle but the fishing is a bit better near the mouth for sauger, walleye, northerns, ling and catfish.

Robinson Reservoir. See McChesney Reservoir.

Roudebush Pond. A private, 2 acre, muddy bottomed, 16 foot deep with weeds in the shallow end, reservoir in open rolling prairie wheatland, reached by county roads about 28 miles or so east from Fort Benton to the ranch and then a 200 yard hike north from the buildings. It's fair to good fishing for 10 to 14 inch rainbow trout (a few up to 3 pounds or so) and quite popular with local anglers — those with permission.

Courtesy USDA, SCS

Courtesy USDA, SCS

Shonkin Creek.   One of the most popular creeks in this area, although there is nothing but rough fish from its mouth on the Missouri River 3 miles below Fort Benton, for the first 5 miles upstream. The upper 15 miles though are pretty good fishing for 6 to 10 inch brook and 9 to 10 inch rainbow trout. There is a county road all along this stretch, through open foothills below and about 5 miles of narrow steep-sided rocky canyon above — it's mostly too steep to climb in and out of from the road — to its headwaters in the Highwood Mountains.

Small's Pond.   Take the Fort Benton road about half way from Highwood, turn off to the west at the Birkeland Ranch and take a truck trail for about 2¼ miles north and then ¼ mile west and you're there, but it's a private and you can't fish it. It's only about an acre in a sharp open farmland coulee, was stocked with brook trout in 1967, and still has some nice lunkers (recorded to 2 pounds) from an old plant.

South Fork Cow Creek.   Heads in the mostly open foothills of the Bearpaw Mountains and flows 7 miles east to join with the North Fork at the head of the main stem. There are some beaver ponds here and there along the lower 5 miles of fair fishing water for 6 to 9 inch brookies — with permission only. It's a popular spot for weekend campers who drive 13 miles south from Lloyd on county roads to the Cow Creek crossing, and then another couple of miles south and west where they take a jeep road back north into the middle reaches of the South Fork.

South Fork Little Belt Creek.   Only about one mile or less of small brook and some cutthroat trout fishing here, in timbered Highwood Mountains reached (but seldom) at the mouth by county road 11 miles east from Armington.

Stafford (or North Winifred) Reservoir.   One of the few real recreation areas in the vicinity, in open grassland an eighth of a mile north of Winifred; 35 acres with lots of willow around it, water skis on it, and probably eat'n size rainbow in it — but not necessarily. It was poisoned out in 1966 and planted with 6 inchers in '67. It used to be a Montana State Water Board reservoir but looks like it may end up as a State Fish and Game responsibility beyond which its piscatorial development is conjectural. P.S. There are no facilities, but it's so close to town you can make a quick "end run" to a service station should the need arise.

176

Courtesy MDFWP

Surprise Creek. There are about 10 miles of good fishing here, for pan-size brookies (and a few cutthroat trout in the willow-bordered, beaver-dammed headwaters), but only the middle and upper reaches are accessible by road northwest from Stanford on U.S. 87 for 6 miles to the creek and then upstream on gravel and dirt roads. It hasn't attracted many fishermen in the past, but if the Surprise Creek Reservoir produces well, the creek, too, should get more attention.

Surprise Creek (or Lone Creek or Hutterite) Reservoir. Take U.S. 87 six miles northwest from Stanford, and then a good gravel road 3 miles to the southwest through open grazing land to this multiple—named stock reservoir which is on the middle reaches of Surprise Creek, 10 acres by 20 feet deep with "clear" water, gravel and mud bottom. It is stocked annually with cutthroat, but is only so-so fishing for 8 to 10 inchers, plus a few brookies migrated in from the creek.

Thain Creek. Is very small, in a rocky timbered canyon, debouches to Briggs Creek at the Thain Creek Campground, is followed up the east side by a USFS trail, has a couple of miles of fishable water for very small brook trout, and is very seldom bothered.

Troy Creek. A small tributary of the South Fork of the Middle Fork of Sixteen Mile Creek. The South Fork isn't much in the way of fishing, but there are a couple of miles of small beaver ponds on Troy Creek and, although they're seldom fished, they do support some fair to good populations of 6 to 10 inch cutthroat trout. It's available by jeep road to about the middle of the fishing area in open pastureland. You can ask directions at Maudlow, but there are better places to go.

URS Pond. Go 4 miles north on a gravel road through rich wheatland from the town of Coffee Creek, then 3 miles east by jogs, and finally turn due north and then take off ¼ mile cross country on the left side of the road — and you'll be there. It's 8 acres behind an earth dam in a steep-sided little coulee, is stocked annually and is pretty good fishing (and moderately popular) for 12 inch rainbow trout and up to 16 inches on occasion.

Valley Reservoir. About a 40 mile drive southwest of Glasgow on Willow Creek road, this 20 feet maximum depth lake is about 7 or 8 acres in size. Planted annually with fingerling rainbow, it is good for trout all the way to 5 pounds. Let the good times roll!

Watt's Reservoir. Only about 10 years old, ten acres by 20 foot maximum depth stock reservoir out on the open prairie 10 miles by county road north of Brusett. It is planted with rainbow fingerlings that provide sport for quite a few folks — for trout ranging from about a foot long up to a record 3½ pounder.

177

West Fork Poplar River. The prettiest little clear water creek you ever saw (in this part of the state) flowing southwestward from Canada for about 50 miles across the open prairie and crossed 6 miles above the mouth by State 13 about 17 miles south of Scobey. There is generally poor access via jeep trails across the wide open spaces for about 15 miles of pretty nice fishing for walleye and northern pike. It used to have some browns, has been planted with brookies and smallmouth bass, and is also fair to good for them now. There are very few fish upstream of cottonwood creek. All in all, a decent little stream, moderately popular.

Wheatcrofts Reservoir. An old reservoir now owned by Paul Gray, reached by State 20 twelve miles southwest from Jordan and a dirt road 3 miles to the northeast. It's on the Steve's Fork Creek drainage, in open rolling grazing land — not a tree in sight, is getting weedy around the edges and is fair fishing (and moderately popular with local residents) for northern pike that average around 20 inches but occasionally run up to maybe 30.

Whitetail Reservoir. Is right on the south side of Whitetail (7 miles north of Flaxville by oiled highway) which is 7 miles south of the Canadian Line and 55 miles west of North Dakota. A WPA project, about 20 acres with gradual dropoffs to a maximum depth of 9 feet (it's silting in badly), is marshy on the southwest end and is aerated to keep it from freezing out in winter. There are picnic tables, outhouses, some cottonwood shade trees and willow all around, and used to be heavily fished for rainbow trout but is now changed over to northern pike and large yellow perch. This pond is a real contribution to local recreation.

Wolf Creek. You can wade this one in overshoes. It goes dry in places, including the lower mile in the Missouri River bottoms just west of Old Town and Wolf Point, but is about all the local people have and is heavily fished (here and there for about 10 miles upstream) for fair, at best, catches of 8 to 9 inch brook and rainbow trout. It's paralleled by county road at distances up to ½ mile, along the west side out across the open prairie. Northern Pike have been known to "run up it."

SPRING & SUMMER STREAMFLOW

AVERAGE CONTRIBUTION —

5 - 15%   FROM MOISTURE IN SOIL

50 - 75%   FROM WINTER SNOW PACK

20 - 30%   FROM SPRING PRECIPITATION

Courtesy USSCS

GATES OF THE MOUNTAINS LIMESTONE
Courtesy USFS

GATES OF THE MOUNTAINS
Courtesy USFS

The Upper Missouri River

Probably no other similar sized section of a Montana river offers more varied fishing and recreation than the 200-mile stretch of the Missouri River from Three Forks to Great Falls. This reach contains three major reservoirs and almost 135 miles of free-flowing wild trout water. To call it an angler's paradise would be an understatement. Let's take a closer look at this remarkable river.

Three Forks, Montana gets its name from the nearby junction of the Gallatin, Madison and Jefferson rivers which form the Missouri. The Missouri Headwaters State Monument just north of Three Forks silently attests to this fact and provides the first access point to the river. The next 20 miles, however, are relatively remote. The Fairweather Fishing Access Site near the railroad siding of Clarkston, provides the only public vehicle access between the headwaters and Toston Dam. Unless one takes out at Fairweather, it is best to allow a full day for this float but a fully relaxing day of floating and fishing in quiet and solitude is hard to find nowadays, and harder to beat.

The 22-mile stretch of Missouri River from Toston dam to Canyon Ferry Reservoir is a favorite haunt for the floater and fisherman alike. There is river access either at the Highway 287 bridge at Toston or at Toston Dam. A gravel road heading east off Highway 287 a short distance south of Toston leads to the dam.

The area immediately below Toston Dam is a real hot spot in the fall when big brown trout move up river to spawn. A big muddler or other large streamer fished near the bottom is particularly effective then, as well as various other types of hardware and bait.

A comfortable day's float from Toston will put you at the Indian Road Recreation area at the north edge of Townsend while the river's large meanders take you well away from the highway and railroad. If you don't have a full day, the river obligingly comes back near the highway at about the middle of this stretch at the Deep Dale Fishing Access Site.

The Missouri River from Townsend to Canyon Ferry Reservoir, while less than two miles of length should not be overlooked by the serious angler. A fall run of rainbow trout from Canyon Ferry invades the many channels of this braided section, and the action can be fast and furious from mid-September through mid-November. Browns are also taken as they pass through this area on their journey upstream.

There are three major reservoirs near the middle of this reach: Canyon Ferry, Hauser and Holter. Canyon Ferry, completed in 1954, is the largest of the three. This attraction of Canyon Ferry Reservoir lies in the wide variety of recreation it offers: its excellent fish populations, the associated public waterfowl and wildlife management area at its upper end, its abundant camping and access areas, and its close proximity to major population centers. While boating, water skiing, canoeing, ice fishing, ice skating, camping and sailing are all pursued with vigor, fishing is probably the most popular pasttime.

Shortly after ice break-up in the spring, anglers flock to the reservoir. The shore fisherman plies the rocky shoreline for cruising rainbow, while the boat angler works the deeper areas. Rainbow trout in the one to two pound category comprise the bulk of the catch, although brown trout are occasionally taken. It would be a good challenge for some enterprising angler to figure out a way to catch brown trout in the reservoir, since they are far more abundant than their presence in the creel indicates. Fishing tapers off somewhat during the hot summer months, but a good percentage of fishermen still come off the reservoir with good catches.

As fall approaches, the angler's ranks thin a bit when the temptations of deer, pheasants and elk take hold but those dyed-in-the-wool fishermen who stick with it through the fall enjoy remarkable success. Often the gunner and the angler can be seen walking side by side from the parking area at the upper end of Canyon Ferry; one seeking pheasants and the other after the fall runs of brown and rainbow trout.

Winter brings out the ice fisherman and this hardy breed of angler seems to grow in numbers every year. If the dry fly fisherman is the purist of the angling fraternity, then the ice fisherman is the gadgeteer. More variety and homemade inventions are seen in ice fishing equipment than in most other aspects of the angling scene. The gourmet ice fisherman seeks out schools of perch and the action is often fast and furious. Fish on or near the bottom for perch, or spice up your life a little by fishing 8 to 12 feet deep for rainbow trout.

Immediately downstream from Canyon Ferry are Hauser and Holter, two long, narrow reservoirs owned and operated by the Montana Power Company. They provide a haven for the work weary fisherman to renew his spirit – or shatter his ego; depending on whether the fish are hungry or not. Though smaller in size than Canyon Ferry, these reservoirs offer similar angling and recreational opportunities. Furthermore, the narrow canyons where the reservoirs lie add sheer cliffs to the scenic vistas that echo with history. Holter Reservoir's "Gates of the Mountains," named by the Lewis & Clark expedition as it forged upstream, must be seen to be appreciated.

Tucked away between these reservoirs are two short reaches of Missouri River which knowledgeable anglers consider to be prime "lunker" trout water. A short reach below Canyon Ferry and about 3½ miles of river below Hauser Dam are the favorite spring hot spots for big rainbow and for a fall bonanza of even larger browns. Pete Test, co-founder and past president of the Missouri Chapter of Trout Unlimited, has angled extensively throughout several western states, and he considers this area "the best trophy trout water I have seen." Browns over four pounds are not uncommon, and every year fish in the ten pound plus category are taken.

The mouth of Beaver Creek, a tributary entering the Missouri 1½ miles below Hauser Dam, is one of the most popular fishing spots in the region. You can reach Beaver Creek by walking down from the east side of Hauser Dam, or by road via the town of York.

Below Holter Dam the Missouri flows for some 90 miles before it reaches Great Falls. The first 25 miles follow a picturesque mountain canyon with several fishing access sites scattered conveniently along the way. Below Sheep Creek, the river abruptly leaves the mountains and meanders through a wide, flat prairie. Willow and cottonwood bottoms prevail in the prairie, and brushy islands are found along this whole stretch.

The fish populations are excellent throughout much of this reach with mountain whitefish, rainbow trout and brown trout the most common catch. The upper 60 miles from Holter Dam to the mouth of the Smith River are classified "Blue Ribbon" trout water, and walleye, although rare, are sometimes taken below Holter.

Just as in the upper reaches of the river, "lunker" browns will make an occasional guest appearance at the business end of your fishing tackle but their stay is often disappointingly short. Still the side channels around the many islands are favored haunts of big browns in the fall, as the fish seek out suitable areas for spawning.

Although many types of lures and baits can be effective, bumper crops of the mayfly Tricorythodes which emerge in late summer and fall make this one of the superb dry fly fishing rivers in the state. A river this large can accommodate a lot of fishing pressure without feeling "crowded."

An added attraction is the abundance of waterfowl throughout this area. Your fishing experience can be immeasurably enhanced by a close-up encounter with a pair of mallards or the music from a flight of geese right overhead. Mallards, mergansers, Canadian geese and teal nest along the river on islands, backwater areas and sloughs, and some even spend the winter along ice-free areas of the river. During spring migration, the river is often an important resting area for thousands of pintails, mallards and other waterfowl headed north to nest.

Access to the river is good throughout the area. There are several public access points along the upper half of this reach. Old U.S. Highway 91 now designated as a recreation road parallels considerable portions of the river and also provides easy access. River flow is always good for floating and many take advantage of this sport. The outstanding scenery and fishing only add to the enjoyment of a float trip.

The upper Missouri River offers you a wide variety of angling and other recreational opportunities – so don't overlook it.

Larry G. Peterman

Missouri River — Upper Drainage

Avalanche Gulch Creek. Heads on Avalanche Butte in the Big Belt Mountains and rushes down a steep-walled partly timbered rocky canyon for about 10 miles and then 4 more out across a broad grass and sagebrush covered coalescent alluvial fan to Canyon Ferry Reservoir. It's crossed a couple of miles above the mouth by a county road 7 miles east and south from Canyon Ferry, and followed upstream by a jeep road to perhaps a ¼ mile string of small headwater beaver ponds. These are fair fishing at times for small brook and 5 to 10 inch cutthroat-rainbow hybrids but are not often bothered. The lower reaches are dewatered for irrigation. Reports indicate the 1981 flood tore this creek up badly and may have ruined it for the next few years.

Battle Creek. A "jumpable" stream in open rolling grassy hills east and south of Grassy Mountain. It flows south for 11 miles to Sixteen Mile Creek at Sixteen and is accessible all along to within ½ mile by county and private roads. It's pretty good early spring fishing (in a limited way) and is moderately popular with local folks for small brookies.

Beaver Creek. Provides 10 miles of good fishing for 10 to 12 inch rainbow and brown trout (these latter range up to a couple of feet in length), plus some small brookies in the upper reaches; available by USFS road up to a spectacular limestone cliff canyon with as much as 1500 feet of local relief. It's in semi-arid country but with some brush along the creek, a few old beaver dams near the Checkerboard Ranger Station (6 miles above the mouth on the Missouri River a mile below Hauser Dam) and some more beaver dams 1½ miles upstream. The lower reaches used to be heavily dewatered for irrigation but were sold to the USFS by a warm hearted land owner, and this takes in most of the really good fishing water which is a real contribution considering that Beaver and Trout Creeks are the only REAL fishing creeks in the neighborhood. Yet to be assessed is some 1981 flood damage.

Beaver Creek. Heads below High Peak on National Forest land and flows to the northeast for 9 miles to U.S. 10 North near Diehl, and then 6 more out across open prairie grazing land (good antelope hunting here) to the Missouri River 2½ miles by county road above Canyon Ferry Reservoir. The upper reaches look good, but aren't. The lower, brushy reaches are fishable for 7 to 10 inch rainbow and brook trout. The whole bit is accessible by gravel and dirt roads but the lower reaches are severely dewatered at times. The upper reaches also get some usage and are good for small brookies.

Big Sheep Creek. Flows east down a rocky little canyon 6 miles to Prickly Pear Creek and U.S. 287, twenty-one miles north of Helena. If you drive a couple of miles up Little Sheep Creek and then north for 2 more you'll cross it a couple of miles above the mouth and from here down there is some fair (but limited) fishing for 6 to 8 inch cutthroat trout.

Big Tizer Creek. The outlet of Tizer Lake, it's crossed by jeep trails in a couple of places and followed by trail for 4 miles to its mouth at the head of Crow Creek a mile and a half above the Crow Creek Falls, all on national forest land. It's mostly fished in the lower reaches (for about a mile above the mouth) but is fair all the way to the lakes for 6 to 7 inch cutthroat and brook trout.

Boulder Lakes. Four, but only the second one up has fish. It's 4 acres in heavy timber on the upper slopes of Boulder Mountain, reached by foot trail 2 steep miles above the end of the (barren) Boulder Creek jeep trail (which takes off to the east from the Confederate Gulch road half a mile south of Diamond City). It's seldom fished but for fair 8 to 12 inch brookies.

Canyon Creek. Heads on Flesher Pass and is paralleled by paved and gravel roads for 10 miles to its mouth on Little Prickly Pear Creek near the Canyon Creek Post Office 5 miles north of Marysville. It's a fairly good sized creek in a partly brushy but mostly open valley (some of it posted) and is fished a lot by Helena-ites for 9 to 10 inch rainbow, brook and brown trout that are generally small but range to 3 pounds, and a few 10 to 12 inch cutthroat trout. A nice little stream, handy to town.

Canyon Ferry Reservoir. One of the Bureau of Reclamation's finest, and if not the most popular spot in the entire state — then close to it. Luckily it's big, being over 25 miles long and up to 4 miles wide, because it's busy, swimmers and water skiers using the dam end of the reservoir more than the rest, and fishermen all over, trolling and drifting. It's on good roads, 15 miles east and south from Helena, in the open, windy, in mostly exposed bottomland of the Missouri River. There are over 10 public and private campgrounds and recreation areas scattered along it, and homes, trailers, cabins, a few marinas, and several boat ramps, sometimes well back from the waters edge. The fluctuation is more stable in recent years, about 10 feet, but used to be about 20 feet. Fishing is good except in July and August (fair) for mostly 12 to 16 inch rainbow, yellow perch (mostly winter), and some brown trout, brookies and kokanee. The Missouri River, above and below the reservoir is at times excellent rainbow and brown trout fishing.

In the reservoir the rainbow can run up to a boisterous 7 or 8 pounds very occasionally, and browns to a spirited 10 pounds are living in the lake, but are rarely caught. There are plenty of suckers for them to munch on and they do.

All kinds of anglers, summer and winter, use all types of angling gear and methods and do pretty well from shore and boat. The lake is a "dump-all" for the State hatcheries, from ¾ million (normally) to a high of 2 million (1980) little rainbow fry being stocked annually with many thousands of 2 pound and better trout yearly as an added reward. They grow well here, and make lots of people happy.

Chamberlain Creek. Very small, clear and steep, flowing south through a narrow rocky cleft to Jefferson Creek half a mile above U.S. 89. The cleft opens up above into a narrow timbered canyon and the creek has a few cutthroat trout in it for the first mile. Few people know it's there and even fewer fish it.

Clancy Creek and Dredge Ponds. There's a USFS campground at the head of this creek — up on Occidental Plateau, and a gravel road that follows it downstream through timbered mountain country 11 miles to Prickly Pear Creek at Alhambra Hot Springs. It was dredged for gold years ago and some of the banks are quite steep and rocky — and brushy. However, the bottom's come back, and it's planted off and on with put-and-take 5 to 10 inch rainbow, and you'll likely pick up a few small brookies, too.

Confederate Gulch. Heads up in the Big Belts and is followed south by road 11 miles to its junction with Dutch Creek a mile above the Missouri River a couple of miles north of Kenne. The lower 6 miles (below the National Forest boundary) are dewatered and go almost dry, but there are a few beaver ponds in the upper reaches and they are fair fishing for small brook and cutthroat trout. They were there before the 1981 floods, that is, and the damage is still being documented.

Cottonwood Creek. Pretty tiny, in open rolling hills east of Holter Reservoir and reached by road 6 miles south from the dam. Cottonwood Creek is located on the Beartooth Game Range which is owned and managed by the Montana Department of Fish, Wildlife and Parks. The lower couple of miles contain a good population of 6 to 9 inch brook trout and a few small resident rainbow trout. It's not heavily fished.

Cottonwood Creek. A very small farmland creek flowing east to Canyon Creek 7 miles north from Marysville. It's seldom fished but there are a few 6 to 9 inch brook trout and rainbow trout in the lower reaches (say for 1½ miles up from the mouth).

Crow Creek. Heads below Bullock Hill and is followed by a USFS trail and county roads for 16 miles to Poplar where it (and the road) turns east for another 7 miles to the Missouri River a couple of miles north and across the river from Toston. It's mostly dewatered for irrigation below Parker, but from here on up to the Crow Creek Falls it's very popular and very good fishing for up to 12 inch rainbow and brook trout at a ratio of about 8 to 1, and an occasional brown trout to about 19 inches, usually before and after the severe dewatering that occurs on the lower reaches each year. Mining activity in and near the stream channel is causing concern for this fine fishery. The lower

CANYON FERRY LAKE
Courtesy Jim Derleth

reaches (above Parker) are in low rolling hills, the upper reaches in a narrow, heavily timbered canyon.

Crow Creek lakes. See South Fork Crow Creek Lakes.

Crystal Creek.
You don't really want to fish this one, but if you think you do — it's a very small headwaters tributary of McClellan Creek with about 1 ½ miles of questionable pan-size brook and rainbow trout water. There's a good campground a couple of miles on up McClellan.

Deadman Creek.
Is hardly worth fussing with and most folk don't. It flows east for 5 miles through timbered mountains to Lost Horse Creek, which has even less fishing potential. The lower brushy mile is accessible by road 1 ½ miles up from the end of the Little Prickly Pear road and provides some mediocre fishing for small brookies.

Deep Creek.
Is paralleled by U.S. 12 east from Townsend for about 15 miles, the lower reaches in open valley ranchland, the upper reaches in a deep, rocky, timbered canyon. It's heavily fished above for 6 to 13 inch rainbow, brook to 9 inches, and brown trout to 14 inches. Requires permission. The stream has been altered by highway, severly in some places, and the 1981 flood damaged some areas of the streambed. Most of the Upper reaches are on USFS land, and still pretty fair fishing.

Dry Creek.
Is crossed at the mouth on the Missouri River by U.S. 10A five miles north of Toston and followed by gravel road 14 miles upstream (east) to headwaters. The upper reaches are in open country with lots of beaver ponds; the lower reaches are mostly in a partly timbered canyon and sometimes go dry. It's pretty small but stands up to a lot of fishing pressure for 8 to 10 inch brook and rainbow trout at the ratio of about 1 to 3 (mostly rainbow). The best fishing is above USFS line in the beaver ponds.

Duck Creek.
A very small Big Belt Mountain creek flowing west to the Missouri River 11 miles north by county road from Townsend. It's seldom fished except sometimes in the lower reaches when a bunch of rainbow spawners come up from the river.

Dutchman Creek.
You can drive 3½ miles south from Alhambra Hot Springs to the mouth of Dutchman on Prickly Pear Creek, and then jeep upstream (southeast) through timbered mountains for about a mile of pan-sized brook trout fishing. Not that many people do.

187

East Fork McClellan Creek. Heads in Casey Meadows below Casey Peak and flows through heavy timber for 2½ miles to the main stream at the USFS campground at the end of the McClellan Creek road. There's a jeep trail up it and a little fishing for little fish (small rainbow and cutthroat trout). It's not much.

Elkhorn Creek. A small, westward flowing tributary of no-goodnick Willow Creek on the Beartooth Game Range a mile above Holter Lake, crossed near the mouth by a county road 8 miles south of Holter Dam and followed by a jeep road 9 miles up its open-valley rocky-canyon to headwaters. It's good fishing for small cutthroat above (an artificial barrier installed by the State Department of Fish, Wildlife and Parks about 4 miles above the mouth) and fair fishing for rainbow below. Reportedly the 1981 high waters caused some damage here, extent not yet fully determined.

Faulkner Creek. A tiny, open-prairie sagebrush-meadow stream flowing eastward for 6 miles down the upper slopes of Grassy Mountain to Butte Creek. It's crossed at the mouth by a county road and you can jeep up it for about 2 miles of limited fishing for pan-sized brookies.

Glenwood Lake. This one is hard to find, a half mile cross country up the drainage (south) from Lower Tizer. There's timber in the basin but only a fringe around the lake which is 10 acres and good fishing for 10 to 16 inch cutthroat trout. Stocked in 1972, 1976 and 1979, it's getting to be more popular.

Greyson Creek. Drive 3½ miles south from Townsend on county roads to its mouth on the Missouri River and then 14 miles east by road and logging trail to headwaters. There are about 10 miles of fishing here (especially in a flock of beaver ponds in the upper reaches) for 7 to 8 inch brookies. Quite a few kids and some grownups fish it, but it's too small to stand much pressure.

Hauser Lake. A Montana Power reservoir with overtures to recreation. It's located in the open Missouri River bottoms 6 miles north of Canyon Ferry, 13 miles northeast of Helena by good gravel roads, and is 3720 acres with a mimimal annual drawdown. There are a couple of very nice public campgrounds here (courtesy of Montana Power) and it's heavily used for boating, skiing and swimming as well as fishing which is darned good as a rule for mostly 14 to 15 inch rainbow trout grown up from 4 to 6 inch planters, plus lesser numbers of brown trout, walleye, and some real nice 10 to 11 inch yellow perch if you can catch them. There are also zillions of suckers. This one gets hit but hard through the ice during the winter. The scenery here is not flatlands type, you'll notice. If you can figure out how to take the brown trout here, they can grow up to 10 pounds or so. The river above and below this lake can be exceptional angling at times.

Hay Creek. A jumpable creek, lousy with little brookies for maybe 3 miles up from its mouth on Battle Creek in open (posted) grazing land with all but the first mile accessible by the Horse Creek road. It sees more deer hunters than fishermen.

Holter Dam. A 4800 acre Montana Power Co. reservoir on the open Missouri bottoms backed up above the "Gates of the Mountains" 28 miles north of Helena by oil and gravel roads. There are several nice campgrounds, many cabins etc. The water level fluctuations are minimal and the fishing excellent (at times) for mostly 14 to 15 inch rainbow (planted each year) plus lesser numbers of brown trout and yellow perch, along wth omnipresent hordes of suckers. An occasional jumping rainbow to 4 or 5 pounds and an even rarer bulldogging brown to 7 or 8 pounds is landed here. The scenery is pretty awesome — Gates of the Mountains especially. Holter is also used more than a little bit for water skiing, swimming and just plain boating.

Izaak Walton Kids' Pond. A shallow, one acre "Fair Grounds" pond a mile north of Helena. It's stocked annually with keeper rainbow for kids under 12 years of age and they fish the dickens out of it.

Lake Helena. A 2100 acre, Bureau of Reclamation Reservoir (kind of a septic tank for the Helena valley; you oughta see the blue-green algae), 8 miles north of Helena by good county roads. It's O.K. for swimming, water skiing, and boating but not as a rule for fishing except at times (especially in the spring and fall) in the outlet for some really nice size rainbow trout. Otherwise it's loaded with suckers, carp and chub, along with a few ling, whitefish, and yellow perch. It doesn't generally see much action.

HOLTER LAKE
Courtesy USFS

Little Prickly Pear Creek. Is really larger than (big) Prickly Pear. It heads in timbered mountains at the junction of the South Fork and Lost Horse Creek, and is followed east down a timbered valley above and open grazing land below by a good gravel road for 11 miles to U.S. 91 at Chevalier where it swings to the north for another 18 miles to the Missouri River 4 miles east of Wolf Creek. The lower reaches (below Sieben) were once ruined by poor highway construction practices. However, most of the damaged reach of stream has since been rehabilitated with stream improvement structures designed to improve trout habitat. As a result the lower reach of the stream now contains a good population of resident rainbow and brown trout (mostly 7 to 14 inch fish) as well as a few brook trout. Some brown trout in this reach may be as large as 3 pounds. Fishing is also good above Sieben, especially between Seiben and the mouth of Canyon Creek. Its in a real brushy valley all the way but there are lots of nice holes that are heavily fished and are good producers of 10 to 12 inch brook and rainbow trout, a few 1 to 3 pound brown trout plus some whitefish.

Little Sheep Creek. A very small stream in a narrow rocky little canyon, crossed at the mouth on Prickly Pear Creek by U.S. 91 twenty miles north of Helena and followed upstream by a jeep road for 2½ miles of fair 6 to 8 inch cutthroat fishing. There are a few patches of timber and some brush here and there along the creek which dries up near the mouth in the fall.

Little Tizer Creek. A small timbered mountain stream flowing to junction with Big Tizer Creek a mile upstream from Crow Creek. The lower couple of miles are accessible by foot trail and are fair fishing for 6 to 7 inch brook and cutthroat trout.

Lump Gulch. Drive 8 miles south from Helena on the Butte Highway and then turn right (west) up the gulch for 14 miles through grain fields, meadow and timberland to headwaters. It's not a bad little creek for small brookies, and this along with the easy access draws 'em like flies. It gets hit hard by Helena-ites. P.S. There are 3 nice size beaver ponds ½ mile apart in the headwaters south and west of Park Lake, and another on a small tributary ¼ mile northeast of Park Lake. All 4 were planted with brooks in '64 and are good fishing now but there is no trail and they are not well known — hope 1981's highwater left them intact.

189

Lyons Creek. A fair-size tributary of Little Prickly Pear Creek crossed at the mouth by U.S. 91 three and a half miles north of Sieben and followed upstream by a gated jeep trail for 3½ miles of mediocre (6 to 8 inch brookies and a few good browns) fishing. There is some timber below with open hill country above. Most people pass it by.

Magpie Creek. About 3½ miles of tough, real brushy beaver pond fishing here upstream from its mouth on Canyon Ferry Reservoir just east of the dam for pan-size brookies. There's a jeep trail up its timbered canyon but one look and most fishermen are disenchanted.

Malmstrom Air Force Base Pond. See Runway Pond.

Marsh Creek. There's a jeep road up this brushy creek from its mouth on Little Prickly Pear Creek 8 miles up from U.S. 91, through semi-arid ranching country for 3 miles of fair 5 to 9 inch brook and cutthroat trout water. There are a few beaver ponds about halfway up if the 1981 high water didn't wash them out. Most people pass this one by.

Maupin Creek. Is a very small headwaters tributary of McClellan Creek — crossed at the mouth by the McClellan road 2½ miles below the campground. It's not really fishing water but does have small populations of camp-eating brook and rainbow trout.

McClellan Creek. Is good fishing if you like small brook and rainbow trout, lots of brush, and up to a mile hike from the road. It heads below High Peak and flows north through mostly timbered mountains for 12 miles to Prickly Pear Creek a couple of miles south of East Helena. There's a USFS campground about 8 miles up (at the head of the fishable stretch).

Meadow Creek. A small sagebrush-grazing-land-and-hay-meadow creek followed for 6 miles north to its mouth on Sixteen Mile Creek 3 miles west of Ringling. It's loaded with small brookies but is seldom fished because — it's posted!

Medicine Rock Creek. Is almost imposible to get to because the Interstate fence cuts you off (3 miles north of Sieben on U.S. 91). Perhaps the best way is via the Lyons Creek road. Anyhow, it's very small and seldom fished, although there are 5 to 7 inch brookies here.

Middle Fork Sixteen Mile Creek. Provides about 4 miles of very good fishing for 7 to 8 inch brook and rainbow trout, mostly by local people. It's paralleled by a good gravel road northward to its mouth on Sixteen Mile Creek 3 miles above Maudlow, but is hard to get down to in places (down its rocky, brushy, snake-infested, cow-dunged canyon). You'll need permission.

Morony Dam Impoundage. (Also Black Eagle, Rainbow, Ryan, and Cochrane Impoundages.) Dams; one after the other impounding short stretches of the Missouri River near (east of) Great Falls. Water flows through them so fast that trout fisheries cannot be normally or adequately maintained. Full of carp and suckers, they get used somewhat for northern pike, sauger, ling, and a few rainbow and brown trout. They are no longer stocked regularly, the trout perhaps drifting down — so-called "washovers." Better water is nearby.

Northern Pacific Reservoir (or Quarry Pond). Drive 2 miles south from East Helena on a good road and then another ½ mile on private gravel road to this 15 acre by 20 foot deep pond in low, brushy, rolling hills. It's really popular with local urbanites and good fishing too— for mostly 7 to 10 inch rainbow and an occasional brook trout.

Paddys Run. Very small and steep, accessible at the mouth on Sixteen Mile Creek by county roads 3 miles east from Maudlow and paralleled by logging roads for a couple of miles of fair 7 to 8 inch brook trout and rainbow trout fishing in a timbered canyon at the south end of the Big Belts. It's fished by an occasional logger with time on his hands.

Park Lake. A pretty little (3½ acre) mountain lake just east of the Continental Divide at 6360 feet above sea level, reached by the Lump Gulch-Corral Gulch road 13 miles west from U.S. 91, 8 miles south from Helena. It's in heavy timber but with open shores around the south end and a most·irregular shoreline along the east side. It was dammed for placer mining operations many years ago, but the miners have long since departed. There is a good campground now, with tables, fireplaces and toilets, and the lake is very popular for fishing. It does freeze out over exceptionally

MERIWEATHER CANYON
Courtesy USFS

hard winters but is planted annually and produces good catches of 7 inch to 2 pound rainbow trout, planted as 8-9 inches, about 4,000 each year.

Prickly Pear Creek.
Heads away up in the sticks between Elkhorn Peak and Bullock Hill, flows west for 8 miles to U.S. 91 a mile south of Jefferson City, and then swings north for 15 miles through East Helena and 8 miles beyond to Lake Helena. The headwater reaches (above Jefferson City) are in a brushy little timbered canyon followed by jeep road and trail. The middle reaches (between Jefferson City and East Helena) are in a mostly open farmland, somewhat rocky and brushy little valley with patches of timber, traversed by U.S. 91. The lower reaches (between East Helena and Lake Helena) are all accessible by county roads across open rolling prairie. The upper reaches are moderately popular for such small water and are good fishing for small brookies. There are a few beaver ponds and old gold mining dredge ponds in the middle reaches (with the dredge still sitting in one about a mile above Jefferson City) and they are quite popular with the younger generation and are fair-to-good fishing for mostly 8 to 14 inch brook plus an occasional brown trout. The lower reaches are primarily brown trout water and pretty good fishing for 8 to 14 inchers.

Quarry Pond.
See Northern Pacific Reservoir.

Quartz Creek.
A dinky little timbered mountain open-valley creek, 1½ miles long from the junction of its North and South Forks to its mouth on Clancy Creek 7 miles by road southwest from Alhambra Hot Springs on U.S. 91, 10 miles south from Helena. There are more cows than fish, and there are quite a few fish — brook trout in the 10 inch class — in numerous beaver ponds up and down the drainage.

Runway (or Malmstrom Air Force Base) Pond.
Was a kids fishing pond for Air Force Brats, out on the base in a maximum security area 4½ miles east of Great Falls. It's about an acre, V-shaped in an earth dammed coulee with cattails and grass around it and now kids fish the dickens out of it for planted rainbow.

Russell Fork Deep Creek.
Heads below Edith Mountain (in the Big Belts) and is paralleled by a rough logging road 6 miles due south to Deep Creek. It's a nice little stream in timbered country above and rangeland below. Most people fish it up as far as the rancher's farmyard about ¼ mile above the mouth, but it's good fishing above for 8 to 9 inch brook and rainbow trout. It sustained only minor 1981 flood damage.

Seven Mile Creek.
This one is close to town and quite popular. It's formed by the junction of Skelly and Greenhorn Creeks (both too small for fishing) and is followed by county roads 7 miles east through low, rolling hills to Ten Mile Creek just north of Helena. There are lots of *very* brushy beaver ponds along it and the farther upstream you go the better they get for 7 to 8 inch brook and rainbow trout — plus a good one now and then.

Sewell Lake. See Canyon Ferry Reservoir.

Sheep Creek. Is formed by the junction of its North and South Forks 1½ miles by private road upstream (east) from it's mouth on the Missouri River near Halfbreed rapids 9 miles by county and private roads south from Cascade. There is a chain across the road with seventy-seven locks on it, so it's doubtful that you (you out-lander) are going to fish here. However, it's a clear, steep little stream in a narrow, rocky, sparsely-timbered valley, with a few summer homes (mostly on the South Fork) and pretty fair fishing for small rainbow and some brookies. The lower half mile (which is accessible to the public) is sometimes hot for 2 to 3 pound rainbow.

Silver Creek. Heads up around Marysville and is paralleled by gravel roads eastward down a brushy canyon above, and out across open rangeland below, 17 miles to Lake Helena. It's close to town with easy access and so — is moderately popular, although no better than fair fishing for 6 to 10 inch cutthroat and brook trout for about 5 miles down from Marysville. It dries up below.

Sixteen Mile Creek. Is 50, not 16 miles long from headwaters in good deer and elk country on the northwestern slopes of the Crazy Mountains to its mouth on the Missouri River at Lombard. The headwaters meander across a broad open divide between the headwaters of the northward flowing Smith River and the southward flowing Shields River, and then west to Ringling (the original winter headquarters of the Circus). From here it plunges westward down a narrow, rocky, rattlesnake-infested canyon for 11 miles to Sixteen, 10 more to Maudlow and then a final 17 to Lombard. It's crossed by U.S. 89 and county roads at Ringling, Lombard, Maudlow, and Sixteen respectively, and paralleled all he way by the Milwaukee-St. Paul railroad. The headwater reaches (above Ringling) are so small as to have little or no recreational potential. The lower reaches are good for rainbow from 10 inches to 2 pounds, and foot long browns — once in a while a lunker to 4 or 5 pounds — and whitefish.

The canyon reaches, which are muddy in the spring, clear up around the first of June and are excellent fishing for mostly 10 to 12 inch rainbow and 10 to 13 inch brown trout, along with an occasional whitefish and brookie. There must be darn good fishing because lots of people come here despite the lack of access — and they surely aren't all hunting rattlers. Now and then a nice size fish is taken (to 2 pounds). The stream is well suited to fly fishing; but permission is needed unless you walk the railroad tracks and "drop in" on public land. A knowledge of the area or a good map helps.

CROW CREEK FALLS
Courtesy USFS

THE UPPER MISSOURI
Courtesy Bill Browning

COULTER CAMPGROUND
Courtesy USFS

South Fork Crow Creek. Drains the South Fork Crow Creek Lakes 5½ miles through timber above and open grassland below to Crow Creek 8 miles above Radersburg. It's a little rocky above, has some beaver ponds below, is all small enough to jump, followed by a good gravel road in the middle and upper reaches, moderately popular and fair fishing for 7 to 8 inch brookies.

South Fork Crow Creek (or Crow Creek) Lakes. Upper and Lower, a shallow 3 and 4 acres 100 yards apart in timber a steep ½ mile by foot trail from the living end of the Crow Creek jeep trail. Upper Crow is poor fishing — but for nice fish (14 to 20 inch rainbow). Lower Crow is fair for 8 to 10 inch brookies. Neither one is very popular.

South Fork Little Prickly Pear Creek. Five miles long, the lower (fishable) reaches in open meadow accessible by the Little Prickly Pear road, jumpable, poor-to-fair fishing for camp-fare brook and a very few cutthroat trout. Not much of a creek.

Stickney Creek. The lower reaches (for about a mile above its mouth on the Missouri River 2½ miles north of Craig by U.S. 91) go dry, but the next couple of miles up to the junction of its North and South Forks are fishable for pan-size brookies. It's all in a narrow, flat bottomed, timbered valley accessible by jeep road.

Ten Mile Creek. The Helena Municipal Water Supply and closed to fishing. Heads right on the Continental Divide and is followed by USFS and county roads 11 miles north down a timbered valley above (open below) to U.S. 10 which parallels it in turn 9 miles east down a broad, open, rocky valley to town which it bypasses to the northeast out across open prairie to its junction with Prickly Pear Creek a couple of miles above Lake Helena. It's dewatered below the old Broadwater Hotel (just west of Helena) but has been fair fishing for about the next 10 miles of real brushy water for mostly pan-size rainbow, cutthroat and brook trout. A few kids still fish it when no one's watching.

Tillinghast Creek. A nice little tributary of Belt Creek, the upper reaches mostly in private meadowland, the lower reaches in a narrow rocky canyon. There are 2 cataracts a few miles up from the mouth with about 4 miles of good brook and rainbow trout fishing in beaver ponded meadowland reaches above — if you can get permission. It used to be cutthroat water but there are only a few left now in the uppermost headwaters.

193

Tizer Lakes. Lower and Upper, 3 and 5 acres, a mile apart in steep rocky terrain with heavy timber all around, reached by a d----- poor jeep road 10 miles east up the Prickly Pear Creek road near Jefferson City. The fishing isn't anything to write home about — 8 to 10 inch brookies plus a very few cutthroat trout in the upper lake. A few hunters try it — between shots. The road is very, very rough, and the USFS may have put a closure on it — I'd check first.

Trout Creek. Take the Hauser Lake road east from Helena across the lake to the mouth of this turbid (because of housing developments above) creek and then a USFS road on up its beautiful (not yet despoiled) partly timbered canyon for 10 miles to the Sunshine Ranch. There are some nice beaver ponds 6½ miles up and these, along with the creek itself, are good producers of 10 to 12 inch brook, rainbow, and perhaps a few brown trout. A popular stream, rightfully. Hope the 1981 flood didn't create havoc here.

Willow Creek. Willow Creek is a small tributary of Holter Reservoir located in the rolling hills of the Beartooth Game Range east of Holter Reservoir about 8 miles south of Holter Dam. The lower few miles of this stream contains a very good population of 6 to 10 inch brook trout and a few resident rainbow trout up to 12 inches long. The lower ½ mile of the creek flows through a "delta-like" area comprised of small channels and beaver dams impounding some large pools. For anglers willing to work their way through a dense willow brush, brook trout as large as 1½ pounds are found in some of the beaver dam impoundments.

Virginia Creek. A small stream, poor-to-fair fishing for pan-size cutthroat and brook trout followed by State 279 from its headwaters on Stemple Pass 6½ miles east down a rocky, very brushy little canyon to Canyon Creek at Wilborn. It's not worth much for recreation, and most folks know it, and pass it by.

Warm Springs Creek. Is paralleled by a good gravel road 4 miles west from junction of its North and Middle Forks down a partly timbered, partly open-meadow draw to Prickly Pear Creek and U.S. 91 at Alhambra. It's pretty small to be a fishing creek but does have a few small brookies. You can safely skip it.

Wolf Creek. Fourteen miles long from headwaters on Rogers Pass to its mouth on Little Prickly Pear Creek at Wolf Creek, and all paralleled by gravel road. It's mostly in timber but opens up in the lower reaches, is pretty small and only poor-to-fair fishing for 6 inch or so rainbow, brook trout, and a few browns coming up from Prickly Pear. Not very popular.

Take No More Fish Than You Can Use.

Release Fish Carefully

UPPER MO
Courtesy Jim Derleth

OUT OF SEASON
Courtesy Jim Derleth

Musselshell River

From its origins high in the Crazy, Castle, Little Belt and Snowy Mountains, the Musselshell River flows some 250 miles before emptying into Fort Peck Reservoir. The gently moving river meanders through wide, peaceful valleys that give little hint of the sometimes violent past when warring Indian tribes, traders, wolfers and mountain men wintered in the sheltered bottoms and herds of buffalo grazed the shortgrass hills.

The Musselshell has three predominant water types: 1) the cold water zone extending from the confluence of the river's north and south forks to Barber, Montana; 2) the transitional zone from Barber to Roundup; 3) the warm water zone from Roundup to Fort Peck Reservoir. Brown trout dominate the cold water zone with rainbow trout in lesser abundance. Mountain whitefish are also quite common. The transitional zone is presently characterized by few game fish; however, numerous forage minnows make it a candidate area in which to establish smallmouth bass or other desirable game species. Sauger, channel catfish, black crappie and smallmouth bass are found in the warm water zones, and ling (burbot) northern pike, walleye, carp, goldeye and numerous forage fish are also represented. This portion of the river is an important nursery and spawning area for channel catfish and sauger from the Missouri River. Some tagged catfish were recaptured 180 to 200 miles from the tagging site on the Missouri. An added bonus to the warm water fisherman are the snapper and softshell turtles, delicious when chicken fried.

Smallmouth bass were introduced in the Musselshell by the Montana Department of Fish, Wildlife and Parks in 1977 through 1981. The bass have established themselves in the stream section between the towns of Shawmut and Melstone. Growth rates have been excellent and fish up to 16 inches have been taken. Wanted –bass fishermen!

Biologists have done considerable work on the Musselshell, using fish traps and electrofishing techniques to learn more about fish populations. Fish have been marked with plastic tags, weighed and measured to give better ideas of species, growth, reproduction and migration habits. Some of the large fish captured and released by the biologists would excite any fisherman. They include catfish up to 16 pounds, brown trout at a hefty 14 pounds, sauger in the 4 pound class and brook trout up to 1½ pounds. Not bad from this unassuming fishery.

The upper reaches of the stream provide excellent fly fishing after the spring run off in June. The girdle bug, Al's hopper, muddler minnow, the Adams and a variety of woolly worms bring excellent results for the fly fisherman.

Lake fishermen will find Bair, Sutherland, Martinsdale and Deadman's Basin Reservoirs will offer plenty of opportunity to catch rainbows and an occasional trophy-sized brown trout. Selkirk fishing access is located west of Twodot and provides limited camping and picnic facilities. Be sure to bring plenty of insect repellent for this one – the mosquitos are bait-sized.

In addition to excellent fishing, the fertile Musselshell valley abounds with mule and white tailed deer, while the surrounding mountain ranges support a healthy elk herd. Black bear, mountain lion and mountain goat complete the big game list. Some of the state's finest pronghorn antelope habitat can be found in the rolling sagebrush hills of central Montana. Small game includes sharptail and sage grouse, pheasants in river bottoms and prairie areas, and blue and ruffed grouse in the mountain and forested terrain. Late season hunting for mallards is unequaled on the numerous sloughs and warm-water springs throughout the area. Canada goose hunting can be productive for the nimrod with plenty of patience.

Remember, much of the hunting and fishing in Musselshell country is on private land and the sportsman always obtains permission from the landowner to enter and enjoy his chosen sport. Courtesy, consideration and common sense are the key words to open unlimited recreational opportunities.

For an unsurpassed outdoor experience, get acquainted with the Musselshell River and the Montana heartland through which it flows.

Roger Fliger

Musselshell River Drainage

Agnes Creek.   A small tributary of American Fork that more or less parallels the main creek at a distance of about half a mile for 8 miles from headwaters to its mouth about 20 miles southwest by mostly good gravel roads from Harlowton, and is followed upstream by a private ranch road. The lower 4 miles are gravel bottomed, meandering with grassy banks and overhanging clumps of willow, and good fishing for pan-size brookies. Too bad it's posted!

Alabaugh Creek.   A small (mostly jumpable) stream that heads below the southern peaks of the Castle Mountains and flows west for 11 miles to the South Fork of the Musselshell River near Lennep. The lower 5 miles are in open hay meadow and grazing land, are paralleled at a distance of a few feet to ½ mile or so by a gravel road out of Lennep, are "posted," and are lousy with pan-size brookies and also fair fishing for 8 to 10 inch rainbow trout. Because of the fishing potential and in spite of the posting (permission to fish is usually granted upon request), it is moderately popular.

American Fork.   Heads in the Crazy Mountain foothills at the junction of the South and Middle Forks, and flows for 30 miles to the northeast to the Musselshell River just south of U.S. 12, five miles east of Harlowton. The lower 6 miles are real bushy with willow and cottonwood along the creek bottom in open prairie "private" rangeland, are quite slow with gravel bottom, and are fair fishing for browns that average around a foot long and occasionally run up to 20 inches, and 10 to 12 inch brook trout. There are cow paths but not much in the way of roads — but it's crossed by State 19, about 12 miles south of Harlowton. The next 6 miles go dry. The upper reaches (about 18 miles) flow through open parkland and scattered timber, are mostly accessible by jeep roads and trails and are fair fishing for 8 to 10 inch brookies.

Basin Creek.   See Lebo Creek.

Bair Reservoir (or Harris or Durand Lake).   A very popular State Water Conservation Board reservoir in open rangeland on the Musselshell River (U.S. 12) 20 miles east of White Sulphur Springs. The lake is 272 acres with mostly shallow dropoffs to a maximum depth of 40 feet behind an earth fill dam, and is stocked every year with rainbow trout. Brook trout (from the inlet stream) make up about half the catch, now running around 10 inches long; the rainbow run between 8 and 14, with a large rainbow to five pounds being netted on a really rare occasion. The stocked 4 inch rainbow grow slowly, competing with a lake full of suckers. Brown trout are being stocked (in 1981) in small numbers to help control the suckers and add to fishing enjoyment, if you can catch 'em. There are public toilets, a campground and boat launching space available here.

Ben Hill Pond.   Here's a pretty fair stocked pond right at the edge of the Judith Mountains reached by county and ranch roads about 3 miles south from a point on U.S. 87 about 8 miles east of Lewiston. It's only a couple of acres and 8 feet deep — but it's in a very fertile coulee, is real mossy, and is fished more than somewhat summer and winter for 8 to 10 inch rainbow plus an occasional lunker up to 2 pounds.

Berg Reservoir.   Two and a half miles north by good road from Lennep on Bonanza Creek, in open meadowland on the Bonanza (Berg) Ranch — permission required. It's 7 acres, 20 feet maximum depth with as much as 8 foot of drawdown, fair fishing summer and winter for rainbow that average around 12 inches and range up to 16 inches, and brook trout in the 10 to 14 inch class, and is stocked every year with 4 to 6 inch rainbow. This is a good example of a successful, multi-purpose (irrigation and recreation) reservoir.

Big Elk Creek.   A real pretty creek that heads in the Crazy Mountains and is mostly paralleled by a secondary road for 22 miles northeastward to its mouth on the Musselshell River at Twodot. It's mostly in open rangeland with some cottonwood along its course, is pretty fast (and too wide to jump), and mostly posted which is just as well because the brookies don't get much longer than 4 to 6 inches here, although it's not bad fishing for 11 to 12 inch browns. There are private roads all through the area.

Blacktail Creek.

A brushy little meadow and farmland creek, flowing north through the Little Snowy foothills for 8 miles to the South Fork McDonald Creek 4 miles west of Grass Range. It's followed upstream by a jeep road for a couple of miles and provides a little fishing near the mouth for 6 to 8 inch brookies, and a stray rainbow trout up from the main stem. The road is partly private and requires permission.

Bonanza Creek.

A small stream heading in the Castle Mountains and flowing for 9 miles down a timbered canyon above and open (kind of bushy at the lower end) meadows through the Berg Reservoir below to the South Fork of the Musselshell River 4 miles east of Lennep (½ mile north of the highway). It has about 5 miles of fishable water on the Bonanza (Berg) Ranch (permission required) but is only fair for pan-size brookies. So — despite its easy access by good road north from Lennep, it's fished only lightly. There's a county road above the ranch, but even poorer fishing.

Box Elder Dam.

Is in Box Elder draw and backs up the creek to form a 25 acre reservoir in open grazing land half a dozen miles north of Winnett by good gravel road — and a half mile east. It's used a moderate amount and produces good catches of 10 to 14 inch rainbow and a few fair sized ones. There are no facilities — pack it in — pack it out.

Bozeman Fork Musselshell River.

Heads on the northern slopes of the Crazy Mountains and flows north through open foothill "deer" country for 10 miles to junction with Warm Springs Creek at the head on the South Fork Musselshell River 5 miles by good county road west from Lennep. There are about 6 miles of "jumpable" fishing water that is mostly accessible by jeep and trail and fair in the spring (before it warms up) for 8 to 10 inch brookies along with a few cutthroat trout in the upper reaches. Watch for "private roads" in the area sometimes posted to no trespassing.

Broadview Pond.

Was built years ago in an old dredge pit by the Great Northern Railroad and then given to the State which in turn gave it to the town of Broadview, for its recreational assets. It's about 4 acres and quite deep, with steep drop-offs in grassy farmland on the west side of the railroad tracks with the highway a few hundred feet farther over — maybe a quarter of a mile north of town. It's stocked with rainbow yearly, has some brook trout and is quite popular and good early in the season (before the creeks open) but gets warm and mossy later on.

Burnett Reservoir.

Take U.S. 87 for about 18 miles east from Lewistown and then a good gravel road 2 miles north, a private road 2 miles east to the ranch buildings, and finally a jeep trail for a couple of miles across open grazing land to this dammed sagebrush coulee with its 2½ acre mud bottomed reservoir. It's stocked off and on and is not bad fishing for 8 to 12 inch rainbow trout —mostly by the ranch hands.

Careless Creek.

Is a fairly small, easily wadeable stream that heads in a forested basin below Windy Point on Knife Blade Ridge in the Big Snowy Mountains and flows for 35 miles to the south and east to the Musselshell River on the south side of State 6 about 4 miles east of Ryegate. The upper 3 or 4 miles are in a timbered canyon and are poor fishing but in good deer hunting country. The next 12 miles are in brushy (willow, aspen and some cottonwood) bottom foothills and here it is moderately popular and pretty good fishing for 8 to 10 inch brookies in the spring and early summer. The lower 20 miles or so are slow and muddy in a sagebrush, grazing land, prairie country that is more productive of rattlesnakes and sagehens than the creek is of fish.

Castle Creek.

Here is a little bitty tributary of Alabaugh Creek (its mouth is 6 miles west of Lennep by county road) that flows through the ghost town of Castle down its brushy little valley for about 4 miles of fair pan-sized brook trout fishing. It's paralleled all the way by a good gravel road but is not as popular as the ghost town — there's better fishing downstream.

Castle Lake.

Is only 3 acres by 20 feet deep with steep dropoffs all around, in a rocky, forested, glacial cirque below Elk Peak in the Castle Mountains at the head of Alabaugh Creek in good deer and elk country. Recommended to walk in on old "jeep" road (really poor) which runs 6 miles off the Warm Springs Creek road from a point about 4 miles upstream from its mouth. Stocked with cutthroat every other year it is good fishing for fish to 15 inches; quite a few hardy souls "have at it," despite its relative inaccessibility.

RAINBOW TROUT
Courtesy USFS

Checkerboard Creek.
From White Sulphur Springs take the Harlowton road, Route 12 for 20 miles to the mouth of Checkerboard Creek a mile east of Lake Harris on the Musselshell River. It's crossed several times by USFS and private roads on its way to the headwaters up its fairly brushy little canyon, and the lower 6 miles are quite popular in spring and summer 'cause they're full of pan-size brookies and it is a pretty little creek that is nice and clear and easy to fish.

Christensen Pond.
A dammed, 4 acre, 12 foot deep with shallow dropoffs, irrigation reservoir with about 4 feet of normal drawdown in open grazing land with a dirt road right to it about a mile off (south of) Route 12 at a point 1 mile east of Lake Harris. It's on private land and permission for trespass must be solicited and granted — but this one is fair fishing both summer and winter for 10 to 14 inch rainbow and 6 to 10 inch brook trout at a ratio of about 2 to 1. It could stand more pressure than it gets.

Clark Reservoirs.
Two of them, about ¼ to ½ mile across open rangeland above and below the ranch buildings which are about 3 miles south of Fergus by gravel and dirt roads. The upper one is about 4 acres, the lower 3; both are around 15 feet at the deepest with mud bottoms and are fair fishing for 8 to 10 inch rainbow trout — plus once in a while one that'll weigh in at a couple of pounds. Quite a few of the Malta and Lewistowners hit this one.

Comb Creek.
This is a clear little stream heading in the northern slopes of the Crazy Mountains and flowing for 9 miles to the Musselshell River (and State 6) 2 miles east of Lennep. The lower 3 miles are private with permission only, are crossed here and there by ranch roads, are mostly in an open draw (brushy in spots) in cattle country and are fished occasionally for fair catches of 6 to 10 inch brookies.

Cottonwood Creek.
Here is a small, easily wadeable and easily fishable, easy access stream moderately popular with local fishermen. It is crossed at its mouth on the Musselshell River by State 6 five miles into the Crazy Mountains. It's all fair-to-good fishing in the lower (brushy) reaches for brook, rainbow and a few brown trout that'll average around 12 inches, and in the upper (conifer bordered) reaches for small cutthroat.

Cottonwood Lake. See Forest Lake.

Daisy Dean Creek.
Flows south from behind Daisy Peak in the Little Belt Mountains for 20 miles to the Musselshell River, 15 miles west from Harlowton on State 6. It's a small, fairly muddy stream in mostly private (posted) open meadowland, is crossed here and there by county and ranch roads, and is marginal water in relation to its value as a fishery. Nothing much in the way of trout would do well here except brookies, and they do very well indeed (8 to 10 inches) for about 8 miles upstream — but they don't attract many fishermen.

Deadman's Basin Lake. A State Water Conservation Board reservoir, windy, 1890 acres, 90 feet deep, 20 miles east from Harlowton just off U.S. 12 (north 1 mile). It's a natural open basin dammed and fed by water ditched in from the Musselshell River. MDFWP has planted shade trees, provided cabin sites, fireplaces, toilets and boat ramps for the campers, fishermen and multitudinous water skiers (it's worth your life to fish it). A popular recreational reservoir, it is planted with 4 to 6 inch rainbow by the many thousands every year and is fair-to-good catching for 8 to 16 inch rainbow; brown trout from 1 to 2½ pounds (occasionally one to 10 lbs.); kokanee salmon (silver) to a couple of pounds. It was last stocked in 1977, and all in all, a little better fishing in the fall.

Durand Reservoir. See Bair Reservoir or Harris Lake.

Finley Reservoir. Drive due north on State 19 from Grass Range for 15 miles on a good oil road through open, rolling grazing land, then turn right for 1 mile on gravel that peters out into a couple of buggy tracks out across the earth dam that holds up this 20 acre haven for suckers. It was planted with rainbow back in the mid-50's but "Alas, poor Yorick," they are no more. The Fish and Game Department offered to rehabilitate this one, but some of the locals prefer the suckers — so! And anyhow, it's posted.

Fish Creek. Is a fair-size creek (you can't jump it) about 45 miles long (double that if you measure all the crooks and turnings) from its mouth on the Musselshell River 33 miles east of Harlowton on State 6 to its headwaters below Porcupine Butte in the eastern slopes of the Crazy Mountains. The upper 6 miles flow clear and fairly fast through foothill country, the next 4 run slower in open prairie meadowland where there are lots of nice holes and beaver ponds — and where it has a silty bottom due to poor irrigation practices. It's crossed near the bottom of this 10 mile stretch by State 10 fourteen miles south from Harlowton, near the middle and upper end by county roads 20 miles or so south from Twodot. The entire stretch is fair fishing for 8 to 10 inch brookies but isn't frequented a lot, due no doubt to the relatively small local population, and the presence of other equally good or better streams in the vicinity. The lower reaches have little or no recreational value.

Flagstaff Creek. There's about 5 miles of fishable water in this little stream that flows through the Castle Mountain foothills, open hay meadows and the Holiday Reservoir to the Musselshell River and State 6 four and a half miles east of Lake Harris. It's a very fertile stream (flows over a series of limestone reefs), is followed along the east side by a dirt road, and is "home" to multitudes of 3 to 20 inch brookies. They come in all sizes here and are real easy to catch but — you'd better check with the owner before rigging up.

Flagstaff Reservoir. See Holiday Reservoir.

Flatwillow Creek. Heads in a timbered canyon at the junction of the North and South Forks between the Big and Little Snowy Mountains and meanders out across farm, range and meadowland for 48 airline miles to junction with Box Elder Creek about 10 miles southeast of Winnett. It's paralleled by county and ranch roads from its headwaters for about 20 miles downstream to a crossing with U.S. 87, twenty-five miles north of Roundup. This gravel bottomed, beaver dammed stretch is fairly brushy but easily wadeable, fair for rainbow, and is moderately popular with local fishermen, having a few brook and brown trout, too.

Forest (or Cottonwood) Lake. Is a rock-slide lake, long, narrow, 10 acres by 50 feet deep, in a timbered mountain (Cottonwood Creek) canyon below (east of) Virginia Peak in the Crazy Mountains. Reached by a mountain road 10 miles or so up the creek from the main highway at a point 5 miles west of Martinsdale, stopping at the primitive 10 site USFS campground and taking the trail the last few miles in to the shore. In good deer hunting country, truly scenic, the lake receives some pressure from fishermen (some hunters, too) who harvest 12 to 14 inch cutthroat at a fair catch rate, with the chance of a lunker adding to the anticipation and challenge. The 71 Ranch Company (Jack Galt-Louise Rankin) owns the upper end; it may or may not be posted.

Grebe Reservoir. Take State 6 three and seven tenths miles west from Sumatra, turn north on an unimproved county road for ⅛ mile and take the right (east) fork which swings due north for 3¼ miles, where you take off to the right again a final 2½ miles across the open prairie to this 4 acre reservoir on the headwaters of (barren) Rattlesnake Creek. Lots of Roundupers come here for the excellent ½ to 1½ pound rainbow fishing.

202

STATE RECORD BLUEGILL
Courtesy MDFWP

Half Moon Canyon. Heads in the Big Snowy Mountains and flows down a fairly steep, rocky, timbered canyon for about 8 miles to the head of North Fork Flatwillow Creek. It is real small and mediocre fishing in the lower 3 miles or so for 8 to 9 inch rainbow trout. No trail — not many applicants! Shhh — listen closely — the upper reaches of this stream have some fairly nice catchable cutthroat wherever you can find enough water.

Harris Lake. See Bair Reservoir.

Haymaker Creek. A small, slow, posted, open meadow (with some brush here and there and a few meanders) stream heading in Six Shooter Springs in the Little Belt Mountains and flowing south to the Musselshell River where it's crossed by State 6 near the Twodot crossing, 11 miles west of Harlowton. The lower 5 miles produce a few 6 to 8 inch brook trout — and there are a few pan-sized cutthroat trout in the headwaters.

Holiday (or Flagstaff) Reservoir. About 1½ miles up Flagstaff Creek by dirt road to this 10 acre by 20 feet maximum depth, weedy bottom, chuck full of rainbow and brook trout up to 2 feet long, PRIVATE but with fishing generally allowed if you ask permission reservoir, in open farmland with a road up the south side and across the dam. A nice place to go; about the only way you could avoid getting your limit would be to leave your tackle at home.

Hopley Creek. Twelve miles of open prairie stream from the junction of its East and West Forks to its mouth on the Musselshell River 3 miles east of Harlowton. Only the lower 4 miles (crossed near the mouth by State 6) are fished a little for fair-to-middling good populations of 7 to 9 inch brook and ½ to 4 pound brown trout. The creek is real brushy here with lots of beaver ponds and marshy stretches but there's a trail up the west side.

Hyde Creek Pond.
Also known as Gap or Peterson Pond, it's right beside (maybe 350 yards north) of a missile site less than ½ mile east by the missile site road from U.S. 191 about 1½ miles north of Judith Gap. It's a 2½ acre stock pond, 7 to 8 feet deep behind a Soil Conservation Service earth dam in an open coulee, is spring fed, and highly productive of 12 to 14 inch rainbow. This one is really a recreational asset to the "fly boys."

Kincheloe Reservoir.
Used to be a real good large mouth bass and crappie pond (in the 40's and 50's) but they're badly stunted now — and the pond is almost never fished. It's 4 acres in a big, dammed, shallow, sagebrush coulee accessible by trail after about 15 miles of wandering around the open prairie. If you're still interested, you cross the Musselshell River at Melstone and take off to the north along its east side — good luck! Whatever happened to the northern pike planted in 1971? Beats me!

Kizer Pond.
Is 2 acres by 10 feet deep in an open pasture earth-dammed coulee, about 5 miles south by gravel road from the Cheadle School crossing on U.S. 87 twelve miles east of Lewistown. It's not very inspiring aesthetically, has been stocked with rainbow and no doubt would provide some fishing if anyone cared to try it — but few do.

Krause Pond.
A private 2 acre, 10 feet deep pond between Bob and Hank Krause's houses on the North and South Banks of Painted Robe Creek 5 miles south of Lavina on State 3, and then a couple of miles east and south on county roads. It reportedly has good populations of largemouth bass and bullhead.

Lebo (or Basin) Creek.
A small stream that heads in the Crazy Mountain foothills and meanders to the northeast for 20 miles across the open prairie and one ranch after another to American Fork 4 miles south and a little east of Harlowton. It's crossed every 5 miles or so by county roads. The upper reaches are rocky with gravel bottom but the lower reaches are mostly mud bottomed. It's generally good fishing for 8 to 10 inch browns and 7 to 8 inch brook trout at the ratio of about 10 to 1 — but is not heavily fished due to posting.

Lebo Lake.
Reached by good gravel road 8 miles south from Twodot, in rolling grassy rangeland. This is a natural lake that has been dammed at the outlet and raised about 12 feet. It's fed by Little Alkali Creek, covers about 700 acres, has mostly gradual dropoffs to about 14 feet and is considered good fishing by more than a few people — for rainbow trout averaging a foot long and once in a great while a brown up to 5 pounds. It's stocked every year with 4 to 6 inchers. I wonder how northern pike or walleye would do here?

Lion Creek.
This brushy little creek is only about 5 miles long (in a timbered Little Belt Mountain canyon) and flows to the Musselshell River 4 miles above Lake Harris on U.S. 12 about 20 miles east of White Sulphur Springs. The lower 3 miles are followed by logging road and trail, and are fair fishing in spring and fall for pan-size brookies. This is good deer and elk hunting country, too. So good that the creek doesn't get fished much in the late season. There are two primitive USFS campgrounds up the Jamison Trail on Lion Creek for roughing it.

SHARPTAIL
Courtesy Harley Yeager

HIKING
Courtesy USFS

Maginnis Creek. Little-bitty and away back, heads in a timbered canyon on the southern slopes of the Judith Mountains. There's a ½ mile string of small beaver dams with large populations of stunted brook trout that are really hot for a fly or anything else that's eatable. You get there by taking U.S. 87 thirteen miles east to the Cheadle School crossing, turning left (north) on a gravel road for 12 miles to the Fort Maginnis School and a quarter of a mile beyond where you bear right at a fork for a mile and then take an unimproved road left for ½ mile and finally turn north again for a last very long mile to the canyon — and you'd better either ask permission, bring a hacksaw, or come prepared to hike because somewhere along the route you'll likely find a locked gate. It's really not worth the effort.

Martinsdale Lake (or Reservoir). Used to be if it rained forget going here (or leaving) but the road in has been improved (now gravel) and the lake is accessible all the way around by secondary roads, about a mile southeast of Martinsdale off U.S. 12. This is a State Water Board irrigation reservoir of about 985 acres and 120 foot maximum depth with steep dropoffs behind a rock filled WPA dam — in open range country with grassy banks right to the water's edge. There are tables and toilets now and good fishing for 9 to 16 inch rainbow (stocked annually as 4 to 6 inchers by the many thousands), plus brown trout that come in the inlet and average over a pound and are not uncommon in the 5 to 10 pound class, although not too frequently caught. With so many suckers to eat, the browns aren't often hungry. With better access and good catches year round, the lake's popularity has been enhanced manyfold.

Maybee Reservoir. On Indian Creek in open sagebrush country reached by county gravel roads 4 miles north of Kolin. This one is a 4 acre, 15 foot deep stock pond that has been stocked (in 1967) with rainbow and is fair fishing now for 8 to 10 inchers. It's fished somewhat but is nothing to write home about.

McCurtney Creek. A pretty little crystal clear, although fairly brushy, stream that heads in a spring in the foothills of the Big Snowies and meanders eastward to the North Fork Flatwillow Creek — and is accessible by trail from the end of the Flatwillow road. It furnishes some real good fishing and is moderately popular the first week of the season for 7 to 8 inch brook trout — but the owners are a little owly and you'd better ask permission.

McKenna Reservoir. Some pretty good fishing here — 18 miles east on U.S. 87 from Lewiston, then 3½ miles north to the Pleasant Plains School and finally another mile or so by "ranch" roads. It's a 3 acre stock pond, 18 feet deep in a steep-sided open coulee, fairly mossy — and produces some good catches of nice fat rainbow for the locals.

Courtesy USSCS

Middle Fork American Fork.   About 8 miles long from its headwaters below Sunlight Peak (elevation 10,087 feet) to its junction with the North Fork. It's pretty much in a timbered canyon and the lower 4 miles (which are more or less followed by jeep road) are fair fishing for 6 to 10 inch brook trout. It doesn't get too much pressure and wouldn't stand it if it did — besides it's mostly private anyhow.

North Fork American Fork.   A tiny, Crazy Mountain creek about 4 miles long in a narrow timbered canyon. No road, no trail, a few 6 to 8 inch brookies in the lower mile and a very few fishermen, mostly private, and hard to find.

North Fork Flatwillow Creek.   Heads in the Little Snowies at the junction of McCurtney and Half Moon Creeks, and flows mostly down a timbered canyon above (for 5 miles) and a brushy coulee below for another 5 miles to the South Fork Flatwillow and the head of the main stem. It's followed to headwaters along the north side by the Flatwillow road, is wadeable and is fished a lot in early season for good catches of 8 to 10 inch rainbow. It also has 6 to 10 inch brooks, and a few brown trout waiting to be creeled. Like the South Fork, it's pretty small and plays out early — besides which it gets a little warm in the summer.

Petrolia Lake.   A State Water Board irrigation reservoir that was formed by damming Flatwillow Creek 8 miles above its junction with Box Elder Creek, reached by a state road 6 miles south from Winnett and then county roads west for about an equal distance to the shore. It's 510 acres in size, has a 35 foot maximum depth and is sometimes drawn almost completely down. In 1980 it was drained completely. Being used more for water skiing and swiming, it was only fair fishing (in the past) for walleye and yellow perch. There's plenty of open space to park but the camping facilities consist of one lonesome Chick Sale. The MDFWP stocked 20,000 rainbow trout 4 to 6 inches long in 1981 and the fishing should be good now if the suckers and carp don't take over again.

Rindal Pond.   About 5 miles north and a little west of Roy by county and ranch roads; 5 acres with shallow dropoffs to a maximum depth of 15 feet in a dammed, shallow coulee in sagebrush grazing land on the Rindal Ranch. It's now being planted annually with a couple thousand or so 4 to 6 inch rainbow and is good for 8 to 12 inchers.

South Fork American Fork.   Is about 8 miles long in scattered timber and park country, mostly accessible by jeep, floats a few pan-size brookies in the lower reaches, and is mostly private.

Courtesy Ernst Peterson

South Fork Flatwillow Creek. Heads below Lost Peak (elevation 8933 feet) in the Big Snowy Mountains and flows fairly rapidly for 5 miles through the mountains, then 8 miles through foothills, and finally a couple of miles of open coulee country eastward to the main stem — there's a trail all the way. There's lots of timber above and quite a few quaking aspen below. The middle and upper reaches are fished a lot in early season for good catches of 8 to 10 inch rainbow and some small brook trout. However, there's not enough water to stand the pressure and it plays out quickly.

South Fork McDonald Creek. Is a small, silty, brushy, meandering, farmland stream that is followed by a gravel road (and the Great Northern Railroad tracks) for 14 miles between Grass Range and Forest Grove. It's not much for fishing.

South Fork Musselshell River. Is formed by the junction of Bonanza and Warm Springs Creek 4 miles west of Lennep, is followed by good county roads for 20 miles to junction with the Musselshell River 2½ miles northeast of Martinsdale. It's mostly in open meadow and grazing land but with brush and cottonwood along its meandering course, and there are lots of nice deep holes that are good producers (and fished more than somewhat) of 12 to 20 inch brown and 10 to 16 inch rainbow trout along with some small brook trout in the upper reaches. Inasmuch as it's almost all on private land, it wouldn't hurt to ask permission — in fact, it's necessary! There have been plenty of litter problems in the past, you know.

Spring Creek. A small, moderately popular stream that heads in the Little Belt Mountains and flows for 9 miles southward through open park and timber foothills (above) in good deer and elk hunting country to open grazing land and the Musselshell River about 6 miles east of Lake Harris on Route 12. The lower end dries up, but the middle and upper reaches (which are paralleled by a good USFS road) are fair fishing for pan-size brookies. Part of its popularity is no doubt due to a good USFS campground.

Swimming Woman Creek. The upper 3 miles are in a timbered canyon on the southern slopes of the Snowy Mountains below Greathouse Peak (elevation 8736 feet), but from here down it flows slowly southward for 23 miles down a broad, open (mostly private ownership) valley to junction with Careless Creek practically beneath the Great Northern Railroad 2½ miles along the track northeast from Ryegate. It's accessible here and there by ranch roads and trails, is mostly

207

clear with lots of meanders and brushy beaver ponds, and is fished a fair amount (considering its locale) for good catches of 8 to 9 inch brook and a very few rainbow trout.

Voldseth Reservoir.
Drive east from Lennep for 1 mile and then take a good secondary road 1¼ miles to the Voldseth Ranch and from there over a rough road for another mile east to the reservoir which is about 5 acres, in open grazing land just east of Comb Butte, has a maximum depth of 14 feet behind an earth dam and about 4 feet drawdown for irrigation. It's excellent fishing for mostly 14 inch rainbow and some brook trout but seldom sees a hook — then with permission only.

War Horse Lake.
Drive 12 miles west from Winnet on U.S. 87 to Teigen and then turn north on a county road for another 8 miles across open rangeland to this 1468 acre irrigation (and National Wildlife Refuge) reservoir on (barren) Little Box Elder Creek. It is in open sagebrush flats, has a maximum depth of 10 or 12 feet behind a badly-in-need-of-repairs dam, is covered with weeds and at present supports bullheads and suckers. Great Falls and Billings anglers used to fish it heavily for bass and northern pike, but no more. The bass died out in the 70's and the pike winterkilled in 1978. It figures — with the lake being drawn down at times to only 5 or 6 feet deep. There are no present plans for restocking.

Warm Springs Creek.
Heads below Elk Peak (elevation 8606 feet) in the Castle Mountains and flows slowly for the most part through private foothill, grazing and hay-meadow land eastward for 10 miles to junction with Bozeman Fork Musselshell River 4 miles by good county road west from Lennep. It's followed by a ranch road along the lower reaches, and a trail to headwaters — the lower 4 miles have a few pan-size brookies. It's seldom fished and is mostly private with permission needed.

West Fork Cottonwood Creek.
Here is one you can jump across. It's a 5 miles long, fair fishing for pan-size brook trout in the first 2 miles above the mouth, and is in a little timbered canyon that is good deer hunting and easily accessible by logging road and trail.

West Fork Flagstaff Creek.
A clear, rocky bottom with a few willows along side, little creek in open rolling rangeland in the Castle Mountain foothills — flowing to Flagstaff Creek near the end of the road. There are only about 3 miles of fishing water here but it stands up well under moderate pressure and produces good catches of rainbow and brook trout that average around 12 and 10 inches respectively.

Willow Creek.
This stream heads in the Little Snowy Mountains and flows for about 35 airline miles out across the range through Lake Masen and eventually into the Musselshell River east of Roundup. Only about 4 miles of the upper timbered canyon foothill reaches are good trout water. Here it's a small, fairly fast stream with good gravel bottom and willow cover and supports a moderate amount of pressure by local anglers for fair catches of 6 to 8 inch brook trout, really more of a picnicking-kids creek than anything else. To get there take county roads north from Roundup to the Al Elseline Ranch and then a private trail on in — after you get permission.

JUST ARRIVED
Courtesy Craig Black

Courtesy Montana Fish, Wildlife and Parks

Yellow Water Lake. A State Water Board irrigation project in open rangeland 7 miles south of Winnett by oil roads and then 6 miles west on gravel. It has a surface area of about 150 acres behind an earth dam on Yellow Water Creek, is sometimes drawn way down and (as the name implies) is not entirely lacking in silt and mud. It is, however, stocked annually with 30,000 or so rainbow trout 4 to 6 inches long and is really good fishing (and catching) for 10 to 20 inch fish, with a not uncommon eye-popping solid-hitting five or even ten pounder to tackle your outfit here. Also caught are ½ to 1 pound bullheads. Small wonder it's popular for anglers as far away as Billings and Roundup. P.S.: The bad winter of 1978 killed some trout here but most of the larger fish apparently survived, luckily.

Know The Fishing Regulations

LOOKOUT
Courtesy USFS

Red Rock River

As you head eastward out of Monida on the gravel road which leads to the heart of the Centennial Valley, the headwaters of the Red Rock River, your car becomes a time machine as you drift back 100 years. Bordered on the south by mountains as spectacular as the valley they were named after, the only hints of civilization lie among the few scattered summer cattle ranches and the headquarters of the Red Rock Lakes National Wildlife Refuge. Besides the refuge personnel and several hearty ranching souls, the moose, trumpeter swan, coyotes and arctic grayling rule this valley during the winter months. Waters originating in Hellroaring Creek, a headwater stream to the Red Rock, travels nearly 4,000 miles to reach the Gulf of Mexico, the third longest river journey in the world.

The upper valley provides a variety of challenges for the fishing enthusiast, the avid birdwatcher stalking the sandhill crane and curlew or the adventurous canoeist wishing for a wilderness wetland experience paddling from the upper to the lower lake on the refuge. Brook trout, fat and sassy, lie under deeply undercut banks in many of the streams draining into the refuge. And you don't really know what a brookie can do till you try your luck in the Widow's Pool. Hot fishing in Elk Lake for cutthroat, grayling and lake trout and in Hidden Lake for lunker rainbows will keep the chill from float tube fanatics. Last, but not least, are colorful Arctic grayling migrating from the refuge lakes into Red Rock Creek on their annual spawning run. Because the refuge was originally established to resurrect the endangered trumpeter swan, fishing regulations are set according to the swan's breeding season. Be sure to stop in at refuge headquarters before sampling the waters.

Red Rock Creek becomes a river once it leaves the lower refuge lake. The river meanders and finds its way through open pasture to Lima Reservoir, a dam constructed for irrigation purposes. Although too warm to support a trout fishery, Canada geese and other waterfowl utilize this area extensively during their spring and fall migration. The Snowcrest Range looms over the valley to the north.

Below the dam, the river, as well as the fishery, changes character on its last leg of the journey to Clark Canyon Reservoir. The high red cliffs which gave the river its name break up the landscape here. Cutthroat and rainbow trout are the fish hitting your flies. A side trip up Big Sheep Creek could land you a brown or rainbow well worth the detour. Traveling downstream, brown and rainbow trout numbers and size increase as does productivity. Although most of the lower river is posted, the stretch on the Bureau of Reclamation land directly above the reservoir can provide all the angling excitement you need for an afternoon. Your trip wouldn't be complete without a stop at the infamous Henry-Wombacher's fly shop on old Highway 91 above the reservoir – full of his outstanding and well known fly patterns. Whether you are seeking a weekend full of outdoor entertainment for the entire family or that quiet solitude between you and your fly rod, the Red Rock country offers something for everyone.

Janet Decker-Hess

RED ROCK RIVER
Courtesy Bridenstine Studio

Red Rock River Drainage

Bar Pits. See Borrow Pits.

Bear Creek. Not many fishermen make it to this little Beaverhead Mountain stream which drops from 9000 feet at its headwaters below Eighteen Mile Peak on the Continental Divide eastward to 7500 feet at its mouth on Nicholia Creek 4½ miles downstream. The upper reaches are steep and fast, but it flattens out and slows down below in open rolling foothills — intermontane basin country. The Nicholia road crosses it at the mouth and the Harkness Lakes road follows the middle reaches for almost a mile. It's fair fishing too (from here down) for 5 to 12 inch cutthroat trout.

Beaver Creek. Don't confuse this Beaver Creek with the one that junctions with (barren) Deep Creek at the head of Junction Creek. This Beaver Creek heads at the mouth of Big Beaver Creek and flows to the northwest across open rolling rangeland for 5½ miles to Junction Creek just south of Interstate 15, seven miles east of Lima. It's a small stream with lots of brushy beaver ponds, is mostly accessible by a jeep trail, but is very seldom fished even though you can fill your basket with pan-size brookies and possibly a stray cutthroat trout or two. It's just too small a stream, too far away from civilization, and suffering from too much competition from better water.

Big Sheep Creek. See Sheep Creek.

Blair Lake. A fairly deep, 9 acre cirque lake with maybe a couple of acres of weeds near the outlet, in alpine timber at 8140 feet above sea level just north and a little below the Continental Divide. You can get to within ½ mile of it with a good jeep up the Snyder Creek-Keg Spring jeep trail on the Idaho side of the hill, but a few Montanans go in as follows: drive 15 miles east from Lakeview or 2 miles west of Red Rock Pass. Here you shoulder "ye old pack" and strike out to the south and east up Hell Roaring Canyon for 2 miles till you come to the Canyon from the lake which you follow upstream for a final steep ½ mile to the shore. It's a nice hike in, fairly popular, and fair fishing for ½ to 1½ pound cutthroat trout when you get there.

Borrow (or Bar) Pits. These are really irrigation ditches along either side of old U.S. 91 (Interstate 15) in open ranchland a couple of miles south of Dell. There is a lot of watercress in them, and lots of 10 to 12 inch brook, rainbow and brown trout hiding in them. The tourist types especially just can't pass 'em by (among others).

Breneman's Lake. Drive 17 miles east up the Centennial Valley from Monida to (barren) Windslow Creek a mile west of the Doyle School. Here you take a dirt jeep road southeast for 2 miles, then the left hand fork for 5 crooked miles up a mostly open ridge to the dammed lake. Once there, you'll find it's in timber, 6 acres with quite a bit of vegetation in the shallows, and has been fair fishing in years gone by for 2 to 6 pound rainbow trout that were planted long ago. It's present status is non-pro-quo. P.S. There's a gate down the road that is sometimes locked. Better ask permission.

Buck Pond. See McDonald's Pool.

Clover Creek. Flows south from the Clover Divide (twixt the Red Rock and Blacktail drainages) for 9 miles to the Red Rock River 1½ miles east of the Lima Reservoir. The upper reaches are paralleled by the Divide road; it's mostly diverted for irrigation below. The upper (fishing) reaches are all in open, rolling rangeland with lots of willow along the creek and a few small cutthroat and brook trout in it. Nobody in the know fishes it.

Corral Creek. A very small northward flowing tributary of Red Rock Creek. Only the lower 1½ miles in "Alaska Basin," open bottomland reaches, are fishable. There's a county road all along the south side (13 miles east from Lakeview) and a darn good population of small brookies and a few cutthroat trout. Funny but few people stop to try it.

Culver Pond (or Widow's Pool).   Is a shallow, 29 acre, ¾ mile long spring-fed pond right at the base of the hills on the north side of the open, grassy Red Rock River bottoms 3½ miles east of Upper Red Rock Lake, 14 miles east and north by county and private ranch roads from Lakeview. The water here is as clear as mountain air and full of 9 to 19 inch brookies plus rainbow, cutthroat and their hybrids, and grayling. It's excellent for seeing fish but not necessarily for catching them. This has been one of the best lunker brook trout fisheries in the state and is still good if you hit it just right.

Deadman Creek.   Drains Deadman Lake away up in the Beaverhead Mountains, 8 miles northward to its mouth on Sheep Creek right in the middle of the upper canyon reaches. It's reached at the mouth by the Sheep Creek road and crossed a couple of miles upstream by the Medicine Lodge (Bannock) Pass road. The rest is all accessible by trail in an open, rocky canyon below and a partly timbered, brushy canyon above. There are a lot of beaver ponds in the middle reaches and they are easy fishing for good catches of 5 to 12 inch cutthroat, rainbow, and hybrids. Truly a nice little stream, and the hiking cuts way down on the fishing pressure. The area is also good mule deer, elk and grouse hunting (in season).

Deadman Lake.   Take the left-hand (south) road off the Sheep Creek road at the junction of Nicholia and Cabin Creeks, go ½ mile and take the left fork again for about a mile where you turn right onto the Henderson Gulch jeep road 9 crooked miles into Deadman. It's in a small, mostly open ravine between rolling sagebrush hills but with fairly steep, sparsely timbered slopes to the east. It is an elongated 8 acres with steep dropoffs (some over 15 feet deep), is spring fed, weedy, and overpopulated with 9 to 10 inch cutthroat trout. In addition to the easy access and good fishing, there are acres of grassland for camping and plenty of wood for fires, so — it gets used aplenty.

East Fork Clover Creek.   Flows five miles into Clover Creek with an unimproved road in the lower 1½ miles and trails on above. Mostly small brooks taken here and some cutthroat (both to 10 inches or so) trout. This little stream gives up easy limits of fine eating fish (though very few fishermen bother it).

East Fork Little Sheep Creek.   A tiny creek with very limited recreation potential, perhaps a mile of fair fishing for 6 to 7 inch brook trout in an occasional beaver pond. There is a USFS campground on it which is accessible by road about a mile up from its mouth on the Middle Fork, a half mile up from the junction of that creek with the West Fork.

MOUNTAIN GROWN TROUT
Courtesy Bridenstine Studio

214

DEADMAN LAKE
Courtesy Bridenstine Studio

Elk (or Elk Springs or Shitepoke) Creek. Is the outlet of Elk Lake which it drains west for 5 miles to Upper Red Rock Lake. The upper 1 mile is in open grassland within a narrow canyon. The lower 4 miles meander slowly through marshland within the Red Rock Lakes Migratory Bird Refuge. The upper mile is paralleled by a poor county road 14 miles east and then north from Lakeview. There are a whole flock of beaver ponds here and they vary all the way from fair-to-excellent fishing for rainbow and brook trout mostly in the 12 to 14 inch class but occasionally up to 1½ and 3 pounds respectively. There used to be cutthroat and grayling, but the newcomers squeezed them out. Don't know if the creek can take the usage, as creels show few bigger fish of late.

Elk Lake. Elevation 6800 feet above sea level, 2½ miles long, 235 acres with about 40 in weeds and lilies, 70 foot maximum depth, in a little draw west and below the Hidden Lake bench and reached by the Elk Creek road. There's a 3 foot dam in the outlet (south end), muddy shoal bottom at the north and with gravel bottoms and steep dropoffs elsewhere, bare rocky hills to the west and patches of timber and aspen to the east.

Elk Lake. In 1954, 1955 and 1957 grayling were stocked here and can be readily caught up to 17 inches long (some of State's largest grow here). Cutthroat trout are stocked annually (currently 35,000 or so) furnishing good sport for 10 to 20 inch (up to a recorded 3 pounds) fish. A little harder to catch are the lake trout to 20 inches and the burbot (ling). You can live it up here at the Elk Lake Resort, a fourth of the way up the west shore, or continue on to Hidden, Goose or Otter Lakes up on over the hill in the Madison River drainage (a bunch of people go this way).

Elk Springs Creek. See Elk Creek.

Game Warden's Private Pond. See Shultz Pond.

Hackett Creek. See Picnic Creek.

Harkness Lakes. Three, 3 to 20 acre by 18 feet deep glacial potholes, at 8140 foot elevation, a few hundred yards apart in open, hummocky grazing land at the end of the Bear Creek road. They were planted with rainbow in '66, still had 'em in the 70's and may be good fishing now — if they haven't frozen out.

Hellroaring Creek. Heads between Mount Jefferson and Reas Peak practically on the Continental Divide and flows northward down its steep, rocky, (Hellroaring) canyon for 5 miles and over 100 foot falls which form a barrier to fish migration to the open rolling Alaska Basin bottoms for a final couple of miles to junction with Red Rock Creek. It's crossed by a poor county road ½ mile below the falls and there is a trail of sorts upstream. The upper reaches (above the falls) provide some fair 6 to 16 inch cutthroat trout fishing in occasional holes and beaver ponds. The lower reaches are excellent fishing for 9 to 10 inch brook and 10 to 20 inch cutthroat, especially in late spring.

Kitty Creek.

Maybe a mile of fishing here — upstream from its mouth on Bloody Dick Creek a mile below and across the water from Hughes Cow Camp. It's "in the woods," no trail, seldom sees a line but is good fishing for small brookies.

Little Beaver Creek.

A pretty small stream that junctions with (barren) Sawmill Creek to form the headwaters of Junction Creek. There are maybe a couple of miles of brushy beaver ponds in the lower reaches and they could provide a limited amount of excellent fishing for pan-size brookies — but seldom do. You can jeep to its mouth if you want to try, 1½ miles south of Lima on Interstate 15, then right (southeast) on a poor dirt road 8 miles in.

Little Sheep (or Middle Fork) Creek.

A very scenic Douglas fir and open sagebrush foothill stream that is seldom fished. From Lima, drive due west for 2 miles on a county road, to the Little Sheep road which you follow upstream (south) for 5 miles to the junction of the Middle and West Forks. Take the left-hand fork for another 4 miles up Middle Creek to the end of the road and then another 7 miles of trail to headwaters below Garfield Mountain. The roaded reaches are dewatered for irrigation, but the upper (trail) reaches are good fishing for 8 to 9 inch cutthroat trout, especially in the many beaver ponds up and down the creek. It's also a prime deer and elk hunting area.

Long Creek.

A small, relatively slow stream that is paralleled south by the Ruby River — North Centennial Valley road through open grass and sagebrush hills for 10 miles to its mouth on the Red Rock River 5 miles east of the Lima Reservoir. About 6 miles is fishable for fair catches of 10 to 14 inch cutthroat and brook trout, plus lesser numbers of rainbow-cutthroat hybrids (not many rainbow but enough to cross). It also used to have lots of grayling, but they are no more. Not many people stop by.

Lousy Springs.

See Schultz Pond.

Lower Red Rock Lake.

An 1126 acre, real marshy Federal Migratory Bird Refuge accessible by road 23 miles east across open grazing bottomland from Monida. The average depth is only 3½ feet, which is splendid for waterfowl but not for fish. There are lots of suckers though, and some cutthroat, grayling and ling that you can't fish for because — it is closed water. A bird watcher's paradise.

Courtesy Montana Fish, Wildlife and Parks

STRUTTING
Courtesy USFS

BLAIR LAKE
Courtesy Bridenstine Studio

McDonald's Pool (or Buck Pond). A great little seven acres of water with abrupt 7 foot dropoffs to a gravel and mud bottom, fed by Elk Springs Creek (below Elk Lake) and drained by Elk and Shitepoke Creek (see Elk Creek). There is some rainbow reproduction here. The pond was built in the 50's by the U.S. Fish and Wildlife Service, and was stocked in 1955, 1957 and 1961 with grayling, since died out. Excellent fishing for 10 to 22 inch rainbow trout (and the ubiquitous sucker). Droves of anglers gamble for the prize of a husky 4 or 5 pounder, with the more tenacious — or just plain lucky — now and then being rewarded.

Middle Creek. Has 2½ miles of small brushy beaver ponds from its mouth near the head of Beaver Creek upstream to the mouth of Poison Creek. It's crossed at the mouth by the Beaver Creek road and you can jeep it up and down across open grazing land — and fish it too for lots of little brookies. Few do!

Middle Fork Creek. See Little Sheep Creek.

Morrison Lake. A 24 acre glacial lake below (east of) Baldy Mountain at 8120 feet above sea level. It is bordered by open hummocky moraine to the north, lies at the base of sparsely timbered mountain slopes to the south, is fed by springs and runoff and has no outlet. In general, the dropoffs are steep to a maximum depth of 50 feet. There are quite a few water plants along the northeast side, and there do not appear to be any spawning grounds; the lake was stocked until 1971 with rainbow. In the past it has given up trout to 8 lbs., but very rarely, having been only poor to fair fishing. It is now good fishing for cutthroat trout stocked in 1972, 1976, 1979 and 1981. They'll run about a foot long, but once in a while, to 3 pounds or so. Come in at the Sheep Creek-Sweeney Ranch road 30 miles southwest from Dell by pickup if it's dry — otherwise 4 wheels.

Nicholia Creek. Heads away up on the eastern slopes of the Continental Divide and is followed by dirt and gravel roads for 9 miles southward to junction with Cabin Creek at the head of Big Sheep Creek. The upper reaches are in a sparsely timbered semi-open little valley, the lower reaches in open, grass and sagebrush covered foothills. It's not fished much and the few that do try — don't get much — a few pan size rainbow and rainbow-cutthroat hybrids. Notice to hunters: this is good mountain goat country.

O'Dell Creek. A small clear, 12 mile long stream that heads on the southern slopes of the Centennial Range and debouches to Lower Red Rock Lake. The upper reaches are in a semi-open, timbered canyon and are accessible by trail. The lower reaches flow through the marshy bottomland of the Centennial Valley where they are crossed by a poor county road near Lakeview. It is good for mostly brookies averaging about 8 inches, a few cutts and grayling, and merits more usage than it gets, having a pretty fair game fish population, and only a few happy fishermen.

Picnic (or Hackett) Creek. The very small 2½ mile long outlet of the Widow's Pool to Shitepoke Creek. It's all in open grassland on the east side of the Centennial Valley at the base of the Deer Mountain foothills. Real pretty water, easy to fish, moderately popular, and fair fishing too in a limited sort of way — for 9 to 10 brook, 10 to 13 inch rainbow, and a "very" occasional lunker.

Poison Creek. Is NOT poison but its not much of a creek either. It flows eastward from its headwaters below the Continental Divide through a passel of small brushy beaver ponds across open grazing land 3½ miles to the upper reaches of Middle Creek. There is no trail, but you can jeep it if you're interested; few people are, although the beaver ponds are loaded with small brook trout.

Red Rock Creek. Heads up on Squaw Pass (on the Continental Divide) and meanders to the west for 7½ miles through the open hay meadow and grazing land of the Alaska Basin, and then another 8 miles down the marshy bottomlands of the upper Centennial Valley to Upper Red Rock Lake. It's crossed here and there by county and private roads and in those localities provides some good fishing for mostly 6 to 12 inch brookies, along with a few 12 to 14 inch grayling and, rare cutthroat trout. Where you have to hike — it doesn't get fished.

Red Rock Lakes. See Upper, Lower.

Sage Creek. Rises in a small alpine meadow on top of the Red Rock Mountains and flows for 26 miles through open, sage covered foothills above and hay meadows below in a great semicircle from east-to-south-to-west to the Red Rock River 2 miles north of Dell. There are about 6 miles of fair fishing in the lower reaches — for 8 to 12 inch rainbow plus a few brown trout that grow like snakes to maybe 15 inches, and some small brookies.

Schultz (or Warden's or Game Warden's Private) Pond (or Lousy Springs).

Is on the Schultz Ranch and was originally planted with rainbow trout by a local game warden for his own "private" fishing, hence the names. It's only 2½ acres and less than 6 feet deep, in open, rolling hills accessible by a poor dirt road 14 miles north across the Centennial Valley from the county road at the Doyle School 18 miles east of Monida. The owner uses it for watering stock (there's a sheepshed handy) but there's been public access since 1951. Informed "locals" have been pulling 'em out of here for years — up to better than 10 pounds — but there are very few if any of these lunkers left. It is really a marginal fishery.

Courtesy Danny On

Shambo Pond. Closed — never fished! It would be good, if you could, for 9 to 15 inch brook trout. Shambo is 7 acres, 2 to 3 feet deep, in the Upper Centennial Valley bottoms ¼ mile west from Upper Red Rock Lake just north of the road 3 miles east of Lakeview, within the Federal Migratory Waterfowl Refuge.

Sheep (or Big Sheep) Creek. A nice-size, easily accessible stream that is good fishing for 9 to 20 inch rainbow, and 10 to 24 inch brown trout. Go south from Dell ½ mile on Interstate 15, turn to your right (southwest) and you can drive right up the full length of it across open grazing land on the Red Rock River bottoms for 3 miles, and then a narrow rocky, brushy little canyon for 5 miles, a narrow flat bottomed valley for another 5, and a final couple of miles through another rocky canyon to its head at the junction of Cabin and Nicholia Creeks. Some of it is hard to fish because of the excessive brush and willow but lots of people bring their trailers and have-at-it. The larger rainbow (to 20 inches) and brown (to 24 inches) are mostly taken in spring and fall.

Shineberger Creek. A little bitty stream with limited recreational potential flows north through open rangeland to Beaver Creek. It's accessible by jeep or pickup from the Beaver Creek jeep trail and has a flock of small, really brushy beaver ponds that are good fishing for small fish (brookies of course).

Shitepoke Creek. See Elk Creek.

Swan Lake. The smallest of three lakes on the Federal Migratory Waterfowl Refuge in the upper Centennial Valley 30 miles east of Monida. It is a very shallow, marshy 600 acres, fed by Elk Creek and draining to Upper Red Rock Lake. This is the place to come if you want to photograph swan, pelican, crane, geese, or almost any of Montana's migratory waterfowl. P.S. Closed to fishing.

Tom Creek. A small stream flowing for about 5 miles northwesterly before entering Upper Red Rock Lake, with access from a county road nearby. Offers fair stream and beaver pond fishing for small eastern brook trout to about 11 inches. There's better water not far away.

Upper Red Rock Lake. A marshy, 2206 acres on the Federal Migratory Waterfowl Refuge at the head of the Red Rock River reached by county road 5 miles east of Lower Red Rock Lake (which is also a waterfowl refuge of similar characteristics). Excellent for observing swan, pelican, geese, ducks, etc. but — closed to fishing. It contains 10 to 17 inch grayling, cutts and brooks to 17 inches, is mostly shallow, and a waterfowl paradise.

RED ROCK LAKE
Courtesy Bridenstine Studio

Courtesy Wes Woodgard

"FOOL" HEN
Courtesy USFS

Warden's Pond. See Schultz Pond.

West Creek. Heads on the southern slopes of Antone Peak in the Snowcrest Mountains and flows south through open, rolling, sagebrush and grass covered hills toward the Red Rock River 3½ miles above (east of) Lima Reservoir, but it's dewatered about 2½ miles upstream and very little water ever gets to the river. There's a little poor fishing above for 6 to 8 inch cutthroat, but they're seldom if ever bothered. If you like it lonesome, there's jeep access.

West Fork Little Sheep Creek. Provides perhaps 2 miles of fair fishing for small brook trout in headwater beaver ponds above the end of the West Fork road (which you get to a couple of miles west from Lima and then 5 miles up the Little Sheep Creek road). The fishing reaches are in timbered mountains just east of the Continental Divide below the Four Eye triangulation station — in real fine elk hunting country.

Widgeon Pond. Just off a county road between Widow's Pool and McDonald's Pond, established in 1964, this little pond used to have a few brooks but for diversity in the area, MDFWP planted cutthroat in 1979 and 1980 and you can catch 'em up to 18 inches now with an added bonus of an occasional fat brookie up to 18 inches. It's easily fished and good, too, though not too well known, which is sure to change if the fishing holds up.

Widow's Pool. See Culver Pond.

MORRISON LAKE
Courtesy Bridenstine Studio

BLACK BUTTE
Courtesy USFS

Ruby River

If you are one of those people that enjoys standing shoulder to shoulder with your fellow angler while working trout waters, skip the Ruby River on your next trip through southwestern Montana. If, however, gazing up to vistas crowded with the spectacular Tobacco Roots and Gravelly ranges, listening to the prehistoric call of the sandhill crane as it flies overhead, or catching a trout or ten appeals to you, come take a journey through the Ruby River Valley.

The upper 14 miles of river and tributaries offer fair fishing for pan size cutthroat and rainbow trout. The spectacular vistas of the Snowcrest and Gravelly offer an added bonus to the angler. Unfortunately, highly erosive soils and poor land use practices in the past have had adverse impacts on trout habitat and aquatic insects in the upper drainage. Once the clear and nutritionally rich waters of Warm Springs Creek join the river, the trout population increases ten fold. Here angling for 10 to 14 inch rainbow trout with the occasional larger brown trout creates an exciting day for the devotee of smaller-water fishing. Between the USFS boundary to the south and the Ruby Reservoir to the north, the river banks are privately owned and permission from the landowners must be granted. Fee fishing has been instigated by several ranchers in the area.

The flowing journey of the river is temporarily impounded behind Ruby Reservoir, located seven miles south of the town of Alder. Built for irrigation purposes, the reservoir may be severely drawn down by late summer. As a result, expect only fair fishing for wild brown trout and stocked rainbows and cutthroat.

Below the reservoir, the wiley brown trout reigns as king until the Ruby's convergence with the Beaverhead River three miles south of Twin Bridges. Although access is provided by several county roads with bridges, permission must be obtained from the landowners. Chances are, once you wet your line and feel the first familiar tug, a rewarding afternoon of angling for 1 to 3 pound trout awaits you. Check with the Four Rivers Fly Shop in Twin Bridges for tips on flies and lures and tales of local fishing lore.

Nestled between the nationally famous waters of the Madison, Big Hole, and Beaverhead Rivers, this sleeper continues to remain undiscovered. The Ruby not only offers superb fishing but gives you that feeling of "being there first."

Janet Decker-Hess

Ruby River Drainage

Alder Gulch Creek (or Virginia Dredge Pond). Rises on the northern slopes of Baldy Mountain and is followed to the west by road for 14 miles down an open sagebrush-and-rattlesnake infested gulch past the old (restored) capital of Montana territory, Virginia City, to an 8 mile stretch of gold dredge tailings. Here it percolates through a series of willow fringed dredge ponds north of Alder. Upon leaving the ponds, it flows for a final 2 miles to the Ruby River just west of Laurin. This creek is quite small. It, and especially the dredge ponds, are excellent fishing for 10 to 14 inch rainbow and an occasional 8 to 10 inch brook trout. There's heavy pressure from anglers on vacation.

Barton Gulch Creek. A small creek that heads on the timbered, northern slopes of Baldy Mountain and is followed by a truck road down the gulch for 4 miles west to the edge of the timber and then 2 more miles through open, rolling foothills to mile-long dredge tailings eventually to the east side of the Ruby Reservoir, a mile above the dam. It's not fished much but is fair in early season for small brookies.

California Creek. This is a small (8 miles long and you can jump it anywhere) open, foothill creek that flows west from below Ramshorn Mountain to junction with Harris Creek (which has next to no recreational value), a mile east and another north from Laurin by county road. There are a few cottonwood and willow along the banks to ward off the sun's rays (and snag your fly). It's seldom fished but does float a few small brook trout in the lower couple of miles.

Cottonwood Creek. A steep, little foothill stream flowing to the west from below Big Horn Mountain for 10 miles to the Ruby River at Cottonwood Camp — but only the lower 3 miles, up through and including a mile-long beaver ponded marshy area, are fishable. Not many people fish this creek; it's poor for 8 to 10 inch rainbow and a few cutthroat trout.

Divide Creek. Here is a rapid, clear little alpine stream that heads at the south end of the Snow Crest Range between the Ruby and Red Rock River drainage and is followed by road along its north side for the last mile to its mouth on the upper Ruby River road, about 35 miles above Alder. There's a USFS trail on upstream. The first 2 miles above the mouth are fair fishing for pan-size brook and cutthroat trout, especially in a few beaver ponds up and down the creek. Very few people stop here.

Courtesy US Fish and Wildlife

Courtesy Danny On

East Fork Ruby River. This stream is pretty small (too big to jump, but you can easily wade it) to be the East Fork of a river. It heads below Monument Hill and flows fast and clear down a willow-sagebrush and conifer lined course for 7 miles west to the Three Forks Campground on the Upper Ruby River road. There are quite a few beaver ponds along the lower and middle reaches that are poor fishing for rainbow, cutthroat, hybrids and camp-fare brookies. Not very many people fish here. Access is by road for about a mile, the rest by foot or horse.

Granite Creek. This creek is a small (jumpable) stream that heads in alpine timber on the southern slopes of the Tobacco Root Mountains and flows 7½ miles down through grass and sagebrush foothills (with patches of conifers here and there) to Alder Gulch Creek just west of Adobe. There are a few beaver ponds along it and a fair population of 7 to 8 inch brook trout. It is accessible by a county road, but the lower reaches of the stream are posted.

Greenhorn Creek. A small (jumpable) stream without a heck-of-a-lot of recreation potential but it is fished a little for 6 to 8 inch brook trout along the lower grazing land reaches (3 miles or so). It's easy to get there; just take the Upper Ruby River road 7 miles south of the Ruby Reservoir and turn right (east) up the creek.

Indian Creek. This is a small stream that heads far back in the Tobacco Root Mountains and flows west near (½ mile north of) the town of Sheridan to its mouth on the Ruby River. It's dammed up above and constitutes the city water supply, hence — no fishing and just as well because it never was a world beater.

Johnson Lake. A quarter acre brushy beaver pond on Indian Creek with a road nearby. This lake is part of the Sheridan city water supply and is off limits. But it's "reliably reported" to be fair fishing for pan-size brook trout. Now who would be silly enough to risk a large fine to catch a small fish?

Ledford Creek. Rises below Hogback Mountain in the southern Snow Crest Mountains and flows by the Devil's Hole on its way north down a park and timbered rocky canyon above and open, fenced, grazing land below to the Ruby River 10 miles distant and 7½ miles south of the Ruby Reservoir by the Upper Ruby River road. Several brushy beaver ponds, scattered along the lower 6 miles, are fair-to-good fishing for 9 to 10 inch brook and rainbow, and small cutthroat trout. There's a gravel road along the creek, but not many people use it.

Middle Fork Ruby River. Poor at best for rainbow trout up to 11 or so inches with a cutt taken now and then. This little creek flows for 9 miles converging with the East and West Forks to form the Ruby River. A road roughly parallels the stream, most of which is on Forest Service land (in good hunting country), if you want to bother. You can drive here from the Ruby Reservoir proceeding south on that road about 30 miles or come in from the Lima Reservoir area of the Centennial Valley going north just east of the reservoir. Stay north for about 20 miles.

Mill Creek. Runs through the town of Sheridan for 17 miles from its headwaters below (north of) Ramshorn Mountain to the Ruby River 5½ miles west of town. It's fast and clear, in a rocky, timbered canyon above and flows out across a great open fan below to the Ruby River bottoms. There's a good road up it and two USFS campgrounds 5½ and 8 miles up from Sheridan. There are a few beaver ponds below the lower campground. Vacationers fish it frequently from the lower campground down to town; local children fish it below town. Unfortunately, the fishing is only poor-to-fair for 4 to 10 inch brook and a few rainbow trout.

Noble Lake. You can 4-wheel to this one, a mile from Sheridan and then 7 more up the Wisconsin and Noble Creek roads. The lake is 8 acres in a barren cirque at 9000 feet elevation below Spuhler Peak on the western slopes of the Tobacco Roots. There are some scrub trees around it. The bottom drops off to a maximum depth of 55 feet, and it was planted with cutthroat in the summers of 1976, 1978, and 1981. It is good now for 8 to 16 inch trout.

Robb Creek. Heads below the rocky northern slopes of Olson Peak in the southern Snow Crest Range and flows north for 15 miles through scattered timber above and open grazing land below to the Ruby River 7 miles south of the Ruby Reservoir on the Upper Ruby River road. There is a poor county road up it and some fair-to-good fishing for 10 inch brook and rainbow and an occasional 6 to 7 inch cutthroat trout in brushy beaver ponds scattered along the lower 5 miles.

Romy Lake. This lake is fed and drained by Warm Springs Creek — but to get there you drive south up the Upper Ruby River road for 14 miles above the Ruby Reservoir and then the Timber Creek jeep road to your left (east) for another rugged 5½ miles to the dam astride the lake's outlet EXCEPT WHEN IT'S WET. It lies at 7000 feet above sea level at the head of a broad, alpine valley below Green Horn Range and the Gravellys. It is below some pretty steep slopes to the east and west, but there's a nice flat to the north. There is quite a lot of brush and aspen around, the dropoffs are shallow, the bottom silty and the water full of moss by late summer. All in all, it's hard to fish and only fair for 6 to 12 inch cutthroat, which is one of the reasons most people pass it by. The other is that it's privately owned and access is restricted.

Ruby Reservoir. Three miles long by ½ mile wide behind an earth dam built for irrigation by the State Water Conservation Board, Ruby Reservoir is at 5392 feet elevation in open pastureland 6 miles south of Alder on State Highway 287. The road follows the full length along the east side, and the west side has a county road in the upper end and the middle section with a jeep trail running about halfway along it, so access is generally available. This reservoir is drawn down extremely at times (exposing huge mud flats) making boat access for water skiers and fishermen difficult, and having a very detrimental effect on game fish. However, it is still fair (can be good in spring) fishing for rainbow (to 3 pounds), cutthroat to a foot long (stocked in 1980 and 1981 in large numbers), and brown trout from a pound to an explosive 10 pounds on occasion. The browns are naturally hook shy and full of suckers (so is the lake), not making them any easier to catch. The usage is fairly heavy and if the cutthroat do well here (rainbow stocked last in 1980 as 5 inchers) and the word gets around, look for increased angling despite poor launching facilities for boats. Could be better winter fishing coming up, too, as these cutthroat begin to be caught.

South Fork Warm Springs Creek. If you drive 2½ miles up the mainstem you'll hit the mouth of the South Fork coming in from the south across ½ mile of sagebrush and grass flat. Here, there is a little mediocre fishing for small brookies. No locals would bother it, and a stranger couldn't find it.

Sunrise Lake. Sits in a high (elevation 9320 feet) cirque below great rocky talus slopes east of Sunrise Peak in the Tobacco Root Mountains. It's 4.3 acres, as much as 15 feet deep with steep dropoffs along the north side but shallower to the south, was planted with cutthroat fingerling in 1967, '70, '72, '76, '78, and is fair-to-middling good fishing for 10 to 12 inch trout now. You can drive to within ⅛ mile of it — up the Wisconsin Creek jeep trail ½ mile above the Jackson Lake turnoff and then "shanks mares" over the ridge to the south.

Sweetwater Creek. This spring-fed creek rises in the Sweetwater Basin. Upon leaving the Basin, it flows to the southeast for 4 miles and then turns abruptly at right angles to the northwest for another 8 miles across open grass and sagebrush covered flats to the Ruby River 3½ miles above the Ruby Reservoir on the Upper Ruby River road. There are about 5 miles of barely fishable water here — for 4 to 10 inch brookies. It's seldom visited.

HUNTERS' LUCK
Courtesy Meir's Studio

Twin Lakes (Lower). Upper twin has been planted a couple of times with rainbow but is too shallow for fish. Lower Twin is a horse of a different color. It's only 4 acres by 16 feet deep but doesn't generally freeze out, even at 8760 feet above sea level. It lies below a great rock slide and talus at the crest of the Tobacco Root Range. It has a few rainbow in it from an old plant, and was stocked with cutthroat in '70, '76, and '78. It's good for small cutts and hybrid trout up to a foot long, but averaging about 8 inches, and gets it's share of visitors. If you want to try it, take the Wisconsin Creek road to the (barren) Ziegler Reservoir turnoff and then on for 3 miles to the end where you proceed south by foot trail another ½ mile to the shore.

Virginia Dredge Pond. See Alder Gulch Creek.

Warm Springs Creek. Now hear this — here is a stream that feeds Romy Lake and it has fish, has 2 forks (Middle and South) and they both have fish, but the mainstem is not much. There are some warm springs a couple of miles above its mouth (1½ miles north of the Vigilante Experiment Range Headquarters on the Upper Ruby River road). There are a few fish below, mostly brown trout, with not many more rainbow and whitefish above. It's just poor fishing.

West Fork Ruby River. This fork of the river rises high in the Snow Crest Range between Hogback Mountain and Olson Peak and flows a fast 7 miles eastward through timber above and open grass and sagebrush below to the mainstem at the Three Forks Cow Camp 4½ miles above Cottonwood Campground on the Upper Ruby River road. There's a road up the creek for about a mile and cow trails along it. The lower reaches get fished a little for poor catches of 6 to 15 inch rainbow, cutthroat, rainbow-cutthroat hybrids, and mountain whitefish. The best stretch is approximately the lower mile where there are some beaver ponds — use of the word "best" is relative.

Wisconsin Creek. This is a small stream, the outlet of (barren) Crystal Lake below Mount Jackson in the Tobacco Root Mountains. The upper 8 miles are through open foothills for 12 miles to its mouth on the Ruby River a few miles south of Twin Bridges. It's followed clear to the lake by road — but isn't fished much because there's not much here, only a small population of 6 to 8 inch brook and rainbow trout.

Don't Be A Litterbug

ELK AND HAREM
Jim Derleth photo

St. Mary River

Paralleled by unimproved dirt roads and (a mile or two to the west) by the Blackfeet highway from the outlet of St. Mary Lake in Glacier Park northward down a broad cottonwood-and-quaking-aspen-bordered valley for about 15 miles to Canada, this is a wide, fairly fast mountain stream with some rapids and nice holes. Mostly too large to wade, the water level fluctuates, depending on water released through the (upstream) Swiftcurrent Dam, with some discoloration at times. You'll need a Blackfeet permit to fish the St. Mary River. It is best with bait in spring and flies later on, good in mid-summer for 10 to 16 inch rainbow and cutthroat trout (occasionally to 4 or 5 pounds), fair for small brook trout, very good for 2 to 4 pound ling, fair for small whitefish, fair for northern pike, and some bull trout. It has a reputation for being somewhat hard to fish – check at Babb for local and seasonal conditions.

St. Mary River Drainage

Beaver Lakes. Two little lakes, about 1½ acres each, at the top of a ridge just south of the Kennedy Creek oil-well road about 6 miles in a north-south loop — a couple of miles northwest from Babb. The upper lake is too brushy to fish but does have some — same as the lower lake which is the best early season fly fishing in the region — for 10 to 16 inch cutthroat trout. It has a muddy, weedy bottom with shallow dropoffs; is moderately popular and becoming more so all the time. Its outlet also supports a fair population of small brook trout but is very small and brushy and almost never fished. May now be restricted by private ownership so best to check at Babb and not waste the trip.

Boulder Creek. Heads in an unnamed lake and flows around Flattop Mountain to the "Glacier Park" boundary from which point it flows for about 3½ miles through rough foothill country to Swiftcurrent Creek just above the Many Glacier Road bridge a couple of miles southwest from Babb. An old sheepherders road follows it upstream for about 1½ miles. The lower reaches (outside the Park) are fast with only a few scattered holes, and are only fair for cutthroat, dolly varden and northern pike. The 1975 flood channelized much of the habitat. Don't forget to get your Blackfeet permit. The creek is not fished that much, then mostly by locals.

Duck Lake. Is reached by a good graded road through open hill land on the Blackfeet Indian Reservation 6 miles east of Babb. It is 2½ miles long in an east-west direction by a maximum 1¼ miles in width, has a maximum depth of more than 80 feet with lots of weeds around the shallows and cottonwood and quaking aspen around the shore. In the summer months it can be success-fully fished from shore (many prefer marshmallows for bait) but is mostly fished from boats with cowbells and flatfish (there is a boat livery and a large public campground). Stocked annually with thousands of 7 to 11 inch rainbow trout, you'll need a Blackfeet tribal permit to join the crowd. The excellent catches usually consist of 1½ pound-or-so, now and then 5 or 6 pounds and very exceptionally to as much as 15 pounds — rainbow trout. Wintertime fishing is also excellent, most people preferring to jig with lead-weighted imitation fresh-water shrimp, with or without added grubs, maggots, rockworms or other bait. Needless to say, this one is hit hard the year around.

East Fork Lee Creek. This moderately popular, small, brushy, rolling rangeland stream heads on Chief Mountain and flows northward (across the Chief Mountain highway about 10 miles north from Babb) for 6 miles to the Canadian line. There are lots of beaver ponds along it and they're good fishing for 8 to 10 inch brook trout, and fewer cutts.

Goose Lake. A very poor dirt road takes you northward from the west end of Duck Lake for about 2 miles around the west side of Goose Lake, and then swings to the east for another 6 miles to the Galbreath Ranch (on the North Fork of the Milk River). Goose Lake lies in rolling cottonwood-quaking aspen parkland. It is 300 acres, about 20 feet at maximum depth, spring-fed with lots of aquatic plants, planted annually with eastern brook trout that really grow fast here. Catches are really good (especially in the fall) and you may get a brookie with real "shoulders" (up to 7 pounds recorded) every now and then. They'll average about 13 inches or so, anyway. Some years winterkill gets some of the larger fish. You'll also need a tribal permit here.

Kennedy Creek. A fairly fast and rocky (but with some nice holes), easily wadeable foothill country stream that heads in a Glacier Park lake of the same name and flows northward across the Blackfeet Indian Reservation for about 8 miles to St. Mary River. It's more or less followed by an old oil-well road (about 4 miles north from Babb on the Chief Mountain road); is moderately popular for 1 to 2 pound dolly varden (recorded to 8 pounds) in the slower reaches above and some rainbow and a few cutts to about a foot long below. The 1975 flood disturbed the creek a bit; it used to be better. You'll need a Blackfeet permit.

Lee Creek.   There is only about ½ mile of this fairly fast mountain stream outside the Park in Montana — before it flows into Canada. It's fair-sized but wadeable; in a pine covered canyon; is crossed (in the Park) by the Chief Mountain highway about 15 miles north-northwest from Babb (just below the border); and is seldom if ever fished but good for 8 to 10 inch brookies, plus a few cutts.

Lower St. Mary Lake.   A large lake, 6 miles long by as much as a mile wide and good and deep but with mostly shallow dropoffs; just outside Glacier National Park in a forested canyon but with lots of quaking aspen and cottonwood around the east side; reached by the Blackfeet highway about 30 miles northwest from Browning. The settlements of St. Mary and Babb are located about a mile above and below the lake, which is accessible by U.S. 89 along the east and by a graded Bureau of Indian Affairs road on the west side. There are quite a few summer homes here. It's becoming more popular all the time (for water skiing as well as fishing) and is very good fishing indeed — in the backwater bays for 2 to 5 pound lake trout (especially through the ice in winter), and fair to good fishing for 10 to 12 inch rainbow trout, some cutthroat, ling, northern pike, and bull trout in the summer. Don't forget your permit. Incidentally, lake whitefish are fished for commercially here.

Middle Fork Lee Creek.   A small, brushy, beaver-dammed stream that heads on the northern slopes of Chief Mountain and flows northward across fairly level rangeland for about 5 miles to Canada. It's crossed near the middle by the Chief Mountain highway about 12 miles north from Babb; is moderately popular for such a small "way-out" creek; and is good fishing for 8 to 10 inch brook trout, and a few cutthroat.

Otatso Creek.   A fair size, easily wadeable stream (the outlet of Otatso Lake in Glacier Park). It flows eastward down a narrow canyon for about 6 miles to junction with Kennedy Creek about a mile west of the Chief Mountain highway 5 miles north of Babb. If you proceed on up the highway for another 4 miles you'll come to a poor dirt road taking off to the left (west) and this parallels the upper reaches. It's moderately popular — both with the local people and with visitors — for good catches of 8 to 9 inch (and a few maybe a foot long) cutthroat trout with some small bulls in the upper reaches only.

ST. MARY LAKE
Courtesy Ernst Peterson

231

MULE DEER
Courtesy USFS

STOP RIGHT THERE
Courtesy USFS

Pike Lake. Is a popular pike lake; about ¾ of a mile wide in rolling foothills with quite a bit of brush around the shore. It has a very weedy bottom with lots of surface vegetation too, and is darned good fishing for northerns that will average between 2 and 6 pounds and sometimes go to as much as 20. You'll need a Blackfeet Indian Reservation permit and also the permission of the landowner. Get these first — then the tackle-busting pike.

Pine Coulee Creek. A small, slow, beaver-dammed "pickup" creek fed by springs below Duck Lake and flowing for about 3 miles down a small brushy canyon through hilly country to St. Mary River about a mile east from Babb. The lower reaches are paralleled (at a distance of about half a mile to the south) by the Duck Lake road — and it's good fishing (though very seldom bothered) for mostly 6 to 10 inch brook trout plus an occasional 10 to 11 inch cutthroat trout and some whitefish.

Roberts Creek. There are about 3 miles of good fishing here, for 9 to 10 inch brook trout, but this little creek heads below the Chief Mountain highway and few people know of it. The upper reaches flow across fairly level, brushy country; the lower reaches in a small, timbered canyon with lots of beaver ponds along its course. It flows to Pike Lake, but the pike fishermen generally aren't interested.

Swiftcurrent Creek. A nice looking stream that flows for about 5 miles down a timbered canyon (outside Glacier Park) from Sherburne Lake to St. Mary Lake and is paralleled upstream from Babb by the Many Glacier "park service" road. It is subject to such rapid and extreme water-level fluctuations, however (via Swiftcurrent dam), that the fishing is very poor — for a few 10 to 11 inch cutthroat and even fewer rainbow trout. A few ling have also been observed just below the dam in the fall months. It all adds up to another erstwhile excellent fishing stream that now has very little recreational potential — courtesy of the Big Dam Builders! The stream is totally dewatered below the dam (we are told) for about 5 months each year. If you want to bother, you'll still need a Blackfeet permit.

Respect Private Property!

QUIET PLACE
Courtesy H.L. Hasler

SHIELDS RIVER INTERLUDE
Courtesy Bill Browning

Shields River

The Shields River drainage begins in the northern end of the Crazy Mountains and flows west, then south for approximately 60 miles where it meets the Yellowstone River 6 miles east of Livingston. The river and it's tributaries drain the Crazy, Bridger and Bangtail Mountains as it grows from a small stream to a medium sized river.

The upper ¼ of the river is a mountain stream which supports a pure strain of Yellowstone cutthroat trout. These trout commonly run from 5 to 13 inches. Although their numbers decrease in a downstream direction, the chances of catching a larger cutthroat are better in the lower reaches of the river.

The lower ¾ of the Shields River flows through pastureland and grain fields as it changes to a more diverse fishery dominated by mountain whitefish and brown trout. Brook trout are common in the Wilsall area and run from 5 to 10 inches. Brown trout from 5 to 20 inches are the most prevalent trout in the rest of the drainage. They are not as easily caught as the other trout because of their habit of hiding in streamside brush. In the fall, migrating brown trout up to 5 pounds are caught in the lower reaches of the river. Rainbow trout are uncommon except in the lowest 5 miles of the stream where they run between 5 and 15 inches.

The Shields River is not fished heavily due to the fact that water levels become very low in late summer in the Wilsall-Clyde Park area. The river is characterized by eroding banks with large piles of trees and brush in the river channel.

Access to the river is good. U.S. 89 and good gravel roads parallel the river for its entire length. Most of the river is on private land; however, most landowners allow fishing with their permision. There is a public rest area about 4 miles south of Clyde Park.

Chris Clancy

SHIELDS RIVER RANCH
Courtesy SCS

Shields River Drainage.

Bangtail Creek.   A small, brushy stream that flows eastward for 11 miles from a timbered canyon in the Bridger Range through mostly open rangeland to the Shields River 10 miles up U.S. 89 from U.S. 10 (41 miles east from Livingston). It's accessible all along by jeep roads and is fair fishing for 6 to 8 inch cutthroat and some brook trout — but not too many people try it.

Bennett Creek.   A very small, spring-fed headwaters tributary of the Shields River in the northern Crazy Mountains. The Bennett Guard Station is located ½ mile above the mouth; the lower mile is more or less accessible by road and is poor-to-fair fishing for pan-size cutthroat. It used to be good but is all frigged up from poor logging practices and has little recreational value now.

Brackett Creek.   Heads at the junction of its South, Middle, and North Forks near the Brackett Creek campground on the eastern slopes of the Bridger Range and is followed by a road for 14 miles through open bottomland with sparsely timbered hillsides to the Shields River a couple of miles south (below) of Clyde Park where it is crossed by U.S. 89. It's mostly all on private land (permission usually granted on request), the upper reaches are bordered by heavy growths of willow, and the lower reaches by scattered willow and aspen. Not heavily fished, it is good for 6 to 11 inch brook and cutthroat trout and an occasional brown to 14 inches or more, with quite a few whitefish caught also. It's best in the lower reaches.

Buck Creek.   This is a sizeable little Crazy Mountain stream flowing north to the head of the Shields River 25 miles by road above Wilsall. It used to be good fishing, but the habitat was ruined by poor logging practices and there are now only a few pan-sized cutthroat left — in the upper reaches. It's seldom, if ever, used for recreation now.

Cache Creek.   Heads below Sacajawea Peak in the Bridger Range and flows east and north for 9 miles to Flathead Creek about 8½ miles west from Wilsall. The middle reaches (which are accessible by road) are mostly in open rangeland and are fair fishing for 8 to 10 inch cutthroat. It's very seldom visited, however.

Canyon Creek.   A small, hilly rangeland stream flowing to the Shields River 3½ miles below Clyde Park. There are about 5 miles of fair fishing here for small brown and cutthroat trout. It's accessible all along by road or trail and sustains a moderate amount of fishing pressure.

Cottonwood Creek.
Heads in Cottonwood Lake and flows for about 5 miles down a steep, Crazy Mountain canyon to the Shields River valley, and then for 12 more southwestward to the river at Clyde Park. Both the upper and lower reaches are heavily dewatered for irrigation, but the middle reaches are moderately popular and fair too — for 8 to 9 inch rainbow and cutthroat, plentiful brookies (in the beaver ponds) and some brown trout to 16 inches. It's accessible all along by country and private farm roads.

Cottonwood Lake.
A 9 acre, cirque lake in talus, scree, and alpine grass high in the Crazy Mountains at 8550 feet elevation, about 36 feet deep at the most, snowmelt from Grasshopper Glacier watering it and its plentiful denizens of the deep — cutthroat trout. Planted in 1969, 1972, 1976 and 1979 (a limited spawning potential exists here) the lake is used quite a bit for good catches of "mountain grown" trout averaging around a foot long, and up to a couple pounds if you're lucky. Go to the end of the Cottonwood Creek road, and then a USFS trail four miles in (and up).

Cottonwood Reservoir.
A small open grazing land irrigation reservoir located just off U.S. 89 three miles north of Wilsall on private (you'll need permission) land. It is full of suckers but gives up a few cutthroat for the few that fish it.

Crandall Creek.
You can drive almost to the mouth of this small (3 miles long), brushy, southward-flowing stream just across the river from the Shields River Campground on State 293 about 22 miles north and west from Wilsall. If you don't mind getting your feet wet you can wade it; there's a trail on up for about 2 miles of fair-to-good fishing for small rainbow trout.

Daisy Dean Creek.
Flows from the Crazy Mountains west to the Shields River valley and then across hilly open rangeland to the river itself near Wilsall. There are about 5 fishable miles of water here (in a willowed-up draw paralleled by road) that is seldom bothered, but fair for pan-sized cutthroat.

Deep Creek.
A small stream, swift and clear, crossed by a good dirt logging road at its mouth on the Shields River 19 miles above Wilsall, and by a USFS road a mile upstream. It's in a timbered semi-canyon above, grass and timber bottomland below. The lower couple of miles are lightly fished for small cutthroat trout.

Dugout Creek.
In scattered timber, small, only about 2 miles of seldom-fished water for pan-size cutthroat; crossed at the mouth by a USFS trail a mile above the end of the Shields River road.

Elk Creek.
A small open rangeland stream flowing southwestward across the hilly east bench of the Shields River valley to the river 1½ miles above Wilsall. It's paralleled by road for its full length (3 miles), is moderately popular and good fishing for mostly small cutts plus here and there a brown, rainbow or brook trout.

Fairy Lake.
With a nearby campground, a blue-green scenic 12½ acre lake with a shallow 25 foot wide shelf most of the way around except for the west side where it drops off steeply from the shore. Nestled below steep cliffs east of Hardscrabble and Sacajawea Peaks, it is about 40 feet maximum depth, and is almost reached by road (300 yards or so short) 35 miles north from Bozeman — the last seven miles bumpy dirt and rock. Many people fish here for fair catches of 6 to 14 inch cutthroat planted in 1977, 1979 and 1980. Plenty of mule deer and bear sign around here.

Fairy Lake Creek.
The small outlet of Fairy Lake, flowing down a timbered canyon above and through open hilly rangeland below for 7 miles to Flathead Creek. There are a couple of miles of beaver ponds on the lower end (accessible by road) that are seldom fished but fair for 6 to 10 inch cutthroat trout.

Falls Creek.
A small creek flowing southwestward for 12 miles from headwaters in the Crazy Mountains, across open hilly rangeland in the Shields River valley to the river itself about 5 miles north from U.S. 10 and U.S. 89. The lower reaches are drained dry for irrigation, but there are a few small cutthroat in the upper reaches, which can be driven to via county and logging roads, but seldom are.

FAIRY LAKE
Courtesy USFS

WINTER OUTING
Courtesy USFS

Flathead Creek. Heads at the junction of its North, Middle and South Forks 5 miles below Flathead Pass, and is paralleled by road for 13 miles through mostly hilly pastureland to the Shields River a mile north of Wilsall. Infrequently fished, it is only poor to fair for cutthroat and eastern brook to 11 inches and whitefish and brown trout to maybe 16 inches or so (mostly much smaller).

Horse Creek. A very small, seldom fished stream that heads in the Crazy Mountains and flows southwestward for about 6 miles to Horsefly Creek (which isn't worth mentioning). It is reached at the mouth by a good county road 5½ miles due east from Wilsall and is followed upstream by an old road through open pastures for about 3 miles of poor-to-fair 6 to 12 inch cutthroat fishing.

Landers Reservoir (or Kistler-Hardy Dam). Take U.S. 89 1½ miles north from Wilsall and then turn left up the poor Muddy Creek road seven miles to this heavily fished, slightly turbid 60 acre reservoir in flat grassland and sagebrush country. It's been planted with cutthroat and rainbow — reproduction up Muddy Creek is good and it now provides good fishing for 1 to 2 pounders. Best get permission (no boats allowed) as it is on private land.

Little Cottonwood Creek. Hardly a fishing stream but the lower couple of miles above its mouth on Cottonwood Creek (a mile hike across the flats from the road 9 miles northeast from Clyde Park) are fished once in a while for a few small cutthroat trout.

Middle Fork Flathead Creek. The lower mile or so of this stream is followed by road through hilly, open pastureland and supports a small population of small cutthroat trout which seldom see a hook.

North Fork Brackett Creek. The lower 1½ miles of this clear little creek are accessible by road from the Brackett Creek campground, are bordered by enough willow to sometimes make it difficult to fish, and are moderately popular for 8 to 10 inch brook, cutthroat, a few brown trout, and whitefish.

North Fork Elk Creek. A clear little stream that flows southwestward across the hilly east bench of the Shields River valley to Elk Creek 5 miles north of Wilsall, and is paralleled by a good county road. It was planted with brook trout in the middle '50s but is only poor fishing now and seldom bothered.

North Fork Flathead Creek. A little spring-fed stream, only about 2½ miles long in rolling grassland and sagebrush country, reached by road a mile north of Sedan. It's not often fished but is fair for small brown, a few cutthroat and here and there a brook trout.

238

North Fork Willow Creek. About 4 miles of fishable water, accessible here and there by mostly private roads and trails — in the open bottomland of the Shields River valley. It seldom is fished but does support a few small cutthroat trout.

Porcupine Creek. Take U.S. 89 up the Shields River 7 miles north from Wilsall to the mouth of Porcupine and then a good gravel road that jogs about in a general northeastwardly direction across the east bench of the Shields River valley to the head of the creek 7½ miles upstream. It's a small clear creek whose lower reaches are heavily dewatered, but the middle and upper reaches have lots of nice holes with good cover. They're good fishing below for brook and cutthroat trout — and for cutthroat only above. The middle reaches give up some whitefish to 15 inches and an occasional fair-sized brown.

Rock Creek. The outlet of Rock Lake, flowing for 6 miles south down a steep timbered canyon in the southern Crazy Mountains and then for 12 miles southwestward across hilly "flatland" to the Shields River 3 miles south of Clyde Park. U.S. 89 crosses the mouth and various county roads "hit" the creek in places. There's a USFS trail the last 6 miles to the lake but as recently as 1980 access became a problem in the lower private lands. A fair sized moderately popular stream fished in the lower reaches for small brown and a few brook trout, but only lightly fished for 5 to 11 inch brooks and a few cutthroat up above.

Rock Lake. Six steep miles by USFS trail above the end of the Rock Creek road (check local USFS Ranger Station for any possible access problems), this lake lies a mile northwest of Iddings Peak below steep barren rocky slopes, is 58 acres, at 8550 feet elevation, with steep dropoffs mostly and a 90 foot maximum depth. Stocked with cutthroat in 1963, 1978 and 1981, the fishing is fair to good for 6 to 12 inch trout. A tunnel bored into the mountain from the west in the dam area results in water level fluctuations of about 40 feet (for irrigation) with catastrophic results to the fishery reported in the past. What the future holds here — with this, and possible access problems —?

Skunk Creek. Flows north from Grassy Mountain for 3 miles to Brackett Creek — 12 miles upstream from the Shields River. There are a few pools here and there among the willows and they provide a few 7 to 9 inch cutthroat and brown trout for the even fewer fishermen. There's a logging road all along it.

Smeller Lake. One hundred ten feet maximum depth, 32 acres, 9500 feet elevation, a high cirque lake in rugged alpine country at the southern end of the Crazy Mountains; reached by a USFS pack trail 6 miles up from the end of the Rock Creek road at the old campground. Used a bit for darn good catches of cutthroat planted in 1972, 1976 and 1979 (the most recent). You could possibly latch on to a brawling cutt with shoulders (occasionally to about 5 pounds) but more than likely a bunch of splendid eating-size trout is what you'll get. While planning your trip, it's wise to check with the Big Timber Ranger District for any possible current access problems.

Smith Creek. After following the Shields River 15 miles by good road north of Wilsall turn right (east) for about 3 miles, then go past the creek for 2 miles, and bear (left) north on a good logging road 5 miles to headwaters. Not many people bother but from the beaver ponds (3 or 4 miles in) on down, it's good fishing for 6 to 14 inch cutthroat, quite a few 6 to 11 inch brookies and an occasional brown trout to 15 inches.

South Fork Elk Creek. Is followed by a dirt road for 3 miles across the East bench of the Shields River valley to its mouth 4½ miles northeast from Wilsall; is really willowed-up so that it's difficult to fish for the few undersize brook trout it supports, and is not exactly overrun with fishermen.

South Fork Shields River. Heads below (not in) Campfire Lake and flows north for 6 miles down a narrow canyon below Black Mountain and Bald Ridge, and finally for 1½ miles across open rangeland to the Shields River 15 miles by good road above Wilsall. It's seldom fished, but the lower 3 miles are fair for 6 to 9 inch cutthroat and 5 to 8 inch brookies. It could be good if it wasn't dewatered so completely for irrigation.

South Fork Willow Creek. A couple of miles of fishable bottomland-willow-bordered creek; accessible by private road and cow trails but seldom fished for the few small trout it has to offer.

THE SHIELDS RIVER
Courtesy Bill Browning

Sunlight Creek. A very small, seldom fished tributary of Deep Creek; reached at the mouth by a logging road and poor-to-fair fishing in the lower mile for pan-size cutthroat. Not much of a recreational asset.

Trespass Creek. A very small mountain tributary of Cottonwood Creek that is reached at the mouth by the Cottonwood Creek trail and followed by another for 4 miles to headwaters. It's seldom, if ever, fished but does contain a few small cutthroat.

Willow Creek. Is followed by mostly private roads from its headwaters at the junction of its Middle and South Forks, across hilly bottomland to the Shields River about 8 miles up U.S. 89 from U.S. 10. Only the extreme lower end of this stream is dewatered for irrigation and there are about 6 miles of fair, open meadowland fishing water for 6 to 8 inch cutthroat plus an occasional 10 to 12 inch brown trout.

Release Fish Carefully!

THE KING AND FAMILY
Jim Derleth photo

THE SMITH RIVER
Courtesy Bill Browning

Smith River

The Smith River originates near the town of White Sulphur Springs and meanders northwesterly for 121 miles before emptying into the Missouri River near Ulm. The upper 30 miles of river meanders through a broad, gently rolling mountain valley, flanked by the Castle, Big Belt and Little Belt Mountain Ranges. Here, the river is relatively small and flows lazily through mostly brush-lined banks. Many deep pools and shallow riffles provide excellent habitat for trout and mountain whitefish. This section of river is the stronghold for brown trout. The deep brushy-covered pools harbor many 2 to 3 pounders, with an occasional 6 or 7 pounder taken by a lucky angler. Rainbow trout are abundant but do not reach the trophy size of the brown trout. The meadow portions along the upper end of this reach also harbor brook trout up to about one pound. Here the river can be easily fished; it's an ideal place to teach a youngster various techniques of stream fishing.

The next 67 miles of the river is mostly entrenched in a deep mountain canyon. Except for the upper 10 miles of this reach, the river is mostly inaccessible; however, it offers excellent floating opportunities. Two Department of Fish, Wildlife and Parks access areas 18 to 26 miles northwest of White Sulphur Springs provide good spots to camp or to embark on a float trip down the Smith. A small take-out access is available near the Eden Bridge about 2 miles below the mouth of Hound Creek.

River flow dictates the length of the floating season on the Smith. By late July the river often becomes too low for successful floating. Floaters using rubber rafts should have plenty of repair materials because some riffle areas hide sharp rocks and snags. Long, deep, lazy pools and riffle areas are characteristic of the canyon zone of the river. Some right angle turns at the end of fast riffle areas often create sudden unexpected excitement for those not familiar with the river. Spectacular scenery, composed of colorful limestone cliffs interspersed with clumps of evergreens, meadows and flowering shrubs keep the trip interesting. The float through the canyon requires at least two days. There are several marked areas where overnight camping is allowed. Floaters should watch carefully for signs that warn of wire fences crossing the river.

Rainbow trout comprise the bulk of the fishery throughout this stretch of the river. One-half pound rainbows are common with a few individuals reaching two pounds. Brown trout again achieve trophy size up to eight pounds, but one to three pounders are the rule. Hoardes of one to two pound mountain whitefish frequent the pools and deep riffles throughout the river. Large wooly worm flies and small spinners appear to be the best lures during high water conditions. These continue to work well after the river drops and the water becomes crystal clear. Early morning and late evening dry fly fishing is unsurpassed in the runs at the head and tail ends of the many deep pools.

Below the Eden Bridge access, the lower river meanders through an agricultural developed valley. Cottonwood and boxelder trees frequent the river banks, which in places, are somewhat rip-rapped and heavily eroding. Few trout are found in the lower half of this reach above the Missouri River. Some persistant anglers make good catches of browns and rainbows in the early spring and fall.

Although the Smith River does not take the spotlight as a nationally famous river, it does offer fine fishing and floating, wilderness scenery, and probably the best of all, quiet restful solitude.

Al Wipperman

Smith River Drainage

Baldy Lake. This high mountain lake lies about ½ mile above Grace Lake in scenic mountain goat country. Backpack to this one from the Duck Creek pass on an improved Forest Service trail past Hidden and Grace Lakes, and then crawl — it's steep. Planted every other year with cutts, it should be good fishing for the hardy hiker.

Beaver Creek. Here is a beaver dammed little creek that is good fishing on timbered USFS land above, and on open private rangeland below, for mostly 6 to 12 inch brookies and a few small cutthroat trout. It rises below the crest of the Little Belt Mountains and meanders eastward below the southern slopes of the Dry Range for 12 miles to the Smith River 21 miles west and north by good gravel roads from White Sulphur Springs. There is good access here and there by county and private roads, but — it doesn't get fished much, mostly by local folks in early spring. The middle 6 or 7 miles usually go dry.

Benton Gulch. You can drive the full length of it (6 miles) 3 miles west from the Old Fort Logan Military Reservation in mostly open meadowland with occasional patches of timber. You can step across it anywhere. Not many people stop, but there is a little fishing here for 6 to 8 inch brookies, and 8 to 12 inch rainbows.

Big Birch Creek. Here is a fast little timbered mountain and real brushy valley above to open grazing land below stream (the outlet of Edith, Grace and Hidden Lakes) that is full of beaver ponds and excellent fishing for brook trout ranging from 8 inches to a foot long. The stream is moderately popular with the local ranchers and townspeople who get there by driving 8 miles due west from White Sulphur Springs to the mouth of Little Birch Creek, and then on up and downstream for a total of 12 miles of fishing. If you don't get lost in the swampy, brushy bottoms — 10 pounds of brookies (a limit) may be a reality.

Black (or Butte) Creek. This is a clear but very small open timberland stream that heads below Black Butte and flows slowly to the northwest for about 9 miles to Sheep Creek 6 miles above the stream's mouth. There are about 4 miles of fair fishing here for native cutthroat, but it's just too small to stand much pressure. After all, it's never planted and you can step across it anywhere. If you're still of a mind, you can get to the middle reaches by taking the Smith River road 20 miles west and north from White Sulphur Springs to the Whitetail Creek crossing and then the right (north and east) crossroad 9 miles on in.

Boundary Lake. Drive 15 miles north on the main drag from White Sulphur Springs, turn right on the Newlan Creek road for 3 miles, leave the car and hike another 3 miles west to this little 2 acre lake that used to be held up behind an old earth dam that is now about washed out decreasing the depth of water to about 2 feet. It's in a timbered mountain valley right on the southern boundary of the National Forest. Was once a black spotted cutthroat hatchery (rearing pond) but there probably aren't a dozen of them left now.

Butte Creek. See Black Butte Creek.

Camas Creek. Drains Camas Lake below Mount Baldy for 20 miles a little east and then due north to the Smith River near Old Camp Baker 17 miles northwest by paved road from White Sulphur Springs. There's a gravel road near the creek which is mostly in open grazing land (you'll need permission there) but with some timber and brush above. There is fair 8 to 10 inch brook and rainbow trout fishing along the lower 11 miles, but not many people "hit" it.

Camas Lake. Take the Camas Creek road as far as you can up the creek and then a USFS horse trail for 3 miles on in to the shore. The lake lies in a great rocky cirque below slide rock to the west and scrub timber on around. It's about 5 acres, 14 feet deep with steep dropoffs to the north but is shallow and somewhat marshy to the south. What with the superb scenery, easy access and good population of 10 to 14 inch cutthroat, it sees its fair share of fishermen. Note: Don't bother with the 2 smaller lakes above; they're barren.

BEAUTIFUL HIT
Courtesy Phil Schlamp, USFS

Deadman Creek. A small fast stream about 4 miles south of Kings Hill east of U.S. 89. Two miles long, a tributary of Sheep Creek, it is accessible all along by a good USFS road (not much room to park) and is only fair for brookies up to 8 inches long.

Deep (or Dry) Creek. This one goes dry, but there are about 2 miles of good fishing for small cutthroat trout in the upper reaches of both the North and South Forks. Here the water is clear and fast with lots of small holes in a narrow timbered valley reached by horseback (or tote goat if you must be mulish about degrading the natural beauty that attracted you here in the first place). Not too many people make it. Drive north of Monarch on U.S. 89 for 3 miles, turn west on Logging Creek gravel road for 18 miles, then hike west over a mountain on a good USFS trail and down the north fork for three miles. See why?

Divide (or North Fork Eight Mile) Creek. See Eight Mile Creek.

Dry Creek. Is small enough to jump but is not dry. Fact is there are some 5 miles of good 6 to 7 inch brook trout fishing here in open timber reached by a jeep road at the mouth and about ⅓ of the way upstream 6 to 7 miles off U.S. 12 a mile east of Sutherlin Reservoir. It receives a fair amount of attention for such a small stream.

Eagle Creek. A small westward flowing tributary of the Smith River, crossed about a mile above the mouth by the Smith River road 26 miles west and north from White Sulphur Springs. It's crossed by the Eagle Creek Ranch road about 3 miles farther upstream, and from here on down there are lots of small beaver ponds that are fair fishing for 9 to 10 inch rainbow below and 6 to 8 inch brook trout above. The entire stretch is in open grazing land but is semi-brushy along the banks. It's too small and remote to attract a great deal of attention.

East Fork Hound Creek. A brushy, meandering, foothill grazing land creek that is accessible neither by trail nor road up the main stem but rather by a ranch road 7 miles southwest from the West Fork crossing. There are a few beaver ponds along and 3 or 4 miles of good (mostly 6 to 12 inch brookies plus a few rainbow) fishing — better than camp fare for a stray sheepherder now and then.

Edith Lake. A high alpine lake in a great rocky basin below Mount Edith in the Big Belts, reached by foot trail 1½ miles east and south of Grace Lake. It's 13 acres with steep dropoffs, in timber all around, stocked in '73, '75, '77 and 1979 with air-dropped cutthroat and fair fishing for 8 to 12 inchers.

Eight Mile Creek. This westward flowing stream is only a mile long from the junction of its North (or Divide Creek) and South Forks to its mouth on Southerlin Reservoir. It and the first couple of miles up both forks are in mountain meadows, are readily accessible by U.S. 12 which parallels the main stem and crosses the South Fork a mile above its mouth. The South Fork and the main stem are fair fishing for 7 to 8 inch brook trout. Eight Mile itself is also full of spawning suckers in the spring. None of this water has much recreation potential.

Elk Creek. This brushy little stream is not fished much and wouldn't stand much pressure if it was, although there are about 5 miles of fair-to-middling 8 to 9 inch brook trout water upstream from its mouth on Camas Creek right on the Old Fort Logan road 16 miles northwest from White Sulphur Springs. The lower reaches are crossed here and there by private, open rangeland roads. The upper reaches are on USFS land.

Elk Creek Reservoir. This is a very popular summer and winter fishing spot reached by a good gravel road in open rangeland a couple of miles above the mouth of Elk Creek about 18 miles northwest from White Sulphur Springs. It's about 4 acres by 20 feet deep behind an earth dam — and it needs every inch of it because it is sometimes drawn down as much as 15 feet, although generally for only short periods of time. It's stocked annually with rainbow and provides fair fishing for 10 to 12 inchers, plus occasional 8 to 10 inch brookies from the creek.

Four Mile Creek. U.S. 12 crosses this little, open grazing land creek a mile upstream from its mouth on the North Fork Smith River 6 miles east of White Sulphur Springs, and it's followed to the southeast by gravel roads to the Grasshopper Campground 3 miles above the highway. Near and above the campground for a couple of miles there is fair fishing for 6 to 10 inch brookies. The lower 2½ miles of this stream goes dry most summers.

Freeman Creek. This is a hard to get to stream if you're a stranger. Perhaps the easiest way in is to drive to the Old Fort Logan Military Reservation 16 miles northwest from White Sulphur Springs, go on west for a couple of miles, then a mile north where you take the left (west) fork and more or less follow your nose in a roundabout fashion for 22 miles north where you finally cross the creek about 4 miles above its mouth on the Smith River. There's a jeep trail on upstream for a total of perhaps 7 miles of fair 9 to 10 inch rainbow fishing along with a few small cutthroat in the upper reaches. The whole bit is in an open prairie canyon above, and a real rugged rocky canyon below. You won't be bothered by a lot of jerks fouling your line.

Gipsy Lake (or Gile Reservoir). You take the Big Birch Creek road 8 miles above the mouth of Little Birch Creek to get to this pretty little natural lake that has been dammed at the outlet to provide additional storage for irrigation water, raising the level about 6 feet. It is timbered on the south side but open on around. The water is a little cool for swimming and is weedy, especially along the south side. It is planted annually with 6 inch or so rainbow trout and is good fishing (especially so in early spring) for fish up to a foot long. It is fair ice fishing, getting some winter play, and is quite popular in early spring and summer.

Grace Lake. There is an old USFS horse trail to this one, in a rocky, partly timbered cirque a mile south of Hidden Lake. Maybe 2 acres, it's deep enough to keep from freezing out with no apparent reproduction by its finny inhabitants. So in 1973, 1975, 1977 and 1979 the lake was stocked with tiny cutthroat and the angling (and catching) is good for 6 to 15 inch "mountain grown" trout.

Guise Creek. This is a typical, small, timbered mountain stream flowing south to the North Fork Smith River 4 miles above Southerlin Reservoir and crossed by a logging road at the lower end. There's maybe a couple of miles of fair pan-size brook trout fishing here, but it's more popular as a whitetail deer hunting area.

Hidden Lake. This is a 5 acre alpine lake that is quite deep below a boulder field around the west end, in a partly timbered, rocky cirque below the northern slopes of Mount Baldy in the Big Belts — reached by trail 4 miles above the end of the Big Birch Creek (Duck Creek Pass) road. Not many get here, but those that do find it good fishing for 10 to 16 inch rainbow trout. The scenery alone is worth the trip.

Hound Creek. Twelve miles of tremendous fishing in mostly posted, rattlesnake infested, open grazing land from the junction of its East and Middle Forks northward to the Smith River 7 miles west from Eden by county road. The stream is slow and clear with some meanders and a little brush here and there and — it's jam packed with trout. Mostly 12 to 14 inch browns below and 6 to 8 inch brook trout above, almost as many as there are suckers, and — it's not overrun with fishermen.

UPPER SMITH RIVER
Courtesy H.L. Hasler

Indian Creek. There is no road to this brushy, little timber and park, mountain valley stream, but you can get to it a couple of miles above its mouth on Sheep Creek by jeep trail 2½ miles east from the Calf Creek Ranger Station (7 crooked miles north from the Schmidt Ranch on the Sheep Creek road). There are a few small beaver ponds along the lower couple of miles and some good enough fishing for eating-size brookies. Not many people find it — let alone fish it.

Jumping Creek. The name is apropos. You can jump it anywhere up and down its brushy little timbered canyon that debouches to Sheep Creek at the Jumping Creek Campground 9 miles southwest from Kings Hill by USFS road. You find a little mediocre small-fry brook trout fishing for the next mile above the mouth — or at least some folks do.

Keep Cool Reservoir. Take off from White Sulphur Springs by auto 16 miles northwest to the Old Fort Logan Military Reservation, drive through it and on west for 2½ miles on a gravel road and then a final mile by jeep trail to this one. It's on private (posted) grazing land. A good place to fish and camp but may be closed to the public at any time due to litterbugging and general lack of concern for private property by the "sporting" public. Too bad because it's a nice and deep, 5 acre pond that is very popular and provides good fishing for mostly rainbow in the 12 to 18 inch class. It's stocked every year with 6 inchers.

Lake Creek. Flows south from a timbered canyon to (barren) Boundary Lake and then across mountain meadows for 5 miles to the North Fork Smith River a mile below Southerlin Reservoir. The Studhorse Creek road crosses it about a mile above the mouth 8½ miles northeast from White Sulphur Springs and it's fished more than somewhat considering its size — for mostly 6 to 8 inch brook and a sprinkling of small cutthroat trout.

Lamb Creek. A very small, brushy, beaver-dammed, timbered mountain tributary of Sheep Creek accessible at the mouth by a USFS road 6 miles south from Kings Hill. There's a trail up it for a couple of miles of small brook trout fishing.

Little Birch Creek. Drive 8 miles due west on gravel roads from White Sulphur Springs and you're there, at the mouth of Little Birch on Big Birch Creek. There are about 4 miles of fishable water upstream (to the southwest, up a draw) all available by cow trails across open grazing land below but with some timber farther up. The creek is a little brushy along its margins but good fishing (with permission from the Zig Ranch) for 7 to 8 inch brook trout, and a few cutthroat are caught in the upper reaches. It's fairly popular with local fishermen.

Middle Creek Lake. Is on Middle Creek of the West Fork of Hound Creek in the northern Big Belt foothills reached by county and private roads as follows: 1¼ miles south from Cascade, then 4 miles east to the Bird Creek turnoff and south for 25 miles to the Sieban Ranch buildings.

248

Stop here and ask permission before you drive a final 6 miles south across open rolling rangeland to this irregularly shaped 42 acre by 18 foot maximum depth, with steep dropoffs at the lower (northeast) end, muddy-bottomed reservoir. It's fed by the Middle Fork and three smaller streams, maintains good populations of 10 to 13 inch rainbow trout and is heavily fished "for this neck of the woods." P.S. In years past the owners kept a skiff on it, but it's easily fished from shore.

Middle Fork West Fork Hound Creek.
A dinky little creek but full of 5 to 7 inch brookies, probably introduced from the reservoir above. There is 2¾ miles of fishable water, all in open grazing land and all posted. For access see Middle Creek Lake.

Moose Creek.
Take the Sheep Creek road to the Schmidt Ranch then drive downstream to the north on a good USFS road for 2 miles to the mouth of Moose and on up this creek for about 4 miles of fair 8 to 10 inch cutthroat, brook and rainbow trout fishing. It's a fairly brushy, timbered mountain stream in good deer hunting country. There's a campground a couple of miles above the mouth.

Newland Creek.
Here is a meandering little beaver-dammed timber-canyon creek above, and mountain-meadow creek below that is excellent fishing for 10 to 12 inch rainbow in the lower 8 miles, and lousy with 6 inch brookies along the upper 4 miles — the entire bit easily accessible by road. If it weren't almost entirely posted you could just drive 5 miles northwest from White Sulphur Springs, take the right hand fork in the road for a couple of miles and be on your way to a delightful day.

Newlan Creek Reservoir.
A 300 acre, 2½ mile long reservoir (completed in 1976) accessible by a county road about 12 miles north of White Sulphur Springs off U.S. 89. Turn west for a couple of miles and be prepared to share the fabulous fishing with hordes of anglers. Both rainbow and cutthroat were planted in good numbers in 1978, 1979 and 1980 and are caught regularly 10 to 17 inches long with occasional bragging size fish reported taken. A few nice eastern brook averaging about 10 inches and up to a couple pounds are also caught. It's a popular place.

North Fork Deep (or Dry) Creek.
See Deep Creek.

North Fork Eight Mile Creek.
See Eight Mile Creek.

North Fork Rock Creek.
A Rankin Ranch creek that is "kind of hard" to get to, either by truck or jeep up an old abandoned logging road from the head of the Rock Creek road. It's not very big when you do get there but supports a moderate amount of fishing pressure for mostly 8 to 12 inch rainbow, and some 6 to 8 inch cutthroat and brook trout, along the lower 3 miles of its course.

ONE MORE ON THE SMITH
Courtesy USFS

WHAT A LIFE
Courtesy USFS

North Fork Smith River.

Heads in the Little Belts near Ant Park and flows southwest through timbered mountains on USFS land for 9 miles to the upper end of the Southerlin Reservoir — and out the far side through open rolling hills for another 13 miles to the main river 3 miles below White Sulphur Springs. The upper reaches are literally crammed full of 6 inch brookies, and 8 to 12 inch rainbows. The lower stretch is good (and popular) for mostly 6 to 16 inch rainbow, plus an assortment of 6 to 20 inch brown, 14 inch or so whitefish and small brookies. Much of it is on posted land here, but all of it is more or less accessible by paved, oil or gravel road.

Rock Creek.

A very popular, easily wadeable stream in good deer hunting country on the eastern slopes of the Big-Belt Mountains "over the hill" from Hauser Reservoir by the Trout Creek jeep road and trail. The main stem heads at the junction of the North and South Forks and wanders north down a more or less timbered canyon for 13 miles to the Smith River 11 airline miles north of the Old Fort Logan Military Reservation. It's crossed by a county road at the Lingshire Post Office and followed all up and down by county roads and jeep trails — all of it on the Rankin Ranch. There used to be hoards of beaver here but they ate themselves out of house and home so that there are only a few brushy ponds left. They and the creek are good fishing for mostly 10 to 12 inch rainbow, some 10 to 16 inch brown and a few pan-size cutthroat and brook trout in the headwaters.

Sheep Creek.

This is probably the most diversified of all the Smith River tributaries. It heads on Kings Hill below Porphyry Peak in the Little Belts, and flows for 33 miles through a variety of timbered valleys and canyons above and open rolling sagebrush and grass-covered hills below to the main stem 24 miles northwest by county roads from White Sulphur Springs. The middle and upper reaches are more or less paralleled by county and USFS roads, but the lower reaches (from a couple of miles above the mouth to the Calf Creek Guard Station) are mostly a mile or more from auto access. There are three USFS (Public Recreation but with a fee attached) campgrounds in the upper reaches. There the stream is quite small but heavily fished by tourists for 8 to 10 inch rainbow and some 6 to 18 inch brook trout and whitefish. The middle "canyon" stretch is harder to get to and seldom fished but does harbor a fair population of 8 to 14 inch rainbow. Above Lamb Creek is good brookie fishing usually. The lower (open foothill) reaches are moderately popular and good fishing for 8 to 14 inch rainbow and an occasional 2 pound brown trout. It's planted twice a year near the campground with rainbow.

Smith River Reservoir. See Sutherlin Reservoir.

South Fork Deep (or Dry) Creek. See Deep Creek.

South Fork Eight Mile Creek. See Eight Mile Creek.

TIME TO RELAX
Courtesy Phil Schlamp, USFS

SHEEP CREEK
Courtesy USFS

South Fork Rock Creek.
Drains the Jim Ball Basin on the northeastern slopes of the Big Belts 5½ miles east to junction with the North Fork at the head of the main stem in good deer hunting country. It's a nice little mountain stream (jumpable in places if you're the athletic type), with conifers and willow along its course, and about 4 miles of fair 6 to 8 inch cutthroat and rainbow fishing. There's a jeep trail up it if you can find your way in up the Rock Creek road. For such a little creek — quite a few do.

South Fork Smith River.
Heads on the Shields River divide 4 miles north of Ringling (where the circus used to winter) and flows north through open meadow grazing land for 17 miles to junction with the North Fork 3 miles west of White Sulphur Springs. It's paralleled all the way by U.S. 87 and county roads. The lower 7 or 8 miles (below the junction of U.S. 87 and 12) are good early spring fishing for 6 to 14 inch brookies, but it gets too low and warm in the summer for anything but weeds and suckers. You should also note: There's a stretch or two here that is posted.

Spring Creek.
Here is a slow, marshy little tributary of the Smith River (2 feet wide by perhaps 2 feet deep) in open meadowland crossed near the mouth by a county road 11 miles northwest of White Sulphur Springs. It's posted at the lower end but provides about 5 miles of fair fishing (if you can get permission) for 8 to 10 inch brookies.

Sutherlin Reservoir (or Smith River Reservoir).
Drive 9½ miles east of White Sulphur Springs on U.S. 12 and just to the north side of the highway you will find this 272 acre, 80 foot maximum depth with as much as 60 foot of drawdown irrigation reservoir on the North Fork of the Smith River in open grazing land. There are toilets and tables, and plenty of people come here to fish (also in winter when the water is colder, the fish bite better and they taste better, too) for rainbow trout (stocked in quantity as 4 or 5 inchers on an annual basis) that grow fast here and usually run between 9 and 15 inches with now and then a big 'un taken. Some 8 to 12 inch brookies are caught, along with 15 to 20 inch burbot (ling) to keep things lively for the squeamish. The suckers do well here, too but the ling may be helping to hold down their numbers. Although certainly not pretty, burbot are excellent table fare.

Tenderfoot Creek.
You drive on a gravel and dirt road down the east side of the Smith River for 20 miles north of Old Fort Logan Military Reservation and come in on the Tenderfoot 5½ miles above its mouth at the Conway Crossing. It's accessible below the crossing by trail, and upstream by logging road. There is a 10 foot falls a mile below the crossing and from here on down it's good fishing for mostly 8 to 12 inch rainbow plus fewer 8 to 10 inch cutthroat and whitefish. Above the falls it is fair for 8 to 10 inch cutthroat and rainbow. Some of its tributaries, Rugby, Bolsinger and Iron Mines Creeks are good small cutthroat angling. You *must* stop at the ranch and sign in before proceeding to the creek.

Thompson Gulch. Drive 8 miles northwest of White Sulphur Springs to a fork in the road right on the east bank of the Smith River. Take the left (south) fork across the river in a U turn to the second left fork (a jeep trail) and west along it for 3 miles to the Gulch. The little creek in the bottom of the Gulch doesn't look like much, but it does not go dry — usually. In fact the lower 4 miles is "home" to a small population of brook trout, but they don't lure many fishermen in.

Trout Creek. This little tributary of the North Fork of the Smith River is a "sleeper" only 4 miles north of White Sulphur Springs by a good county road. There is about 3 miles of easily fishable water here, in open grazing land with not too much brush along, and a good population of 8 inch brookies — especially in early season, and — it's all posted — no trespassing.

Trout Creek. About 12 miles in length, draining east to the Smith River south of Milligan Hill about 40 miles southeast of Ulm, this very small creek contains good fishing prospects for small brookies up to a foot long. It crosses the county road at the Anderson Ranch — better get permission.

West Fork Hound Creek. From Cascade drive south for 1 mile, then go east for 4¼ miles to the first right hand (west) turnoff beyond Willow Creek. Now hang on and follow the road for 13 miles to the West Fork about 2½ miles up from its junction with the East Fork. It's wadeable here, and mostly jumpable above. The lower 3 or 4 miles of fishable water is in open rolling foothills on the north end of the Big Belts. There are a few brushy beaver ponds and they — and the intervening stretches — are fair fishing for rainbow and brook trout that run anywhere from 8 to 16 inches. Too bad it's mostly posted!

GOD'S COUNTRY
Courtesy Phil Schlamp, USFS

Whitetail Deer Creek. About 7 miles of fair fishing here, from its mouth on the Smith River 4 miles by county and private roads below the Old Fort Logan Military Reservation turnoff, eastward to its headwaters back up in the timbered foothills of the Little Belts. It's mostly accessible to within a mile by county and private roads, is slow, brushy along the middle reaches, and fair fishing for brookies that run around 8 inches but range upwards to 12.

Whitetail Reservoir. Drive 16 miles northwest on a paved road from White Sulphur Springs to the Old Fort Logan Military Reservation, turn right (due north) for 2 miles where you take the right hand (east) fork 3 miles and you're about there. It's in open grazing land but brushy around the upper (east) end, 4 acres, 20 feet deep with a 10 foot drawdown and gradual dropoffs, moderately popular and fair winter fishing for 9 to 10 inch rainbow (stocked annually as 6 inchers), and brook trout.

Willow Creek. Here is a very small (jumpable) open grazing land, northward flowing, Castle Mountain foothill tributary of the North Fork Smith River that is crossed at the mouth by U.S. 12 a couple of miles east of White Sulphur Springs and followed upstream by private roads for 3 or 4 miles of pan-size brook and a very few cutthroat trout fishing. It's really good in the spring, and fair in summer — if it doesn't dry up — has a few good beaver ponds, but is posted. Fishing, if any, is with permission only.

Take A Kid (Or An Oldtimer) Fishing!

OSPREY AND NEST
Courtesy USFS

IMPASSE FALLS
Courtesy USFS

Stillwater River

The Stillwater River heads in really high spectacular country, running off Sunset Peak as snow melt (3 miles north over Mineral Mountain from the town of Silver Gate) and flowing north and east for 70 miles to the Yellowstone River at Columbus.

Trout ripple the water of many high lakes in the awesome rocky area this underrated little river drains. Varying from rugged scenic mountain terrain to a quieter valley river, this stream has much to offer. The upper reaches dash through timbered mountains, give up fair catches of 6 to 10 inch rainbow, cutthroat and brook trout and are accessible by USFS trail. The middle reaches are heavily fished and fair for brown, rainbow and some brook trout; some of the browns may reach 3 pounds, but are mostly smaller. The lower reaches are moderately popular and good angling for mostly brook, rainbow and brown trout from 8 to 14 inches average size with an occasional brown to 4 or 5 pounds. The whitefishing is good here, too. Most of the lower reach is on private land – 'nuff said.

Stillwater River Drainage

Antelope (or Morris) Creek.   Flows to East Rosebud Creek at Roscoe and is followed upstream through pastureland and open meadows by a fair dirt road. There are a lot of beaver ponds along the lower 4 miles of this little stream, and they're heavily fished for good catches of 6 to 8 inch brook trout.

Anvil Lake.   To get to this one just keep on hiking west-northwest for 1¼ miles across the Stillwater Plateau (including a way-to-hell-and-gone climb down-into-and-up-again across Good Creek canyon from Mutt and Jeff Lakes). Anvil is 9430 feet above sea level and you'll know you've been someplace when you get there. It's in timber all around, has a little rocky knob at the bottom of the anvil, used to be barren but was planted with cutthroat in 1968 and 1974, and is good fishing for mostly 12 to 14 inch trout (some bigger). It's not overfished — you won't have much company. P.S. You can also get there (if you are young and strong and full of vinegar) about 3 miles east and a like amount north from Lake Abundance in the Yellowstone drainage.

Arch Lakes.   Take the East Rosebud trail ¾ mile above Elk Lake to (barren) Arch Creek and then fight your way up that drainage over cliffs and waterfalls for 3½ miles to Lower Arch Lake (in timber) and another mile upstream to Upper Arch (in talus) at around 10,000 feet above the sea below Phantom Glacier. These and 2 other lakes nearby used to be barren but were planted with cutthroat in 1971 and 1977 and (at last report) were good fishing for trout to a couple of pounds. Sure an' they'll not likely be fished out.

Assure Lake.   See West Rosebud Lake.

Bad Canyon Creek.   Heads below Limestone Butte and is followed by a good USFS trail for 10 miles through timber above, and open rangeland below to the Stillwater River (and road) at Beehive. There are several fair-sized gorges along the middle reaches, but the lower end (all on private land) is fair fishing for 6 to 10 inch brook and brown trout. There are a few cuts up above.

Barrier Lake. Is a "slide lake" on the North Fork Wounded Man Creek, about ½ mile long and maybe 20 acres in size, lying below barren talus slopes almost all around (except at the eastern, lower end). It's real good fishing for 6 to 12 inch rainbow-golden hybrids but is not often visited because, along with the miniature trout, it's reached by trail 1½ miles north from Jordan Lake to Jordan Pass — and then east another ¼ mile cross-country and 2000 feet *down* to the shore, at 8150 feet elevation.

Beauty Lake. Is about 6 acres, 35 feet maximum depth, mostly in timber with some talus to the north side, at 9200 feet elevation, reached ½ mile cross-country from Anvil Lake. It was stocked with cutthroat in 1967-8 and is excellent fishing for trout that'll average around 14 inches long — for "them what gets there." 'Reproduction here appears fine.

Big Park Lake. Is a shallow (only a few feet deep), 10 acre lake in timber (but with a big grassy park on the southwest side) a half mile above Lake at Falls by a new USFS pack trail. It used to be fished off and on for goldens, but may be barren now.

Butcher Creek. A small stream flowing through open rolling rangeland to the head of Rosebud Creek, at the junction of the East and West Forks. It's paralleled by road for about 10 miles of poor fishing for 6 to 9 inch brook, brown and some cutthroat trout, but there is better water in the vicinity, and it's not bothered much.

Cairn Lake. Take the Dewey Lake (misnamed Medicine Lake on many maps — Medicine is the next lake up the drainage ¼ mile to the north) trail 1¼ miles northeast from Fossil Lake and then proceed cross-country 2 miles northwest to the unnamed outlet of Cairn Lake to the shore at 10,186 feet elevation. This one is in a barren, rocky cirque away above timber line. It's maybe 100 acres, good and deep with an almost baldheaded island jutting out from the north side, and had a fair population of hard-to-catch nice-sized goldens. Is poor fishing now for fair-sized brook trout.

Castle Creek. Heads in timbered country below Picket Pin Mountain and flows 15 miles east (through mostly posted irrigated farm-and-pastureland) to West Fork Stillwater River, 2 miles above Nye. The lower couple of miles (which are known locally as Limestone Creek) are followed by a county road and are lightly fished by mostly local folks for catches of 8 to 16 inch brown and small brook trout.

Cirque Lake. Follow the westernmost inlet of Jordan Lake upstream crosscounrty through scrubby timber for ¼ mile to this not-too-deep 2 acre lake that is almost never fished. One trip several years ago resulted in a pair of cutthroat (2 and 3¼ pounds) in two hours — and no others were seen. According to recent reports it's barren now.

Crazy Mule Lake. See Pentad Lake.

Crow Lake. Is reached by a good USFS trail 4 miles east from Alpine on East Rosebud Lake, 6 miles west from the end of the West Fork Rock Creek road. A deep, 11 acre alpine lake, it lies in scattered timber and rock but has some nice meadows for horse pasture on the north end, is excellent fishing for 12 to 13 inch brook trout but isn't fished much.

Crow Lake. See Favonius Lake.

Dewey Lake. Is up to 95 feet deep, about 37 acres, at 9340 feet elevation, in alpine country just at timberline, reached (somewhat) by trail 1½ miles below Fossil Lake, ¼ mile cross-country southeast from Medicine Lake. Swimming in its greenish-gray (from glacial silt) waters are a fair number of hard-to-catch ½ to 1½ pound cutthroat (it was planted in 1968) that mostly drifted down from Fossil Lake. Called Medicine Lake on some maps.

East Fiddler Creek. Not a bad little stream but only lightly fished; it's more or less followed by road through open foothill (but brushy) country for 4 miles upstream from the main creek 6 miles above Fishtail — and heads in rough, heavily timbered country on the northern slopes of the Fishtail Plateau. The lower reaches are fair fishing for mostly browns up to about 1½ pounds, a few 8 to 12 inch rainbow, and some 10 to 12 cutthroat trout above.

East Fishtail Creek. A small stream flowing north to join West Fishtail in open farmland at the head of the main Fishtail Creek road. The lower 3 miles are fished now and then for 8 to 12 inch brook trout, but it's a marginal fishery and not recommended.

ON THE STILLWATER
Courtesy USFS

AVALANCHE LAKE
Courtesy USFS

East Rosebud Creek. Heads-away-to-heck-and-gone up on the Beartooth Plateau in Cairn Lake from whence it flows southeastward for about 15 miles across open alpine country through Medicine, Big Park, Lake at Falls and Rainbow Lake to timbered country, and then for another 6 miles into and out of Rimrock and Elk Lakes to East Rosebud Lake — and finally for 20 miles northeast to West Rosebud Creek at the head of the Rosebud River 2½ miles above the old Crow Agency. It's followed by road to East Rosebud Lake, and by a USFS trail on up as far as Medicine Lake. The lower 5 miles are mostly pastureland and are good fishing (with permission) for 1 to 6 pound brown and quite a few 8 to 9 inch brook trout. The middle reaches (below East Rosebud Lake) meander for several miles across an old lake bed behind a breached terminal moraine — a beautiful stretch of water that is heavily fished for fair-to-good catches of 10 to 12 inch rainbow and brown trout.

East Rosebud Lake. A ¾ mile long by ½ mile wide spot formed by the natural damming of East Rosebud Creek at the mouth of Spread Creek. It is 6208 feet above sea level, 112 acres, about 20 feet deep, and lies mostly in timber but has some big meadows on the east side (with about 30 or 40 summer cabins) and has cliffs along the west side. You can drive right to it 14 miles up from Roscoe and lots of people do — for fair catches of cutthroat and rainbow in the 8 to 12 inch class (Cutts planted in 1975 and 1976) and browns all the way up to a recorded 10 pounds and better. Stocked as 4 inchers in the late 1970s, they appear to be doing well.

Echo Lake. Follow Granite Creek 1¼ miles upstream from Big Park Lake to Echo at 8486 feet elevation, 4 miles east and 4307 feet below Granite Peak. It's maybe 12 acres, 21 feet deep, in talus to the south and an old burn to the north but with some timber near the outlet. It used to be barren but was planted with cutthroat in 1971 and is (or should be) good fishing now for everything up to 16 inches. You'll not have much competition here.

Elk Lake. A shallow, 7 acre lake, mostly in timber but partly open on the north side, in a glaciated U-shaped valley 3 miles by trail above East Rosebud Lake. It's moderately popular with folks on their way through to the lakes above, and good fishing for pan-size brook trout.

Emerald Lake. Is followed around the north side by the West Rosebud road 35 miles south from Columbus; is in timber on the south, open meadows to the north, 28 acres, so shallow (7 feet maximum depth) you can almost wade across, and is at 6310 feet elevation. There is a USFS campground near the upper end and another at the outlet end. It is stocked annually with several thousand 9 to 10 inch rainbow trout, is heavily fished for excellent catches of 10 to 15 inch rainbow plus a few browns up to 1½ pounds.

Favonius (or Crow) Lake. 25 acres, reached by trail a couple of hundred yards south up the drainage from Pentad Lake. It's bordered by sparse timber on the north side, mostly grassy park on the south, and is good fishing for cutthroat that range up to 2½ pounds, but run generally smaller, about 10 to 12 inches.

Fiddler Creek. A small stream. The lower 4 miles are mostly in mixed pine and pastureland and are followed by the West Rosebud-Stillwater road and fished more than you'd think for fair catches of pan-size brook trout.

Fishtail Creek. About 15 miles of fishing here, mostly in open (much of it posted) rangeland, paralleled by an oiled road for 9 miles from Fishtail upstream to Dean, and gravel roads and jeep trail above. It's fished a moderate amount and is fair-to-good for rainbow trout that average 10 to 12 inches, and browns up to as much as 2½ pounds.

Flood Creek. This stream is the outlet of Pinchot Lake and flows to the Stillwater River 4 miles south by trail above the end of the road. It's fair-sized but too steep in the lower reaches to fish. The upper reaches, however, below Pinchot Lake and immediately above and below the 6 small unnamed lakes strung out downstream to the east over about 4 miles, are fabulous fishing for golden trout — many of which are crossed with rainbow and cutthroat. The best way in is by a fisherman's trail from Wounded Man Lake, a half mile northwest across a shallow saddle to Pinchot Lake.

Fossil Lake. So named because of its extremely irregular outline resembling nothing living or dead. At one time it had scrappy 2 to 6 pound goldens and no usage to speak of, but the goldens are gone and the usage is way up. The lake squats on a flat mountain top at 9920 feet elevation, is about 165 acres, over 150 feet deep and is just a mile north by trail from Bald Knob Lake in the Clarks Fork of the Yellowstone drainage. Planted in 1972, 1977, and 1980 with McBride cutthroat trout, Fossil regularly gives up good catches of 8 to 16 inch fish. Being out in the open and far above tree line, even in summer (defined here July to August), Fossil can be windy and cold.

Froze-to-Death Lake. Cold, windy, sitting in a boulder-strewn, barren cirque, 195 feet deep, at 10,156 feet, the lake is reached by a 750 foot scramble one mile south-southwest up the drainage from Phantom Lake — by those in shape, or just plain stubborn. Few sample the decent cutthroat, planted in 1978, trout 15 inches or so. The lake is reported to have had grayling in the past, but they are gone now.

Goose Lake. Here is a deep, 102 acre lake you can jeep right to — and many do — 7½ miles north over the Beartooth Plateau from Cooke City. It lies in a wide grassy meadow at 9800 feet, a couple of miles south of Grasshopper Glacier, is heavily fished by all kinds of people, and is fair to good for cutthroat that average 10 to 12 inches and range up to 3 pounds.

EAST ROSEBUD LAKE
Courtesy USFS

ELK LAKE
Courtesy USFS

TRAIL'S END AT STAR LAKE
Courtesy Bill Browning

Huckleberry Lake. Would drain southwest if it drained at all, to the Stillwater River via Goose Creek; but is reached cross-country across a shallow saddle ¾ mile northeastward up the inlet from Long Lake in the Clarks Fork of the Yellowstone drainage. It lies in a bedrock-meadow basin at 9500 feet, is 15 acres with a small island in the west end, and you could call it excellent fishing — I guess — for zillions of 4 to 9 inch brook trout. Practically nobody ever comes here, and it's too bad because if half of them were caught the rest could grow up.

Hudson's (Ernie) Reservoir. Considered at one time one of the best rainbow "fishing holes" in Montana, when the mayfly hatch was on, the leviathans that inhabited these waters (20 to 30 inchers) sounded like a bunch of grunting hogs, sucking in the flys — and looked like a fleet of subs. Strictly private, reported nearly fished out by oil crew people mostly, it can be found by going to Fishtail, inquiring, and following county roads about 5 miles west to the ranch buildings. Jerry Ragman bought the spread from Ernie Hudson in 1981, and if it is eventually restocked, you'll need his permission for sure to fish it. The fishing hole is just over a rise from the ranch, nary a tree in sight, is maybe 7 or 8 acres with a mud-to-weedy bottom. A small spring fed little stream keeps it wet.

Ingersoll Creek. Very small, but a fooler. Ingersoll flows north through mostly open rangeland to the West Rosbud 4½ miles above Fishtail and is followed upstream by road for 1½ miles. The lower 4 miles are lightly fished (a lot of it is on posted land) and are fair for 8 to 12 inch brown, rainbow and a very few brook trout.

Island Lake. Take the USFS trail up around the south side of Mystic Lake and a few hundred yards beyond and across some beaver dams to the lower end of Island Lake which lies in a timbered canyon, is 1¼ miles long, almost ½ mile at the widest, heavily fished (and excellent fishing, too) for 10 to 12 and up to 16 inch rainbow and a few cutthroat trout. The stream above is also excellent fishing. Island Lake is at 7717 feet elevation, is 144 acres, and has a maximum depth of 45 feet.

Jasper Lake. See Tumble Lake.

Jeff Lake. See Mutt and Jeff Lakes.

Jordan Lake. Is 15 acres, elevation 8850, in timber all around, and is reached by the Middle Fork Wounded Man Creek trail 1½ miles below Pentad Lake. It's fished off and on for 8 to 12 inch cutthroat trout, taken in good numbers from this self-sustaining little fishery.

Lake at Falls. A very beautiful, very deep, 50 acre alpine lake at 8150 feet above sea level; reached (but seldom) by the East Rosebud trail 1 mile above Rainbow Lake. There's slide rock all along the north side, scrub timber and slide rock along the south side, and a fair population of hard-to-catch golden trout (up to 3 pounds) and cutthroat to 1½ pounds, and some hybrids.

259

GOOSE LAKE
Courtesy USFS

Lightening Lake. A really deep (122) feet, 61 acre cirque lake at 9340 feet in some scattered alpine timber. (Seldom) reached by following the West Fork Stillwater trail about 8 miles above the end of the road to a point one mile beyond the mouth of (barren) Lightening Creek, and then hiking and scrambling 2000 feet up in 2½ miles due south to the shore. *Stay out of the (awful) creek drainage.* Hear tell there is an easier way in from the other direction — if you're an Indian scout and know the country. The lake has a good population of golden trout that are seldom in the mood to bite. A 2½ pound golden is considered a respectable trophy and reliable reports indicate there are husky fish many times that size here — but so far they've been seen only, not caught.

Lily Pad Lake (Lower). Take a poor (an old oil rig) jeep road 7 miles above the mouth of Fiddler Creek clear to the end of the north shore of this shallow (no more than 15 feet deep, even in the middle), 20 acre lake. It is surrounded by dense timber, is beautiful in summer when the lilies are in bloom away out from shore — and is barren.

Lily Pad Lake (Upper). This is just a large, marshy beaver pond with a 150 foot or so dam, reached by foot trail ¼ mile from the south end of Lower Lily Pad Lake. It's in a pinched-in canyon, is bordered by grass and timber and is barren.

Limestone Creek. Is not so named on many maps but is local terminology for the stream formed by the junction of Castle and Lodgepole Creeks — flowing through mostly posted farm and pasture land for 2 miles to the West Fork Stillwater River a couple of miles above Nye. It's paralleled by a county road and is lightly fished by mostly local folks for good catches of 8 to 14 inch (maximum reported to 4 pounds) browns and some small brook trout.

Little Goose Lake. Eight acres, at 9835 feet above sea level, 23 foot maximum water depth, in an open alpine meadow above tree line ½ mile above and cross-country from Goose Lake, it looks as though it should freeze out but doesn't. It's well used and excellent, too, for 8 to 14 inch cutthroat trout.

Little Lightning Lake. Is 17 acres, at 9280 feet elevation, just below timberline, about 12 feet maximum depth, and if you struggle to Lightning Lake it is a nice little bonus as it is fair fishing for small golden trout that not many humans get to see. It's a few hundred yards down drainage from Lightning Lake.

Little Rocky Creek. A small stream meandering northward across irrigated pastureland for the last mile above its mouth to the Stillwater River a couple of miles below Nye. This section is lightly fished (mostly by locals) for pan-size and a few up to maybe 16 inches or so browns, and rainbow or cutthroat now and then. The stream used to be good fishing above but was reportedly ruined by pollution from a sawmill near the headwaters.

YOUNG GOAT
Courtesy USFS

LAKE AT FALLS
Courtesy Dick Behan

Lodge Pole Creek.
Flows north to the West Fork Stillwater River 4½ miles above Nye and is followed upstream by a county road. The lower 3 miles of this little creek flow through mostly posted pasture and meadowland, are moderately popular (with those who can get permission), easily fished and is really good fishing for pan-sized brown, brook and rainbow trout in decreasing order of abundance.

Lost Lake.
Take the East Fishtail Creek trail 2 miles south above the end of the road and then a poor fishermen's trail a half mile east to this one. It lies in a timbered valley, is about 10 acres, shallow, and used to have nice rainbow but is now barren.

Medicine Lake.
At 9906 feet elevation, 127 foot maximum water depth, 30 acres, mis-named Dewey Lake on some maps (or vice-versa), has some beautiful waterfalls, about 80 feet high, splashing into its upper end and is reached (somewhat) by going up the outlet of Dewey Lake (by the East Rosebud trail 2 miles above Big Park Lake). Planted with cutthroat in 1971 and 1978 they run between 9 and 14 inches and up to now have been easy to catch.

Middle Fiddler Creek.
Not a bad little stream but only lightly fished. It's more or less accessible by road for 5 miles of fair fishing in open foothill country (but brushy along the creek). There are mostly brown trout here, up to 1½ pounds, a few 8 to 12 inch rainbow, plus some 10 to 12 inch cutthroat trout in the upper (fishable) reaches.

Morris Creek.
Flows to East Rosebud Creek at Roscoe and is followed upstream through pastureland and open meadows by a fair dirt road. Permission is needed and usually granted to fish this nice little stream, mostly in the beaver ponds in the lower four miles. Plenty of people try 'cause the catching is excellent here for 6 to 11 inch brook trout.

Mutt and Jeff Lakes.
Two fairly shallow 2 acre lakes, ⅛ of a mile apart in an alpine meadow ½ mile west-northwestward cross-country from Huckleberry Lake. They are seldom visited but excellent fishing for camp-fare brook trout.

Mystic Lake.
A Montna Power Company reservoir, over 2 miles long by ½ mile wide, reached by trail 2½ miles above the Mystic Lake hydroelectric plant at the end of the West Rosebud road. The trail follows around the south side of the lake, in timber all the way, although there is some fairly open country across the water. This reservoir, at 7673 feet, 435 acres, is 205 feet deep with as much as 85 feet of water level fluctuation. It's popular with people who hike in from the several campgrounds below (at West Rosebud and Emerald Lakes), and is good fishing at the upper end, especially below the mouth of Huckleberry Creek for 10 to 12 and some to 16 inch rainbow, along with a few cutthroat and hybrids.

TERRACED LAKES
Courtesy USFS

Pentad (or Crazy Mule) Lake. Near the top of the timber at 9382 feet above sea level, reached by the Middle Fork Wounded Man Creek trail 7 miles above the Stillwater River — or you can come over Columbine Pass from the East Boulder. It was originally named Pentad for the 5 points around the shoreline and was subsequently renamed Crazy Mule by a local packer who was so unfortunate as to have one get spooked into it and drown. It is 21 acres and good fishing for 11 to 12 inch (maximum reported to 3 pounds) rainbow trout.

Phantom Lake. This one is a honey to get to. It lies in a hanging glacial pocket on the east side of Froze-To-Death Mountain at 9400 feet above sea level. From Slough Lake follow Phantom Creek 1½ miles west to the forks, then take the left (south) fork upstream for a rugged 1650 feet-in-one-mile climb to the shore. It's 20 acres, good and deep, in timber all around below high barren cliffs, and fair fishing for 10 inch cutthroat trout — a fairly popular hike.

Picket Pin Creek. A small stream in timbered country; reached at the mouth by the Castle Creek road and mostly paralleled (for about 10 miles) by mining and USFS roads. The upper reaches are mostly too steep to fish, but the lower 1½ miles flatten out and are fair fishing for small brook and brown trout, and quite a few cutthroat and rainbow here and there.

Picket Pin Lake. Used to have large beautiful silver-colored rainbow trout to 3 pounds or more, but they supposedly winterkilled. Planted with cutthroat in 1972 and 1979, this 6 acre lake is of medium depth, but with shallow dropoffs. It is in real rough timbered country reached to within ¾ of a mile by the Picket Pin road (may get closed; check USFS Ranger District) and then south cross-country to the shore. The fishing is a bit slow but the fish can be nice — to a couple pounds.

Pinchot Lake. A moderately popular 54 acre lake that is 30 feet deep with steep dropoffs on the east and south, timbered on the east, and has open grassy banks (below timber) on around. It's reached by a fisherman's trail (which you don't really need because it's only sparsely timbered) ¾ of a mile northeast from Wounded Man Lake. The fish (which average less than a pound and range up to a couple of pounds) are mostly golden and rainbow, plus some cutthroat trout and hybrids of all three species.

Princess Lake. See Slough Lake.

Rainbow Lake. Is 58 acres, 180 feet maximum depth and nestles at 7670 feet in some pretty country, a mile long by ½ mile wide lake in a deep U shaped, glaciated canyon, mostly open around the shores but with timber above; reached by the East Rosebud Creek trail 5 miles above East Rosebud Lake. It's real popular and excellent fishing for 9 to 14 inch rainbow, golden and rainbow-golden hybrids.

EAST ROSEBUD HEADWATERS
Courtesy USFS

Rimrock Lake. A 25 foot deep, 34 acre lake with steep dropoffs all around, right in the timbered canyon of East Rosebud Creek; reached and followed around the west side by trail 4½ miles above East Rosebud Lake. It's fished quite a bit by people going on through to Rainbow, Lake At Falls, Big Park, Medicine and Dewey Lakes and is fair for 8 to 14 inch rainbow and cutts.

Rosebud River. A fair size stream but a small river, formed by the junction of its East and West forks near the Rosebud community center and followed by a paved road for 3 miles south across open farmland to the Stillwater River just below the Old Crow (Absarokee) Agency. It's very good fishing (with the land owner's permission) for mostly 1 to 2 pound brown trout and 10 to 14 inch rainbow trout.

Shadow Lake. A deep, 5 acre lake with steep dropoffs below open banks all the way around. It's excellent fishing for brook trout but the way in is rugged, a half mile up Armstrong Creek from the lower (northwest) corner of East Rosebud Lake, and then a 2 mile cross-country climb up the first tributary to your right (west) side. The fish are small — and few people bother.

Silver Lake. A 21 feet deep (maximum) — but with shallow dropoffs — 73 acre lake at 7820 feet above sea level reached by the West Rosebud Creek trail 1½ miles above Island Lake. It lies in a steep-walled, glaciated canyon with talus slopes to thé east and timber on around — and is fished quite a bit for fair catches of 8 to 12 inch rainbow. Reports of 15 pound trout hooked and lost in the past may be true but only a very occasional rainbow to 3 or 4 pounds is currently taken. Some fine cutthroat fishing not well known is said to exist if you take off up the shallow draw almost due west for 1¼ miles and a tough 1500 foot climb. Are you a gambler?

Sioux Charley Lake. A half mile long, swampy "wide spot" in the Stillwater River reached by road and trail 3 miles upstream from the Woodbine Campground. It's fished a lot and is good for pan-size brook trout 8 inch average.

Slough (or Princess) Lake. Leave your car ¼ mile below East Rosebud Lake and take the Armstrong Creek (Phantom Creek) trail 2¼ miles west to this heavily fished lake. It's in timber all around, about ⅛ of a mile long by a couple hundred yards across, very shallow with marshy country just above — and is excellent for 6 to 10 inch brook trout.

Snow Lakes. Take the East Rosebud trail 1½ miles upstream above East Rosebud Lake and then climb (that's the correct word) for another real rough 1½ miles east and south — and 3500 feet up — to these two lakes about 400 yards apart in mostly barren alpine country with some scrub timber close enough for firewood, at the foot of Mount Inabnit Glacier. The lower lake is 7 acres, the upper is 8 acres; both are deep enough to keep from freezing out and are fair fishing for 8 to 15 inch rainbow trout — were stocked in 1978.

263

Sourdough Basin Lakes.
Four, unnamed on most maps, in Sourdough Basin a couple of miles south of Courthouse Mountain and 1-2 miles north of Anvil Lake. They range from 7 to 9 acres, at timber line but with enough around for camp fires and a little protection from the wind, and are generally excellent fishing for 10 to 13 inch brookies for them what gets there.

Sylvan Lake.
Elevation 9153 feet, in a barren cirque on the edge of the East Rosebud Plateau at the head of (barren) Hellroaring Creek but reached by a USFS foot trail up (barren) Spread Creek 3 miles east from East Rosebud Lake. It's long and narrow, about 18 acres, deep and good fishing immediately after the ice goes out (say in mid-June or so) for 10 to 14 inch golden trout. Quite a few dudes pack into this one.

Trout Creek.
A small foothill stream flowing to the Stillwater River 2½ miles below Beehive. The lower 6 miles are mostly in open rangeland (with a fair amount of willow and brush along the banks), are accessible by a jeep road and are fairly popular and really good fishing for 6 to 12 inch rainbow, brook and brown trout. In some areas recent high flows have caused some channel disturbance, however.

Tumble Lake (or Jasper).
Drive up the West Fork of the Stillwater River to the Initial (barren) Creek camp, then hike up the West Fork for 3½ miles to Tumble Creek and finally for another 2½ miles up that creek to the lake at 9080 feet elevation in a glacial cirque at just about timberline. It is about 53 acres, really difficult to get to, and is excellent cutthroat fishing for 8 to 17 inch trout stocked in 1968 and 1977. There's some apparent reproduction in the inlet, helping to enhance the fishery. There is a small lake 300 yards up the inlet and another a mile up into the cirque, that may or may not have fish — who knows!

Trugulse Lake.
Lies at a windy 10,206 feet elevation in a great rocky alpine cirque — framed on the north, west and south by Froze-To-Death, Tempest and Peal Mountains, an easy ¾ mile cross-country hike west from Froze-To-Death Lake. It is over 80 feet deep, 83 acres, and receives some pressure (justified) because of the good cutthroat trout fishing; planted in 1978 and still growing.

Unnamed (?) Lake.
(On headwaters of Glacier Creek west of Grasshopper Glacier). From Little Goose Lake hike ½ mile due north across a barren saddle to a shallow barren pond, and then down its outlet (Glacier Creek) for a mile to a fairly deep, long, narrow 6 acre lake in mixed scrub timber and rock a couple of miles west of Grasshopper Glacier. It's very seldom if ever fished, but is excellent for hordes of 8 to 9 inch brook trout.

Unnamed Lakes Near Jordan Pass.
Two, 8 and 12 acres, in timber a quarter mile apart, reached (by few) cross-country (and here you'll hit a trail) 1¼ miles due south from Wounded Man Lake. They used to be real good for 10 to 14 inch cutthroat from a 1969 plant but are almost barren now. There's no reproduction; look for a possible replant.

RAINBOW LAKE
Courtesy USFS

STILLWATER RIVER
Courtesy Phil Farnes

SPARKLING STILLWATER
Courtesy USFS

RAINBOW LAKE
Courtesy USFS

Unnamed Lakes (On Flood Creek).

From Lake Pinchot follow (and fish if you're of a mind to) down the outlet (Flood Creek) for about 4 miles east past six 2½ to 10 acre unnamed lakes in a steep timbered mountain canyon that would be good sheep country, but it's too rough to hunt. All of them are excellent fishing for 6 to 15 inch golden-rainbow-cutt hybrids. The further downstream you go the fewer people you see.

Unnamed Lake One Half Mile South of Favonius Lake.

Lots of outfitters pack their dudes into this one, an easy half mile cross-country south from Favonius. It's 3½ acres, the north shore in timber with rock rubble on around, was planted with cutthroat in the 70's and is good fishing now for 10 to 14 inch fish.

Unnamed Lake One Mile Up Unnamed Creek North From South Fork Wounded Man Creek.

Is 12 acres, maximum depth 40 feet, 80% in timber and the rest below talus slopes on a bench with 200 foot outlet falls; reached by shanks' mares 1¼ miles up the South Fork Wounded Man Creek from its junction with the Middle Fork, and then on up the unnamed tributary coming in from the north. It was planted with cutthroat in 1969 and should be excellent fishing now for anything from fingerling to 16 inchers — if they haven't frozen out.

Unnamed Lakes (Two on the head of Wounded Man Creek — not including Wounded Man Lake).

The smaller lake lies at the head of the northern inlet of Wounded Man Lake a mile to the north and right beside the West Fork Stillwater River trail. It's about 7 acres. The other lake lies at the head of the northwestern inlet of Wounded Man Lake, a mile to the west. It's about 9 acres. Both had a few BIG rainbow (to 5 pounds recorded) and neither is fished much.

West Fishtail Creek.

A small stream flowing northeastward to join East Fishtail in open farm and pastureland at the head of the main Fishtail Creek road. It's drawn way down at times for irrigation but is fished quite a lot for fair catches of 8 to 10 inch brook trout.

West Fork Stillwater River.

Flows to the Stillwater River at Nye and is followed upstream by road for about 5½ miles and thence by trail for 20 miles to headwaters. From the mouth of Cathedral Creek down to the main river (8½ miles) it's fair-to-good fishing (a lot of it is posted) for 10 to 12 to 18 inch brown and rainbow trout in occasional beaver ponds and sloughs. This part is heavily fished. The next 10 miles above Cathedral Creek (mostly in timber) provide fair fishing for 8 to 12 inch rainbow and cutthroat trout — but are only lightly fished.

West Rosebud Creek.

Is formed at headwaters by ice melt from Grasshopper Glacier from where it flows northward for 6 miles to Silver Lake, then eastward for another 6 miles through island and Mystic Lakes, and then northeastward for 25 miles to junction with the East Rosebud just below the Rosebud Community Center 3 miles above Absarokee (the Old Crow Agency). It's followed by a road as far upstream as the Mystic Lake hydroelectric plant a couple of miles below the lake, and by a USFS trail another 7 miles to Silver Lake. The lower 7 miles are in open pastureland (mostly posted) and are lightly fished for good catches of 10 to 16 inch brown and rainbow trout. The middle reaches are heavily fished for good catches of 8 to 12 inch rainbow, small brook, brown trout and some cutts. Above Silver Lake about a half mile (through the jungle) there is some decent small rainbow fishing to be had where the stream meadows out.

West Rosebud (or Assure) Lake.
Shallow, mostly under 6 feet deep, about 19 acres, at 6387 feet above sea level, timbered on the south side, open on the north; reached by road ¾ of a mile above Emerald Lake. There is a nice public campground, the lake is in a very scenic area, it is stocked annually with small rainbow, all of which creates heavy usage for the excellent catches of 8 to 12 inch rainbow plus a few browns.

Wilderness Lake.
A beautiful 30 acre lake with steep dropoffs below cliffs at the upper (east) end — talus on the south side and timber on the north. The lower (west) outlet end is quite shallow. Wilderness is at 9481 feet above sea level on a little unnamed tributary a mile east of (barren) Woodbine Creek but you can't get in that way. Take the Nye Creek trail east from the Stillwater River road 8 miles above Nye for 7 miles upstream past the headwaters and on up until you intersect the "ridge" trail — which can also be reached by trail from the end of the West Fishtail (Benbow Mine) road. From here you head due south over the rolling Stillwater Plateau for about 6 miles and then hike a steep 1½ miles down to the shore. Wilderness is one of the campsites of the Beartooth Guest Ranch (on the headwaters of the Stillwater River), and is fair fishing for 8 to 12 inch cutthroat trout. The 10 acre lake ⅛ of a mile on up the drainage to the southeast is reportedly frozen out, but worth a try anyway.

Wood Lake.
Is 12 acres, 38 feet maximum depth, at 9690 feet elevation one quarter of a mile above Wilderness Lake and is used somewhat (by dudes mostly) for fair catches of foot long cutthroat trout stocked in 1976. It's a little jewel sparkling in a rocky cirque in rugged country up a branch of Woodbine Creek just below Mt. Wood and Mt. Hague. See Wilderness Lake for a way in.

Wounded Man Lake.
An excellent lake for 10 to 12 inch rainbow, cutthroat and rainbow-cutthroat hybrids. It's about 50 acres, with scattered timber back from the shore, has a little island — and a good sized rock — in the south end; is reached by trail above Woodbine Camp at the end of the road — or 9 miles by trail from the Lazy Day Ranch on the Boulder River up (barren) Upsidedown Creek and over the pass. A lot of parties camp here when fishing the neighboring lakes. The elevation here is 9248 feet with the maximum depth 55 feet. If you're ambitious, there are several unnamed lakes nearby (look under unnamed lakes).

Zoetman (Pete) No. 3 Pond.
A shallow, 10 acre pond in scattered timber and grazing land ½ mile west of the Stillwater River road about 2 miles below the Chrome Mine. It's not well known, you can't see it from the road, and it's just as well because it's poor fishing at best — for rainbow trout, some of which are of nice size. By the way, it's private.

Be A "No Trace" Camper

ON GRASSHOPPER GLACIER
Courtesy USFS

GRANITE PEAK
Courtesy USFS

Sun River

The Sun River, as defined here, is that part of the river flowing from Gibson Reservoir eastward for approximately 55 airline miles to its junction with the Missouri River near Great Falls. Gibson Reservoir provides the gateway to the famed Bob Marshall Wilderness Area which abounds with excellent hunting and fishing opportunities.

Between Gibson Dam and Diversion Dam, there are about 2 miles of river and another mile of pool behind the Diversion Dam. This stretch of river (on public land) is reached by county roads 25 miles northwest from Augusta. The Sun River in this beautiful mountainous area flows through a narrow canyon with large, deep pools and turbulent riffles. Flows are dependent upon discharges from Gibson Dam. Good fishing is found in this area, with 8 to 12 inch rainbow most common and a few brook and cutthroat taken occasionally.

At Diversion Dam, water is diverted from the Sun River to two off-stream irrigation storage reservoirs, Willow Creek and Pishkun. Flows in the river are regulated by releases from Gibson and Diversion Dams. Below Diversion Dam, the river emerges from the mountains flowing in a rocky channel surrounded by rolling hills. A few miles downstream the channel is characterized by gravel bottoms and banks which were badly scoured by the 1964 and 1975 floods. The lower reaches are mostly followed by the Great Falls-Augusta highway. Most is on private land, but permission to fish is generally granted upon request. The fishery consists of rainbow, brook, brown and whitefish in the upper portion (a few recorded to 4 pounds and better). The lower reaches produce bragging size northern pike (to 20 pounds) and a few burbot (ling). Historically, grayling were native to the Sun River below Diversion Dam, but few are thought to exist today; one was reported taken in 1970.

Bill Hill

Sun River Drainage

Alpine Lake. By trail about 3 miles above Wood Lake, at 7000 feet, over 10 feet deep, and 3 to 4 acres in size. Used to contain nice cutthroats but may be barren now. In any event, a tough climb in to a scenic lake.

Barr Creek. A small open "Game Range" stream (brushy along the lower reaches) flowing southeastward to the North Fork Willow Creek 10 miles west by county road from Augusta. The lower 5 miles are excellent kids' fishing for 6 to 10 inch brookies, and are accessible all along to within about a mile by road. There are fishermen's trails all over the place.

Barr Lake. A few miles by road above the "Game Range Headquarters" up Barr Creek, it's good fishing for rainbows averaging 11 inches or so.

Bear Lake. A 20 acre lake formed behind a prehistoric rockslide across the headwaters of (barren — it's too small and steep for fish) Bear Creek. It lies north of Prairie Reef at about 7000 feet elevation in steep rock-timber-and-park country reached by a good USFS trail 7 miles west from the upper end of Gibson Reservoir. It has 3 very small inlets, mostly steep dropoffs and a muddy bottom; and has been described as "wonderful" fishing for 12 to 13 inch cutthroat trout.

Beaver Creek. Is excellent fishing and very popular around the last of May — for 10 to 14 inch and once-in-a-while to a couple of pounds — rainbow spawners, plus a few cutthroat and brook trout up from the Sun River diversion reservoir. It's crossed at the mouth by the Sun River road just below Gibson Dam and is followed by a USFS road south up its timbered, sometimes pretty brushy, canyon for about 3½ miles of fishing. Don't hit it later on as it gets very low and the fish all migrate back down.

Big George Creek. Flows due south down a steep, rocky, timbered canyon for 5½ miles to Gibson Reservoir, and is followed all along the west side by a good USFS trail. It comes close to going dry in the summer but the lower couple of miles are sometimes fished and are good in early season for 9 to 11 inch (and a few to 14 or so) cutthroat and rainbow — that come up from the reservoir.

Biggs Creek. A small, clear mountain stream flowing down a very steep and rocky canyon above, and across more gentle but still far from flat, timbered country below, to the North Fork Sun River about 8 miles by pack trail above the upper end of the Gibson Reservoir. The lower couple of miles (below the falls, which act as a fish barrier) are followed by trail and are fair fishing (mostly-if-at-all by hunting parties) for 6 to 10 inch brook trout.

Big Muddy Creek. Is followed by the Great Northern R.R. southeastward from Plummerton across open farmland for about 20 miles to the Sun River near Vaughn, and is paralleled here and there by county and private roads. It's all silted up due to what has been described as "poor farming practices," and is marginal fishing at best for a few 10-14 inch rainbow, and still fewer pan-size brook and brown trout. In terms of recreational attributes — it's nothing to brag about.

Blacktail Creek. A small stream followed all along down its steep, rocky, timbered canyon by a good USFS trail for 8 miles to the Sun River just below Gibson Reservoir. It goes almost dry in summer but is fished now and then in early season for good catches of 9 to 14 inch rainbow, cutthroat, and brook trout that migrate up from the main river.

Blubber Creek. A small, northeastward flowing tributary of Elk Creek, reached to within a few hundred yards of the mouth by the Elk Creek road about 9 miles southwest from Augusta. It's quite brushy, mostly on private grazing land (access usually granted on request) and is followed all along by fishermen's trails for about 4½ miles past numerous beaver ponds that are excellent fishing for 8 to 10 inch rainbow and brook trout.

DIVERSION RESERVOIR ON THE SUN
Courtesy USFS

WHITE TAIL FAUN
Courtesy USFS

Cutrock Creek. A small stream, reached at the mouth on the North Fork Willow Creek by a county road 12 miles west from Augusta, and followed upstream by an old four-wheel drive (PRIVATE) road for 2½ miles up its brushy canyon between Limestone Ridge and Sawtooth Ridge. The lower couple of miles are fair fishing (if you can get permission) for 6 to 10 inch brook trout and a few cutts.

Dickens Lake. On the Sun River Game Range northwest of Augusta, only a short walk from the county road leading to Gibson Dam. Being about five acres in size but only 10 feet deep it gets very weedy by mid-summer and hard to fish. Stocked with fast growing rainbows, it's good for 7 to 15 inchers, with some to 5 pounds, when it doesn't winterkill.

Diversion Reservoir. A heavily fished, summer home, boating (no skiing, though, because the water is too cold), and picnicking reservoir behind a 200 foot concrete dam on the Sun River 20 miles by road northwest from Augusta. It's over 1 mile long by ⅛ of a mile wide, in the Sun River Canyon with lots of aspen, fir, brush and some open banks around. Fishing is good for 8 to 14 inch rainbow and some 8 to 10 inch brookies.

Elk Creek. Heads on the rocky, timbered slopes of Steamboat Mountain and is followed northeastward by a good county road for 22 miles, through Augusta to the Sun River 5 miles east of town. All but the upper 5 miles is in open country, is easily accessible, and is heavily fished in early season for good catches of 7 to 8 inch rainbow and brook trout plus brown trout along the lower reaches. Late in the season the fishing is only fair-to-poor. This stream is usually closed within a mile of town — for kids under 12 years of age.

Elk Ranch (or Swazee) Pond. A 2½ acre MDFWP pond with steep dropoffs but only 10 feet maximum depth, in open rangeland on the south side of the road one mile southeast of the Sun River Game Range Headquarters a couple of miles north of Black Butte on the Rose Creek drainage 14 miles by road west-northwest from Augusta. If you know how to fish this one, it's a good place to go — and lots of people do — for 6 to 12 inch rainbow. Should be too, because it's stocked each year.

Fairview Creek. A small, mountain tributary of Wood Creek, crossed at the mouth by the Bench Mark road 2¼ miles above the Ranger Station and followed upstream for 4 miles to headwaters. It's seldom if ever fished, but there are a lot of small beaver ponds along the first 2 or 3 miles, and they support a fair population of pan-size brook trout.

Ford Creek. Used to flow to Smith Creek but is now mostly diverted to the Nilan Reservoir. It's followed upstream (mostly along the north side) by the Bench Mark road for 10 miles west from the diversion canal practically to headwaters. The lower (beaver-ponded) reaches are on private,

270

rolling meadow and hay land; the upper reaches flow through a narrow mountain canyon. It's moderately-to-heavily fished and good, too — for 10 to 12 inch rainbow and a fair number of 8 to 9 inch brook trout.

Gates Creek. Is reached at the mouth by the North Fork Sun River trail 12 miles north from the upper end of the Gibson Reservoir and is followed by trail beyond the Gates Park Ranger Station to headwaters. There are some falls a couple of miles upstream that act as a fish barrier, but there are numerous small pools in the open valley below that are easily fished for good catches of 6 to 8 inch rainbow, brook, and cutthroat trout.

Gibson Reservoir. Five miles long and averages about ¼ mile wide, real deep but with as much as 50 foot water level fluctuations behind its concrete dam 1½ miles west by road above the Diversion Reservoir. Gibson lies in the bottom of the deep, narrow Sun River canyon between high rocky slopes and cliffs. On the north side of the lake by the dam there are public campgrounds and a good USFS pack trail along the same side takes you past many good camping spots at the mouths of the various tributary streams. The water here is too cold for swimming or skiing, but it supports a good population of 12 to 14 inch rainbow where the creeks come in, plus browns to 15 inches and a very few cutthroat and brooks. The lake is fished — mostly from boats — a fair amount in spring up around the upper end.

Goss Creek. The lower reaches of this little stream flow to the southeast around the southwest side by Haystack Butte to Blubber Creek 2 miles up from that stream's mouth on Elk Creek. No trail here except for the cows', but there are quite a few brushy little beaver ponds along the lower mile that are fished a fair amount for good catches of 8 to 10 inch rainbow and brook trout.

Hannan Gulch. A small stream, similar to Big George Creek, followed northward upstream by a USFS road for half a mile above its mouth on the Diversion Reservoir — to the Hannan Gulch Guard Station, and then for another 3 miles up its rocky, timbered canyon by trail. The lower 3 miles are only lightly fished but good until mid-summer, for most 8 to 12 inch rainbow and brook trout.

Levale Lake. Lies high on the Continental Divide (elevation 7400 feet) a mile west of Signal Mountain; reached by good USFS trails up the North Fork Sun River and then (barren) Open Creek 25 miles north and west from the upper end of Gibson Reservoir. It is spring-fed, about 5 acres, good and deep with steep dropoffs below alpine timber on the north and east sides, and rock and talus on around. It's good for 10 to 12 inch (maximum to 14 inch) cutthroat that really put up a scrap.

Little Willow Creek. Take the Ford Creek road 8 miles west from Nilan Reservoir and you'll come in on and follow the upper reaches of Little Willow for about 2 miles. If you fish downstream (and many do) for a couple of miles to its mouth on Willow Creek — you will arrive at a jeep road that will take you 1½ miles south to the main road again. There are a lot of beaver ponds in the lower pastureland reaches and they're good fishing for mostly 8 to 9 inch (a few to a foot) brook trout.

Long (J.B.) Reservoir. See Totts Reservoir.

Lowry Lake. A natural, 50 acre lake with shallow dropoffs, in open rolling rangeland, reached by a dirt trail a few miles north from State Highway No. 20, perhaps 6 miles west of Simms, or 35 miles west from Great Falls. It used to be (reportedly, that is) good fishing but has been closed to the public for years and is an unknown quantity now.

Mill Coulee. A small stream with little or no brush, in open farmland and grazing land near Sun River 20 miles west on U.S. 89 from Great Falls. It was rehabilitated in 1961 and yields a few 9 to 10 inch brook trout, mostly to the local gentry who fish it in between slugs of mud brought down from irrigation above.

Moose Creek. Is reached at the mouth by the North Fork Sun River trail 7½ miles north above the upper end of Gibson Reservoir, and is followed by trail (but not many people) for 12 miles up its steep, rocky, timbered canyon to headwaters below the Chinese Wall. There are some good holes in the middle reaches and from there on down it's fair fishing for 6 to 10 inch rainbow and brook trout.

MIDDLE REACHES
Courtesy USFS

FAT CUTTHROAT AND RAINBOW
Courtesy Bill Browning

Nilan Reservoir.
A good sized reservoir, 100 acres or so, 1¼ miles long by a third of a mile wide, with a maximum depth of 50 feet behind an earth-fill dam in open rangeland 7½ miles by good county road west from Augusta. It's heavily fished both summer and winter by everybody in the country — because it has produced some of the best fishing in the country — for 9 to 15 inch (occasionally to 5 pounds) rainbow. Nilan was rehabilitated in 1973 and in 1977, and is stocked every year with rainbows, producing lots of fish in the 14 to 18 inch class, and some lunkers. It is excellent fly fishing summer evenings with wooly worms and with lures, or cowbells and worms from a boat during the day. In winter, corn or jigs thru the ice work well.

North Fork Sun River.
As defined here — that stream which rises below the Sun River Pass on the Continental Divide at 7800 feet elevation, and flows southward for about 25 miles down its broad timbered valley to the upper end of Gibson Reservoir at 4750 feet elevation — followed all along by good USFS trails. The middle and lower reaches are fished a fair amount by parties passing through. There are lots of nice holes here with swift clear water that is good late season fly fishing for rainbow in the half-to-two pound class, a few cutthroat, and brookies.

North Fork Willow Creek.
A beaver-dammed, brushy, posted (and they MEAN it), open rangeland creek flowing to the main Willow Creek 1¼ miles above the reservoir. It's crossed in the middle reaches by a county road 8 miles west from Augusta, and is followed upstream for a couple of miles by a jeep trail, and downstream by cow trails. It's seldom fished but is reportedly good for 6 to 10 inch brook trout.

Paul's (or Sink Hole) Lake.
Private, in open grazing land south of the Nilan Road on the intake ditch from Fork Creek about a mile west of the lake. It and the wide spots in the ditch above and below used to be excellent for rainbow trout that sometimes reach 9 pounds or so. Reported to have "killed out," it was stocked with brook trout in 1977, and at this writing was reported to be good for small brookies.

Pishkun Canal.
A large canal 30 to 40 feet wide, that leaves the Sun River ¼ mile below the Diversion Reservoir and is paralleled along its south side by a maintenance road for 9 miles east-northeastward across open rolling grazing and farm land to the Pishkun Reservoir. It's drained each winter but come summer a good population of 10 to 12 inch rainbow soon migrate into it from the river. At that time it's fair fishing, and moderately popular for a "ditch."

Pishkun Reservoir.
A large, (1550 acre) irregularly shaped irrigation reservoir 2½ miles long by 2¼ miles maximum width (including both the east and west ponds), in open grazing land about 20 miles southwest by county roads from Choteau. Up to 80 feet deep with an average drawdown of 10 feet, it occasionally is lowered about 30 feet. Used by Great Falls people a bunch, it is fairly good fishing for northern pike that average 3 to 8 pounds and run up to 30. Rainbow were planted in 1980 and are stocked periodically (when the pike population is low). Fair for 2 to 4 pounders with a maximum of 12 husky pounds recorded. Occasionally yellow perch are taken and

272

IN VELVET
Courtesy Bridenstine Studio

FISHING THE SUN
Courtesy Bill Browning

a few grayling. Kokanee salmon were introduced in 1970 and planted annually. Kokanee fishing is good by trolling and many spawners are taken by snagging in the fall. The state record Kokanee came out of Pishkun in 1976.

Renshaw Lake. A 25 foot deep, 3 acre lake with variable dropoffs, and mud-and-rock bottom beneath rock slides, grass and some scrubby timber at 7400 feet elevation on the east side of Renshaw Mountain — reached by a good USFS trail 6½ miles northeast up Fairview Creek from the Bench Mark road. Planted with cutthroat trout in 1975-77-79, the catching is fair for 8 to 15 inchers; the fish being a bonus as the scenery is beautiful.

Rock Creek. Heads below the Chinese Wall on Larch Hill Pass at the Continental Divide and is followed eastward down its timbered canyon for 12 miles to the North Fork Sun River 10 miles by a good USFS pack trail upstream from the upper end of Gibson Reservoir. The middle reaches are followed by the trail from Gates Park to Spotted Bear Pass, but only the lower 2 miles (below the falls) have trout — 3 to 12 inch cutthroat and rainbow in numerous pools and a nice beaver pond near the mouth. It's very seldom fished.

Rose (Furnam) Creek. A very small (2 to 4 foot wide) brushy tributary of Barr Creek, with lots of beaver ponds along the lower 3 miles of its course. The Sun River Game Range headquarters are on it and the access road (from the North Fork Willow Creek a half mile above the mouth of Barr Creek) parallels the middle reaches for ½ mile. It's fair for pan-size brook trout.

Sink Hole Lake. See Paul's Lake.

Smith Creek. Is reached at the mouth on Elk Creek by a county road 3½ miles southwest from Augusta, and is followed upstream by road for 9 miles through open rolling grazing land, and finally by trail for 8 miles up its steep, rocky canyon to headwaters. The road reaches are very brushy, moderately popular, and fair fishing for 9 to 11 inch rainbow and brook trout.

Sock Lake. Reached by USFS trail, up Red Shale Creek 7 miles west of the Gates Park Ranger Station, this little 4 acre jewel lies under the Continental Divide 2 miles west of Lookout Mountain at 7400 feet elevation. Stocked with cutthroat in 1975-77-79 (has also some natural reproduction), is good for 9 to 12 inchers, and occasionally rewards an angler with a 3 or 4 pounder.

South Fork Sun River. As defined here: that stream which heads at 8500 feet elevation on the Continental Divide between Observation Point and Scapegoat Mountain and is followed by a good USFS horse trail for about 25 miles down its rocky, timbered canyon to the upper end of Gibson Reservoir at 4750 feet elevation. It is heavily fished. The lower five miles (below Pretty

273

Prairie) have many nice pools that are excellent fly fishing in August and September for 1 to 1½ pound rainbow and an occasional cutt or brookie. The next six miles above are only fair. There are no fish above the falls just above Hoadley Creek.

Split Rock Lake.
A shallow 90 acres, the largest in a whole string of ponds on Meadow (split Rock Coulee) Creek, extending 1¼ miles southwestward from Pishkun Reservoir. It's on federal, state and private grazing land, has lots of cattails and rushes around it, and is moderately popular the year around. The fishing is excellent (especially in the winter) for 10 to 11 inch yellow perch and is fair in summer for 18 to 20 inch (the recorded maximum is 32 pounds) northern pike. You can drive to it from the ditch road.

Sunny Slope Canal.
A large canal that carries irrigation water from Pishkun Reservoir to the Fairfield Bench. It can carry any of the several species of fish found in Pishkun Reservoir but also maintains a self sustaining grayling population. Although the canal is shut off in the fall, some isolated pools remain allowing the grayling to survive the winter.

Swazee Pond.
See Elk Ranch Pond.

Tunnell Lake.
A natural, 24 foot maximum depth, 20 acre, gravel bottomed lake on the east side of the Pishkun Canal road ¼ mile east of the "tunnel" in rolling grassland 5 miles west of the Reservoir. Has 2 pound cutts from plants up to 1979 but is now stocked (1980) with rainbow and is fair for 8 to 12 inchers.

West Fork of the South Fork of the Sun River.
Flows to the South Fork a mile above the Pretty Prairie Guard Station and is followed upstream by a good USFS pack trail 13 miles to headwaters below Cliff Mountain on the Continental Divide. From the Indian Point down (for almost 6 miles) there are lots of nice holes, wide gravel bars, and a wide open flood plain between timbered and grass-covered slopes. The fishing here is fairly good for 12 to 14 inch brook trout and pan-size rainbow. The lower mile is heavily fished but the rest of it only lightly if at all.

Willow Creek.
A small stream with lots of beaver ponds (and lots of brush around them) in mostly open pasture and farmland west and north of Augusta. The lower (fishable) reaches flow 10 miles east-northeastward from below McCarty Hill into the Willow Creek Reservoir and out the other side and then for another mile east to the Sun River 4 miles north by county road from Augusta. There are no roads along it, but it's crossed in a few places and there are cow trails, etc. It's moderately popular, fair fishing above but only poor below for 10 to 16 inch rainbow trout. It's mostly posted.

Willow Creek Reservoir.
A 1530 acre irrigation reservoir with a public campground on the southeast end, in rolling grass-covered hills reached by county roads 5 miles north from Augusta. It's popular (with water skiers, too) and pretty good fishing for rainbow 9 to 19 inches and an occasional brown to 20 inches. Trollers with cow bells and worms and fly fishermen do well here, not to mention ice fishermen with jigs or maggots in winter. Suspected to occasionally winterkill, the reservoir was stocked in 1980 with 75,000 little trout 4 inches long — cross your fingers.

Wood Creek.
The outlet of Wood Lake, followed by the Bench Mark road for 6½ miles northwestward down its timbered valley to junction with (barren) Straight Creek just above the Ranger Station. It's easily accessible, moderately popular, and fairly good fishing for pan-size rainbow and brook trout.

Wood Lake.
Lies south of the road in Wood Creek canyon 6 miles above Bench Mark and 1½ miles above Green Timber Lake. The north side is open along the road, the south side is in timber. It's quite shallow (mostly under 8 feet deep) and sometimes freezes out but has lots of feed and lots of fish, mostly 10 to 14 inch rainbow put-and-takers, but there are a few big ones too, although they're so well fed as to be hard to catch. The fishing pressure is extreme for this part of the country. In terms of recreation this is really a valuable piece of water. Oh yes; there's a very nice USFS campground for your pleasure.

Teton River

The Teton River is formed by its north and south forks coming off the east slope of the rocky mountain front approximately 25 miles west of Choteau. It meanders easterly about 175 miles to where it joins the Marias River at Loma.

Historically, the Teton produced good fishing, but nine major floods since the late 1800's have destroyed valuable habitat. Evidence of two recent floods, in 1964 and 1975, is plainly visible.

The river between Choteau and the mountains has been most affected by the floods. This section is characterized by gravelly soils which are easily eroded, and channels change frequently. This portion of river has stretches that fluctuate considerably or are completely dewatered at times due to irrigation demand. The fishery consists mostly of small brook trout, with a few rainbow, brown and whitefish. Rainbow and brown trout numbers and size increase near Choteau where stable water conditions are more likely.

The river below Choteau to its mouth is considerably more stable than above, with a more constant flow. Dewatered areas are not common except in the lower reaches. Fish populations in the first several miles consist of a few rainbow and brook trout, with greater numbers of brown trout and whitefish. Fish are considerably larger in this stretch than above Choteau, with some in the 2 to 4 pound class. Progressing downstream, a warm-water fishery develops, composed of sauger, burbot (ling), channel catfish and northern pike.Carp, goldeye and several sucker species are also common.

Bill Hill

Teton River Drainage

Arod (or Brady or Eyraud) Lakes, (or Kropps Reservoir). Eyraud was one of the early owners of three natural potholes now called Arod, or Brady Lakes, or Kropps Reservoir. To get there you drive 6 miles north from Choteau, turn right and drive 6 miles east, then north again for another 6½ miles to Farmers Coulee where you take a Montana Fish, Wildlife and Parks access road ½ mile east to the lower lake in open cultivated land. It's very irregularly shaped, about a mile long, as much as 25 feet deep near the dam at its lowest (east) end, and normally has about 10 feet of water-level fluctuation. It went completely dry in 1962. The two upper lakes are about ¼ and ⅜ of a mile to the south, about 10 acres each, and 10 to 15 feet deep. All three are fair-to-good fishing for 20 to 26 inch northern pike and 8 to 12½ inch yellow perch (really nice ones). The lower lake is however by far the best fishing, with a pike to brag on being caught now and again. Most people fish here and picnic at the upper reservoir at the MDFWP facilities. (No camping.) Note: There's been a lot of driving across the owner's fields around and about and if it doesn't stop pronto, likely everyone will be booted off.

Brady Lakes. See Arod Lakes.

Bynum Reservoir. Built in 1910; when full, about 4000 acres (2½ by 3 miles), with a 30 foot maximum depth (mostly 15 feet deep, though), behind a ½ mile long earth dam in open rangeland 5 miles by county road southwest from Bynum, this irrigation reservoir has just recently improved access now with a State-acquired right of way to it. It is somewhat turbid most of the time, receives water from the Teton River, and has up and down water levels, dropping to about 8 feet in dry years. Was rehabilitated in 1961 and is planted annually with small rainbow trout now, heavily fished for good catches of mostly 10 to 12 with some up to 16 inch fish. Kokanee plants were discontinued in 1978 but some are taken still (to 3 pounds); whitefish to 1½ pounds are also fairly common. Brown trout are being recommended to try in here (maybe they'll eat on those longnose and white suckers, huh!).

Clark Fork Muddy Creek. Heads on Choteau Mountain and flows east for 11 miles to junction with (barren) Rinkers Creek to form the South Fork Muddy Creek. The Clark Fork is good and muddy as well as brushy and mostly on posted land. The lower and middle reaches are, however, accessible by a truck road and are sometimes fished a little for poor catches of pan-size brook trout.

Cow Creek. Heads below Volcano Reef on National Forest land and flows east through rolling hills for 9 miles to the North Fork Muddy Creek. There are lots of willow and jackbrush along it, and it's crossed and followed here and there by jeep roads. The upper reaches are fair-to-good fishing for 6 to 8 inch cutthroat; the middle reaches are good for mostly small brook and some rainbow trout; the lower reaches are heavily silted and oftentimes go dry.

Deep Creek. A brushy, willowed-up, easily wadeable little stream, about 20 miles long from the junction of its North and South Forks, eastward through open grazing land to its mouth on the Teton River 1¼ miles south-southeast of Choteau. It's crossed here and there by county roads, and is fished a little for an occasional 7 to 8 inch rainbow — and even fewer brook trout and whitefish, along with an overabundance of rough fish.

Eureka Lake (or Reservoir). One and a quarter miles long by a quarter mile wide, in open rangeland just north of (and fed by) the Teton River; reached by a paved road 8 miles northwest from Choteau. It has a maximum depth of about 35 feet; water level fluctuations of as much as 10 feet; and a nice campground maintained by the Dept. of Fish Wildlife and Parks. It has been rehabilitated several times, the last time 1977 with rainbow trout. It is about 275 surface acres in size, and is very heavily used, being good for 7 to 18 inch rainbow, and a few browns to 18 inches. The survival rate of the trout is excellent but the growth is now rated as slow, although some (a few) to 4 pounds are taken. The rainbow are stocked annually at about the 4 inch size (in 1980, 50,000). Some brown trout stocking is also being considered (perhaps to cut down the sucker population?). The lake is also used somewhat for waterskiing and swimming.

Courtesy Ernst Peterson

FISHIN' HIGH COUNTRY
Courtesy Bill Browning

Eyraud Lakes. See Arod Lakes.

Green Gulch. A small, 4 miles long, northward flowing tributary of the South Fork Teton River; reached at the mouth by the South Fork road 5½ miles above the Ear Mountain Guard Station and followed by a USFS pack trail up the east side of its narrow, timbered canyon to headwaters. It's not much of a creek and provides very little fishing except in some brushy beaver ponds about 3 miles upstream. Here you will find a few 6 to 8 inch brook trout — and even fewer fishermen.

Hidden (or Our) Lake. About 5 acres, good and deep with steep dropoffs; in timber on the east side but below cliffs and steep rocky slopes on around with a 300 foot falls at the outlet. Hidden Lake lies just east of the drainage divide between Old Baldy and Rocky Mountain; is reached by a good USFS trail 2¼ miles west and 1500 feet above the end of the South Fork Teton jeep road; was planted with cutthroat away back in the '30s and '40s, "reportedly" with rainbow in the '50s, and with cutthroat again in the '70s. It is fair-to-very good indeed at times for 8 to 12 inch fish — and a very popular spot.

Kropps Reservoir. See Arod Lakes.

McDonald Creek. A very small but fairly popular stream that heads in open rangeland north of Pine Butte and mostly accessible by cow trails and private jeep roads along its entire length (9 miles), east to the Teton River a couple of miles west of Eureka Reservoir. There are a lot of brushy beaver ponds along it that provide fair catches of 6 to 8 inch brookies — plus an occasional cutthroat and/or rainbow trout.

Middle Fork Teton River. Heads below Teton Peak and flows 5 miles east down its fairly brushy, timbered canyon to the North Fork just below Wind Mountain. It's followed all the way by a good USFS horse trail; there are beaver ponds along it here and there for the first couple of miles and it's fair fishing from about a mile above them clear to the mouth — mostly for 8 to 10 inch rainbow plus a few cutthroat and brook trout. The trail is mostly used by parties passing through and the creek isn't fished much.

Muddy Creek. Is formed by the junction of its North Fork and (barren) South Fork 3 miles northeast of Bynum Reservoir, and flows eastward through flat open rangeland for 30 miles to the Teton River 3 miles east of Collins. It's all silted up; sometimes goes almost completely dry; is mostly on posted land and supports only a very few 8 to 9 inch brook trout but a fair population of shiners and other rough fish. It is crossed by state and county roads here and there along its course and needless to say — is seldom bothered.

277

OUR (OR HIDDEN) LAKE
Courtesy USFS

FREEZE
Courtesy USFS

North Fork Deep Creek.
Take the South Fork road to where it "hits" the creek and then fish upstream one mile or so to its junction with the North Fork. There is no road or trail up the creek but the lower 3½ miles or so are in open grazing land, and are poor fishing for 8 to 10 inch rainbow trout and a few cutthroat. Few fishermen are allowed in — anyway, it is posted.

North Fork Muddy Creek.
Is formed by the junction of Cow Creek and Gansman Coulee, and flows eastward through open rangeland for 8 miles to the main creek 3 miles northeast of Bynum Reservoir. It's accessible here and there by road but is very badly silted up and oftentimes goes almost dry. There is a little poor fishing (at times it's good) in the upper reaches for pan-size brook and some real nice rainbow trout — but it's seldom taken advantage of.

North Fork Teton River.
Heads on Bloody Hill in the Great Bear Wilderness Area and is followed by a good pack trail for 6 miles to the West Fork Guard Station and then by a USFS road for 13 miles down its steep timbered canyon south and east to junction with the South Fork at the head of the main river, 22 miles west by county road. It shows the effects of recent floods and is poor at best and only lightly fished — for mostly rainbow, cutthroat and a few brook trout.

North Fork Willow Creek.
A private farmland, brushy little stream that heads on Ear Mountain and flows eastward for 10 miles past Pine Butte to the main creek where it's reached by a county road 15 miles west from Choteau. It's easily accessible (with permission) all along, is moderately popular and fair fishing for mostly 8 to 10 inch rainbow and brook trout — plus an occasional "good" one.

Our Lake.
See Hidden Lake.

South Fork Deep Creek.
A small, brushy, grazing land stream in the lower reaches; reached by a county road 25 miles west from Choteau or about the same distance north-northeast from Augusta. The lower 3½ miles are followed by a jeep road and then there is a good USFS trail on upstream. There are some steep cataracts 5 miles above the mouth and from there on down it is moderately popular but generally only poor fishing for 8 to 10 inch rainbow and a few cutthroat trout. It is "posted" and few fishermen are allowed.

South Fork Teton River.
Heads below Rocky Mountain and is followed by a good horse trail for 3 miles south — then by gravel roads 7 miles east to join the North Fork 22 miles west by county roads from Choteau. It flows down a narrow timbered canyon above, and out across open grazing land below where it's quite brushy, moderately popular, but only poor fishing at best for 10 to 11 inch rainbow along with a few small cutthroat and brook trout.

MOUNTAIN MOOSE
Courtesy USFS

South Fork Willow Creek. Heads at 7000 feet elevation between Ear and Chute Mountains, and flows south-east-north and again east for 15 miles to junction with the North Fork at the head of the main stream 15 miles by county road west from Choteau. The lower 6 miles are mostly on private farmland accessible here and there by county roads. It's quite brushy here but moderately popular and fair fishing for rainbow and brook trout that will average about 9 inches plus a few a little bigger.

Spring Creek. A small, seldom-fished-except-by-kids, farmland stream that flows right through Choteau to the Teton River. It's stocked with rainbow in town and fished heavily too, by "kids only." The water just above and below town is also very good for small brook trout and a few rainbow — except in dry years when the whole shebang gets real low.

West Fork Teton River. A small brushy stream, crossed at its mouth by the North Fork Teton River road ½ mile below the Ranger Station, and followed by a good USFS pack trail for 5 miles up its timbered canyon past Empty Jug Cabin to headwaters and on over Teton Pass. The lower 2½ miles are sometimes fished for small rainbow, cutthroat and a few brook trout.

Willow Creek. Heads a few miles east of Pine Butte at the junction of its North and South Forks and flows eastward for about 10 miles to Deep Creek 6 miles southwest from Choteau by county roads. It's a real brushy stream, mostly on private farmland but moderately popular and fair fishing for 8 to 10 inch rainbow and brook trout — plus an occasional good one to keep you on your toes.

A YELLOWSTONE FISHERMAN
Courtesy U.S. Fish and Wildlife

The Yellowstone River
Park Line to Springdale

A good trout stream ought to be fed by mountain snowmelt to keep it fast-running and cold. It ought to run a course with rapids and holes and riffles and long, flat stretches of water – the type of water fishermen find hard to fish and trout find easy to live in. A good trout stream ought to be able to absorb year around fishing and support the complex food chain that makes it possible. And of course the stream ought to have trout; lots of them. The upper Yellowstone has all this on a magnificent scale. It is a prime example of what a river ought to be.

The Yellowstone makes its Montana debut near Gardiner and flows through a narrow valley before entering Yankee Jim Canyon. Steep walls force the channel a bit to the northwest as the water cascades through white water rapids into deep holes. Emptying into Paradise Valley, the river assumes a northeasterly direction. A series of long, flat runs broken by shallow riffles dominate this stretch, and backwater pockets abound where the river flows around boulders. Near Livingston the river turns briefly to more violent, fast water rapids with holes that make excellent cover for the rainbows and browns. Beyond Livingston the stream gradually flattens and rolls eastward, still cold and fast, but always hinting at the prairie river it will become.

Throughout the section between Gardiner and Springdale the Yellowstone takes on over three dozen tributaries. Mountain streams born in the snowmelt of the Absaroka and Gallatin ranges improve the water quality through Paradise Valley. The Shields River drains the Crazy Mountains and enters from the north below Livingston. This input of mountain water does more than its share to help the upper Yellowstone earn its designation as "blue ribbon" trout water. The 103 mile section is the longest continuous stretch of thus-classified stream in the state and comprises nearly a fourth of Montana's blue ribbon water. Add to these characteristics an abundance of natural feed and it's little wonder the upper Yellowstone's trout population is one of the greatest in the nation.

Brown trout dominate the upper river around Corwin springs and they reach lunker size around Emigrant. The hard to catch, rock-rolling browns feed heavily on mottled sculpins and stone fly larva. Fishermen duplicating natural bait have fair summer fishing for browns up to 4 pounds, with action really picking up in early fall. Cool nights, clear water and frenzied spawning activity combine to give fall fly fishermen the sort of angling memories are made of.

Rainbows share the stream with browns along the entire route. Their numbers increase dramatically, outnumbering the browns by two to one around Livingston. The rough water provides excellent cover for trout, and the acrobatic rainbow takes full advantage of it. A fisherman stands a better chance of catching not only more trout here, but more big trout than elsewhere along the route. Below Livingston trout density declines somewhat, but fishing is still fine for both browns and rainbows.

In the upper river, near the Park line, native Yellowstone cutthroat lay tentative claim to their original niche, though not in the numbers they once did. Cutthroat to 14 inches can be caught high in the stream, but their population decreases accordingly downstream, due primarily to irrigation dewatering in tributaries that once served as spawning beds. A cutthroat caught in the Springdale area is now a rarity.

The Yellowstone's only other native fish, the mouintain whitefish, suffers no such humiliation. The whitefish is the most abundant of fish in the upper Yellowstone. Although they have been the object of more than one oath uttered by dedicated trout fishermen, whitefishing goes a long way toward taking the doldrums out of winter.

That the Yellowstone is a river for all seasons is not the least of what makes it great. Early spring and fall finds the stream clear and wadeable. During the peak run-off in June and early July, bait fishermen hit backwaters with more than limited success. The entire course of the upper Yellowstone is ideally suited for float fishing, and more anglers each year take advantage of the strong summer flow to guide their craft past pocket water and riffles to pick out rainbows and browns waiting there. It would not be difficult at all to spend a year, or a lifetime, on the upper Yellowstone. It is after all, a great beginning to a terrific river.

Jerry Brekke

Springdale to Clark's Fork

Count the number of boats bobbing along the blue ribbon water of the upper Yellowstone some August day and you'd think there was no other water on the river worthy of a float trip. Consider the Yellowstone between Springdale and the mouth of the Clark's Fork, however, and you'll change your mind. Still truly a mountain stream as far as Columbus, the river tends to run deeper along a broadening channel and the longer rolling stretches are more suited to float fishing than wading. A number of bridge crossings and state fishing access sites along the route enhance shore fishing and are spaced at intervals to accommodate float trips of nearly any length.

Between Springdale and the old Highway 10 bridge below Reedpoint, for example, an angler may choose from five access points to begin or end a float. Grey Bear fishing access lies about ten river miles below Springdale, or a boater can continue another 21 miles to Greycliff access. Bratten and Indian Fort fishing access sites break up the distance between Greycliff and the Highway 10 bridge. Cuttthroat to two pounds can be caught on occasion between Springdale and Big Timber. But brown and rainbow trout dominate the entire fifty mile stretch, with Yellowstone's usual abundance of mountain whitefish.

It takes a good person on the oars and a better one at the end of a rod to boat fish between the Highway 10 bridge and Hensley Creek and Cove ditch below Columbus. Ling (burbot), which make their initial appearance in the Springdale to Reedpoint stretch, become abundant now and reach a size of 10 pounds. Their size comes in second to this area's trout, though, with a recent reported rainbow of 12½ pounds and browns to 9½ pounds.

Trout size diminishes a bit between Hensley Creek and Buffalo Mirage fishing access, but there is fair fishing for browns and rainbows in the three- to five-pound class and ling (burbot) to seven pounds. A couple of boating hazards in this stretch are noteworthy. A quarter mile below Henley Creek you can avoid a hazard by floating the river's south shore, and about five miles further the current makes a sharp bend against a rock wall opposite Westover Isle. Stay on the north side of the main channel to avoid this one.

Beyond Buffalo Mirage, trout populations begin to thin as you progress downstream. The Yellowstone here becomes a prairie river. There are still another four access sites to accommodate fishermen between Laurel and Billings. Downstream from Billings Huntley Diversion Dam is a dangerous boating hazard, especially for non-powered craft, and those free-floaters who value life and limb should take advantage of the boat takeout below the east bridge at Billings.

Between Springdale and the mouth of Clark's Fork, the Yellowstone divests itself of the mountains, takes on the responsibilities of agriculture and industry, and becomes more cosmopolitan in nature. Although you won't find the massive trout concentrations of the upper river here, the section is still an exuberant, vital trout stream, and it could probably stand more fishing than it gets.

Jerry Brekke with Steve Swedberg

Clark's Fork to North Dakota Line

While the stretch of the Yellowstone River from Clark's Fork to the Bighorn can't be considered in the same category as the cold, gin-clear trout waters upstream, a good fishery exists. This reach of the Yellowstone is a transitional zone, changing from cold-water dominance to warm-water dominance.

Rainbows, browns, and whitefish are still abundant and an angler can easily "limit out" while in the city limits of Billings. Season this catch with burbot (ling), sauger, and channel catfish and the joys of total angling become a reality.

Fishing in the lower Yellowstone – downstream from the Big Horn – is akin to playing roulette in Las Vegas: with the number of angling opportunities available, you never know what you might pull in. This warm-water giant that meanders lazily across Montana's prairie is home to a more diverse community of game and non-game fish than its cold headwaters. Over 40 species of fish are known to dwell in the lower Yellowstone. Among these are nine species of game fish, ranging from the relic paddlefish to the sleek walleye to the snaky burbot (ling).

Although the usual angling technique for most of these fish is nothing more than still-fishing, drifting a worm or minnow at the foot of a riffle or the mouth of a back water, that is more a matter of tradition than of necessity. Sauger, walleye, northern pike, smallmouth bass, goldeye and even channel cats will smack any lure that resembles a minnow. Setlines, offering the angler up to six opportunities to catch a fish, are also legal.

While anglers push and shove to get a chance at Montana's blue ribbon trout streams, the prairie streams go almost unnoticed. As a result, these waters offer not only good fishing, but also peace and quiet, with little or no competition from fellow anglers. The warm-water streams of the lower Yellowstone guarantee a quality and variety of fishing available in few other places in the United States. Whether you go after ling, smallmouth or sturgeon, once you have fished the plains that rise to meet the Rockies, you'll ask why they've been neglected by anglers for so long.

Al Elser

Yellowstone River Drainage

Aldridge Lake. A narrow, 75 acre, ⅓ of a mile long reservoir behind a 6 foot earth dam in open sagebrush flats, reached by a poor private road ½ mile southeast from the Mol Heron Creek road a couple of miles up from that stream's mouth. The lake has a maximum depth of about 35 feet and the water is murky due to excessive amounts of vegetation. If you get the chance, it's good fishing for 10 to 14 inch rainbow and cutthroat that were stocked in 1978 and 1981.

Alkali Creek. See Clear Creek.

Anderson Creek. A small stream flowing down a steep timbered gorge for 4 miles from its headwaters on the western slopes of Pyramid Mountain — west and then south to Mill Creek, 3 miles by trail above the Mill Creek campground (accessible by road). It's seldom fished, but there is a sheepherder's trail up it for about a mile of poor-to-fair fishing for camp-fare cutthroat trout.

Armstrong Spring Creek. Take U.S. 89 south from Livingston for 4 miles to Carter's Bridge where you leave the main highway and proceed on up the same (west) side of the Yellowstone River to Armstrong Spring and about 2 miles of the top fishing water in the nation, in open river-bottom rangeland. The creek is a novel trout stream for the expert fly fisherman and supports an enormous population of wild trout, many of which range to 4 or 5 pounds. The food is so abundant that even the larger trout live on tiny insects and will readily take no. 16-20 flies. There is no longer a hatchery on the creek, but the rainbow are more abundant (3-1) than the brown trout presently because of many "escapees" in the past. The number of "rods" on the creek is regulated. The current fee is $20.00 a day per rod with reservations the rule — mostly tourists fish here.

Basin Creek. Flows for 5 miles through open rolling foothill country down the east side of the Crazy Mountains — to Sweet Grass Creek about 7 miles northwest from Melville. The lower couple of miles are never more than a few hundred yards hike from the road, are moderately popular, and are excellent fishing for 8 and 9 inch brook trout, plus a fair number of brown and rainbow trout.

Bear Creek. Heads in Fish Lake, in high alpine country below (south of) Monitor Peak and flows south for 10 miles to the Yellowstone River a couple of miles east of Gardiner. The lower 3 miles are accessible by a good road (as far upstream as Jardine) and the upper reaches by a USFS pack trail. The upper reaches are quite small, the lower reaches were polluted with arsenic from the Jardine mine dumps. Since the cleanup of water from old dumps it's fair fishing for 8 to 10 inch rainbow and cutthroat trout. Brown trout and whitefish are caught in the lower reaches. It's not heavily used.

Big Creek. Is crossed at the mouth by road 7 miles up the west side of the Yellowstone River from St. Johns (at the bridge) and is followed upstream by road for 4½ miles through open range and timber (rattlesnake infested) country to the Big Creek campground. A trail takes you on for 9½ miles through alpine "parky" country to headwaters. The lower reaches are easily, but only lightly fished for fair catches of mostly 6 to 10 inch rainbow-cutthroat hybrid. The upper reaches are fair for cutthroat trout. The first 2 miles are posted and somewhat dewatered in season.

Big Bull Elk Creek. A fairly small stream with about 10 miles of fishing water flowing north down a rough, rocky, rattlesnake infested canyon through some pretty rough country in the northern Bighorn Mountains to the Yellowtail Reservoir. There is no trail and it has long been closed to the public by the Crow Indians — but since the building of Yellowtail Dam you can reach it by boat. Fishing is fair at the mouth for rainbow and brown trout to 2 or 3 pounds.

CAPITOL ROCK
Courtesy USFS

LITTLE BIG HORN
Courtesy Bill Browning

Big Drop Reservoir. This year round fishery is located about 20 miles south of Glendive on BLM land in the cedar creek drainage. Access is good year round as is the fishing for rainbow trout that are planted annually and will run up to 3 pounds.

Bighorn Lakes. See Yellowtail Reservoir.

Bighorn Reservoir. See Yellowtail Reservoir.

Bighorn River. This meandering lowland river flows 84 miles before emptying into the Yellowstone River between Custer and Bighorn, having originated (in Montana, that is) at the Yellowtail Afterbay Dam located at Fort Smith. After Yellowtail Dam was built in 1965, the resulting cooler water temperature turned this wide wadeable (carefully) river into a high quality trophy trout "classic." The excellence of the fishing, especially when floating and/or fly fishing, has earned the Bighorn River national recognition and acclaim. The river supports good vegetation and steady insect hatches. The largest problem here is access, since most of its upper 48 miles flow through the Crow Indian Reservation and other private lands. Regulations also bear watching as they vary along the stream.

The fame of the river lies in the consistently large trout caught here — mostly browns with some rainbow averaging 2 to 4 pounds. This excellent water also gives up an occasional 8 to 10 pound battling brown or jumping rainbow, especially in the upper reach to Two Leggins and the middle reach down to Hardin. The third reach, from Hardin on down, due to increased sediment and higher water temperature is only fair for planted rainbow and a few browns. In summer, this stretch is good for channel cats to over 20 pounds and in spring for sauger and burbot.

Access being of utmost importance, listed below by Steve Swedberg of the MFW&P are the seven public access sites on the river:

Afterbay Dam — An NPS-USBR facility. There are toilets and parking areas immediately below the dam on both sides of the river; on the north side there is a boat ramp. An airfield for small aircraft is located on the north side of the Yellowtail Afterbay Reservoir and is within walking distance of the river.

John Linds — Take gravel road 3 miles below Fort Smith for ¾-mile, turn left at corner and drive ½-mile to the river (3¾ miles by boat). An NPS area, undeveloped, with a small boat takeout.

Bighorn Fishing Access — Located 13 miles below Fort Smith (about 11½ miles by boat). A MFW&P area with toilet, parking, camping and boat launching facilities — YOU pack out garbage.

Two Leggins — Eight miles southwest of Hardin at the Two Leggins Bridge, located above the bridge on the north side of the river (about 21 miles below the Bighorn Fishing Access). A MFW&P area and undeveloped with small boat takeout. Floaters — caution — a low diversion dam is ¾-mile above Two Leggins Bridge and immediately below the old county bridge.

Arapooish — Take Hardin-Custer highway north out of Hardin for 1¾ miles, turn right and go 1½ miles and then take a left and go ½-mile. A MFW&P area that is undeveloped — has small bass pond and small boats can be launched at the river.

Grant Marsh — Go 8 miles north of Hardin on the Hardin-Custer highway, then take gravel road east one mile. A MFW&P undeveloped area with natural sites for launching boats.

Manuel Lisa — At the freeway bridge between Custer and Bighorn. A 38 acre MFW&P area with toilet and small boat takeout. Floaters — caution — there are two irrigation diversion dams between this access and the Grant Marsh Access. Kemph Dam is about 18¾ river miles below Grant Marsh and Manning Dam is about 9 river miles below Kemph Dam.

Big Timber Creek.

The outlet of Pear, Druckenmiller (barren), Granite, Thunder, Blue and Twin (barren) Lakes, all clustered around Granite Peak in the central Crazy Mountains. The upper reaches are too fast and cold for fish; the lower reaches are muddled up and dewatered for irrigation. There used to be, however, about 2 miles of pretty fair fishing in the narrow mountain valley above and below the Big Timber campground — which is reached by road 20 miles or so northwest from the town of Big Timber. However, the flood of 1972 pretty well washed everything out and ruined the fishing. It's only fair for eastern brook 6 to 10 inches and a few rainbow and brown trout.

Billman Creek.

Heads on Bozeman Pass and flows eastward through hilly farmland along U.S. 10 for 11 miles to the Yellowstone River on the outskirts of Livingston. There are lots of willows all along and they make it difficult to fish (not many people do). The lower 8 miles are poor-to-fair for 8 to 10 inch cutthroat-rainbow hybrids and an occasional brook or brown trout.

Black Canyon Creek.

A small stream, about 10 miles of fishing water here, on the Crow Indian Reservation and closed to the public. It flows north down a real rugged canyon (lots of rattles if you're tired of fishing) and debouches directly into the Yellowtail Reservoir where you'll reach it by boat. It's fair now for brown and rainbow to 2 or 3 pounds. The best fishing is at Black Canyon Campground.

Blue Lake.

Follow the outlet of Granite Lake a couple of hundred yards east to this 18 acre lake that is fairly deep on the west side beneath scattered alpine timber, is bordered by talus slopes and cliffs on around, and is usually no better than fair fishing for skinny 8 to 10 inch cutthroat plus an occasional lunker to a couple of pounds — stocked in 1977 and 1981. It's mostly fished by dudes.

Bridger Creek.

Take U.S. 10 for 16 miles east from Big Timber to the mouth of Bridger Creek on the Yellowstone River, and then a gravel road south along it for 12 miles or so. There are some beaver ponds about 4 miles up from the mouth, below which the stream dries up in the summer. The next 5 or 6 miles of this small cottonwood, chokecherry bordered stream are in open rangeland (much of it posted) and are good fishing for 4 to 8 inch brookies and a few brown trout. It would not stand much fishing pressure.

Buffalo Fork Creek.

Flows south from the junction of the East and West Forks (elevation 9031 feet) through a series of mountain meadows interspersed with short canyons for 7½ miles to Yellowstone Park (elevation 7535 feet). It is mostly in the Absaroka Primitive area, is followed the full length by a good USFS pack trail 6 miles north from the Slough Creek road (in the Park), and is moderately popular and good fishing for 6 to 18 inch cutthroat-rainbow — all hybrids.

Camp Reservoir.

Located on BLM land about 20 miles south on Glendive in the Cedar Creek Drainage with good access. Planted annually with rainbow that grow fast here, it's a popular spot and good fishing.

Campfire (or Hindu) Lake.

A deep, 20 acre lake in a barren glacial cirque reached by trail 7 miles west above the end of the Sweet Grass Creek road — or — you can come in by trail 6 miles north above the end of the Cottonwood Creek road in the Shields River drainage — or — 4 miles east above the end of the Elk Creek road, likewise in the Shields River drainage. It's fair for cutthroat trout 8 to 12 inches stocked in 1980. It's moderately popular and you may catch a larger rainbow if they haven't died off.

Carpenter Lake.

An excellent lake that is heavily fished (for this part of the country) for 10 to 14 inch cutthroat trout. It's about 10 acres, fairly deep but with shallow dropoffs, in dense timber but with open shores on the north side, and is an easy day's horseback ride in from the end of the Mill Creek road on up the Wallace Creek trail over Wallace Pass and down the Grizzly Creek trail about 15 miles.

Castle Rock Lake (Colstrip Surge Pond). About 170 acres, 70 feet deep maximum, located at the town of Colstrip, with a nice public recreation area developed by Montana Power Co. The lake produces good catches of northern pike to 10 pounds, walleye to 4 pounds, crappie, smallmouth bass recently planted and bluegills (pounders, easy to catch). There is good reproduction, promising fine future angling.

Cave Lake. Take the Middle Fork Sweet Grass Creek trail for 1 mile above the end of the road to the mouth of Milly Creek, and then an old unmaintained (and in places invisible) trail over rocks and deadfalls up that drainage southwest for 3 miles to the shore. It's 22 acres, good fishing at times for 8 to 12 inch cutthroat, stocked in 1980, and very seldom visited.

Cayuse Creek. A small, heavily fished open pastureland stream flowing southeastward to Sweet Grass Creek about 5 miles southeast of Melville. It's crossed by Montana State Highway 18 a short way north of Melville, and is excellent fishing downstream for 8 to 10 inch rainbow, and 11 to 12 inch (maximum 5 pounds) brown trout.

Charlie White Lake. The northwest end of this 8 acre lake is an open swampy area, the lower (and fairly deep) southeast end is in dense timber. The outlet (West Fork Horse Creek) drops very rapidly below the lake and there is no trail along it. There are several trails almost to the lake, though. Perhaps the shortest route is 8 miles by the Bear Creek trail above the footbridge near Jardine — to the head of the West Fork Horse Creek and then 1½ miles down that creek to the shore; or you can come in on the Ash Mountain-Hellroaring Creek trail from Yellowstone Park; or up the West Fork Mill-Monitor Creek trail. Once there you'll have only an occasional sheepherder for company, but it's good fishing for 8 to 10 inch cutthroat trout.

Chico Lake. The 30 yards or so across, water supply for Chico Hot Springs just up the hill behind the lodge. It was planted with brook trout years ago and is deep enough to keep from freezing out so that there are still some swimming around. But you can't catch 'em. It's posted.

Cinnabar Creek. A small, swift, clear stream formed by the junction of Lion Creek (which is too small and steep for fish) and Mill Creek. It flows north and east for 3½ miles through heavily timbered mountains above, and "park and timber" below to Mol Heron Creek a couple of miles above that stream's mouth on the Yellowstone River. There's a road up it all the way and quite a few beaver dams near the headwaters — which are only lightly fished and poor for 6 to 10 inch rainbow trout.

Clark's Reservoir. In open rangeland on the Cherry Creek drainage near Little Sheep Mountain about 20 miles west-northwest from Terry — which is about midway between Miles City and Glendive on U.S. 10. Clark's Reservoir is 18 acres in size, only about 8 feet deep on an average but as much as 15 feet at the maximum and was rehabilitated and planted with rainbow in 1981 — should be a winner soon.

Clear (or Alkali) Creek. A small stream about 14 miles long in a narrow "hayfield-bottomed" valley but with lots of brush and willows along its banks; parallel to and about a mile east of Rock Creek which it joins 8 miles above Boyd. The lower 9 miles are heavily fished but only poor to fair fishing for 8 to 10 inch brook, a few brown and rainbow trout.

Cokedale (or Miner) Creek. Heads in some springs below Center Hill and flows east through brush and open rangeland for 6 miles to Billman Creek 4 miles west via U.S. 10 from Livingston. The lower 4 miles are followed all along (past lots of beaver ponds) by road and they're easily fished (but lightly) for good catches of 6 to 10 inch brookies and cutthroat trout.

Colstrip Surge Pond. See Castle Rock Lake.

Cow Creek Pond or Reservoir. Drive 3 miles east from Ashland to the Otter Creek road, then 20 plus miles to the Cow Creek road (half a mile south of the Fort Howe Ranger Station). Drive on up the creek for maybe 5 miles to the Cow Creek campground. This one acre or so spring-fed reservoir is right in this nice little family-type campground with lots of shade trees, the best drinking water in the country, and is good rainbow angling by mostly local folks for 8 to 12 inchers on up to 3 or 4 pounds.

GRIZZLY TRACKS — GOD ALMIGHTY!
Courtesy Bridenstine Studio

PURTY, AIN'T THEY!
Courtesy U.S. Fish and Wildlife

Crazy Lake. Take the Big Timber Creek road 12 miles north from the town of Big Timber, then the South Fork jeep road 5½ miles west, and finally "shanks' mares" for 6 miles on upstream cross-country to the shore just below Crazy Peak (elevation 11,214 feet). Don't confuse it with the 2½ acre barren pothole ¼ of a mile below. It's a good 15 acres in size, deep with steep dropoffs below talus slopes all around, and is very seldom, if ever, visited although fair-to-good fishing at times for 8 to 14 inch cutts stocked in 1978.

Crisafulli Reservoir. At the Cottonwood Golf Course in open "badland" country about 3 miles east of Glendive; about 8 acres, mostly 6 to 8 feet deep with a maximum of about 14 feet; it's good "kids" fishing for 6 to 8 inch bullheads, bluegill, and other species — a hodge-podge.

Crooked Creek. Flows south and east, mostly in Montana through a narrow sheer-walled canyon, for 18 miles from the Pryor Mountains to the Bighorn River 10 miles south of Millsboro in Wyoming. There are several points of access via game trails — the one at the Wyoming Campground is perhaps the best known. The stream is quite brushy but moderately popular and good fishing for 8 to 9 inch cutthroat above, and brook trout below.

Crystal Lake. Take the Mill Creek trail for about 2 miles above Agate Springs to the 3rd drainage coming in from the north. Follow it up keeping always to the left hand (West Fork) for another couple of miles to this 5 acre lake in a little glacial cirque at 9350 feet above sea level. It's hardly ever fished but was planted with cutthroat in 1976 and 1981 — should be good as of right now.

Cutler Lake. This one used to have a few BIG rainbow trout in it — and just possibly may still have. It's a long narrow 5 acre pothole with lots of rushes around it in open sagebrush country right beside a county road along the west side of the Yellowstone River 4 miles north and across the river from Corwin Springs. It's seldom, if ever, bothered any more. The last I heard it was full of stunted perch.

Daily Lake. Lies 1½ miles east of the Yellowstone River in sagebrush-grassland foothill country at 5000 feet elevation; reached by a good dirt road 5½ miles south from the Historical Marker on the east side of U.S. 89, 25 miles south of Livingston. It's 204 acres in area, a maximum of 24 feet deep but mostly shallow, though with relatively steep dropoffs at the north end. It is good early season fishing and very popular for mostly 7 to 8 inch yellow perch, 10 to 12 inch rainbow trout, and walleyed pike to 15 inches. It's fed by springs, run-off, and a ditch canal from Six Mile Creek. There's a campground out in the open. Watch out for the skiers.

Deer Creek (Upper and Lower). Are ten-twelve miles east of Big Timber, drain into the south side of the Yellowstone, are mostly on private land except at headwaters, fair fishing for 6 to 10 inch brook and a few cutthroat trout, have trails up each of them (horse) and roads lower down are in timber above and rangeland below — mostly fished in upper reaches in rough mountainous country (lots of deer and bear here) on USFS land. Most people miss them.

De-Puy's Hatchery. Originally a hatchery but now a series of ponds for "guest" fishing only — on the west side of the Yellowstone River 7 miles south of Livingston by U.S. 89, county and private roads. See listing for Armstrong Spring Creek.

Dredge Hole. Take a good gravel road a couple of miles south from Chico Hot Springs to this old abandoned borrow pit in open grassland about three miles east of the Yellowstone River (no signs). It's about a quarter the size of a city block, deep and steep-sided all around except on the east end where there is a big sand bar. The local youngsters — and most everyone else — use it for swimming. It also contains a few brookies but hasn't much of a reputation.

Dry Head Creek. A moderately popular stream that heads on the northern slopes of the Pryor Mountains and flows 20 miles east to the Bighorn River 12 miles upstream (as the crow flies) from Old Fort Smith. It's crossed by a road at the old Dry Head Ranch below which is excellent fishing for rainbow, brown and some cutthroat. In the past trout to 8 pounds were caught. It's on Crow tribal land — no permits currently are sold.

Duck Creek. Is only a couple of miles long from the junction of its East and West forks to the Yellowstone River 2 miles east of Springdale across the river (north) from U.S. 10. It's all in open rangeland easily accessible by jeep roads, has quite a few willows along it and lots of beaver ponds in it that are seldom fished but do support a poor to fair population of 6 to 8 inch trout.

East Bridger Creek. A "private land" creek on sheep and cattle range. Only the lower half mile runs all summer and there are a few pools above for a total of maybe a mile of poor fishing for small brook trout. It's reached (should you be still interested) at the mouth by the Bridger Creek road 1½ miles above the mouth of West Bridger Creek.

East Fork Mill Creek. A small stream that is crossed at the mouth by the Mill Creek road and paralleled by road for 2 miles to the Snowy Range Ranch — and then by trail for 7 miles of nice easy hiking or riding up a timbered gorge to headwaters below Boulder Mountain. A fair number of people fish it and the lower 7 miles have a good reputation for 9 to 10 inch cutthroat, plus a few rainbow and brook trout.

East Fork Sweet Grass Creek. A small stream flowing westward through open rangeland to Sweet Grass Creek 8 miles up from that stream's mouth. All but the lower couple of miles go dry in summer (robbed for irrigation) and is all muddied up. It contains only a very few brook trout in the lower reaches and is very seldom fished.

Eight Mile Creek. A small, clear, swift stream, 8 miles long, the headwaters in timbered hill country, the lower reaches in the Yellowstone bottomland 5 miles or so north of Emigrant. There's a private road the first 3 miles upstream and then a posted trail, because of which it is seldom fished. Just as well too because it's no better than fair for mostly 8 to 10 inch brookies, 9 to 14 inch cutts and some rainbow to 10 inches.

Elbow Creek. So called for its right angle turn to the north after leaving the foothills (from the east) of the Absaroka Range. The lower reaches are completely dewatered for irrigation, but if you hike upstream for about a mile above the end of the road (which leaves U.S. 89 some 3½ miles above the Rosedale School) you'll come to a small gorge that extends on for another mile to the "elbow." In this region the creek is lined with willows and cottonwood and, though seldom fished, it supports a fair population of 8 to 10 inch cutthroat.

Elk Creek. A small westward flowing stream that heads below Hummingbird Peak in the Absaroka Range and joins Hellroaring Creek 1¼ miles above the Ranger Station. There's maybe a mile of timbered valley directly above the mouth, and then another mile of open meadows (accessible by trail from Hellroaring Creek). There are some nice holes in the meadow land reaches that are fair fishing — though seldom fished — for 6 to 8 inch cutthroat trout.

CAMPSITE ON THE YELLOWTAIL
Courtesy USBR

Erickson Pond.   Eleven acres by 15 feet deep on the Ed Erickson farm 4½ miles south from Girard, a mile west and another north to the house where you ask permission. It's fair to good fishing for ½ to 1½ pound largemouth bass.

Fish Lake.   A high (elevation 9150 feet) alpine lake just above timberline in a little barren pocket south of Monitor Peak; reached by USFS trail 1½ miles above Knox Lake. It's only 7 acres, barely deep enough to keep from freezing out, poor fishing for 5 to 8 inch cutthroat trout — very seldom visited.

Five (or North Bear Creek) Lakes.   From the footbridge at the end of the Bear Creek road at Jardine, take off cross-country up the North Fork of Bear Creek for 2¼ miles to the second unnamed tributary coming in from the west, which you should follow up for about 2 miles to its head in barren, rocky, but-with-some-scrub-timber country. Then strike off south for ¼ mile to the lakes. The largest (southernmost) is 3 acres, fairly deep with fairly steep dropoffs at the south end, is at 9500 feet elevation, and is fair fishing for 8 to 12 inch cutthroat trout. The next one up, a few hundred yards to the northwest, is only a half acre in size and so shallow that it probably freezes out each winter but must be restocked up the drainage from the lower lake because it too is fair fishing. The remaining three lakes are barren.

Fleshman Creek.   A small, swift stream flowing through hilly farmland and timbered pockets for 7¼ miles east-southeastward to Billman Creek — right in the outskirts of Livingston. It's paralleled all along by a county road, is good fishing for 8 to 9 inch brookies, a few cutthroat trout now and then, and fair sized browns to 2 pounds...right on into town.

Fridley Creek.   The outlet of Fridley and Twin Lakes flowing for a mile east down a timbered canyon above, and through posted farmland below to the Yellowstone River 1¼ miles south from St. Johns. The lower reaches are accessible by road (or would be except that they're posted). The upper reaches are followed by a USFS trail and provide a couple of miles of good fishing for 8 to 12 inch brook trout plus some cutthroat and rainbow.

Fridley Lakes.   Two little 1¼ acre lakes that are fairly deep, about ¼ mile apart (north-south) in high (elevation 9452 and 9250 feet) alpine cirques southeast of Overlook Mountain, and are reached by a good USFS trail 4½ miles above the end of the Fridley Creek road — that is, they are if you can get the owner's permission. They were stocked with cutthroat trout in 1973, 1976, 1979 and 1981. Both are good for 8 to 14 inchers.

Gartside Lake.   A heavily fished, 10 acre, 20 foot (maximum) depth recreation reservoir in open rangeland about a mile north of Crane (which is about 50 miles north of Glendive on Montana State Highway 16). It was rehabilitated in 1963 and has since been stocked annually with 8 to 10 inch rainbow trout. There's a picnic area, trees, and sanitary facilities, all provided by the folks in Sidney.

MEDICINE ROCKS
Courtesy USFS

Glass Lindsey Lakes.   Upper (600 acres and shallow), and Lower (1200 acres and fairly deep towards the outlet), reservoirs ¼ mile apart in pasture and rangeland with a few cottonwoods and willows around. Lower Lindsey is reached by road 8 miles east from U.S. 191, about 15 miles north from Big Timber; and you hike on north to upper Lindsey. Both are only lightly fished although there is a boat ramp at the lower lake — which is poor to fair for 12 to 14 inch rainbow trout, good for 6 to 10 inch (and a few whoppers) yellow perch, and also has some nice browns (to 6 pounds recorded), and a very few crappie. Upper Lindsey is poor fishing for 4 to 5 pound browns and 8 to 10 inch yellow perch. Now hear this! The gates to these lakes are locked, a result of "sportsmens" trespass, without permission.

Granite Lake.   A high, alpine 20 acre lake right under Granite Peak in the central Crazy Mountains — misnamed Thunder Lake on many maps (see listing). It's reached by trail 3 miles up Big Timber Creek from the end of the road at Half Moon Campground. The last half mile to Granite is real steep with lots of switchbacks. The lake is fairly deep all over with a small peninsula at either end, some talus and steep cliffs on the north end, and alpine timber on around. The fishing used to be good but is now only fair for 8 to 10 inch rainbow stocked in 1976 plus a few good ones up to maybe 1½ pounds. Quite a few "guided tourists" make this one.

Grizzly Creek.   Heads at 10,000 feet elevation in alpine country on the southern slopes of Mt. Wallace and flows southeastward for 8 miles to Hellroaring Creek at 7150 feet elevation, 8 miles by trail above the Hellroaring Ranger Station. The lower 3 miles are paralleled by trail through fairly open meadows with fairly shallow gradient, and are moderately popular and fair fshing for 9 to 11 inch cutthroat.

Grosfield (Louis) Reservoir.   Is reached by county roads 10 miles northeast from Big Timber, but is not open to the general public. It's a 1 acre earth-dammed reservoir on Swamp Creek at the foot of the Crazy Mountains; very brushy and swampy around the margins and hard to fish but fair for rainbow trout that run up to a couple of pounds or better. This is fine deer hunting country.

Haughian Trout Pond.   About 40 miles north of Miles City. Take the Cap Rock Road to the Haughian Ranch and ask directions and permission. A nice, clear trout pond giving up fish to 6 pounds.

Hellroaring Creek.   You can reach this one 11 miles by trail east from Jardine (at the head of the Bear Creek road), or up from the Yellowstone River in the Park. The first 4 miles of Montana waters are in a timbered canyon, but the creek flows south into it from another 4 mile stretch of open mountain meadows, and here it is good fishing for 10 to 12 inch cutthroat trout. The Hellroaring Ranger Station is at the head of the canyon and the area is frequented quite a lot by people coming and going from both up and down the creek.

Hidden Lake. Lies in a timbered pocket between a little hill and the side of the mountain ½ mile east and across Buffalo Horn Creek from the trail 3 miles north into the Absaroka Primitive area from the Yellowstone Park boundary. It's about 10 acres, quite deep, with talus slopes to the water on the southeast end and is fished a fair amount for good catches of 12 to 14 inch rainbow trout.

Hindu Lake. See Campfire Lake.

Hollecker Pond. A little reservoir on the outskirts of Glendive, maintained by the Glendive Lion's Club. For the last 15 or so years it has been stocked annually with catchable sized rainbow, providing good angling for youngsters (and oldsters, too).

Homestead Reservoir. A nice reservoir located on BLM land north of Terry about 35 miles near the county road between Terry and Brockway. Stocked in the 1970s with both largemouth and smallmouth bass. Homestead is good bass fishing, kicking out fish up to 4 pounds.

Horse Creek. Heads on the Gallatin Range and flows northward for 8 miles to Tom Milner Creek. The lower, willow-bordered reaches flow through open meadows and are accessible by road. There are 4 old beaver ponds that stretch for a couple of miles at the head of the meadows, but then the creek enters a real narrow, rough canyon and you have a heck of a time even getting down to it. The beaver ponds and meadow reaches are fair (they have been good in the past) fishing for 10 to 12 inch cutthroat trout, but they're seldom fished.

Intake Dam. A 500 foot long, 4 foot high redwood plank "dam" built in 1918 across the Yellowstone River to back the water up for irrigation. It's reached by Montana State Highway 16, 18 miles northeast from Glendive. The river is about 6 feet deep above the "dam" but the fishing (which is very good-to-excellent in the spring) is in the fast water below. There's a picnic area, heavy pressure, and plenty of good "fishermen's luck" for sauger, ling (burbot), catfish, paddlefish and sturgeon.

Johnson's Dam. A 15 acre, 8 to 15 foot maximum depth, W.P.A. reservoir of 1937 vintage; on the (barren) Deer Creek drainage in open grass and farmland 7 miles north and then 2½ miles east by county road from Lindsay, Montana (30 miles northwest of Glendive). Its future fishing potential is dubious because it washed out in 1978. MDFW and P would like to have this northern, walleye and perch fishery rebuilt but no luck so far.

STOCKWATER POND IN BADLANDS
Courtesy SCS

Killen (or Needlebutte) Reservoir. Drive 17 miles on a gravel road due west from Angela, take the left (southwest) fork for 3 more and finally a rough road about a mile northwest to this 12 acre by 20 feet deep, stock pond on the Ryan Fork of Little Porcupine Creek away out in the open rolling prairie. It gets some use from Billingsites because — it produces some nice fat rainbow trout up to 2 pounds.

Knox (or Castle) Lake. A 9 acre wide spot in the drainage, half in timber (to the south) and half in alpine meadow 1¼ miles southeast below Fish Lake on the Bear Creek trail 6½ miles above the Footbridge at Jardine..Part of the south side is deep, the rest is fairly shallow and all of it is excellent fishing (if you wish to call it so) for 6 to 10 inch brook trout. It is heavily fished.

Labree Reservoir. A 20 acre, 15 foot maximum depth reservoir in open rangeland (no trees here) at the head of O'Fallon Creek; reached by a dirt county road maybe 20 miles northwest of Ekalaka (where you can combine your fishing trip with a look at the dinosaurs at the High School museum). It's moderately popular and fair fishing for largemouth bass and bluegill and good for northern pike.

Lake Abundance. Take the Red Lodge highway ¾ of a mile east from Cooke City, then a good mining road north up Miller Creek for 3¼ miles to about ¼ of a mile beyond Daisy Pass, and finally an extremely hazardous jeep road 3½ miles west to the shore at 8400 feet — and the Lord help you if it rains. You can also make it on foot or horseback up the Lake Abundance Creek trail. Once there, it's a 17 acre lake, in timber but with open banks, fairly deep (37 feet) but with shallow dropoffs, moderately popular and fair fishing for 6 to 10 inch cutthroat trout.

Lake Abundance Creek. A small clear stream, the outlet of Lake Abundance and a tributary of Slough Creek. It's followed by trail (but not many people) for its full length of about 6 miles down a narrow timbered canyon to its mouth a mile above the end of the Slough Creek road. The fishing is fair for 10 to 12 inch cutthroat trout.

Lake of the Woods. At 8675 feet elevation, a long 8 acre lake that's right in the "woods" but has mostly open shores — at the head of (barren) Horseshoe Creek, reached by a good USFS pack trail an easy day's ride (18 miles) above the end of the Stillwater road. It's swarming with 8 to 10 inch cutthroat trout — a self sustaining population is only lightly fished.

"LORD OF HIS DOMAIN"
Courtesy Wesgerd

PADDLEFISH
Courtesy Bill Browning

Lindsay Dam. Is 20 acres, 10 to 15 feet deep behind an earth fill dam on Hay Creek in open rangeland ¼ of a mile south across the railroad tracks from the town of Lindsay, about 30 miles northwest of Glendive. There's a road right across the dam. It used to be heavily fished for good catches of trout, but none are left now. It's still moderately popular, though — and good fishing for — bullheads, northern pike and bluegill.

Lisk Creek Reservoir. Located a few miles south of Brockway, this is a nice pond with the county road running across the face of the dam. Annually stocked with rainbow trout, the reservoir produces good catches of 12 to 16 inch fish, giving up a "lunker" on occasion.

Little Big Horn River. A fair size stream followed by Interstate 90 from its mouth near Hardin, south for 50 miles along its broad flood plain to Wyola and on southwest to the Wyoming line. However, much of it is heavily silted due to poor irrigation practices and only about 20 miles or so are "fishing" water — for good catches in the fall below the crow agency dam for burbot and channel catfish and at the dam for brown trout. The crow tribe is not selling permits at present.

Little Mission Creek. Heads below Elephanthead Mountain in the Absarokas and flows north and west to Mission Creek about 7 miles above U.S. 10. Only the lower 2 miles (paralleled by road) are fishable; the middle and upper reaches are too small. Even the lower reaches are seldom fished, but they are good for 9 to 10 inch cutthroat and a few brown trout.

Little Timber Creek. A very small stream that is seldom fished; flowing southward through open farmland for 8 miles to the Yellowstone River, 3 miles west of the town of Big Timber. It's crossed at the mouth, in the middle reaches, and near the headwaters by unimproved roads. The lower reaches are dewatered in summer and there are only a couple of miles above that support fish — a poor-to-fair population of 6 to 8 inch cutthroat and brook trout.

Lodge Grass Reservoir. See Willow Creek Lake.

Lonesome Pond. . The West Fork Mill Creek-Monitor Creek (too small for fish) trail takes you 6 miles above the end of the road to this not-so-very-deep 2 acre pond in such dense timber (right to the shore) that it's hard to fish for the few 10 to 16 inch cutthroat trout that inhabit its waters. It very seldom sees a line.

Lower Deer Creek. Flows north from the Boulder Plateau for 20 miles to the Yellowstone River where it's crossed by U.S. 10 six miles east of Big Timber. It's followed upstream by unimproved roads for about 9 miles, and then by a USFS trail to headwaters. The lower 5 miles are in open rangeland and are so extensively dewatered for irrigation that they have little or no fishing potential — but the upper reaches (in conifer-covered mountains) are excellent for such a small stream and are moderately popular for 8 to 10 inch cutthroat, browns to 15 inches, and some brook trout.

Merrill's Lake. A private, posted, 30 acre lake with lots of willows around it and some trees on the south side, but mostly in open grassland east of Tom Miner Creek a couple of miles upstream. If you can get permission it's possible to drive right to it ½ mile cross-country from the Tom Miner road; but you probably won't. It's really locked up tight, which is unfortunate because there's a good population of 12 to 14 inch rainbow trout here and they're ready and willing to test your tackle. The lake is rumored to also contain walleye.

Middle Fork Hellroaring Creek. Joins the West Fork in a little mountain meadow at the head of the main creek. The USFS Middle Fork trail follows it to headwaters, but only the lower (meadowland) mile is flat enough and large enough to support a fair number of 8 to 10 inch cutthroat trout. Few people hit it.

Middle Fork of Sweet Grass Creek. Heads in Campfire Lake (in the Crazy Mountains) and is followed by a USFS pack trail down its rocky, timbered canyon for 8 miles to the end of the road 18 miles above Melville. It's seldom fished, but the canyon reaches (just below the lake) are fair early spring fishing for camp-fare cutthroat trout.

Mill Creek. A seldom fished little stream that is good for 9 to 10 inch cutthroat in its lower to middle reaches. It heads on the eastern slopes of the Gallatin Range and flows northward down its steep, timbered canyon above — and through a wide mountain valley between conifer-covered slopes below — to Cinnabar Creek at the end of the road and is mostly on private property.

Mill Creek. Heads below Crow Mountain at about 9000 feet elevation in the Absaroka Range. It flows fast and clear for 8 miles west and north down a narrow timbered canyon with lots of deadfalls, then for 5 miles through open sedge meadows in a flat-bottomed valley — another mile through a narrow canyon, and finally for 5 miles out across its wide alluvial fan to the Yellowstone River and U.S. 89 about 19 miles south of Livingston. The lower reaches are heavily dewatered and are fishable only in early season for good-sized brown trout. The meadowland reaches (all followed by road) are fair fishing for mostly 8 to 10 inch cutthroat, plus a few rainbow and brook trout and whitefish. There's a USFS public campground at the head of the meadowland reaches — the canyon above is too steep for fish.

Miner Creek. See Cokedale Creek.

Mission Creek. Is crossed at the mouth (on the Yellowstone River) by U.S. 10 seven miles east of Livingston and followed by roads upstream for 10 miles, and then by trail for another 2½ miles to headwaters on the northern slopes of Elephanthead Mountain. It's mostly in hilly, rocky, cliff country and much of it is tough fishing because of willows and brush along the margins. The lower reaches are heavily fished for good catches of mostly 6 to 12 inch browns, plus a few rainbow trout and rainbow-cutthroat hybrids. The middle reaches are moderately popular, but the fishing is only fair and there are not so many browns. The upper reaches are quite small and only poor-to-fair for mostly 6 to 9 inch cutthroat and hybrids. At the mouth browns to 18 inches are caught and the whole creek is good whitefishing (mountain whitefish).

Mol Heron (or Mulherin) Creek. Flows north from the Gallatin Range in Yellowstone Park for 8 miles to the Yellowstone River. From Corwin Springs on U.S. 89 drive west across the Yellowstone and then north up the river for a mile to the Mol Heron Road and on upstream for 5 miles, and thence proceed by trail to the border. The almost torrential lower (canyon) reaches have lots of excellent cover provided by deadfalls, etc., are good 9 to 10 inch cutthroat fishing. The upper timbered valley and park reaches are not quite so fast but are still swift and provide good fishing for both cutthroat, rainbow, and hybrids. The entire stream sustains a moderate amount of fishing pressure giving up a few browns near the mouth.

ON THE YELLOWSTONE
Courtesy Bill Browning

Moose Lake. A moderately popular, fairly deep, 10 acre lake with mostly shallow dropoffs, below talus slopes on the east side and timber on around; reached by the Middle Fork Sweet Grass Creek Trail 6½ miles above the end of the road — and a half mile below Campfire Lake. It's fair fishing for 8 to 10 inch rainbow trout.

Mud Turtle Reservoir. Stop at Fort Howes for directions to this new reservoir located in the Custer National Forest up Taylor Creek. Planted largemouth bass could provide some good catching by now.

Mulherin Creek. See Mol Heron Creek.

Needle Butte Reservoir. See Killen Reservoir.

Nelson Spring Creek. Drive one mile south past the Suce Creek school on U.S. 89 four miles south from Livingston, and then turn west on a private road for about a mile to the open flood plain of the Yellowstone River and Spring Creek — which has about 1¼ miles of limited access fishing (you have to go through the farmers' back yards to get there) and is fair for 12 to 14 inch (and a few up to 5 or 6 pounds) brown and rainbow. It's mostly fished by out-of-staters now that it is on a "fee" or charge basis.

North Amelong Creek. A very small tributary of Big Timber Creek, crossed at the mouth by the Big Timber road a mile below the Big Timber campground. There is a beaver pond right at the road and it supports a small population of small brookies.

North Bear Creek Lakes. See Five Lakes.

North Fork Bear Creek. Flows swift and clear, southward through conifer-covered hills to the main creek and the end of a good dirt road at Jardine. There is no trail up the North Fork and it's only occasionally fished, but is fair for 8 to 9 inch cutthroat trout. Its principal attraction is that it lies on the route to Five Lakes.

North Fork Deep Creek. Flows from the foothills of the Absaroka Range to the lip of Paradise Valley where it joins the South Fork at the head of the main stream (which incidentally is about all used for irrigation and has no fishing potential). The lower mile is accessible by road, the next 2 miles by trail and there is about a mile of the stream, right at the foot of the mountains before all of the water is taken out, that provides some poor fishing for small cutthroat trout.

North Fork Six Mile Creek.
Is reached at the mouth by the (poor) Six Mile Creek road and is followed by trail up its steep, timbered canyon for about 3 miles of fair-to-middling 8 to 10 inch cutthroat fishing. There are a lot of cascades, deadfalls and brush piles, and all in all it's neither as attractive nor as good as the main stream.

North Fork Sweet Grass Creek.
The outlet of Sunlight Lake (in the Crazy Mountains). It is followed by a fair USFS foot trail for 10 miles down a rocky, timbered canyon to junction with the Middle Fork; is seldom fished — and only poor to fair in early spring for 8 to 12 inch cutthroat trout.

O'Fallon Creek.
A marginal, open rangeland, cottonwooded bottomland stream that runs the year around (but barely) northwestward to the Yellowstone River near Fallon, about midway between Miles City and Glendive where it's crossed by U.S. 10. The lower 10 miles or so (followed by the Chicago, Milwaukee and St. Paul R.R.) support a few cattfish (to a couple of pounds), bullheads (to a half pound), and sunfish. In the spring some nice channel catfish are caught in the lower reaches. For all the fishing pressure they attract, they'll likely stay there.

Otter Creek.
A small stream that heads in the Crazy Mountains and flows east and south for 30 miles through open rolling hills to the Yellowstone, a couple of miles east and across the River from Big Timber. The lower reaches are mostly dewatered for irrigation, but the upper reaches (for about 1½ miles within the USFS boundary) provide a little fishing for little fish — 6 to 9 inch brookies. Access is by fishermen's trails taking off from the end of the road.

Passage Creek.
Heads away up in the Absarokas and is paralleled by a good USFS horse trail for 8 miles down its timbered gorge to Mill Creek a mile above the campground. There are some 60 foot falls two miles upstream and about 4 miles of fair fishing — for 7 to 8 inch cutthroat trout. It's a dead ender, though, and seldom visited.

Pear Lake.
Is pear-shaped, about 40 acres, fairly deep, in a high cirque with talus all around it, reached (by a very few) cross-country up the drainage ½ mile south from Granite Lake. Don't take the drainage coming in from the west or you'll end up at Druckenmiller Lake (misnamed Granite on some maps) and it is barren. Pear Lake was planted with rainbow trout years ago, again in 1978, and is reported to still be good at times for skinny 8 to 10 inchers.

Pine Creek Lake.
Take U.S. 89 eleven miles south of Livingston, then the Luccock Park (Pine Creek) recreational area road 2¼ miles east to the campground and finally a steep horse trail for another 2½ miles on east and 3400 feet up to the lake at 9032 feet elevation in a beautiful semi-barren setting below Black Mountain. It lies in a great glacial cirque with steep talus slopes most of the way around, along with some grass and a few alpine trees, is 28 acres, over 100 feet deep, and has 2 beautiful falls — one above and one below. A lot of people hike in for the scenery, but not many fish it, although it's fair at times for pan-size cutthroat trout 6 to 10 inches stocked in 1976 and 1981.

Powder River.
A quicksand muddy-bottomed creek with a few forks here and there, flowing north through open rangeland and cottonwooded bottoms for about 150 airline miles from the Wyoming line to the Yellowstone River 35 miles northeast of Miles City. It's not hit very hard but is good for catfish in the spring (recorded to 14 pounds), and has produced a very few sturgeon (recorded to 37 pounds), along with a good run of sauger (out of the Yellowstone) in the spring, too. There's a good road along it all the way.

Ringstveidt (Pete) Dam.
Drive north for 35 miles or so from Miles City to Angela, and then west for another 20 to this little (2 acres) stock reservoir in open rangeland. It's an old one, but the sides were recently raised so that it now has a maximum depth of about 12 feet, is moderately used for annually planted rainbow trout, and good too.

Rock Creek.
Heads below Fortress Mountain in the Gallatin Range and flows eastward through heavily forested mountains above, and open rolling rangeland below for 11 miles to the Yellowstone River about 35 miles south of Livingston on U.S. 89. The lower reaches are followed by a logging road, the upper reaches by trail to headwaters. The lower 5 miles are mostly posted, fished a little and are fair for 8 to 11 inch brook and cutthroat trout — excellent for rattlesnakes. The upper reaches are quite fast, seldom fished, and no better than poor for 8 to 9 inch cutthroat trout.

DON'T FENCE ME IN
Courtesy Jim Derleth

Rodgers Reservoir. Located about 1 mile off U.S. 312, twenty miles south of Miles City in some gumbo hills, this little pond consistently produces good catches of rainbows planted annually with a couple thousand 2 inchers.

Rush Hall Dam. A Montana Department of Fish, Wildlife and Parks fishing access site about 10 miles north of Baker on State Highway 7. Watch for the signs. Stocked with rainbows annually, produces good catches.

Sacajawea Park Lagoon. A 3¼ acre, L-shaped pond on the west side of the Yellowstone River flood plain right in south Livingston — deep, stocked with rainbow trout annually, good for 8 to 12 inchers. The Lagoon is fished hard by all age groups and every now and then, a true lunker is beached.

Sage Creek. Starts as a trickle below Crater Ice Cave in the Pryor Mountains and flows west, south and finally east for 30 miles in a big semicircle around the mountains and into Wyoming 4 miles south of Warren. It's accessible by road all the way, mostly to within a few hundred yards, never more than a couple of miles across open farm or rangeland. The upper creek in Montana is very brushy and is heavily fished for good catches of rainbow trout planted yearly, brookies, and a very few cutthroat trout.

Sanburn Dam. Located on Belle Creek, about 30 miles southeast of Broadus on the Belle Creek Road. The MDFWP put in about 4,000 little rainbow every year. Catching is good with an occasional 4 pounder taken.

Schaak (Adolph) Pond. Two, 1¼ and 2 acres, on the East Fork of Pryor Creek just east of the town of Pryor 25 airline miles due south of Billings (or about 35 miles by state, county and private roads). They are private ponds that have been stocked with rainbow trout from a commercial hatchery, and they provide good-to-excellent fishing for friends and ranch personnel only.

Shooting Star Lake. A long, narrow, 3¼ acre lake just east of the crest of the Gallatin Range in high (elevation 8700 feet) alpine, mostly open country. It's reached either by the Tom Miner Creek road and Horse Creek trail or the Mol Heror-Cinnabar Creek road-Lion Creek trail — about a 4 mile hike both ways on old unmaintained and sometimes invisible game and fishermen trails. The lake is fairly deep with steep dropoffs, and it produces a few cutthroat for the even fewer fishermen who hike in for them. It's really off the beaten path.

Silver Tip (or Van Cleve, Phillip) Reservoir. Is 4 acres, in open rangeland about a mile east of Clark's Reservoir. The Terry Rod and Gun Club has been promoting public facilities here. It was planted with largemouth bass in 1963, and they winter killed in 1978-79. The BLM repaired the dam in 1981 — look for a plant of rainbow trout in 1982.

Courtesy MDFWP

Six Mile Creek. Heads below Monitor Peak in the Absaroka Range and is followed by a good USFS trail through steep-timbered mountains 6 miles north to the mouth of the North Fork Six Mile Creek, and then by a poor jeep road 4 miles down a nice little open-bottomed valley — and finally another couple of miles across private farmland to the Yellowstone River and U.S. 89 about 25 miles south of Livingston. The lower reaches are fair for up to 14 inch brown trout. The middle and upper reaches, however, maintain a good year-round flow with lots of nice ponds clear to headwaters. They contain cutthroat and are fair-to-good fishing for 10 to 12 inch trout.

Slough Creek. Heads in a little, unnamed (barren) lake about a mile south of Columbine Pass on the west side of Pinnacle Mountain in the Absaroka Range — from where it flows south for 15 miles down a mostly timbered canyon to Yellowstone Park. It runs full during spring runoff but partly sinks in the fall to form a series of ponds some of which are as much as ¼ of a mile long. The lower reaches used to be accessible by a jeep road north from the Park past the Silver Top Ranch and on upstream for about 5 miles. Then a USFS trail takes you on to the headwaters. The jeep road is now barricaded about 1½ miles up from the highway so you have your choice, sore feet or a sore bottom. The lower and middle reaches (through some big open alpine meadows) are fair-to-good fishing for 8 to 10 inch cutthroat trout — but are only lightly fished. However, if you amble on up the creek for maybe 4 miles or so, it really starts to get better. Here the stream flows through some open meadows and in the pools the trout will average 14 inches and range up to 30 or more. And best of all it's a fly fisherman's paradise although you probably will have company.

Soda Butte Creek. A nice little creek (in the Montana reaches) that heads in Cooke City, flows westward down its wide, timbered valley for 2¼ miles to Silver Gate and leaves the state half a mile beyond. It's followed all along the north side by U.S. 12, is easy to fish with fairly wide banks, nice holes, and a good population of 8 to 9 inch cutthroat trout. How could it be other than popular? If the fish were larger it'd be beat to death.

South Sandstone Reservoir. Seven miles south of Plevna, this 120 acre reservoir has good access and nice recreational facilities. Stocked with walleye in 1977, with northern pike in 1976 and 1980, it provides good fishing for these and also for perch and bullheads. A nice place to spend a few days off the beaten path.

Sunlight Lakes. Two, Upper (3 acres) and Lower (2 acres), shallow lakes ¼ mile apart, 5¼ miles by USFS pack trail up the drainage from the end of the Sweet Grass Creek road. The upper lake is in open park country and is slow fishing for BIG cutthroat trout. The lower lake is in timber all around but has open shores and is good fishing for 10 to 12 inch cutthroat trout. Neither is fished once in a blue moon. They were stocked in 1974 and 1978.

MOUNTAIN SHEEP
Courtesy USFS

Swamp Lake.
Is so named because it lies at the head of Swamp Creek; not because it's a swampy lake, because it isn't. It's a Crazy Mountain cirque lake in rocky, alpine, above timberline country, about 15 acres, fairly deep with steep dropoffs on the west end and rock slides about ⅔ of the way around the shore. To reach it, take the Big Timber Creek road 3 miles north from the town of Big Timber, then the Swamp Creek road 14 miles northwest, and finally a USFS trail 3 miles on in to the shore. Once there you'll find it temperamental but sometimes excellent fishing for 8 to 16 inch brookies, plus occasionally, a truly good one — up to 9 pounds recorded. N.B. Be sure and stop and ask Arnie Grosfield or his son for permission to cross his land. He lives at the head of Swamp Creek.

Sweet Grass Creek.
Heads in the Crazy Mountains and is followed by county, private and USFS roads most of the way (about 50 miles) east and south to the Yellowstone 8 miles east and across the river from Big Timber. The lower reaches are drawn quite low for summer time irrigation, but there is some good fishing in the headwater reaches for a couple of miles on either side of the National Forest boundary. It provides mostly 9 to 13 inch brown and rainbow, plus a few brook trout and whitefish in winter.

Tauck Reservoir.
Is on the ranch belonging to Lyle Tauck, a former — and one of the better — Montana State Fish and Game Commissioners. The best way to find it is to take U.S. 212 to Hammond and inquire there for further detailed directions. It's reached by a private road about 2 miles north through open rangeland, is 25 acres, mostly under 15 feet deep, moderately popular with local residents, and good fishing for northern pike and bullhead.

Ten Mile Creek.
A small, open rangeland stream flowing eastward to Otter Creek, and crossed here and there by county roads 9 miles or so north from Big Timber. The middle and upper reaches are good fishing (using the term in the broad sense) for 4 to 8 inch maximum to maybe 12 inch brook trout.

Thompson Lake.
Eight acres, barely deep enough to keep from freezing out but with shallow dropoffs on the south end only, bordered by dense timber on the west, some beautiful big meadows on the east, and is reached by a good trail (not shown on many maps but it's there) 6½ miles above the end of the West Fork Mill Creek road. It's a lovely place to camp, moderately popular, easily fished, and good for 6 to 14 inch cutthroat trout.

Thunder Lake.
Is practically a 5 acre eastward extension of Blue Lake, mostly in alpine timber but with quite a bit of rock on the southeast side, shallow to the southeast but deeper to the northwest, and fair fishing for skinny 8 to 10 inch rainbow trout plus an occasional good one to 1½ or 2 pounds. It's moderately popular with out-of-staters.

Tom Miner Creek. Flows 13 miles southeastward from Canary Bird Peak through mostly a wide-bottomed open little valley below timbered mountains in the Gallatin Range just north of Yellowstone Park, to the Yellowstone River and U.S. 89 about 38 miles south from Livingston. The lower 6 miles, or as far as the road goes and no farther, are easily fished, moderately popular, and good fishing, too, for mostly 8 to 12 inch cutthroat, plus a few rainbow, brook, and some brown trout in the lower reaches, if you can get on the creek (private).

Tongue River. Flows north-northeast from Wyoming for about 5 miles to the Tongue River Reservoir, and then is followed by roads for about 90 air line miles through open cropland and cottonwood bottoms to its junction with the Yellowstone River at Miles City. It's sometimes clear in the spring but is very muddy in the summer. The first 10 or 15 miles below the reservoir are fair fishing (and moderately popular) for rainbow and brown trout, but there are lots of catfish here too, and rough fish. The lower reaches are good spring fishing for sauger, walleye pike, and fair for catfish, bullhead, perch and rock bass. As the fishing access varies, so does the fishing pressure — from moderate to heavy. Dewatered a bit in its lower reaches, the river's middle reaches are best for northern pike (to 25 pounds on occasion), and really good for strong smallmouth bass to 4 pounds, especially between Ashland and Burney.

Tongue River Reservoir. Is on the river bottom 5 miles north of the Wyoming line in open rangeland but with trees (and picnic areas) around the shore. It's about 5 miles long by ⅛ of a mile wide behind a 50 foot or so high earth-fill dam, but the average depth of water is only about 10 feet. It's accessible by road from either Birney or Decker and is mostly used by Wyomingites for swimming and fishing. It is good for northern pike to 18 pounds; walleye, sauger, and smallmouth bass — also excellent crappie fishing. It's popular.

Trail Creek. A small stream whose lower, willow-bottomed reaches (10 miles are closely followed by road) are heavily fished for good catches of mostly 9 to 10 inch rainbow, cutthroat, and brown trout — equally good for chasing diamondback rattlers. It heads in the Gallatin Range and the lower reaches flow southeastward to the Yellowstone River 14 miles south by road from Livingston. A super abundance of brush makes it a tough one to fish.

Tronrud (Adolph) Ponds. Two little 1 acre ponds in open pastureland reached by a secondary road 8 miles northwest from Melville (which is 20 miles north on State 19 from Big Timber). No public fishing has been allowed and it was just as well because there wasn't much. However, it was drained in 1972 and planted with brook trout fingerling in 1973 and has been good since.

Twin Lakes. Upper Twin (3 acres) and Lower Twin (5 acres). Both are fairly shallow, a few hundred yards apart in high semi-open country below Granite Peak in the central Crazy Mountains; reached by trail 3 miles west above the Half Moon campground at the end of the Big Timber Creek road. They are fished a fair amount by dudes for good catches of 9 to 10 inch cutthroat trout — but have been known to freeze out.

Unnamed Lake (1) Mile North of Swamp Lake. Deep, 6 acres, below barren talus slopes a mile over a high rocky ridge north from Swamp Lake but to get to it you must backtrack a mile down the outlet from Swamp to the first southward flowing tributary, which you then follow up for another mile to the shore. It is practically never fished but was planted years ago and is reported to have some really good ones (rainbow trout).

Unnamed Lakes (5) at Headwaters of Wounded Man Creek. Only the one at the very head of the creek has fish. It's a fairly deep, 31 acre, "wide spot" right on the creek, in timber but with nice open shores; reached by a good USFS trail 3½ miles through some rugged country up from Slough Creek. It's seldom visited, very seldom fished, and no better than fair for camp fare cutthroat trout.

Van Cleve (Phillip) Reservoir. See Silver Tip Reservoir.

West Bridger Creek. Heads in Jim Gulch and flows northeastward through a small, sparsely timbered draw for 5 miles to the main stream 7½ miles by road upstream from U.S. 10. This is a small, cottonwood-bordered stream with lots of beaver ponds in the lower reaches — in which are fair numbers of 7 to 8 inch brook trout. Quite a few people fish it with moderate success.

COOLING OFF
Courtesy Mike Venturino

West Fork Duck Creek. Heads in the southern Crazy Mountains but flows south, mostly through open rangeland with cottonwood and willow along the banks for 14 miles to its junction with the East Fork at the head of the main stream a couple of miles up from the Yellowstone River. There are jeep roads all over the place here but it's seldom fished for poor-to-fair catches of 6 to 8 inch cutthroat, brook and some brown trout.

West Fork Little Timber Creek. Flows for 11 miles from below Kid Royal Mountain in the southern Crazy Mountains, to Little Timber Creek ½ mile above that stream's junction with the Yellowstone River 3 miles west of the town of Big Timber. The lower (fishing) reaches, for about 7 miles, are mostly in cottonwood bottoms, are crossed here and there by roads and are followed along by fishermen's trails (and rattlesnakes), and are subject to moderate fishing pressures for good catches of 7 to 8 inch average (maximum to perhaps 12 inches) brook trout.

West Fork Mill Creek. Is formed by the junction of Thompson and Monitor Creeks, neither of which have fish, but both of which drain lakes (Thompson and Lonesome) that do, at the head of its not too steep but heavily timbered canyon which is followed along by a good USFS trail 4 miles north to the end of the (poor) West Fork jeep road 3 miles up from the main creek at the Bow and Arrow Ranch. The lower reaches support a fair amount of fishing pressure, the upper reaches practically none — for fair-to-middling catches of 8 to 10 inch cutthroat trout.

Westrope Dam. A 20 acre, artificial, "sportsmen's" pond in open rangeland south of Baker. You can drive right to it. It's marshy around the upper end, about 20 feet maximum depth at the lower end, sometimes winter kills but is presently fair fishing for bass. It is "off limits" now — a private club leases it.

Wibaux Fish Pond. Located just south of Wibaux off State Highway 7, this pond originally had crappie which are reproducing. Now stocked with rainbow trout annually, it's worth a try.

Willow Creek Lake (or Lodge Grass Reservoir). Take U.S. 89 forty-nine miles east from Billings to Hardin, then State 90 (twenty-one miles south) to Lodge Grass, and finally a good gravel county road about 13 miles southwest to this irregularly shaped, 600 acre, Bureau of Indian Affairs irrigation reservoir in open rolling hills just east of the Bighorn Mountains. It has a maximum depth of about 50 feet — but also has a 30 foot drawdown; is good fishing for 8 to 10 inch rainbow and some monster brown trout. It gets pretty fair usage year round.

Wounded Man Creek.

A small stream flowing eastward down a fairly steep timbered canyon between Timberline and Horseshoe Mountains for 4 miles to Slough Creek 8 miles above the Silver Tip Ranch. It's followed all along by a USFS trail but is only poor fishing for 8 to 10 inch cutthroat trout and is very seldom bothered.

Yellowtail (or Bighorn) Reservoir.

Yellowtail Dam and Reservoir lie within the Bighorn Canyon National Recreation Area. Main entrances are by paved roads via Hardin, Montana and Lovell, Wyoming.

The Dam was completed in October 1965 and rises 525 feet in the Bighorn River Canyon near Fort Smith, Montana. The dam forms a beautiful blue-green lake which winds about 67 river miles through majestic, precipitous canyon walls and rolling prairies. Access sites on the 195 miles of shore line are located at:

Kane Bridge — 15 road miles east of Lovell, Wyoming, just off U.S. Alternate 14A. Facilities include 39 campsites, tables, pit toilets and boat ramp. No drinking water.

Ok-A-Beh — About 12 miles above Fort Smith, paved road takes off midway between Fort Smith and Government Camp. Facilities include a fish cleaning station, toilets, boat ramp and a courtesy loading dock. Overnight camping is located at the campground on the Afterbay Reservoir.

Black Canyon Campground — About 4 river miles up the lake from the dam, or at the head of Black Canyon where Black Canyon Creek enters the lake. Accessible only by boat; low water level inhibits use until about June 15. Facilities include toilets, tables and fireplaces. This is one of the most scenic spots on the lake.

Additional facilities are at the Afterbay Reservoir, located below Yellowtail Dam at Fort Smith. Facilities include 12 campsites, tables, pit toilets and boat ramp.

A visitors center is located at Yellowtail Dam. Water, gas, fishing licenses, tackle, groceries, meals and information can be obtained at Fort Smith. Motel accomodations are available at Hardin, Montana and Lovell, Wyoming.

Recreational Opportunities:

Fishing — Primarily a walleye fishery, but other species include brown trout, rainbow trout, crappie and perch. Of minor importance are lake trout, cutthroat trout, ling (burbot), sauger, and channel catfish.

Walleye have been taken to 13½ pounds, but the usual catch runs between 1 and 3 pounds. In the spring, fish for walleye near the bottom in 10-30 feet of water, or troll very slowly near the shoreline with weighted line. In summer and fall the walleye are taken in shallow water during late

YELLOWTAIL
Courtesy USBR

evening, but are at 10-50 ft. depths during most of the daylight hours. Best lures and baits are: for trolling, spinner-crawler, helldiver and rapalla; for casting, jug-crawler, spoon or live minnow. Brown and rainbow trout fishing is best in spring and early summer. Both browns and rainbows have been taken to 8 pounds, but the usual size runs 12 to 18 inches.

The lake extends into Wyoming with such popular fishing areas as the "narrows" and Crooked Creek Canyon; but in Montana try such areas as Devils Canyon and Medicine Creek Canyon, or Dry Head Canyon, Bull Elk and Black Canyon.

Other Activities — Lots of water available to give one that feeling of being alone. Watch at sharp elbows on Yellowtail for other traffic and debris lines. Debris from runoff is present on the surface of the lake from June through August. July and August are the best months for water skiing and scuba diving. Boaters plying the lake in May and June should watch for sudden storm fronts which produce strong, gusty winds, hail and rain. Rock hounds can find sedimentary rock containing sea shell and fern fossils along much of the shoreline. Spectacular canyon walls, nearby mountains, panoramic vistas and wildlife offer the photographer a variety of backgrounds and subjects.

STEVE SWEDBERG

Yonkee Reservoir.

A new pond on the Custer National Forest up Taylor Creek. Stop at Ft. Howes for instructions. Now hear this: nestled in the pines, this spring-fed pond has been stocked with some lunker brookies. Trout to 3 pounds are common.

Maps and Other Aids

Over the years, in compiling access directions for this guidebook, more than 400 U.S. Geological Survey topographic maps, 50 USFS planimetric maps and 10,000 aerial photographs were used. All are available to the public. Topographic maps show the configuration of the terrain and elevations as well as roads, towns, trails, etc.; they cost $1.00 and up. Write for an "Index of Topographical Mapping in Montana" and an order form from:

Denver Distribution Center
U.S. Geological Survey
Box 25046
Denver, CO80225

USFS Planimetric maps do not show configurations but do show lakes, rivers, trails, roads, etc.; they cost up to $3.00 each. Stereo-photo maps are available at $1.00 a photo. You must provide the name of the lake, and the section, township and range. These and USFS Visitor Maps and Travel Plan Maps are available from:

Regional Forester
USDA-Forest Service
Federal Building
Missoula, MT 59807

For good detailed color maps, so far free, write: Bureau of Land Management, Montana State Office, 222 North 32nd Street, Billings, MT 59107.

Special note: you may be missing out if you aren't keeping a Fisherman's Log, or Diary — forms available free from:

Fisheries Division
c/o George Holton
Montana Department of Fish, Wildlife and Parks
1420 E. Sixth
Helena, MT 59620

I think you'll find it valuable; and the Department regards it as a significant management tool, helping them with current information.

Jim Derleth